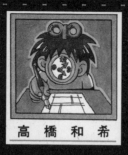

高橋和希

I DO NOT WALK AROUND WITH A CELL PHONE! WHY? BECAUSE MY ASSISTANTS WILL BE ABLE TO FIND ME! WHEN I'M WALKING AROUND TOWN, WHEN I'M MEETING FRIENDS, THAT'S MY TIME OF FREEDOM! BUT THEN I HEAR A VOICE INSIDE ME... "FINISH YOUR SCRIPT! STOP FOOLING AROUND!" AGGH! I WANT MORE TIME TO PLAY! SOMEBODY HELP ME! AND THEN I GOT AN IDEA FOR A CHARACTER: A RUDE GUY WHO BARGES INTO PEOPLE'S MINDS! AND THAT'S THE ORIGIN OF MARIK.
   —KAZUKI TAKAHASHI, 2000

Artist/author Kazuki Takahashi first tried to break into the manga business in 1982, but success eluded him until **Yu-Gi-Oh!** debuted in the Japanese **Weekly Shonen Jump** magazine in 1996. **Yu-Gi-Oh!**'s themes of friendship and fighting, together with Takahashi's weird and wonderful art, soon became enormously successful, spawning a real-world card game, video games, and two anime series. A lifelong gamer, Takahashi enjoys Shogi (Japanese chess), Mahjong, card games, and tabletop RPGs, among other games.

YU-GI-OH!: DUELIST VOL. 15
The SHONEN JUMP Manga Edition

STORY AND ART BY
KAZUKI TAKAHASHI

Translation & English Adaptation/Joe Yamazaki
Touch-up Art & Lettering/Eric Erbes
Design/Andrea Rice
Editor/Jason Thompson

Managing Editor/Elizabeth Kawasaki
Director of Production/Noboru Watanabe
Vice President of Publishing/Alvin Lu
Vice President & Editor in Chief/Yumi Hoashi
Sr. Director of Acquisitions/Rika Inouye
Vice President of Sales & Marketing/Liza Coppola
Publisher/ Hyoe Narita

YU-GI-OH! © 1996 by Kazuki Takahashi. All rights reserved. First published in
Japan in 1996 by SHUEISHA Inc., Tokyo. English translation rights in the
United States of America and Canada arranged by SHUEISHA Inc. The stories,
characters, and incidents mentioned in this publication are entirely fictional.

No portion of this book may be reproduced or transmitted in any form or by
any means without written permission from the copyright holders.

In the original Japanese edition, YU-GI-OH!, YU-GI-OH!: DUELIST and
YU-GI-OH!: MILLENNIUM WORLD are known collectively as YU-GI-OH!.
The English YU-GI-OH!: DUELIST was originally volumes 8-31
of the Japanese YU-GI-OH!.

Printed in the U.S.A.

Published by VIZ Media, LLC
P.O. Box 77010
San Francisco, CA 94107

SHONEN JUMP Manga Edition
10 9 8 7 6 5 4 3 2 1
First printing, June 2006

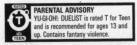

PARENTAL ADVISORY
YU-GI-OH!: DUELIST is rated T for Teen
and is recommended for ages 13 and
up. Contains fantasy violence.

THE WORLD'S
MOST POPULAR MANGA

www.shonenjump.com

www.viz.com

SHONEN JUMP MANGA

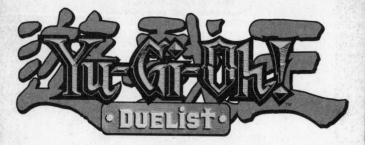

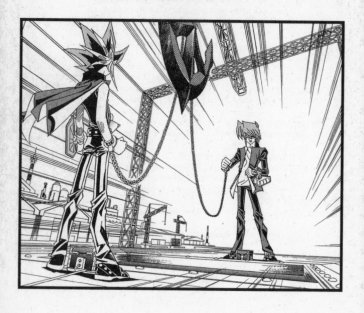

Vol. 15
YUGI VS. JONOUCHI
STORY AND ART BY
KAZUKI TAKAHASHI

THE STORY SO FAR...

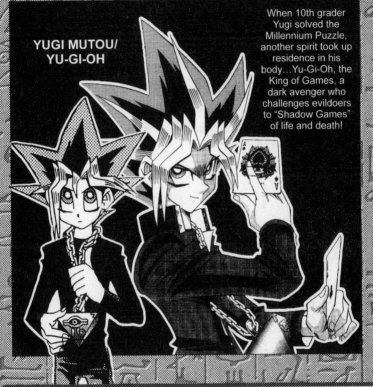

**YUGI MUTOU/
YU-GI-OH**

When 10th grader Yugi solved the Millennium Puzzle, another spirit took up residence in his body…Yu-Gi-Oh, the King of Games, a dark avenger who challenges evildoers to "Shadow Games" of life and death!

YUGI FACES DEADLY ENEMIES!

Using his gaming skills, Yugi fights ruthless adversaries like Maximillion Pegasus, multimillionaire creator of the collectible card game "Duel Monsters," and Ryo Bakura, whose friendly personality turns evil when he is possessed by the spirit of the Millennium Ring. But Yugi's greatest rival is Seto Kaiba, the world's second-greatest gamer—and the ruthless teenage president of Kaiba Corporation. At first, Kaiba and Yugi are bitter enemies, but after fighting against a common adversary—Pegasus—they come to respect one another. But for all his powers, there is one thing Yu-Gi-Oh cannot do: remember who he is and where he came from.

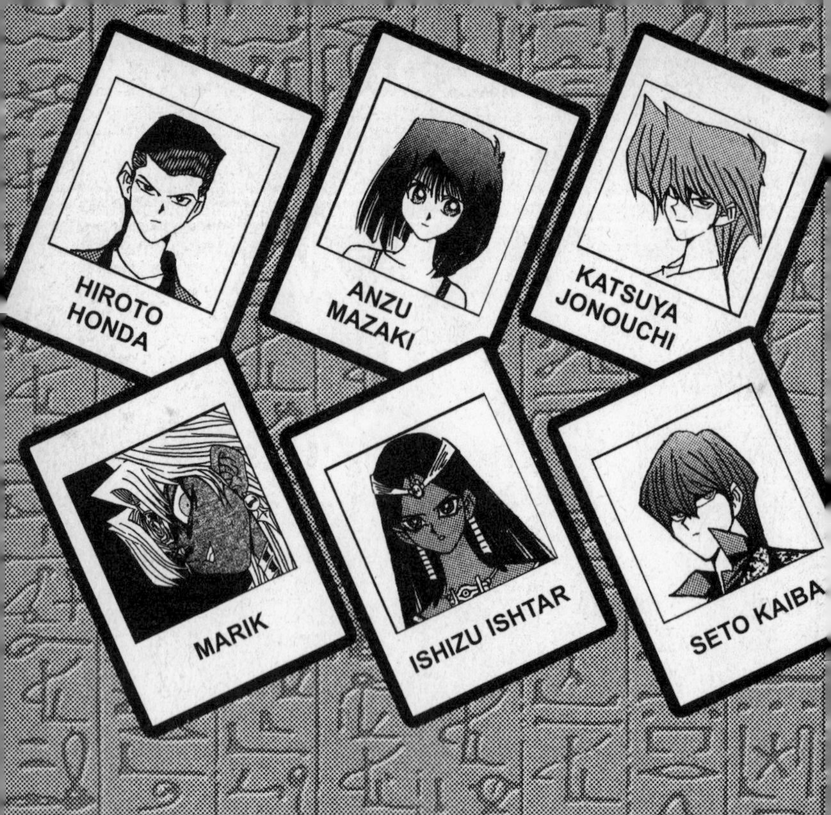
HIROTO HONDA
ANZU MAZAKI
KATSUYA JONOUCHI
MARIK
ISHIZU ISHTAR
SETO KAIBA

THE TABLET OF THE PHARAOH'S MEMORIES

Then one day, when an Egyptian museum exhibit comes to Japan, Yugi sees an ancient carving of himself as an Egyptian pharaoh! The curator of the exhibit, Ishizu Ishtar, explains that there are seven Millennium Items, which were made to fit into a stone tablet in a hidden shrine in Egypt. According to the legend, when the seven Items are brought together, the pharaoh will regain his memories of his past life.

THE EGYPTIAN GOD CARDS

But Ishizu has a message for Kaiba as well. Ishizu needs Kaiba's help to win back two of three Egyptian God Cards—the rarest cards on Earth—from the clutches of the "Rare Hunters," a criminal syndicate led by the evil Marik, Ishizu's brother. In order to draw out the thieves, Kaiba announces "Battle City," an enormous "Duel Monsters" tournament. As the tournament rages, Yugi, Kaiba and Marik struggle for possession of the three God Cards, while Yugi's friend Jonouchi bravely makes his way to the finals. But Jonouchi, too, is Marik's target. Now, Yugi and Kaiba must fight for their lives in a tag-team match against Marik's henchmen...while with every passing second, Marik closes in on Yugi's friends!

YU-GI-OH! DUELIST

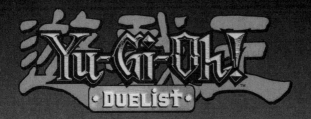

Vol. 15

CONTENTS

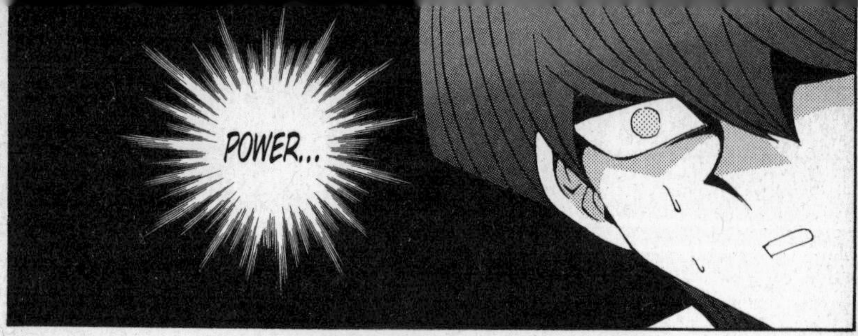
POWER...

Duel 129: Combine Your Power!

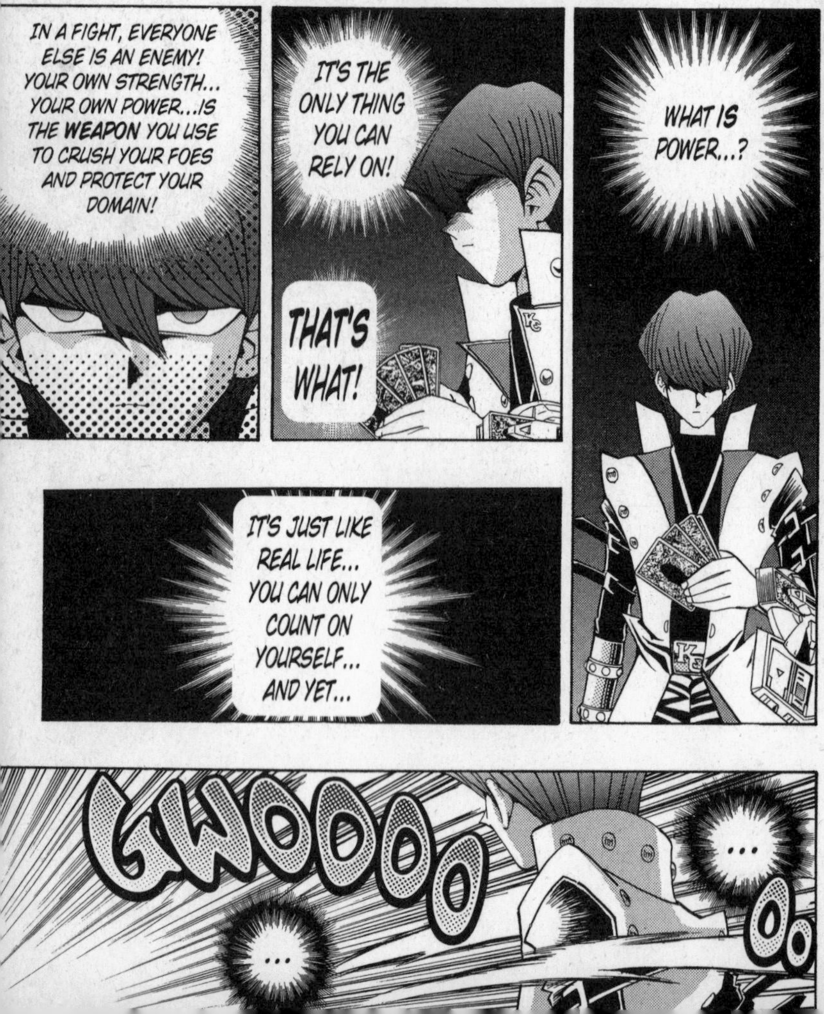
WHAT IS POWER...?
IT'S THE ONLY THING YOU CAN RELY ON!
THAT'S WHAT!
IN A FIGHT, EVERYONE ELSE IS AN ENEMY! YOUR OWN STRENGTH... YOUR OWN POWER...IS THE WEAPON YOU USE TO CRUSH YOUR FOES AND PROTECT YOUR DOMAIN!
IT'S JUST LIKE REAL LIFE... YOU CAN ONLY COUNT ON YOURSELF... AND YET...
GWOOOOOOO
...
...

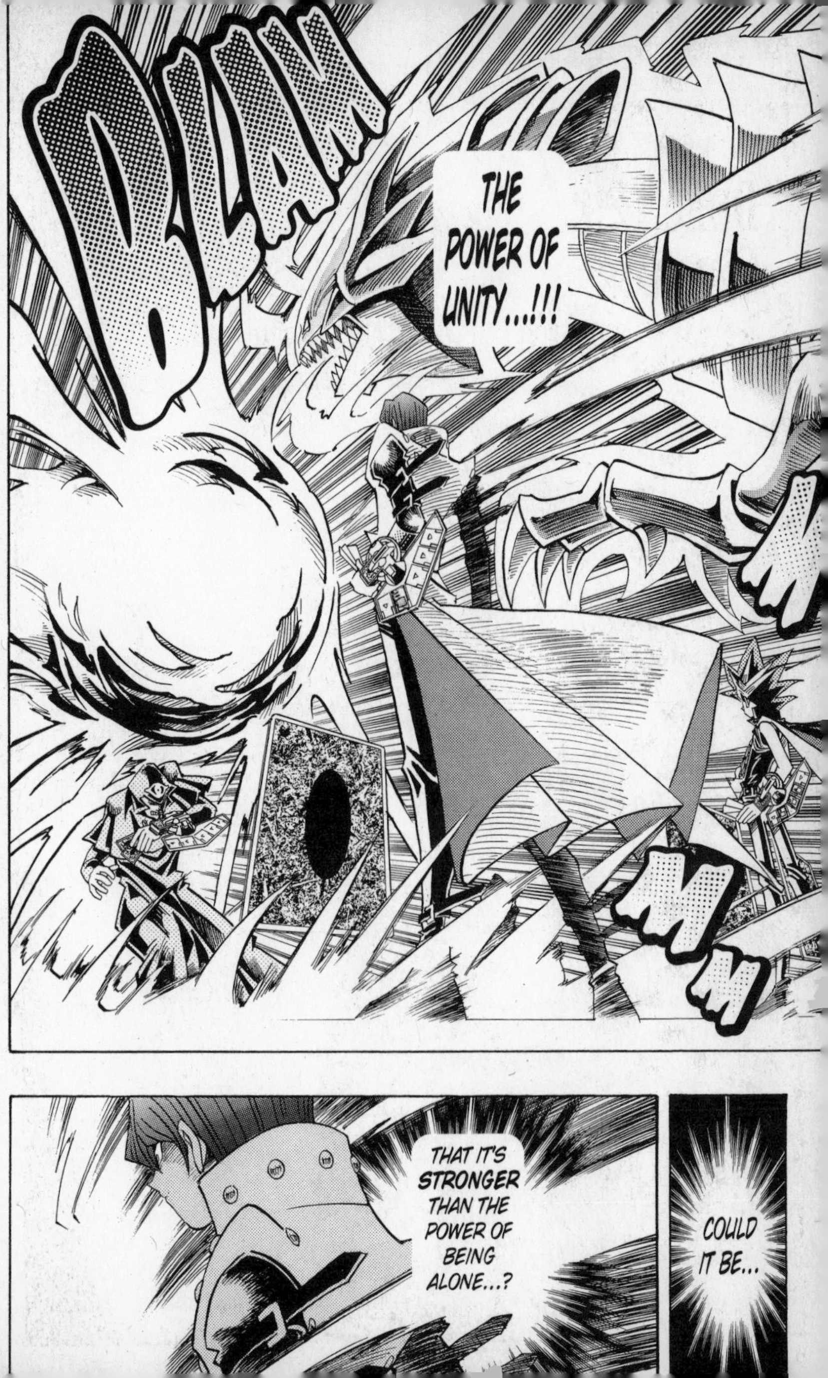
BLAM
THE POWER OF UNITY...!!!
COULD IT BE...
THAT IT'S STRONGER THAN THE POWER OF BEING ALONE...?

Duel 129: Combine Your Power!

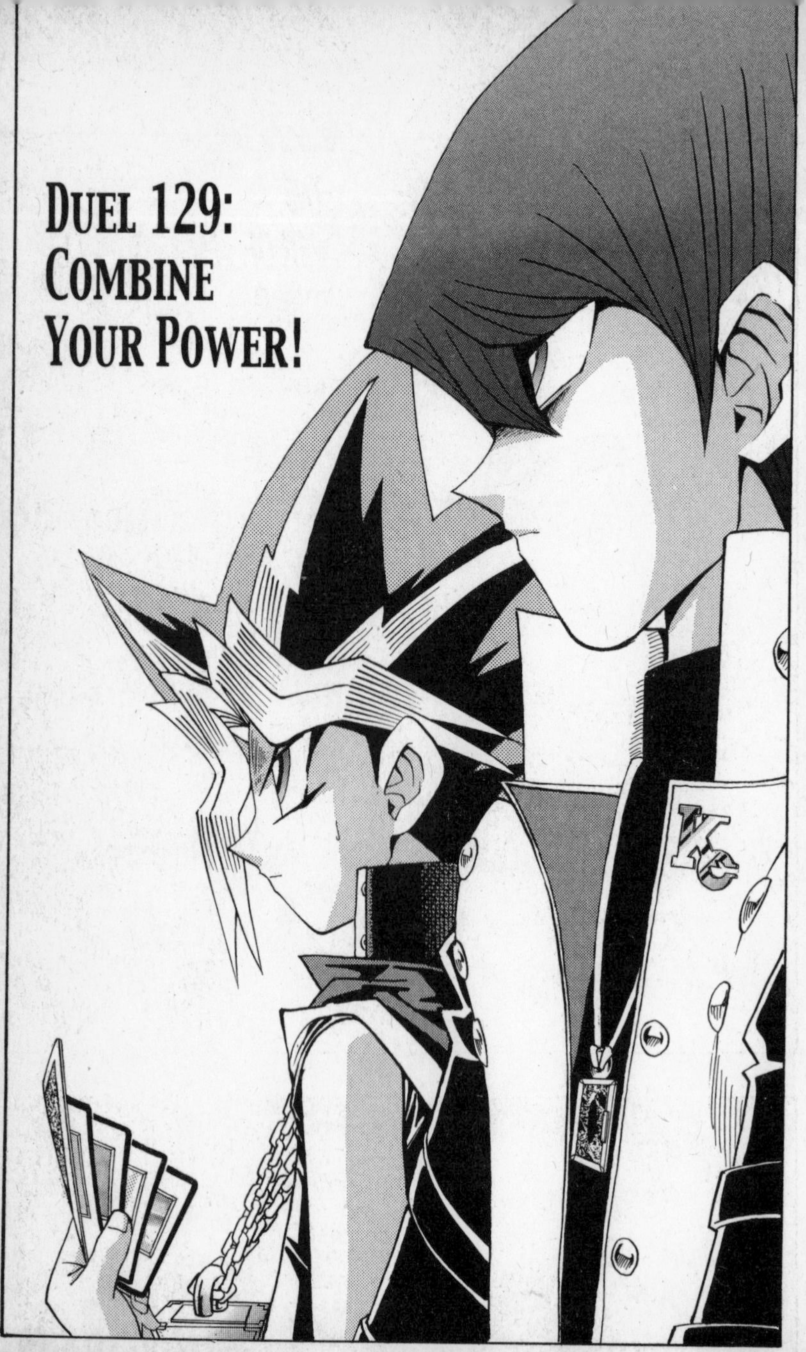

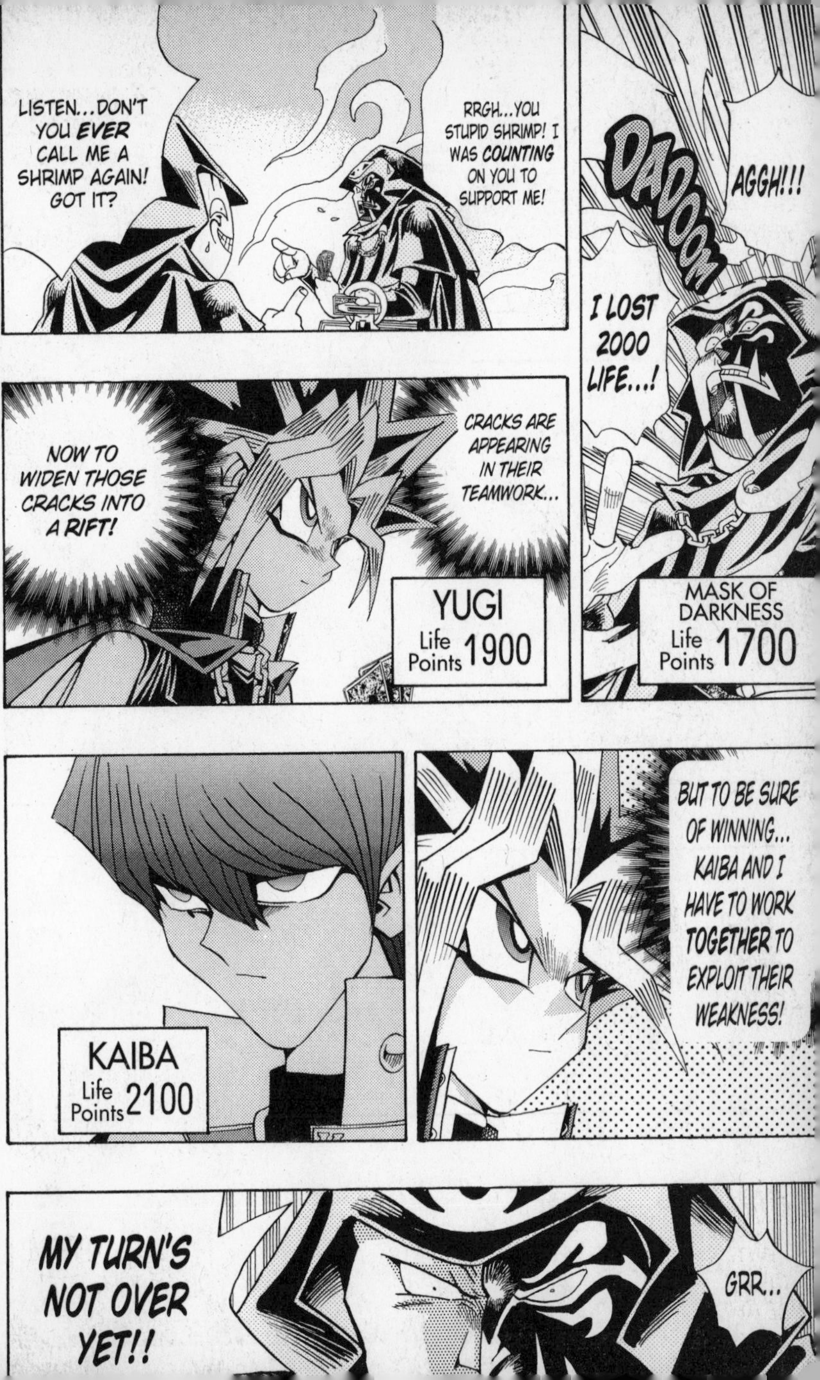
DADOOM
AGGH!!!
I LOST 2000 LIFE...!
MASK OF DARKNESS Life Points 1700
RRGH...YOU STUPID SHRIMP! I WAS **COUNTING** ON YOU TO SUPPORT ME!
LISTEN...DON'T YOU **EVER** CALL ME A SHRIMP AGAIN! GOT IT?
CRACKS ARE APPEARING IN THEIR TEAMWORK...
NOW TO WIDEN THOSE CRACKS INTO A **RIFT!**
YUGI Life Points 1900
BUT TO BE SURE OF WINNING... KAIBA AND I HAVE TO WORK **TOGETHER** TO EXPLOIT THEIR WEAKNESS!
KAIBA Life Points 2100
GRR...
MY TURN'S NOT OVER YET!!

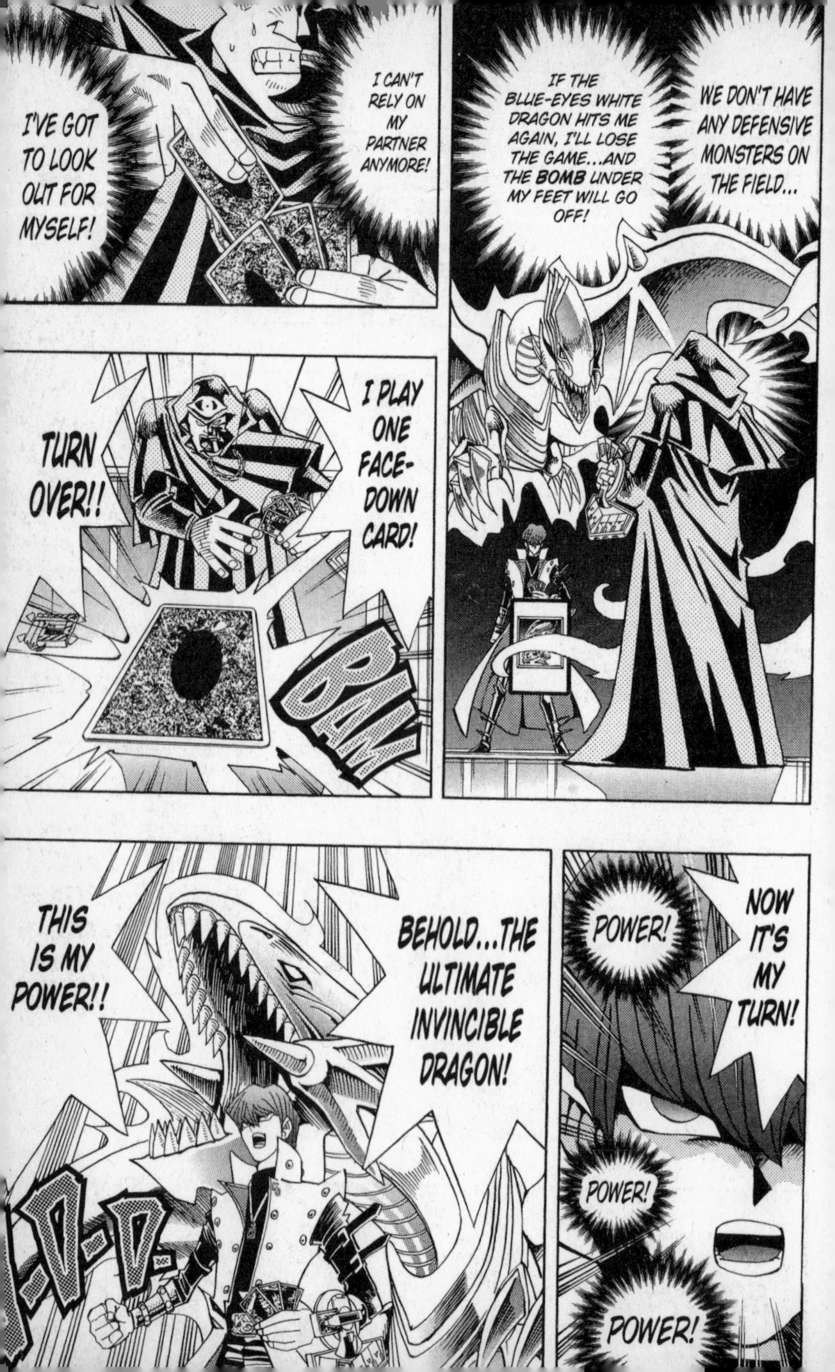
WE DON'T HAVE ANY DEFENSIVE MONSTERS ON THE FIELD...
IF THE BLUE-EYES WHITE DRAGON HITS ME AGAIN, I'LL LOSE THE GAME...AND THE BOMB UNDER MY FEET WILL GO OFF!
I CAN'T RELY ON MY PARTNER ANYMORE!
I'VE GOT TO LOOK OUT FOR MYSELF!
I PLAY ONE FACE-DOWN CARD!
TURN OVER!!
BLAM
NOW IT'S MY TURN!
POWER!
POWER!
POWER!
BEHOLD...THE ULTIMATE INVINCIBLE DRAGON!
THIS IS MY POWER!!

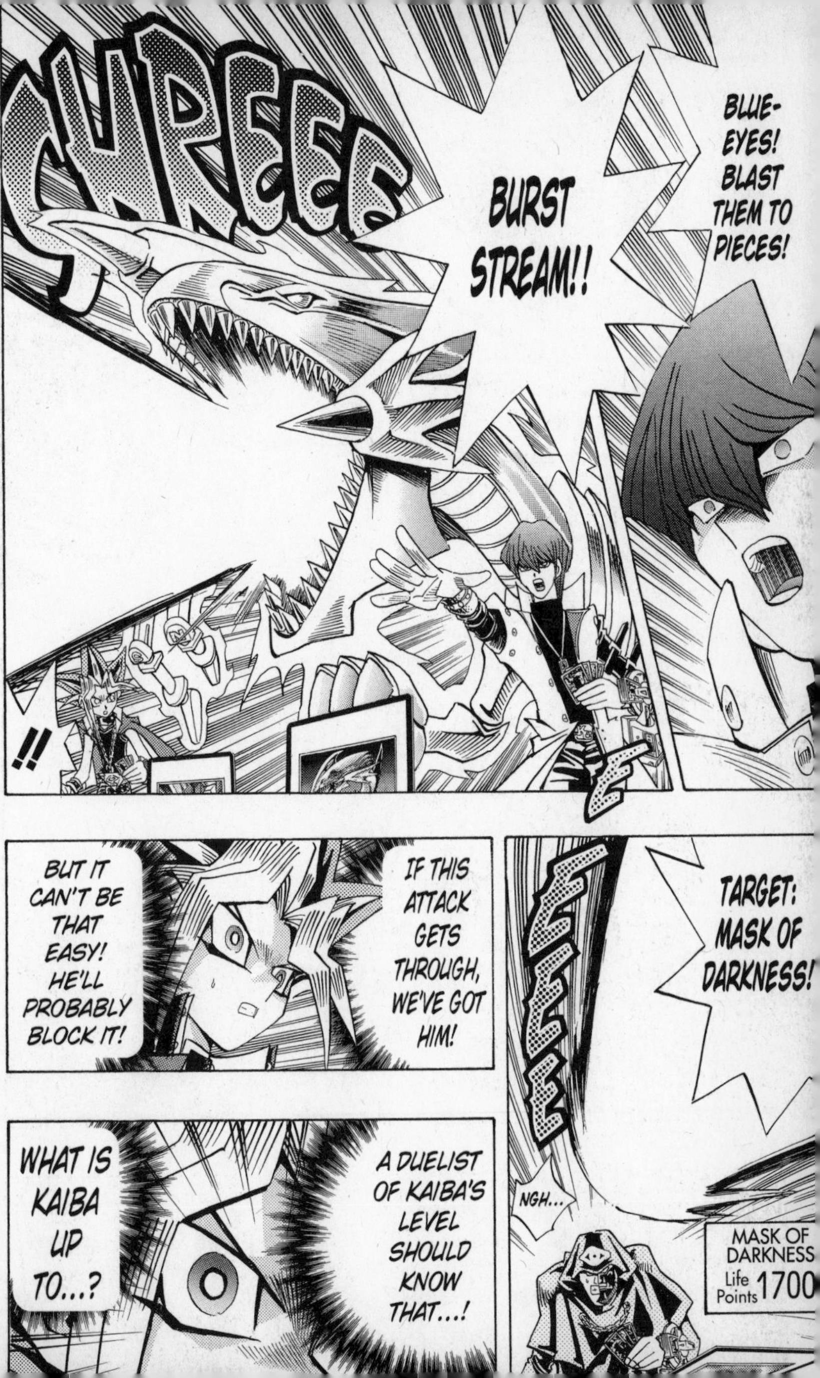
BLUE-EYES! BLAST THEM TO PIECES!
BURST STREAM!!
CHREEE
!!
E
TARGET: MASK OF DARKNESS!
EEEE
NGH...
MASK OF DARKNESS
Life Points 1700
IF THIS ATTACK GETS THROUGH, WE'VE GOT HIM!
BUT IT CAN'T BE THAT EASY! HE'LL PROBABLY BLOCK IT!
A DUELIST OF KAIBA'S LEVEL SHOULD KNOW THAT...!
WHAT IS KAIBA UP TO...?

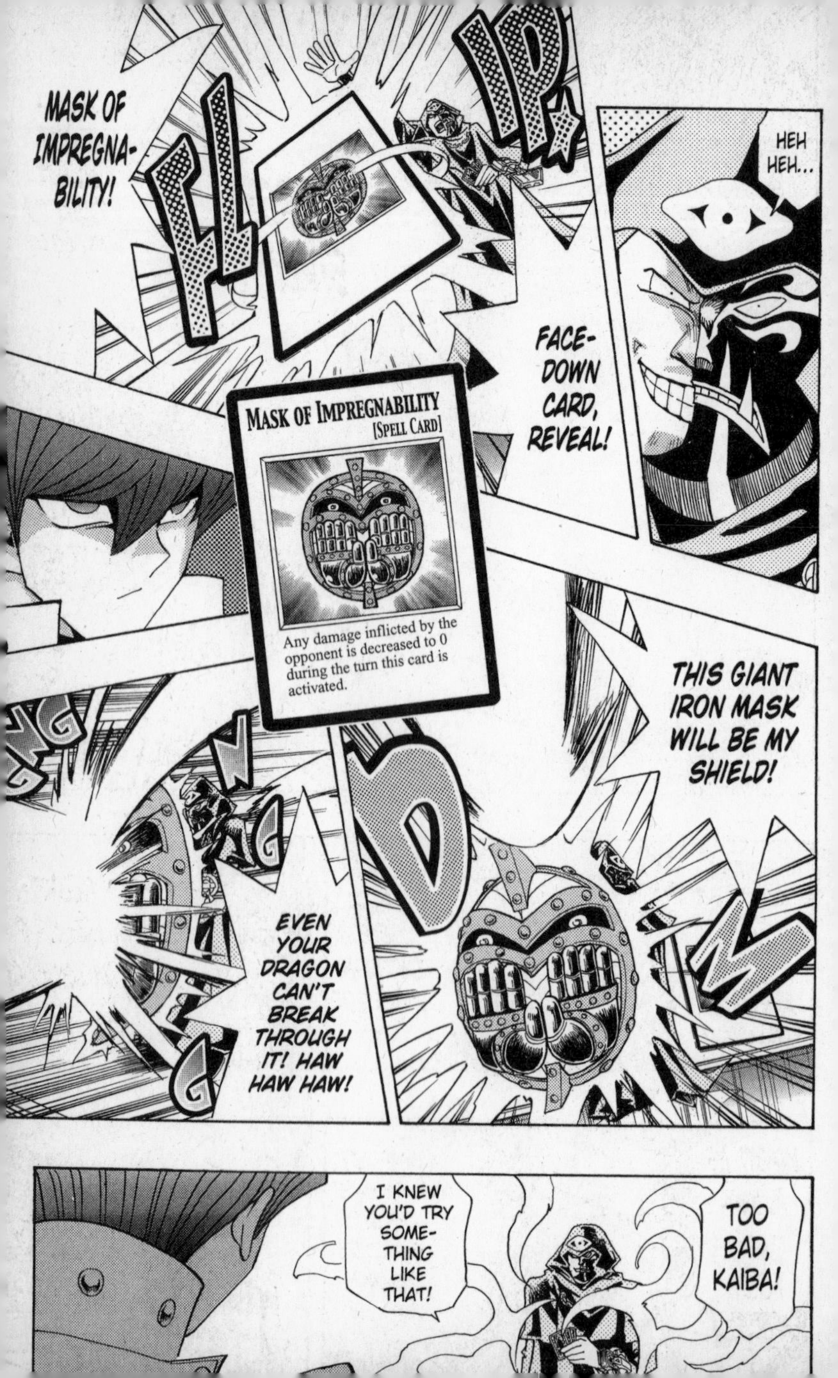
HEH HEH...
FACE-DOWN CARD, REVEAL!
MASK OF IMPREGNA-BILITY!
MASK OF IMPREGNABILITY
[SPELL CARD]
Any damage inflicted by the opponent is decreased to 0 during the turn this card is activated.
THIS GIANT IRON MASK WILL BE MY SHIELD!
EVEN YOUR DRAGON CAN'T BREAK THROUGH IT! HAW HAW HAW!
TOO BAD, KAIBA!
I KNEW YOU'D TRY SOME-THING LIKE THAT!

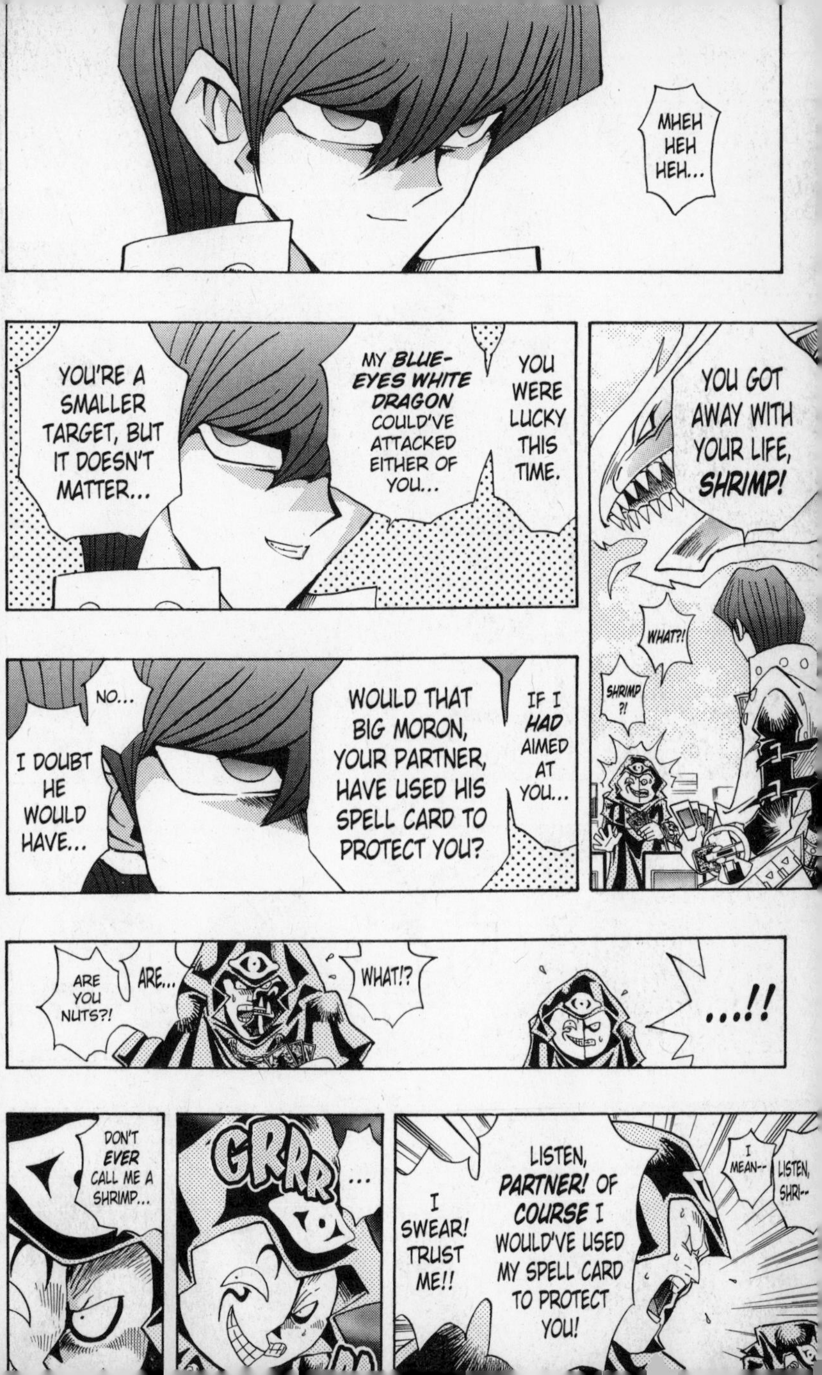
MHEH HEH HEH...
YOU GOT AWAY WITH YOUR LIFE, **SHRIMP!**
WHAT?!
SHRIMP ?!
YOU WERE LUCKY THIS TIME.
MY ***BLUE-EYES WHITE DRAGON*** COULD'VE ATTACKED EITHER OF YOU...
YOU'RE A SMALLER TARGET, BUT IT DOESN'T MATTER...
IF I ***HAD*** AIMED AT YOU...
WOULD THAT BIG MORON, YOUR PARTNER, HAVE USED HIS SPELL CARD TO PROTECT YOU?
NO...
I DOUBT HE WOULD HAVE...
...!!
WHAT!?
ARE...
ARE YOU NUTS?!
LISTEN, SHRI--
I MEAN--
LISTEN, ***PARTNER!*** OF ***COURSE*** I WOULD'VE USED MY SPELL CARD TO PROTECT YOU!
I SWEAR! TRUST ME!!
GRRR
...
DON'T ***EVER*** CALL ME A SHRIMP...

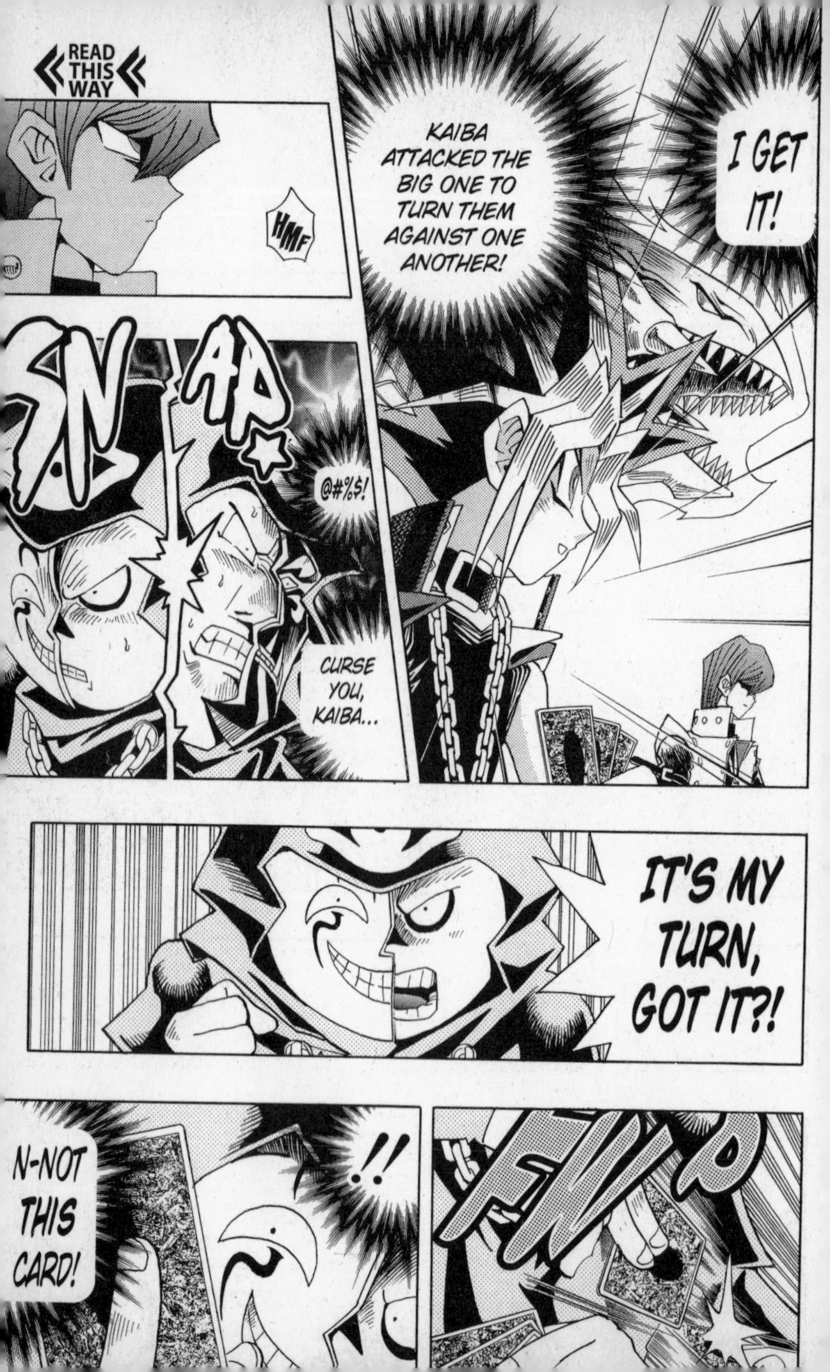
READ THIS WAY
I GET IT!
KAIBA ATTACKED THE BIG ONE TO TURN THEM AGAINST ONE ANOTHER!
HMF
SNAP
@#%$!
CURSE YOU, KAIBA...
IT'S MY TURN, GOT IT?!
FLIP
!!
N-NOT THIS CARD!

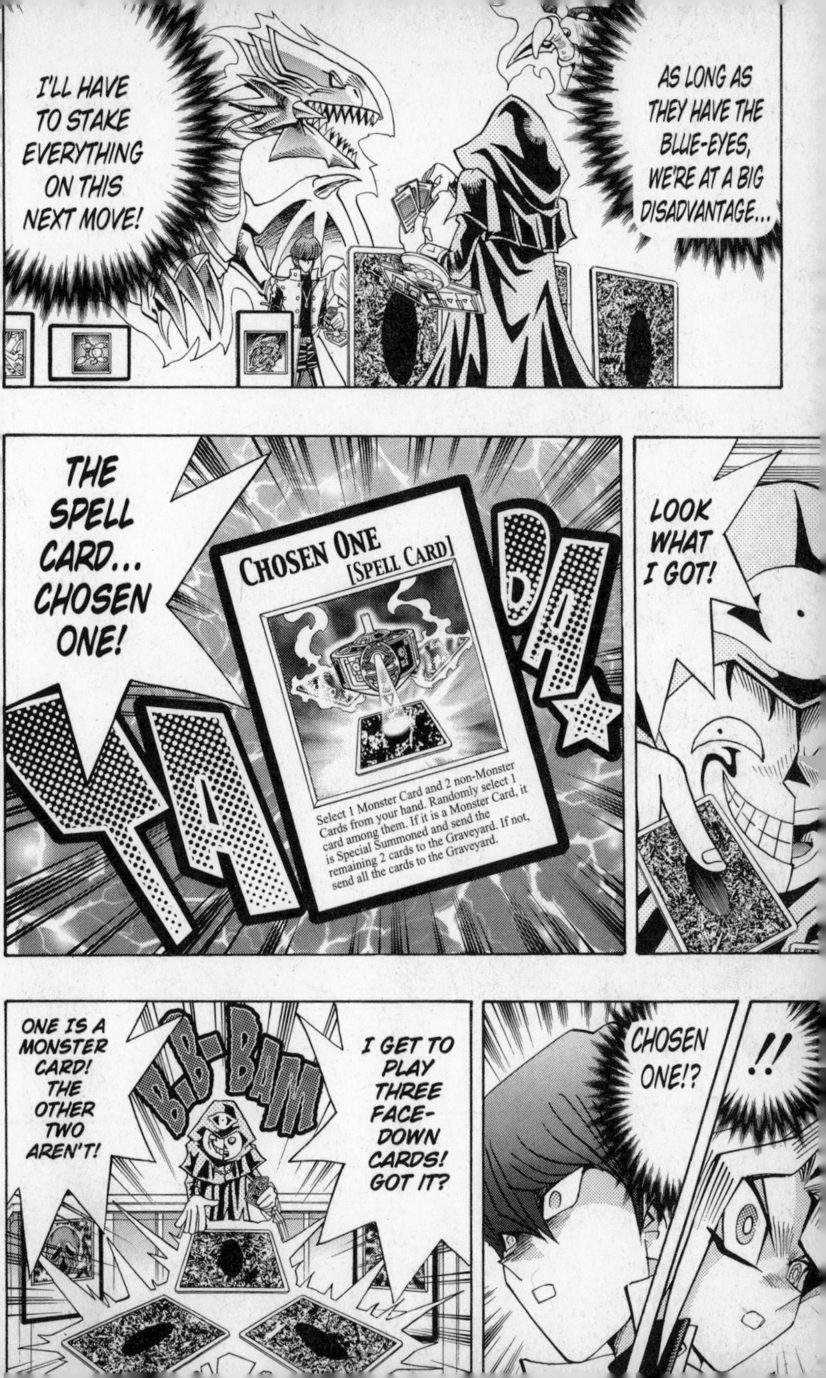
AS LONG AS THEY HAVE THE BLUE-EYES, WE'RE AT A BIG DISADVANTAGE...
I'LL HAVE TO STAKE EVERYTHING ON THIS NEXT MOVE!
LOOK WHAT I GOT!
THE SPELL CARD... CHOSEN ONE!
TA DA
CHOSEN ONE
[SPELL CARD]
Select 1 Monster Card and 2 non-Monster Cards from your hand. Randomly select 1 card among them. If it is a Monster Card, it is Special Summoned and send the remaining 2 cards to the Graveyard. If not, send all the cards to the Graveyard.
CHOSEN ONE!?
!!
B-B-BAM
I GET TO PLAY THREE FACE-DOWN CARDS! GOT IT?
ONE IS A MONSTER CARD! THE OTHER TWO AREN'T!

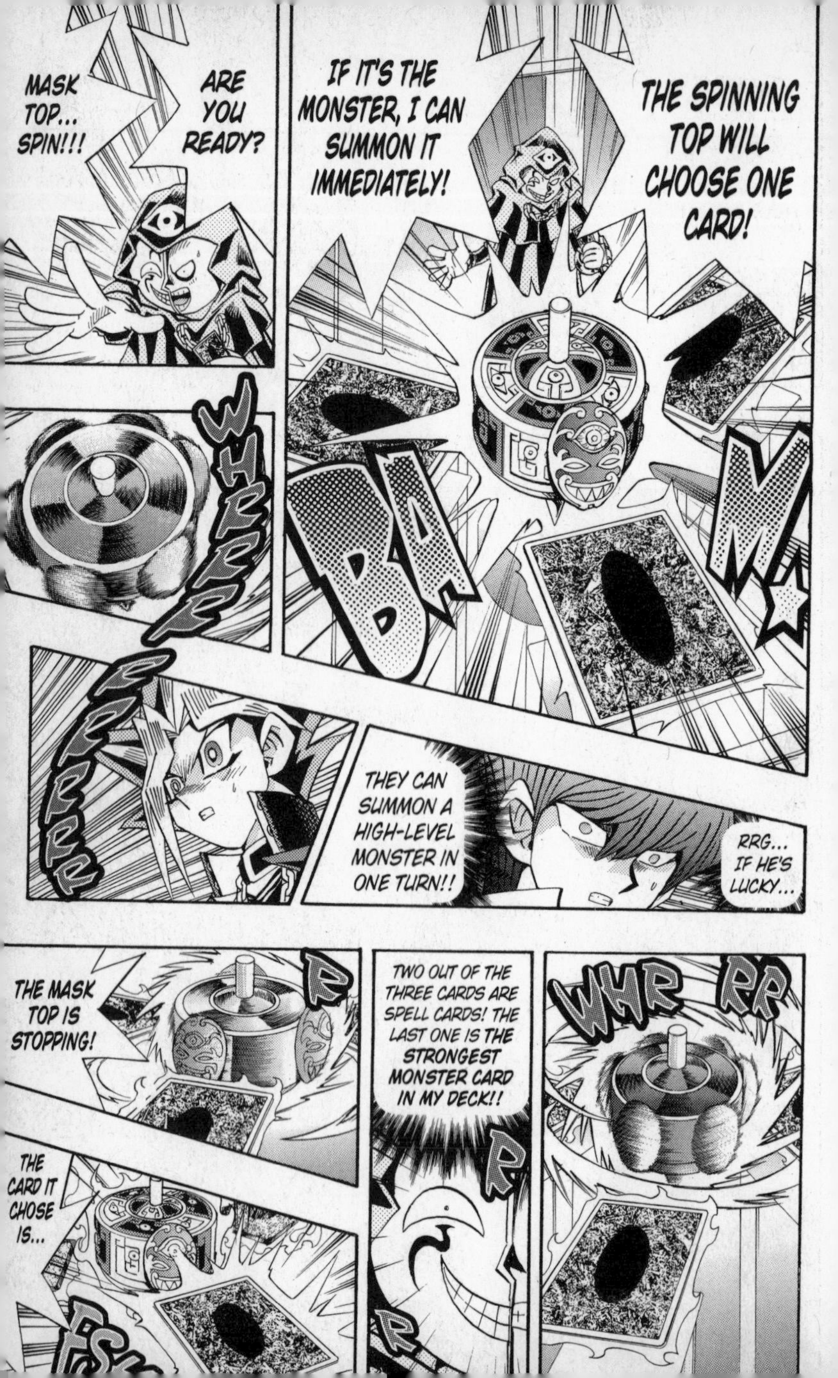
THE SPINNING TOP WILL CHOOSE ONE CARD!
IF IT'S THE MONSTER, I CAN SUMMON IT IMMEDIATELY!
BAM
ARE YOU READY?
MASK TOP... SPIN!!!
RRG... IF HE'S LUCKY...
THEY CAN SUMMON A HIGH-LEVEL MONSTER IN ONE TURN!!
WHR RR
TWO OUT OF THE THREE CARDS ARE SPELL CARDS! THE LAST ONE IS THE STRONGEST MONSTER CARD IN MY DECK!!
R
R
THE MASK TOP IS STOPPING!
THE CARD IT CHOSE IS...

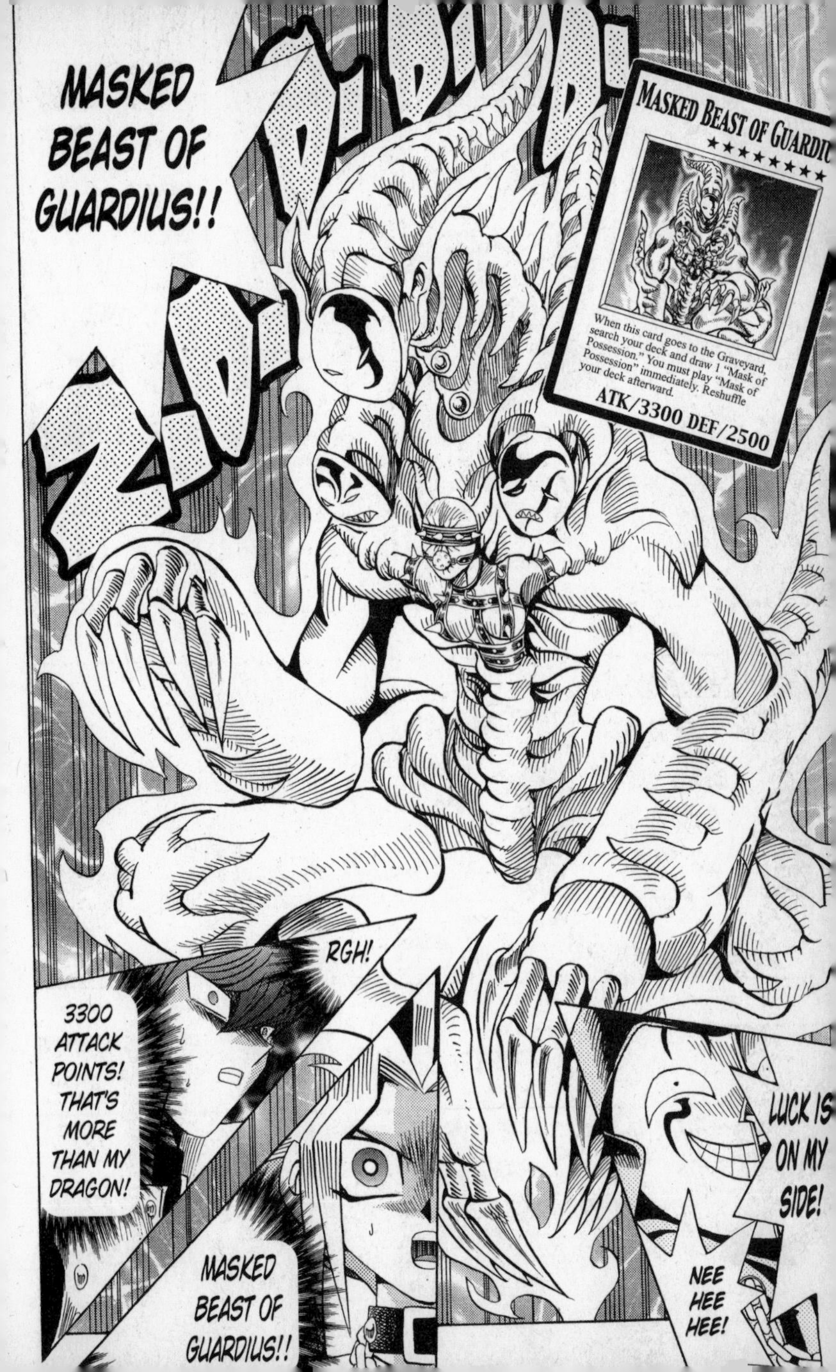
Masked Beast of Guardi
When this card goes to the Graveyard, search your deck and draw 1 "Mask of Possession." You must play "Mask of Possession" immediately. Reshuffle your deck afterward.
ATK/3300 DEF/2500
MASKED BEAST OF GUARDIUS!!
LUCK IS ON MY SIDE!
NEE HEE HEE!
MASKED BEAST OF GUARDIUS!!
RGH!
3300 ATTACK POINTS! THAT'S MORE THAN MY DRAGON!

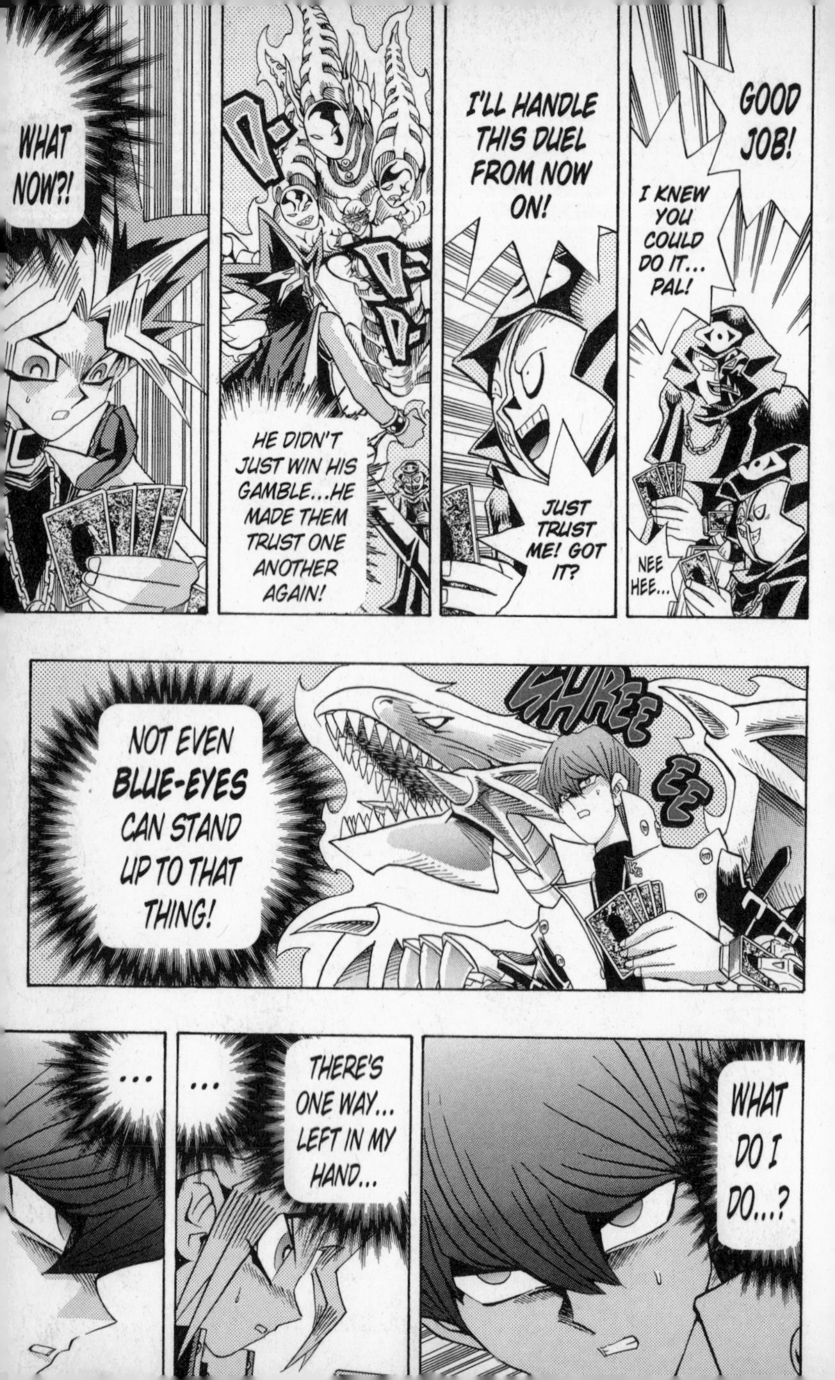
GOOD JOB!
I KNEW YOU COULD DO IT... PAL!
NEE HEE...
I'LL HANDLE THIS DUEL FROM NOW ON!
JUST TRUST ME! GOT IT?
HE DIDN'T JUST WIN HIS GAMBLE...HE MADE THEM TRUST ONE ANOTHER AGAIN!
WHAT NOW?!
SHREE
EE
NOT EVEN BLUE-EYES CAN STAND UP TO THAT THING!
WHAT DO I DO...?
THERE'S ONE WAY... LEFT IN MY HAND...
...
...

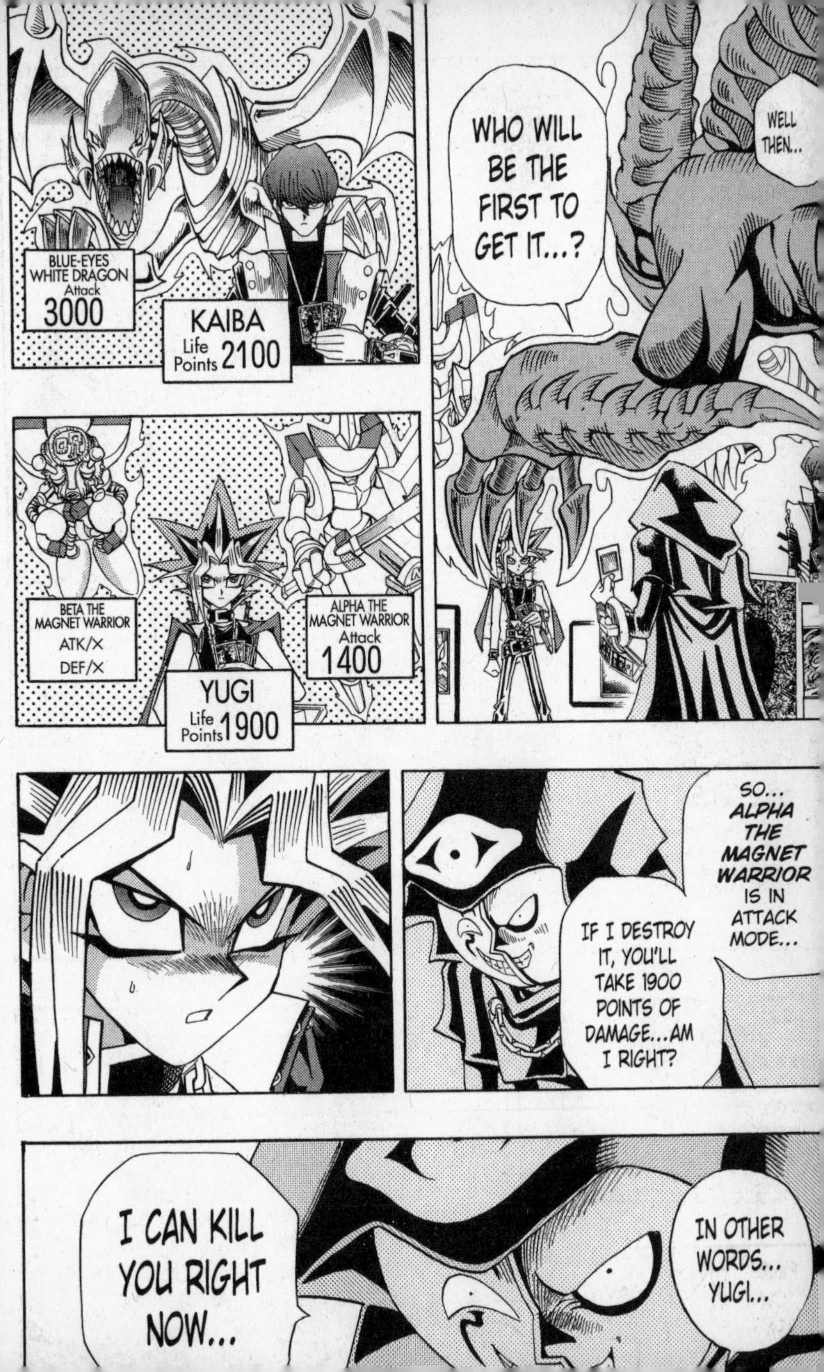
WELL THEN...
WHO WILL BE THE FIRST TO GET IT...?
BLUE-EYES WHITE DRAGON Attack 3000
KAIBA Life Points 2100
BETA THE MAGNET WARRIOR ATK/X DEF/X
ALPHA THE MAGNET WARRIOR Attack 1400
YUGI Life Points 1900
SO... ALPHA THE MAGNET WARRIOR IS IN ATTACK MODE...
IF I DESTROY IT, YOU'LL TAKE 1900 POINTS OF DAMAGE...AM I RIGHT?
IN OTHER WORDS... YUGI...
I CAN KILL YOU RIGHT NOW...

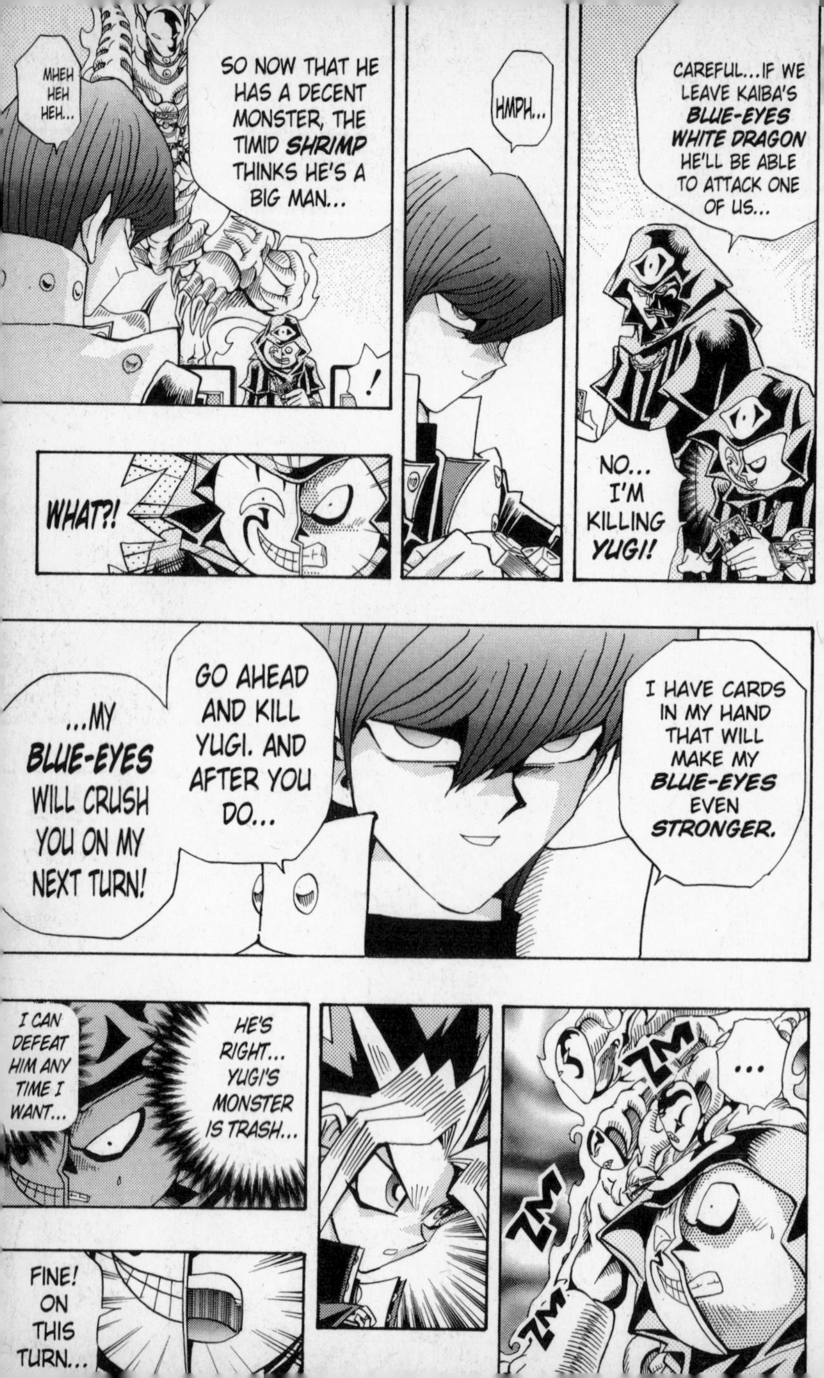
CAREFUL...IF WE LEAVE KAIBA'S BLUE-EYES WHITE DRAGON HE'LL BE ABLE TO ATTACK ONE OF US...
NO... I'M KILLING YUGI!
HMPH...
SO NOW THAT HE HAS A DECENT MONSTER, THE TIMID SHRIMP THINKS HE'S A BIG MAN...
MHEH HEH HEH...
!
WHAT?!
I HAVE CARDS IN MY HAND THAT WILL MAKE MY BLUE-EYES EVEN STRONGER.
GO AHEAD AND KILL YUGI. AND AFTER YOU DO...
...MY BLUE-EYES WILL CRUSH YOU ON MY NEXT TURN!
...
ZM
ZM
ZM
HE'S RIGHT... YUGI'S MONSTER IS TRASH...
I CAN DEFEAT HIM ANY TIME I WANT...
FINE! ON THIS TURN...

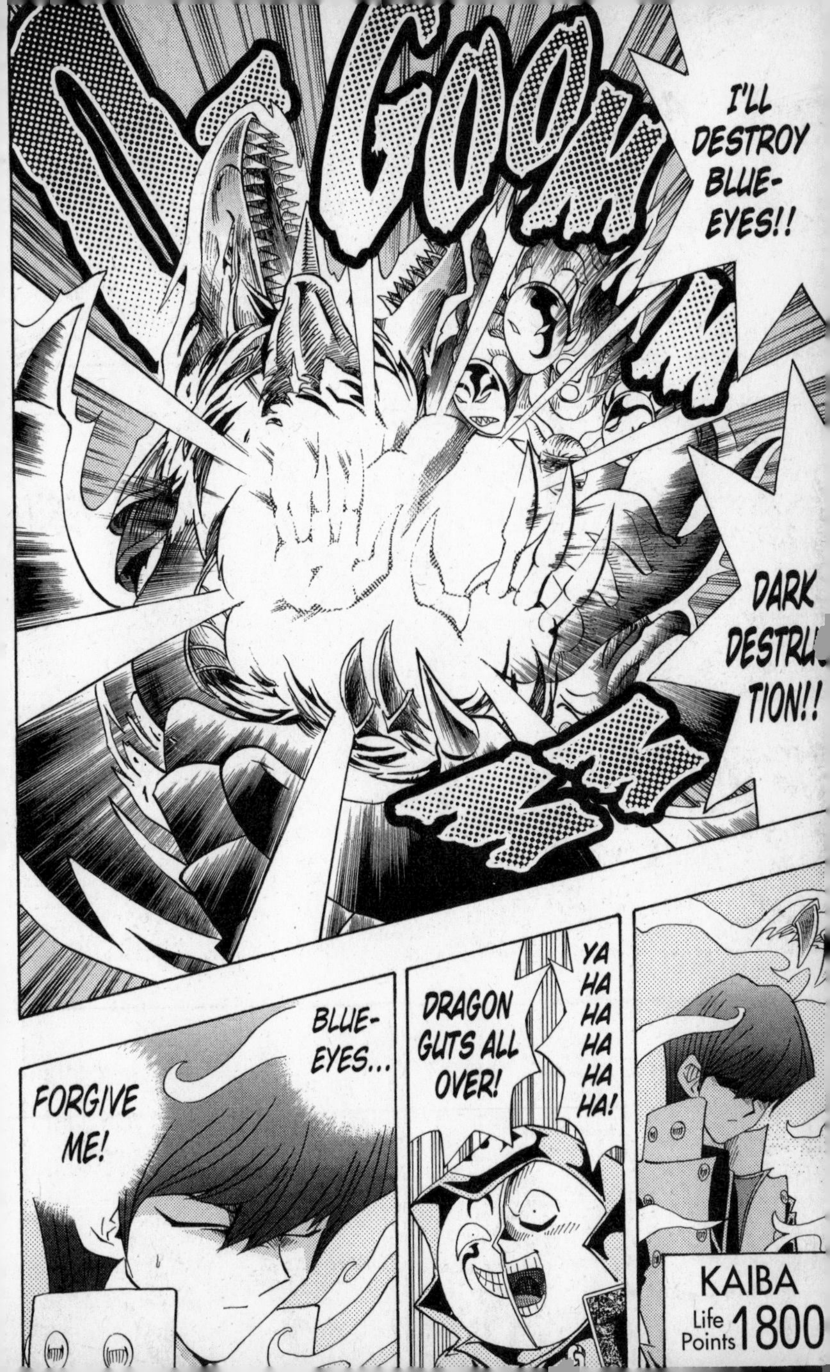
I'LL DESTROY BLUE-EYES!!
GOOM
DARK DESTRU TION!!
KAIBA Life Points 1800
YA HA HA HA HA HA HA!
DRAGON GUTS ALL OVER!
BLUE-EYES...
FORGIVE ME!

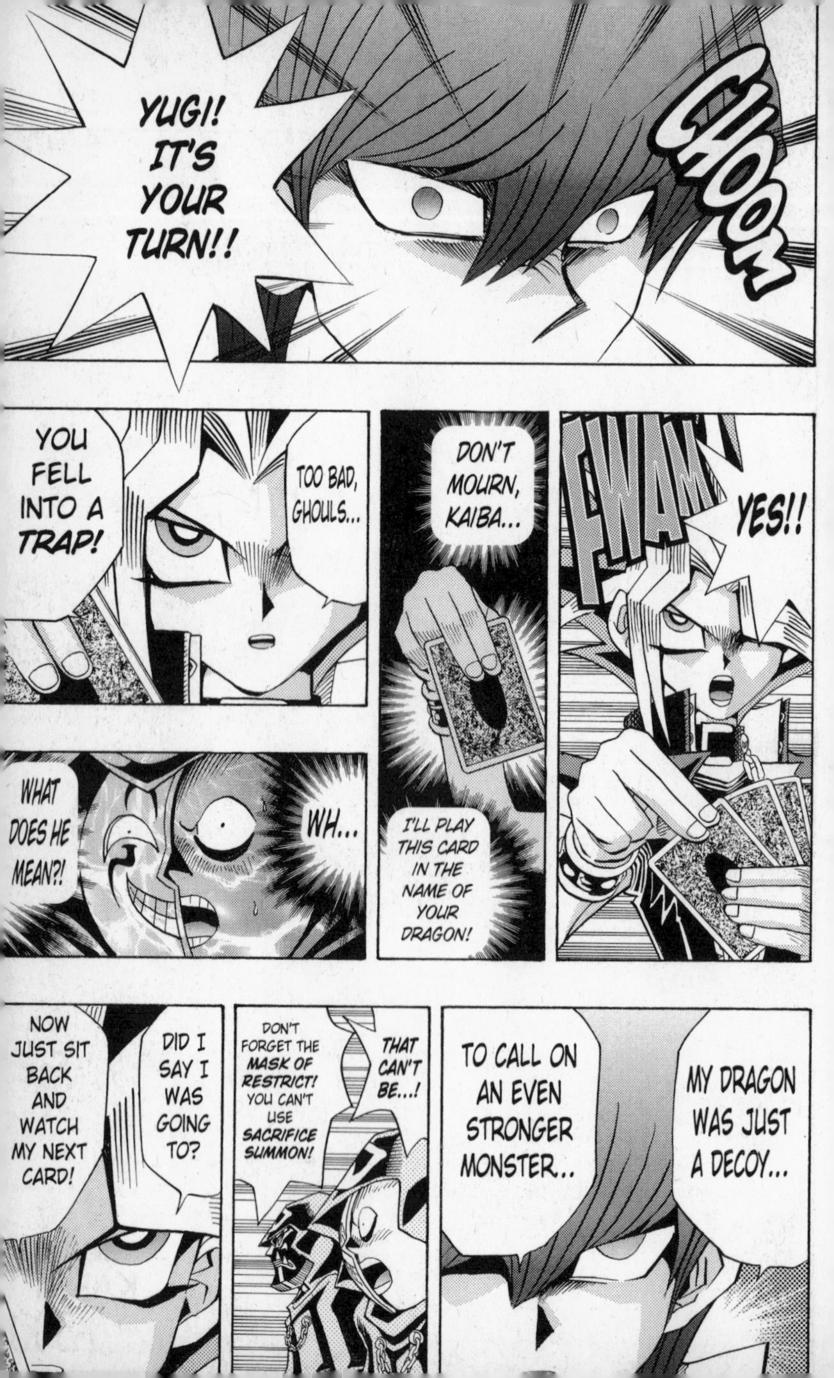
CHOOM
YUGI! IT'S YOUR TURN!!
FWAM
YES!!
DON'T MOURN, KAIBA...
I'LL PLAY THIS CARD IN THE NAME OF YOUR DRAGON!
TOO BAD, GHOULS...
YOU FELL INTO A TRAP!
WH...
WHAT DOES HE MEAN?!
MY DRAGON WAS JUST A DECOY...
TO CALL ON AN EVEN STRONGER MONSTER...
THAT CAN'T BE...!
DON'T FORGET THE MASK OF RESTRICT! YOU CAN'T USE SACRIFICE SUMMON!
DID I SAY I WAS GOING TO?
NOW JUST SIT BACK AND WATCH MY NEXT CARD!

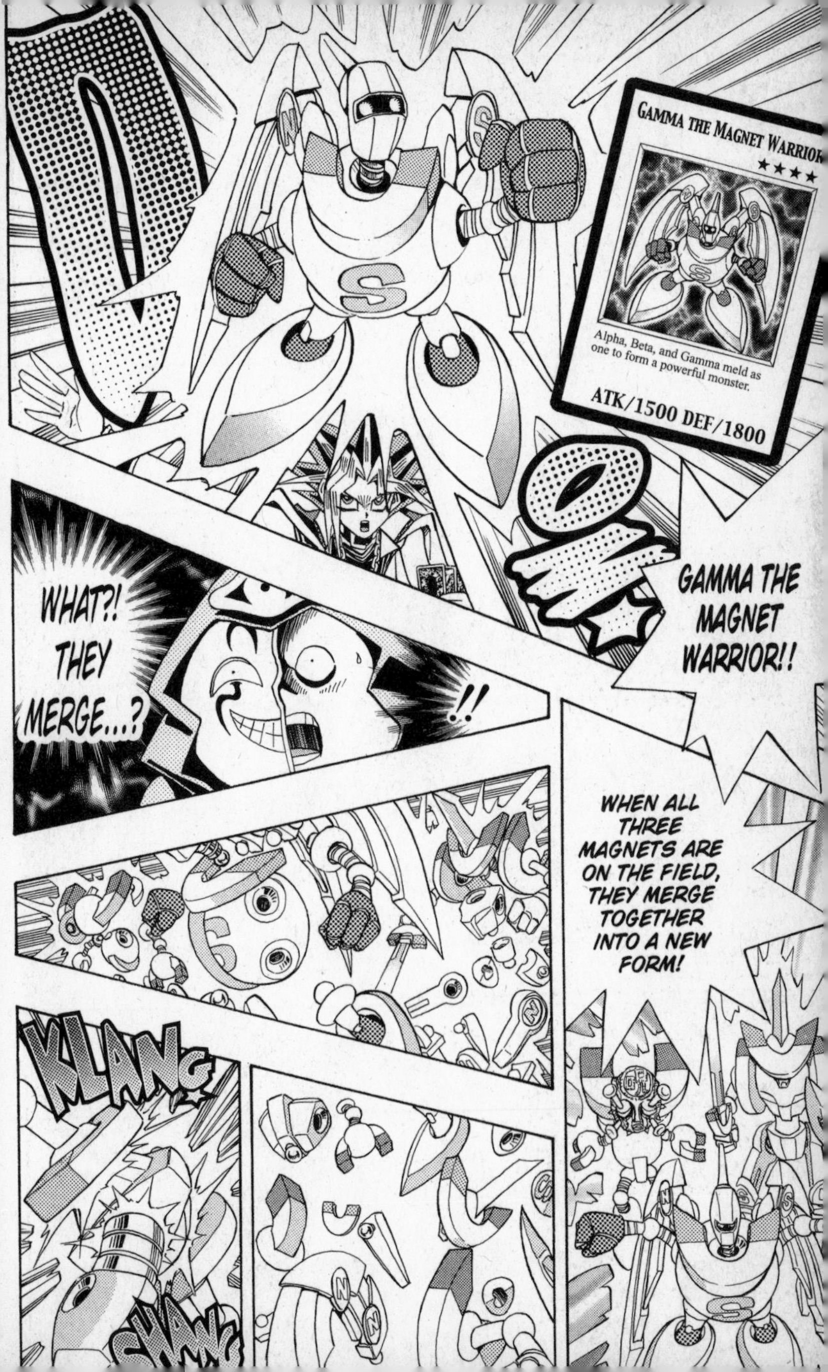
GAMMA THE MAGNET WARRIOR
Alpha, Beta, and Gamma meld as one to form a powerful monster.
ATK/1500 DEF/1800
GAMMA THE MAGNET WARRIOR!!
WHAT?! THEY MERGE...?
!!
WHEN ALL THREE MAGNETS ARE ON THE FIELD, THEY MERGE TOGETHER INTO A NEW FORM!
KLANG

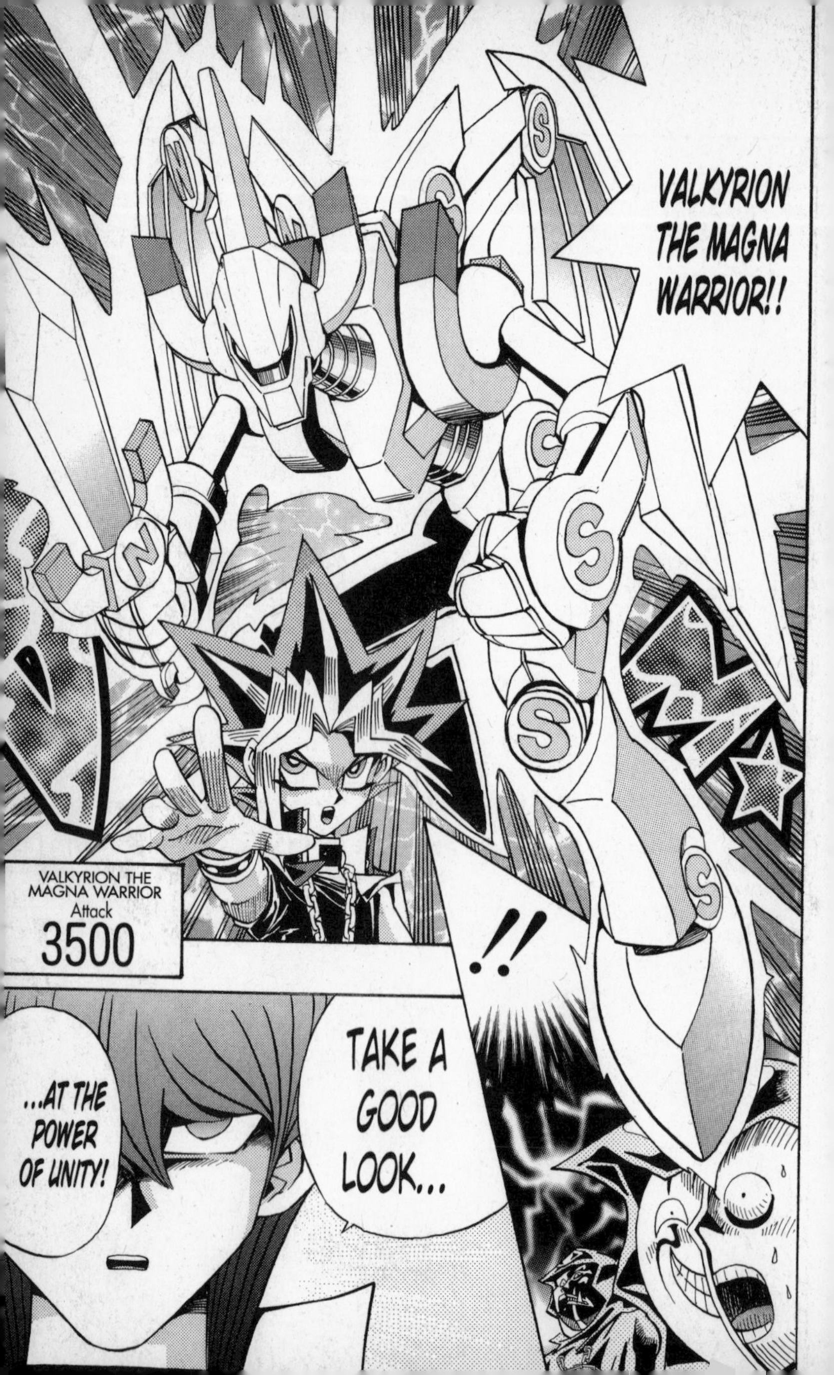
VALKYRION THE MAGNA WARRIOR!!
VALKYRION THE MAGNA WARRIOR Attack 3500
!!
TAKE A GOOD LOOK...
...AT THE POWER OF UNITY!

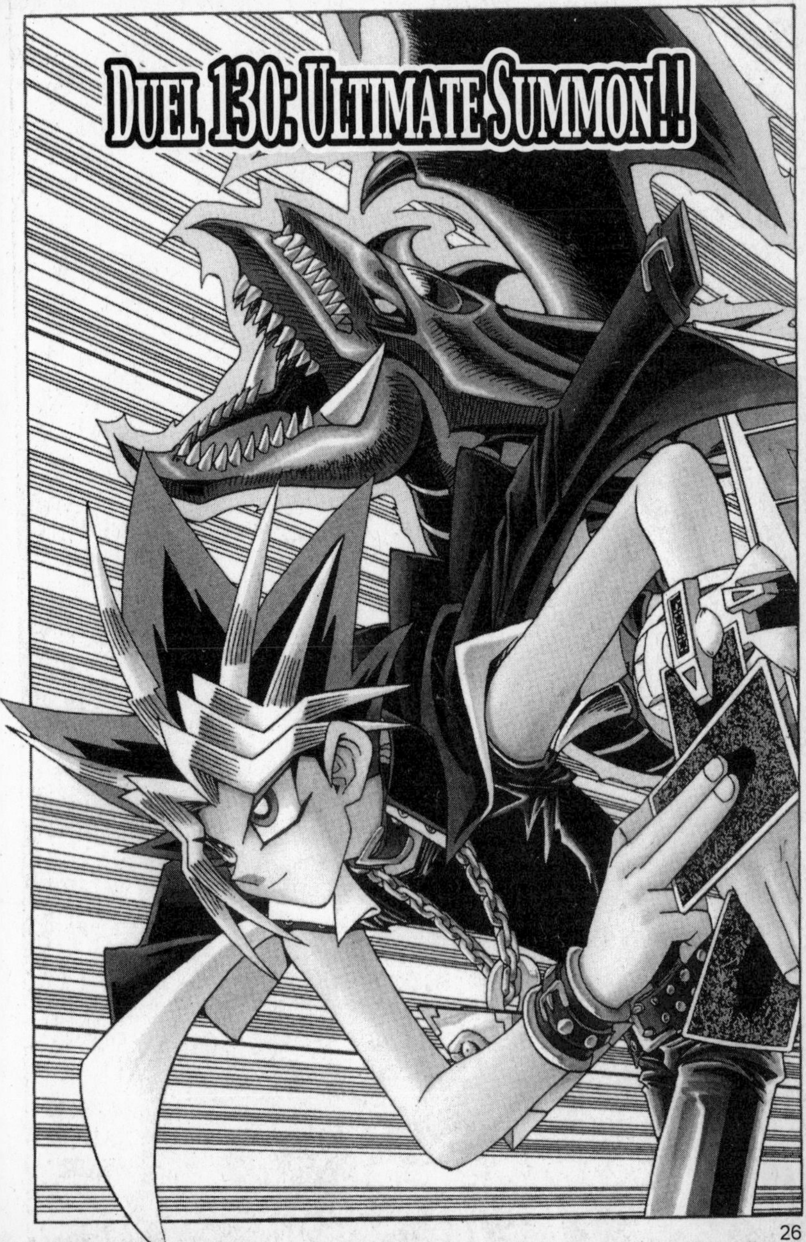
DUEL 130: ULTIMATE SUMMON!!

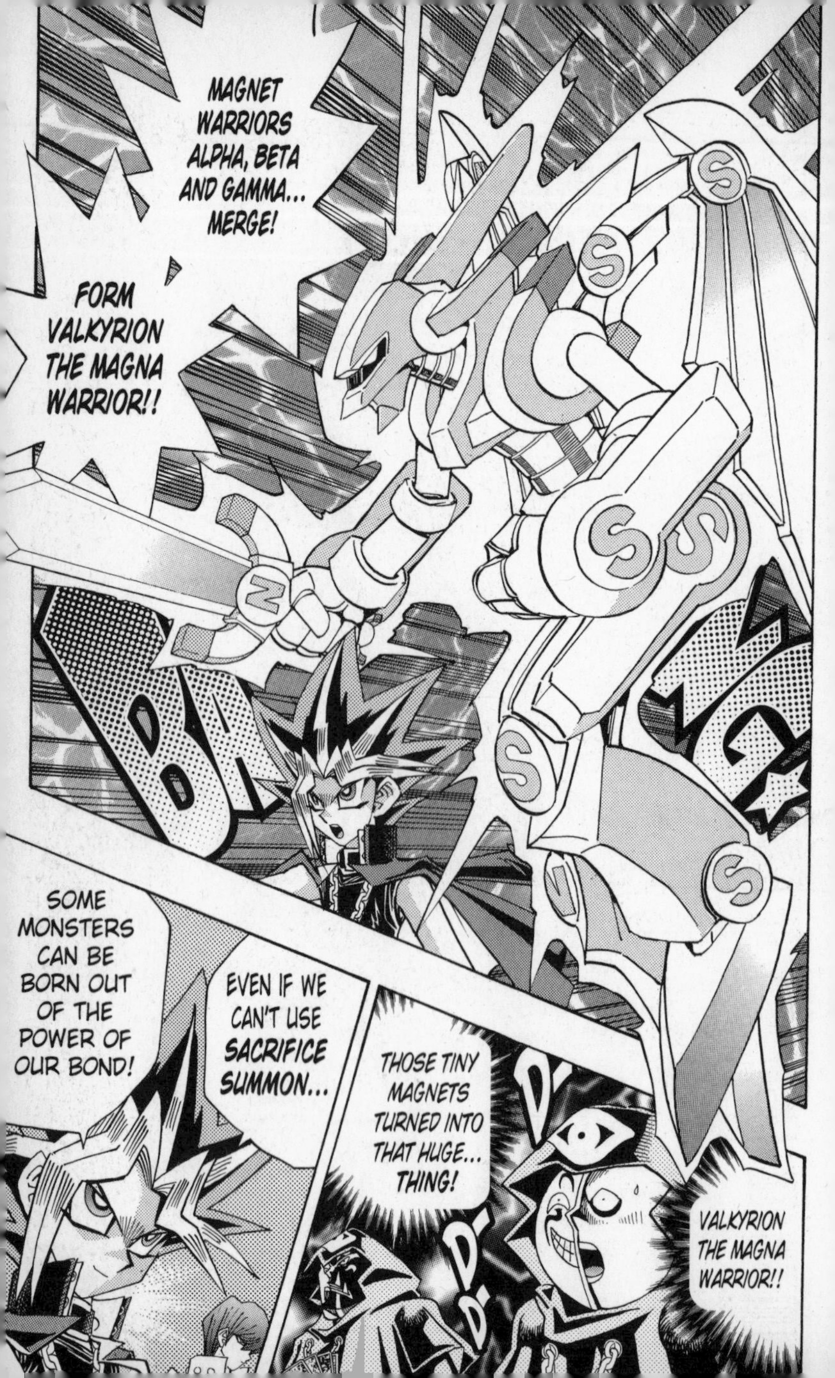
MAGNET WARRIORS ALPHA, BETA AND GAMMA... MERGE!
FORM VALKYRION THE MAGNA WARRIOR!!
VALKYRION THE MAGNA WARRIOR!!
THOSE TINY MAGNETS TURNED INTO THAT HUGE... THING!
EVEN IF WE CAN'T USE SACRIFICE SUMMON...
SOME MONSTERS CAN BE BORN OUT OF THE POWER OF OUR BOND!

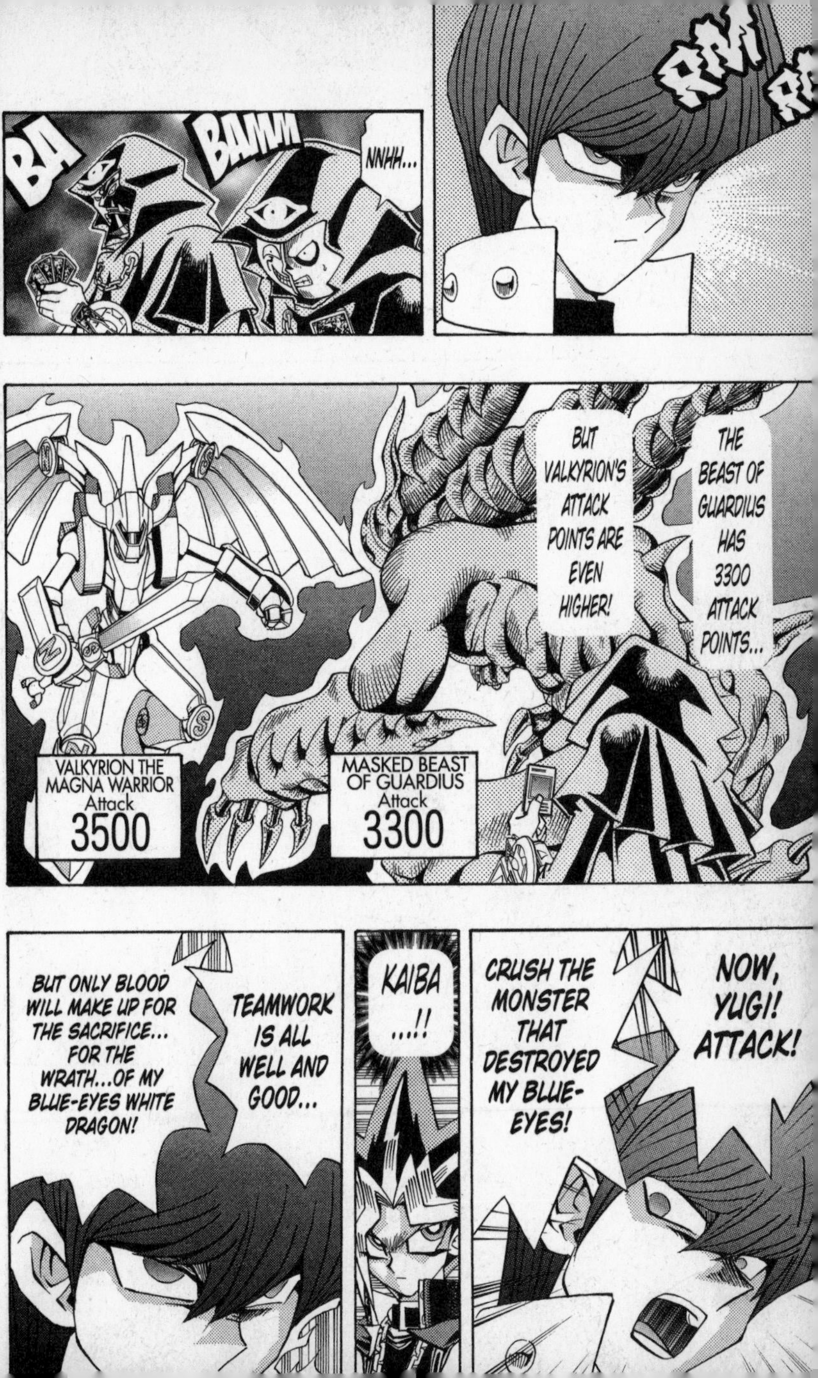
RM
BA
BAMM
NNHH...
THE BEAST OF GUARDIUS HAS 3300 ATTACK POINTS...
BUT VALKYRION'S ATTACK POINTS ARE EVEN HIGHER!
MASKED BEAST OF GUARDIUS Attack 3300
VALKYRION THE MAGNA WARRIOR Attack 3500
NOW, YUGI! ATTACK!
CRUSH THE MONSTER THAT DESTROYED MY BLUE-EYES!
KAIBA ...!!
TEAMWORK IS ALL WELL AND GOOD...
BUT ONLY BLOOD WILL MAKE UP FOR THE SACRIFICE... FOR THE WRATH...OF MY BLUE-EYES WHITE DRAGON!

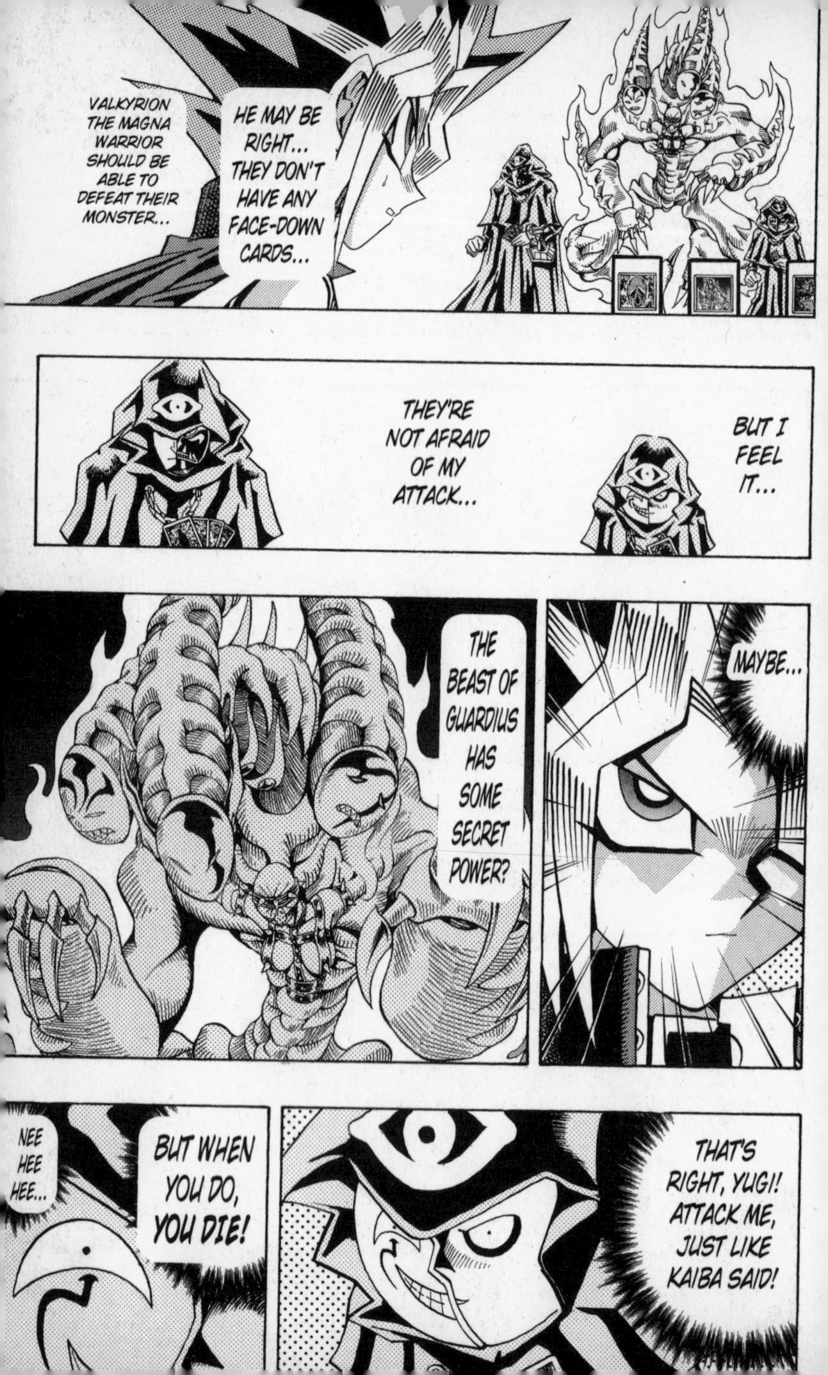
HE MAY BE RIGHT... THEY DON'T HAVE ANY FACE-DOWN CARDS...
VALKYRION THE MAGNA WARRIOR SHOULD BE ABLE TO DEFEAT THEIR MONSTER...
BUT I FEEL IT...
THEY'RE NOT AFRAID OF MY ATTACK...
MAYBE...
THE BEAST OF GUARDIUS HAS SOME SECRET POWER?
THAT'S RIGHT, YUGI! ATTACK ME, JUST LIKE KAIBA SAID!
BUT WHEN YOU DO, YOU DIE!
NEE HEE HEE...

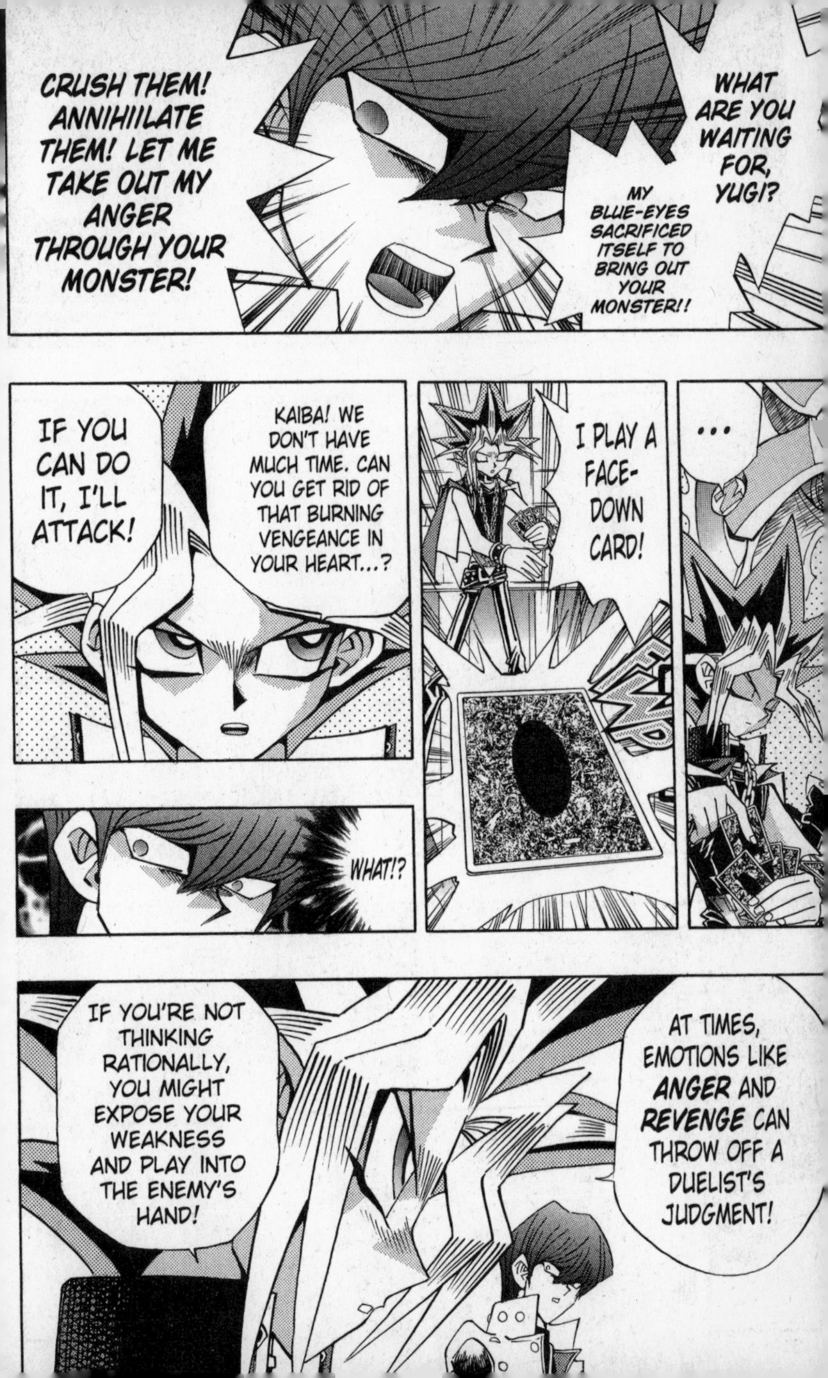

WHAT ARE YOU WAITING FOR, YUGI?
MY BLUE-EYES SACRIFICED ITSELF TO BRING OUT YOUR MONSTER!!
CRUSH THEM! ANNIHIILATE THEM! LET ME TAKE OUT MY ANGER THROUGH YOUR MONSTER!
...
I PLAY A FACE-DOWN CARD!
FWP
KAIBA! WE DON'T HAVE MUCH TIME. CAN YOU GET RID OF THAT BURNING VENGEANCE IN YOUR HEART...?
IF YOU CAN DO IT, I'LL ATTACK!
WHAT!?
AT TIMES, EMOTIONS LIKE ANGER AND REVENGE CAN THROW OFF A DUELIST'S JUDGMENT!
IF YOU'RE NOT THINKING RATIONALLY, YOU MIGHT EXPOSE YOUR WEAKNESS AND PLAY INTO THE ENEMY'S HAND!

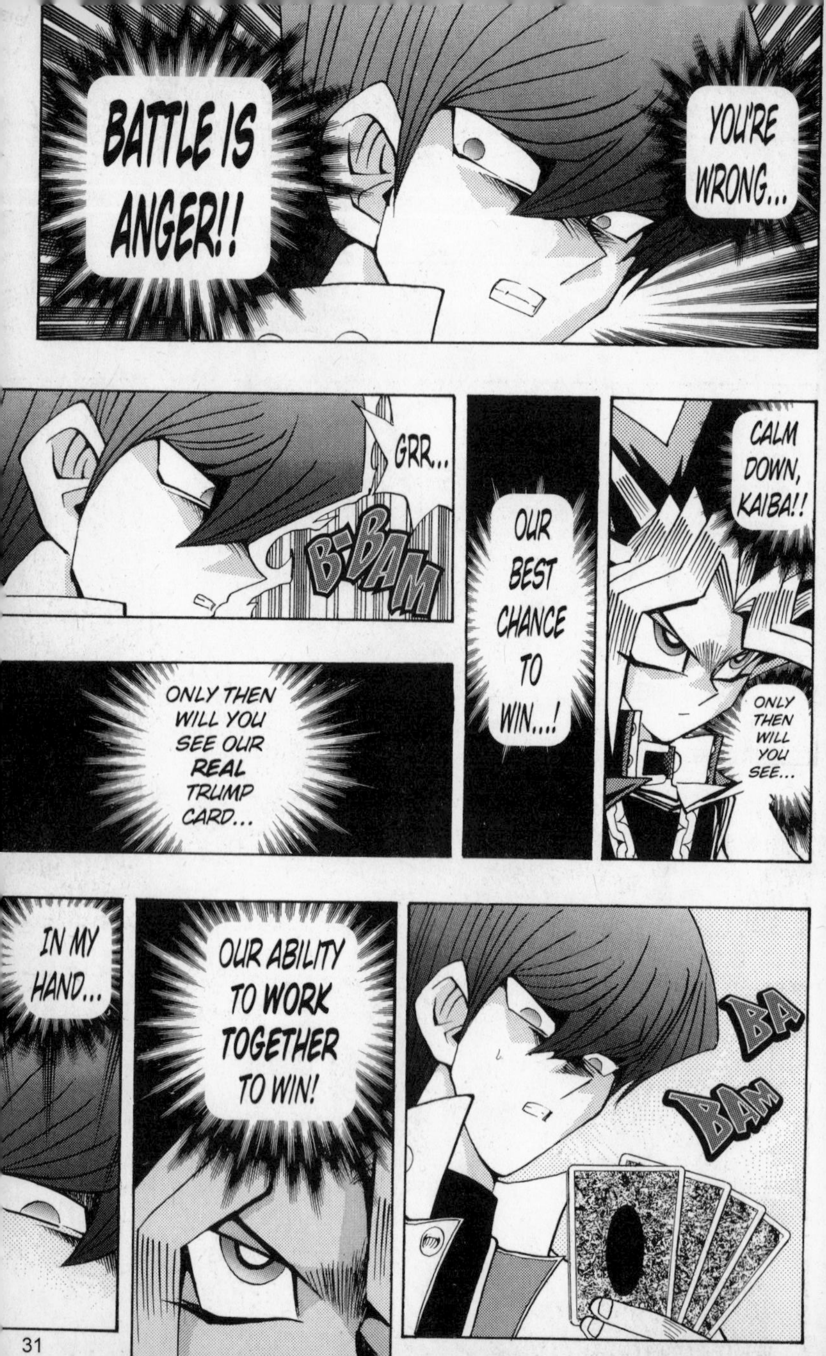

YOU'RE WRONG...
BATTLE IS ANGER!!
CALM DOWN, KAIBA!!
ONLY THEN WILL YOU SEE...
OUR BEST CHANCE TO WIN...!
GRR...
B-BAM
ONLY THEN WILL YOU SEE OUR REAL TRUMP CARD...
BA
BAM
OUR ABILITY TO WORK TOGETHER TO WIN!
IN MY HAND...

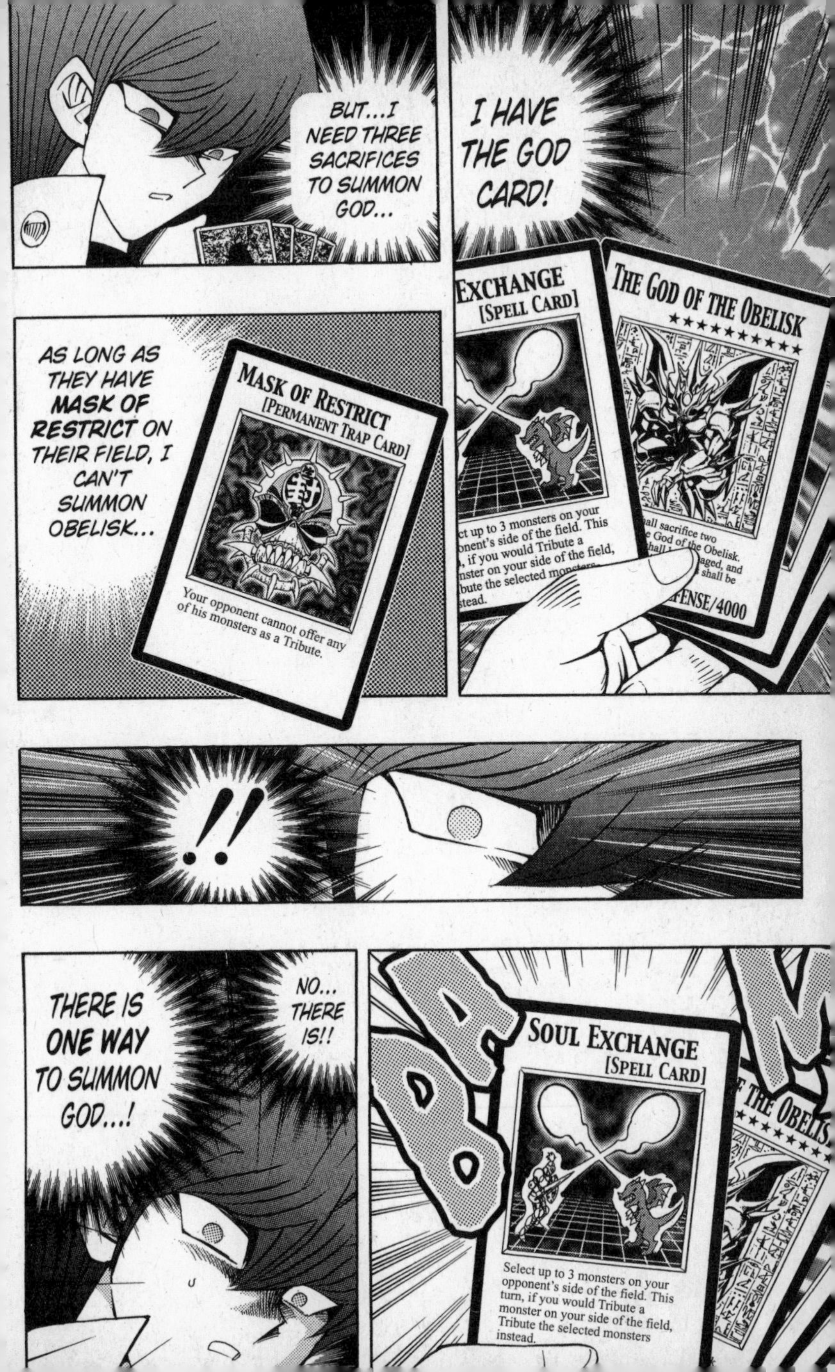
I HAVE THE GOD CARD!
EXCHANGE
[SPELL CARD]
THE GOD OF THE OBELISK
BUT...I NEED THREE SACRIFICES TO SUMMON GOD...
AS LONG AS THEY HAVE MASK OF RESTRICT ON THEIR FIELD, I CAN'T SUMMON OBELISK...
MASK OF RESTRICT
[PERMANENT TRAP CARD]
Your opponent cannot offer any of his monsters as a Tribute.
!!
SOUL EXCHANGE
[SPELL CARD]
Select up to 3 monsters on your opponent's side of the field. This turn, if you would Tribute a monster on your side of the field, Tribute the selected monsters instead.
NO... THERE IS!!
THERE IS ONE WAY TO SUMMON GOD...!

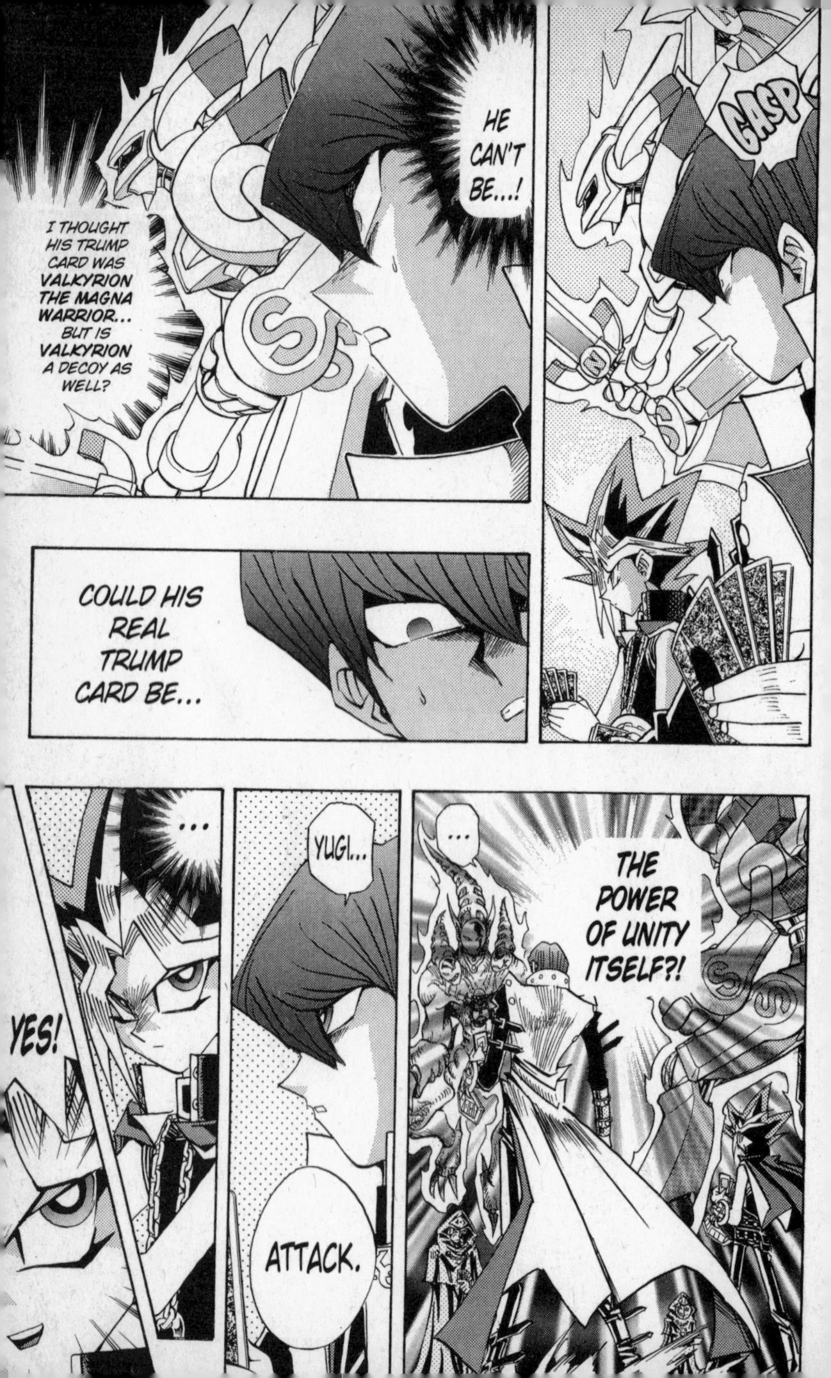
GASP
HE CAN'T BE...!
I THOUGHT HIS TRUMP CARD WAS VALKYRION THE MAGNA WARRIOR... BUT IS VALKYRION A DECOY AS WELL?
COULD HIS REAL TRUMP CARD BE...
...
THE POWER OF UNITY ITSELF?!
YUGI...
ATTACK.
...
YES!

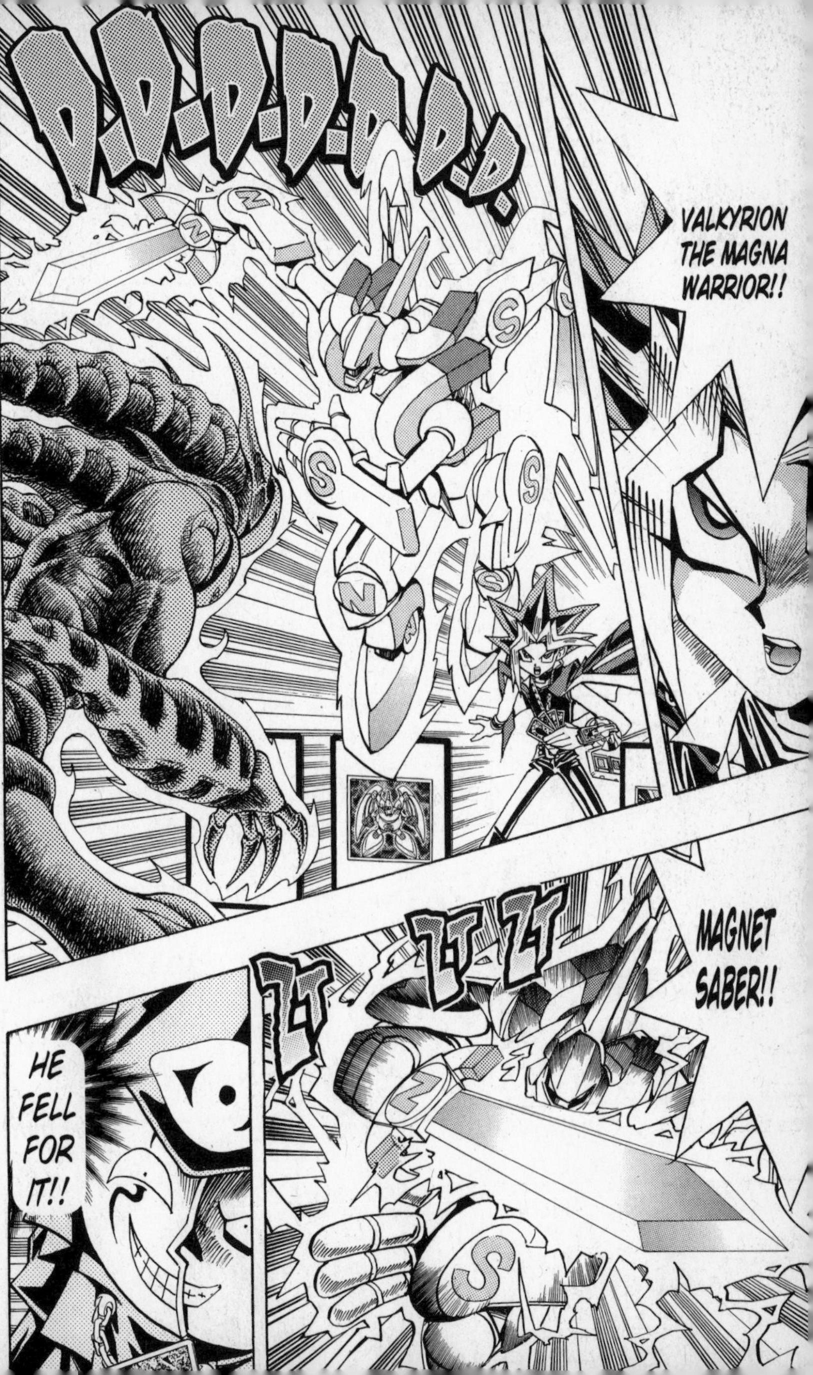
VALKYRION THE MAGNA WARRIOR!!
D.D.D.D.D.D.D.
MAGNET SABER!!
HE FELL FOR IT!!

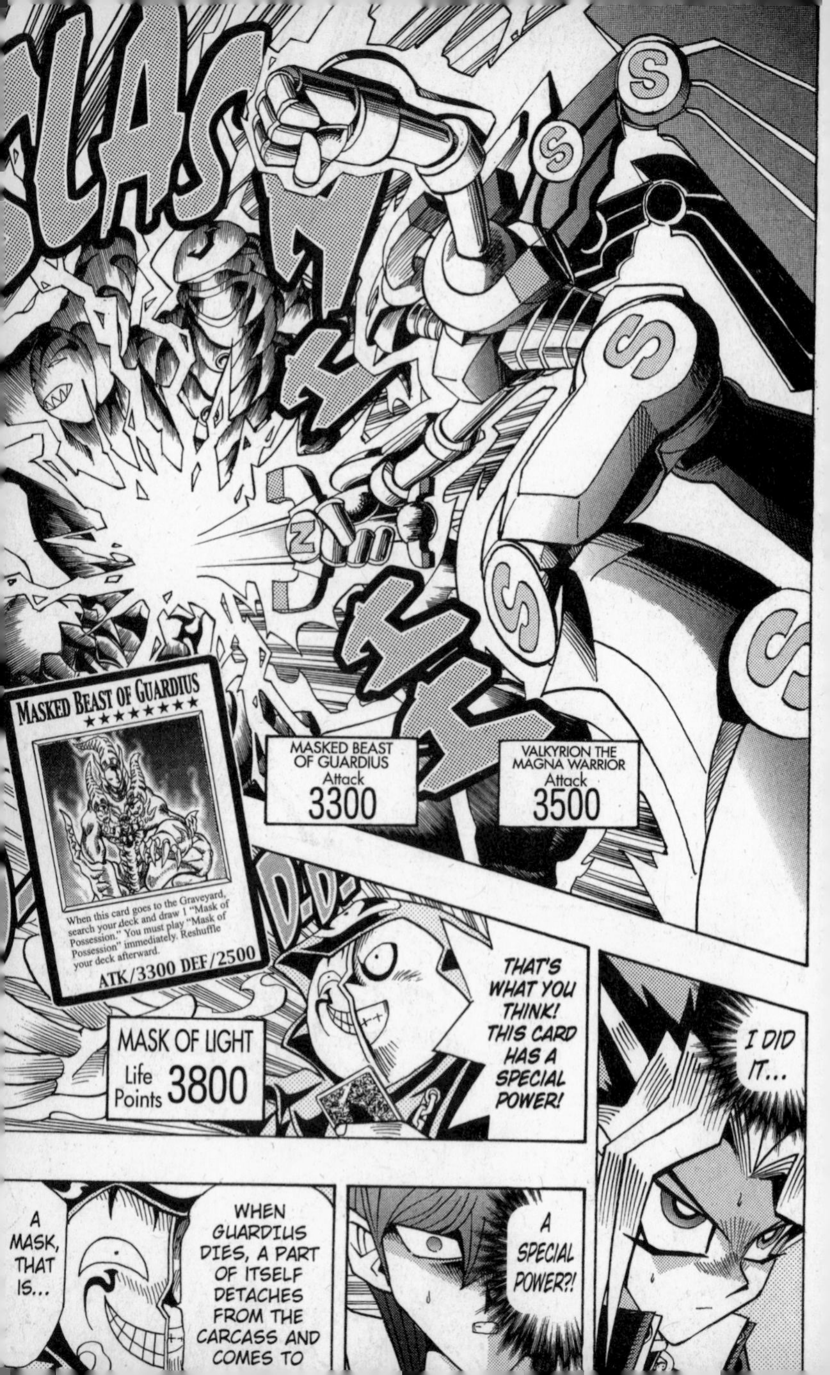

VALKYRION THE MAGNA WARRIOR Attack 3500
MASKED BEAST OF GUARDIUS Attack 3300
MASKED BEAST OF GUARDIUS
When this card goes to the Graveyard, search your deck and draw 1 "Mask of Possession." You must play "Mask of Possession" immediately. Reshuffle your deck afterward.
ATK/3300 DEF/2500
I DID IT...
THAT'S WHAT YOU THINK! THIS CARD HAS A SPECIAL POWER!
MASK OF LIGHT Life Points 3800
A SPECIAL POWER?!
WHEN GUARDIUS DIES, A PART OF ITSELF DETACHES FROM THE CARCASS AND COMES TO
A MASK, THAT IS...

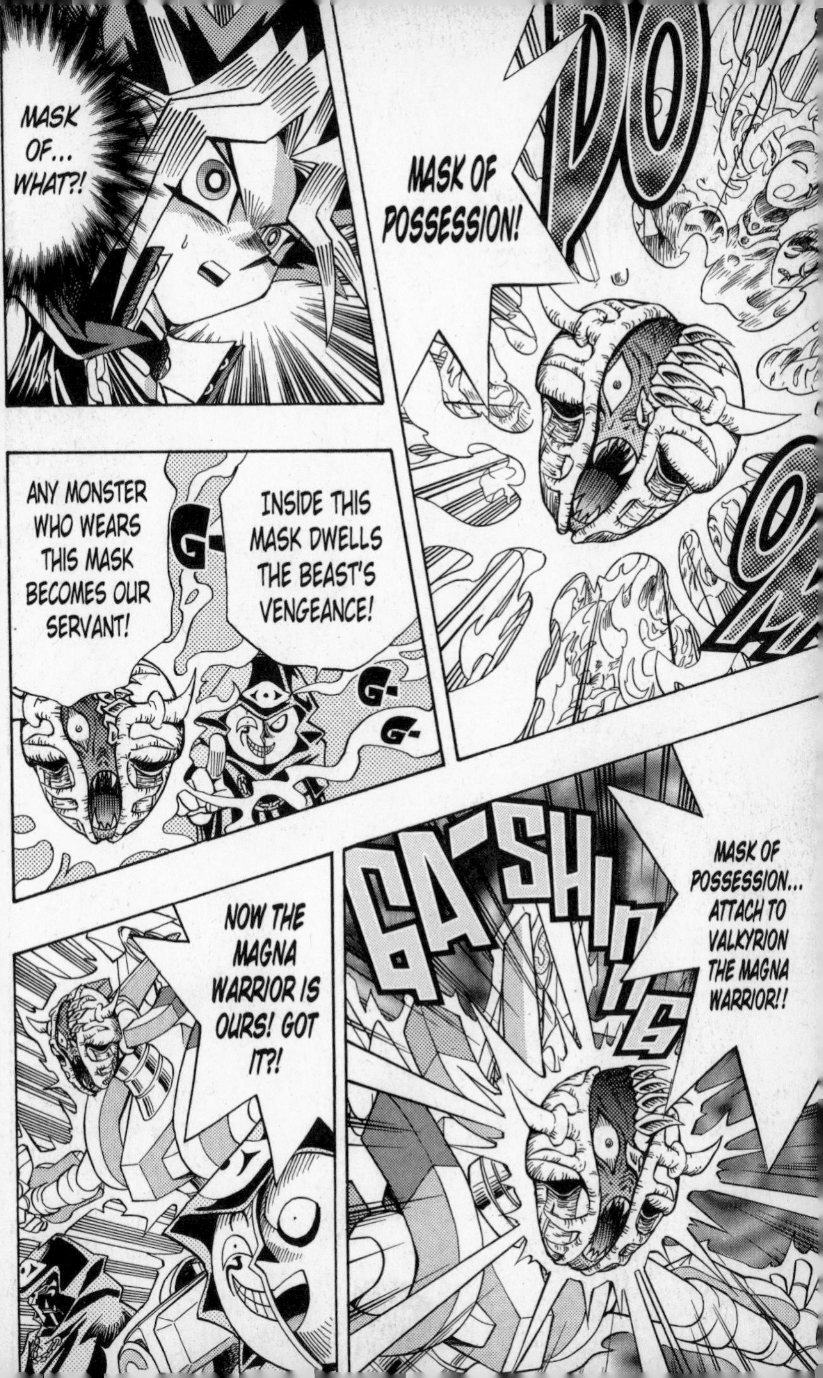
MASK OF POSSESSION!
DO
MASK OF... WHAT?!
INSIDE THIS MASK DWELLS THE BEAST'S VENGEANCE!
ANY MONSTER WHO WEARS THIS MASK BECOMES OUR SERVANT!
G-
G-
G-
MASK OF POSSESSION... ATTACH TO VALKYRION THE MAGNA WARRIOR!!
NOW THE MAGNA WARRIOR IS OURS! GOT IT?!

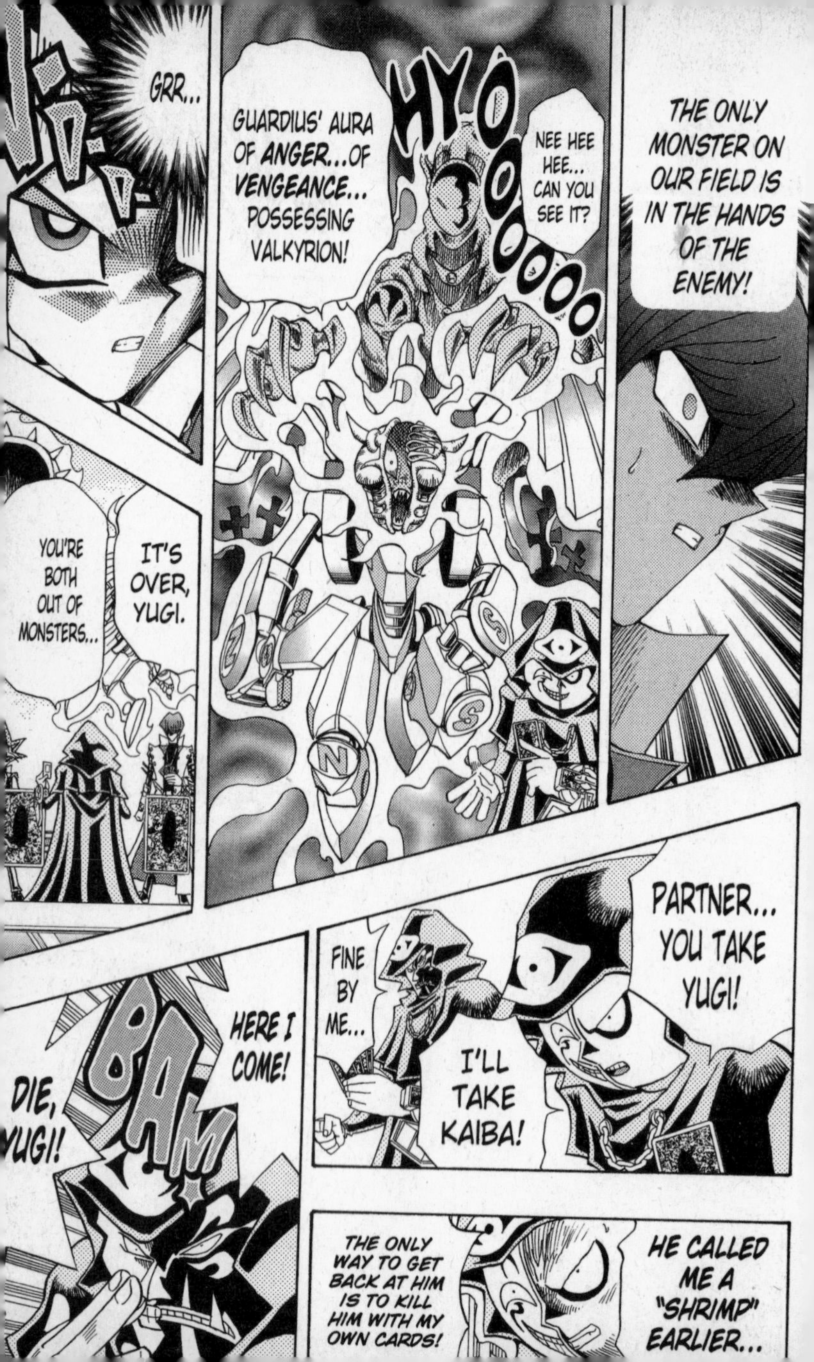
THE ONLY MONSTER ON OUR FIELD IS IN THE HANDS OF THE ENEMY!
NEE HEE HEE... CAN YOU SEE IT?
HYOOOOOOOO
GUARDIUS' AURA OF ANGER...OF VENGEANCE... POSSESSING VALKYRION!
GRR...
IT'S OVER, YUGI.
YOU'RE BOTH OUT OF MONSTERS...
PARTNER... YOU TAKE YUGI!
I'LL TAKE KAIBA!
FINE BY ME...
HE CALLED ME A "SHRIMP" EARLIER...
THE ONLY WAY TO GET BACK AT HIM IS TO KILL HIM WITH MY OWN CARDS!
HERE I COME!
BAM
DIE, YUGI!

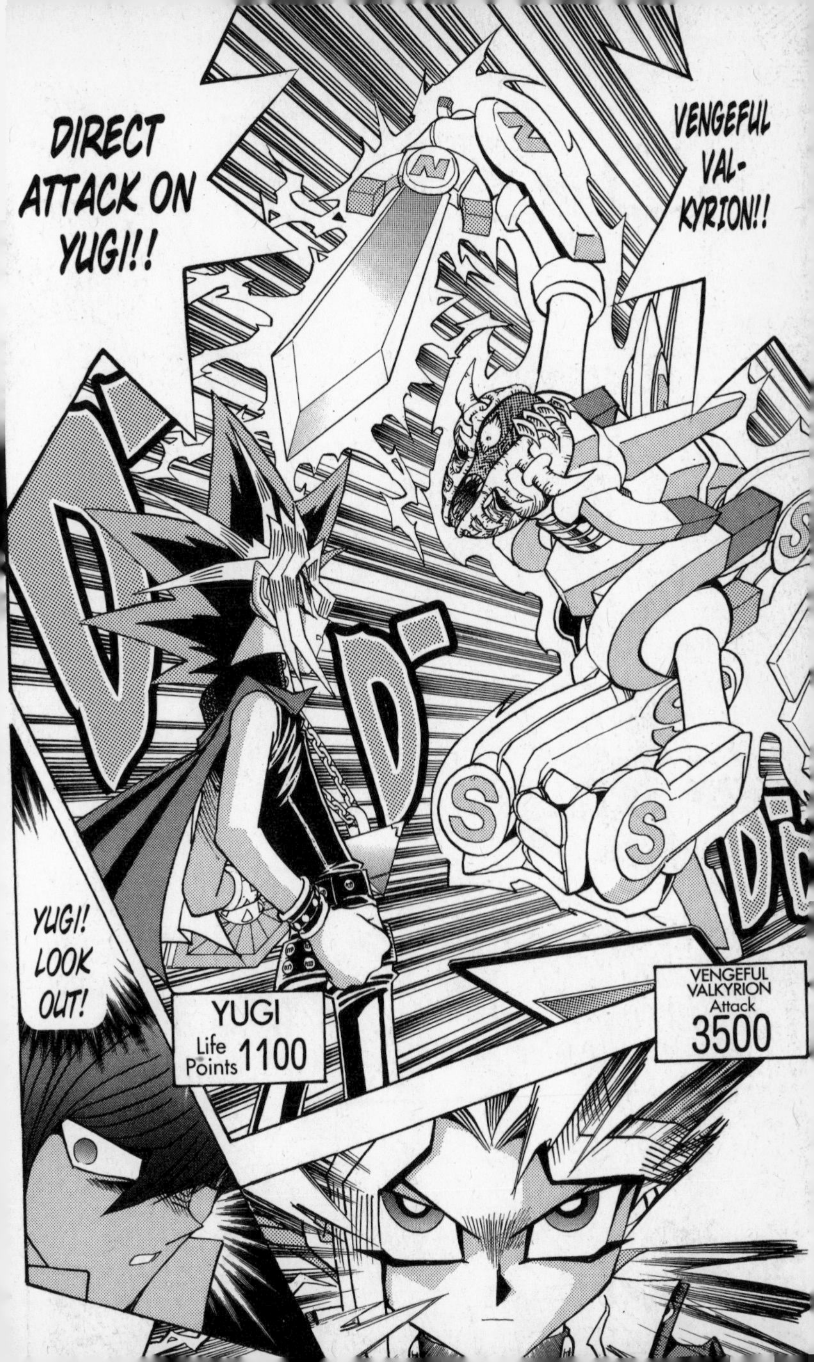
VENGEFUL VAL-KYRION!!
DIRECT ATTACK ON YUGI!!
VENGEFUL VALKYRION Attack 3500
YUGI Life Points 1100
YUGI! LOOK OUT!

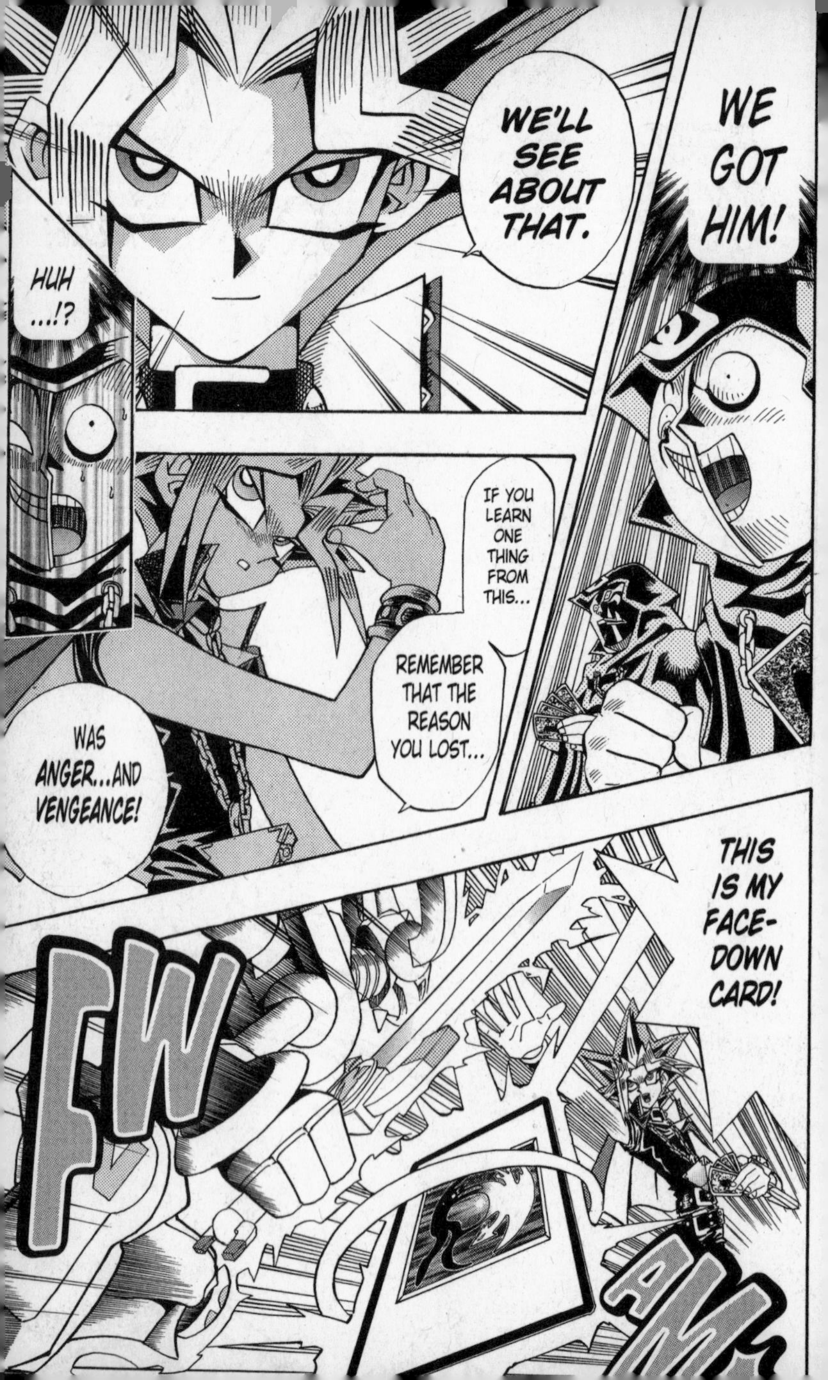
WE GOT HIM!
WE'LL SEE ABOUT THAT.
HUH ...!?
IF YOU LEARN ONE THING FROM THIS...
REMEMBER THAT THE REASON YOU LOST...
WAS ANGER...AND VENGEANCE!
THIS IS MY FACE-DOWN CARD!
FW

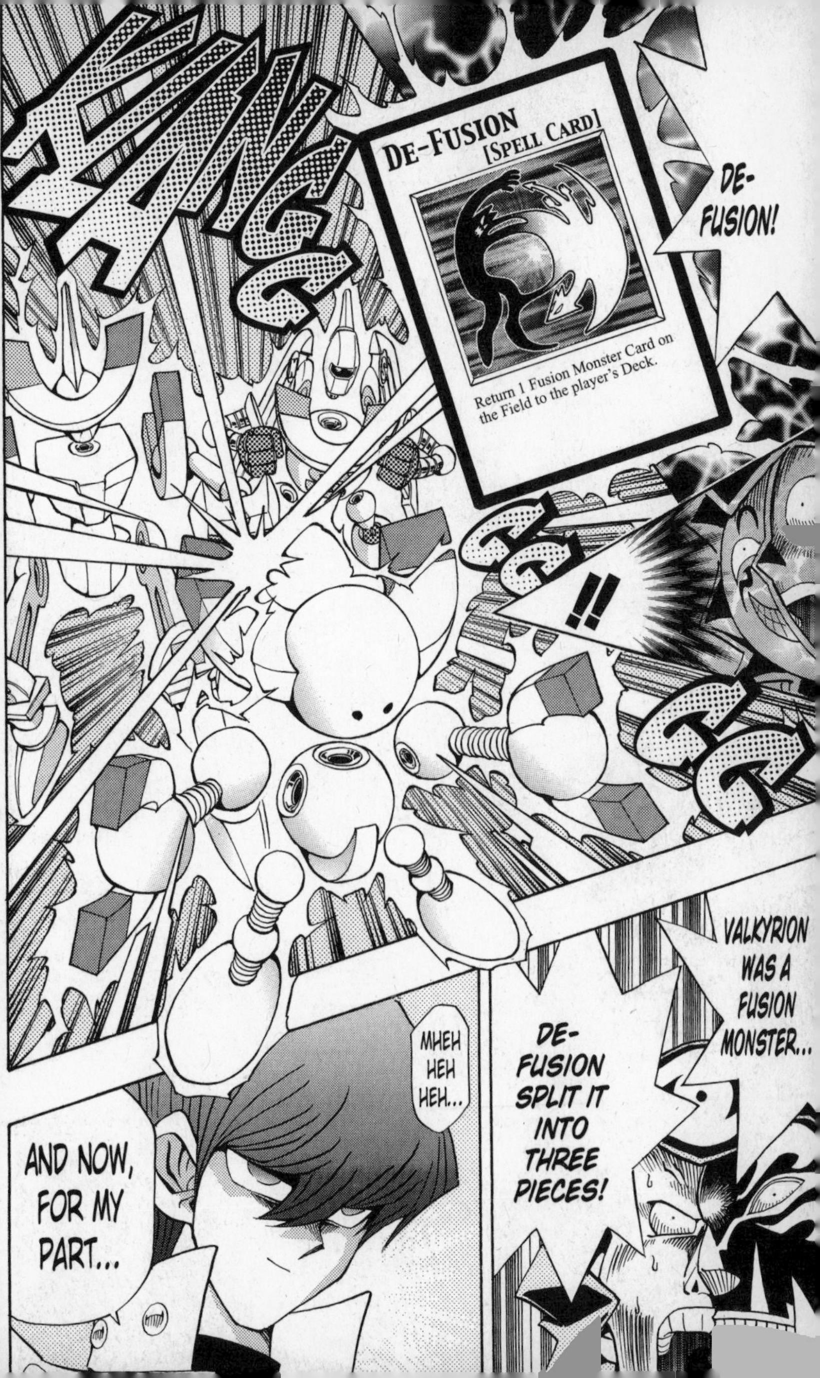
DE-FUSION!
DE-FUSION
[SPELL CARD]
Return 1 Fusion Monster Card on the Field to the player's Deck.
ZANG
VALKYRION WAS A FUSION MONSTER...
DE-FUSION SPLIT IT INTO THREE PIECES!
MHEH HEH HEH...
AND NOW, FOR MY PART...

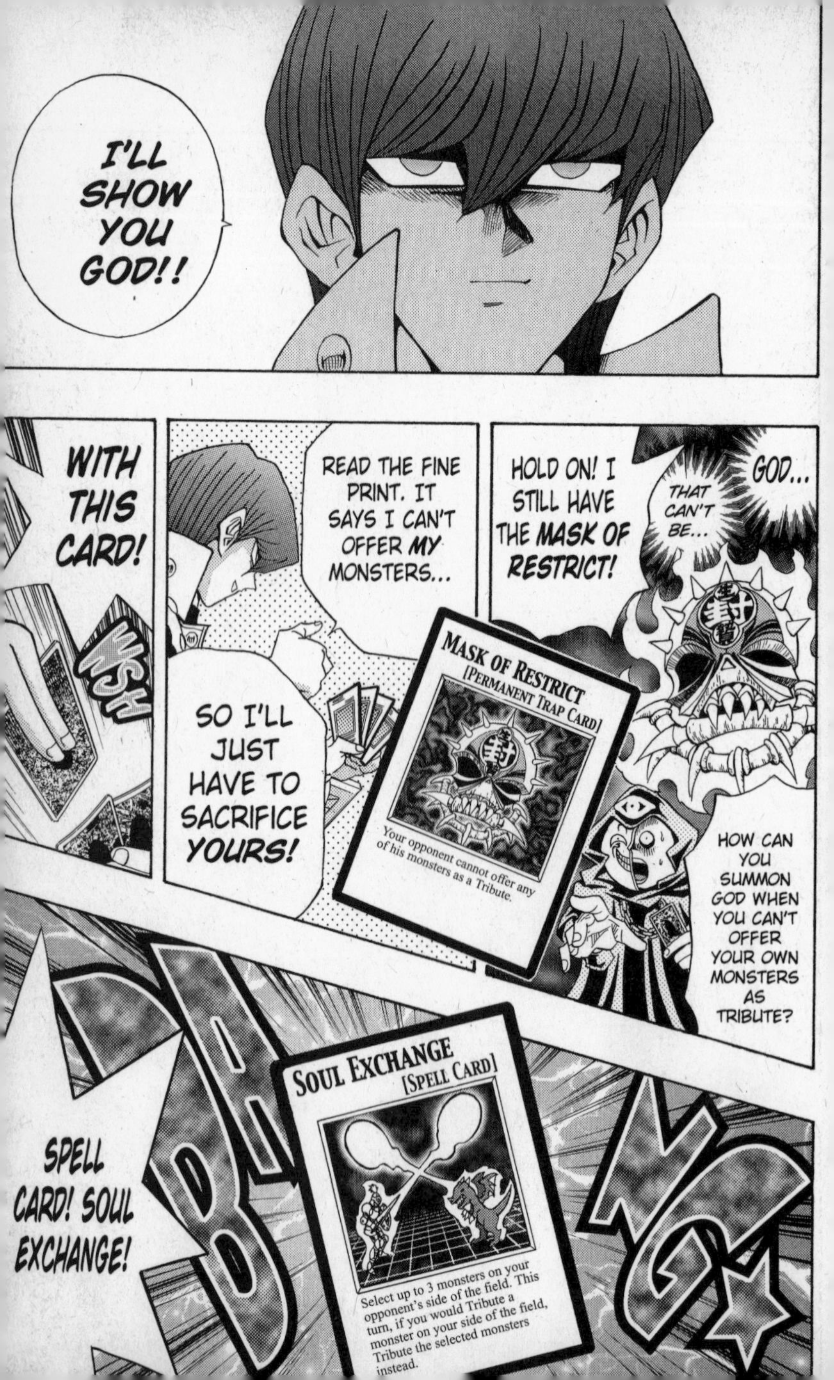
I'LL SHOW YOU GOD!!
GOD...
THAT CAN'T BE...
HOLD ON! I STILL HAVE THE MASK OF RESTRICT!
MASK OF RESTRICT
[PERMANENT TRAP CARD]
Your opponent cannot offer any of his monsters as a Tribute.
HOW CAN YOU SUMMON GOD WHEN YOU CAN'T OFFER YOUR OWN MONSTERS AS TRIBUTE?
READ THE FINE PRINT. IT SAYS I CAN'T OFFER MY MONSTERS...
SO I'LL JUST HAVE TO SACRIFICE YOURS!
WITH THIS CARD!
WISH
SPELL CARD! SOUL EXCHANGE!
SOUL EXCHANGE
[SPELL CARD]
Select up to 3 monsters on your opponent's side of the field. This turn, if you would Tribute a monster on your side of the field, Tribute the selected monsters instead.

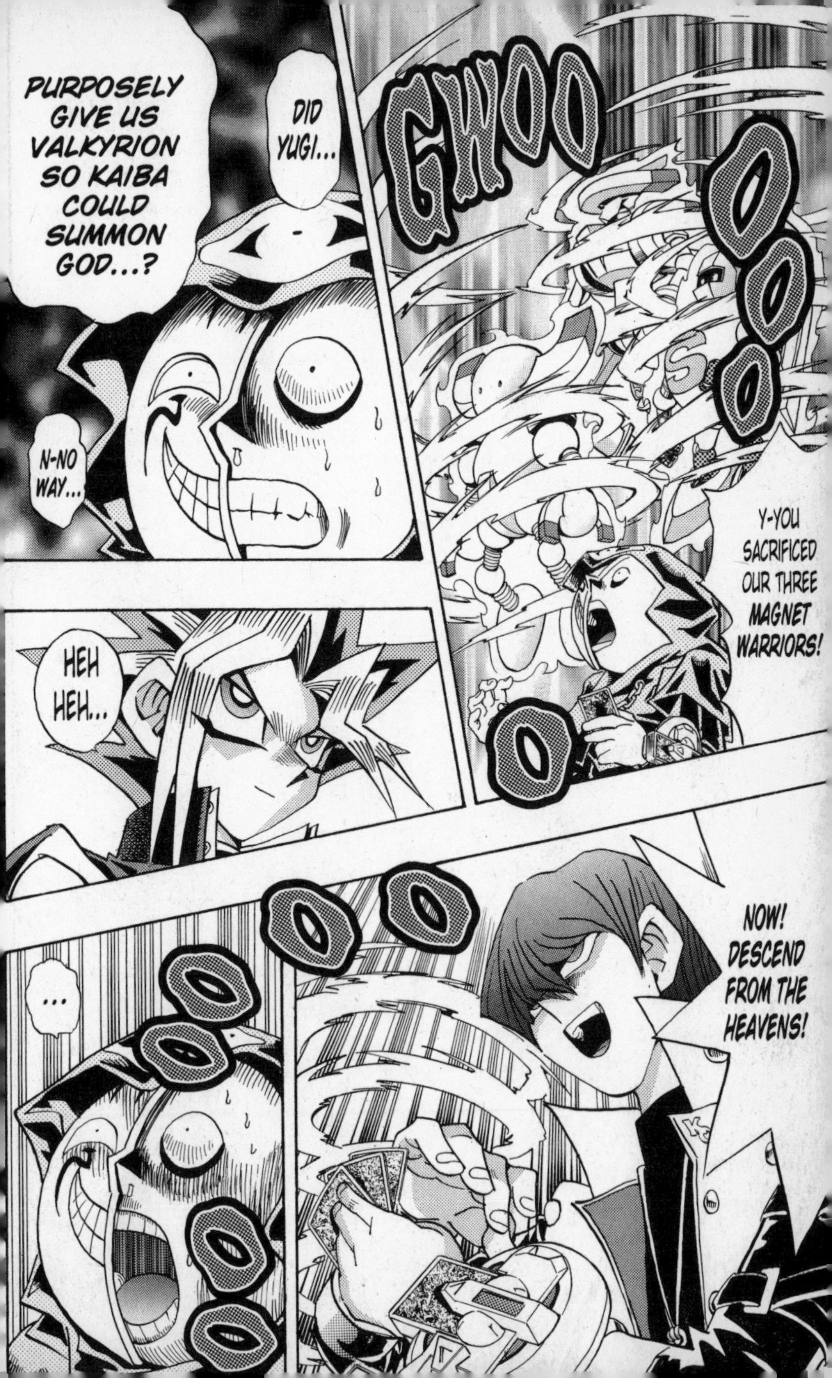
GHOOOOOOO
Y-YOU SACRIFICED OUR THREE MAGNET WARRIORS!
DID YUGI...
PURPOSELY GIVE US VALKYRION SO KAIBA COULD SUMMON GOD...?
N-NO WAY...
HEH HEH...
NOW! DESCEND FROM THE HEAVENS!
OOOOOOO
...

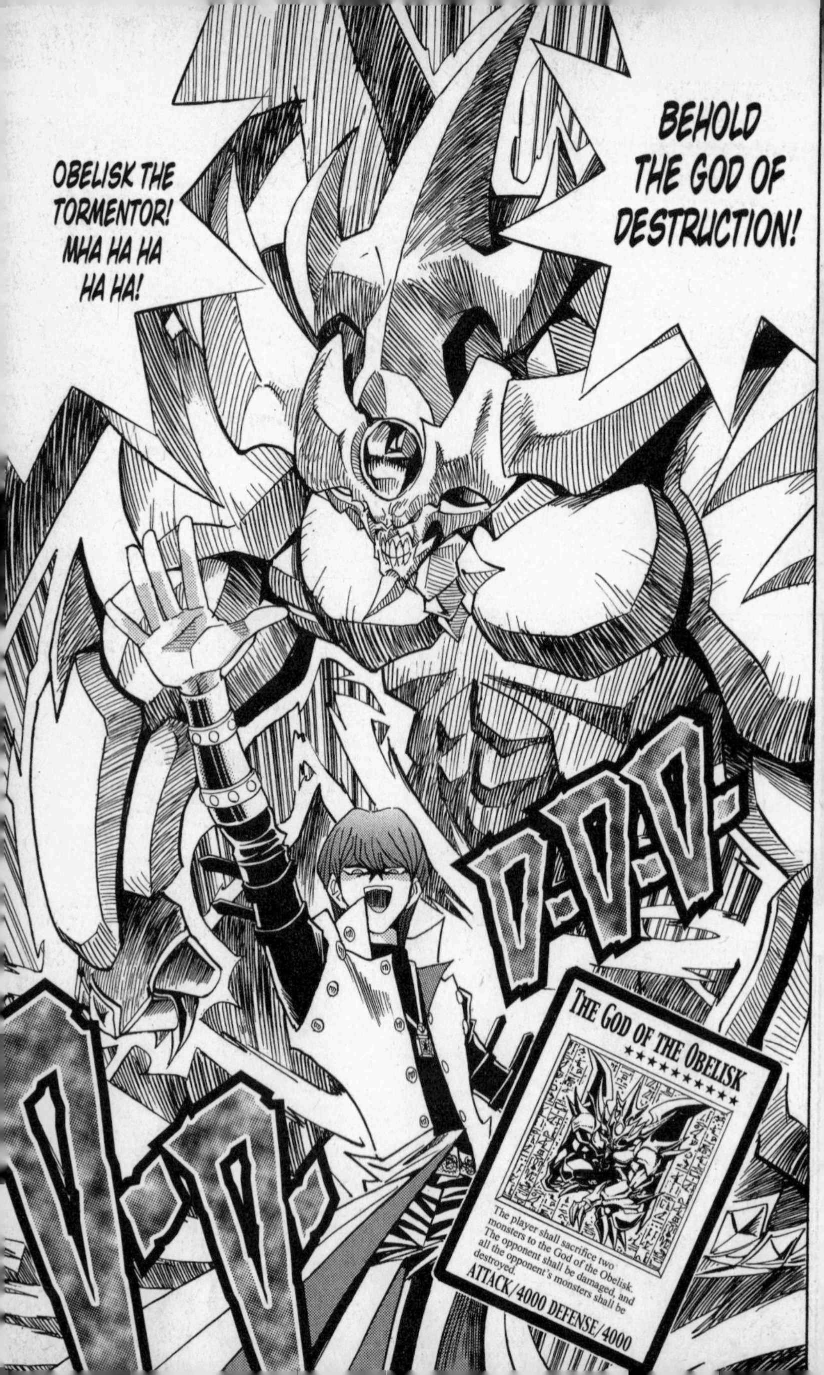
BEHOLD THE GOD OF DESTRUCTION!
OBELISK THE TORMENTOR! MHA HA HA HA HA!
D-D-D-
THE GOD OF THE OBELISK
The player shall sacrifice two monsters to the God of the Obelisk. The opponent shall be damaged, and all the opponent's monsters shall be destroyed.
ATTACK/4000 DEFENSE/4000

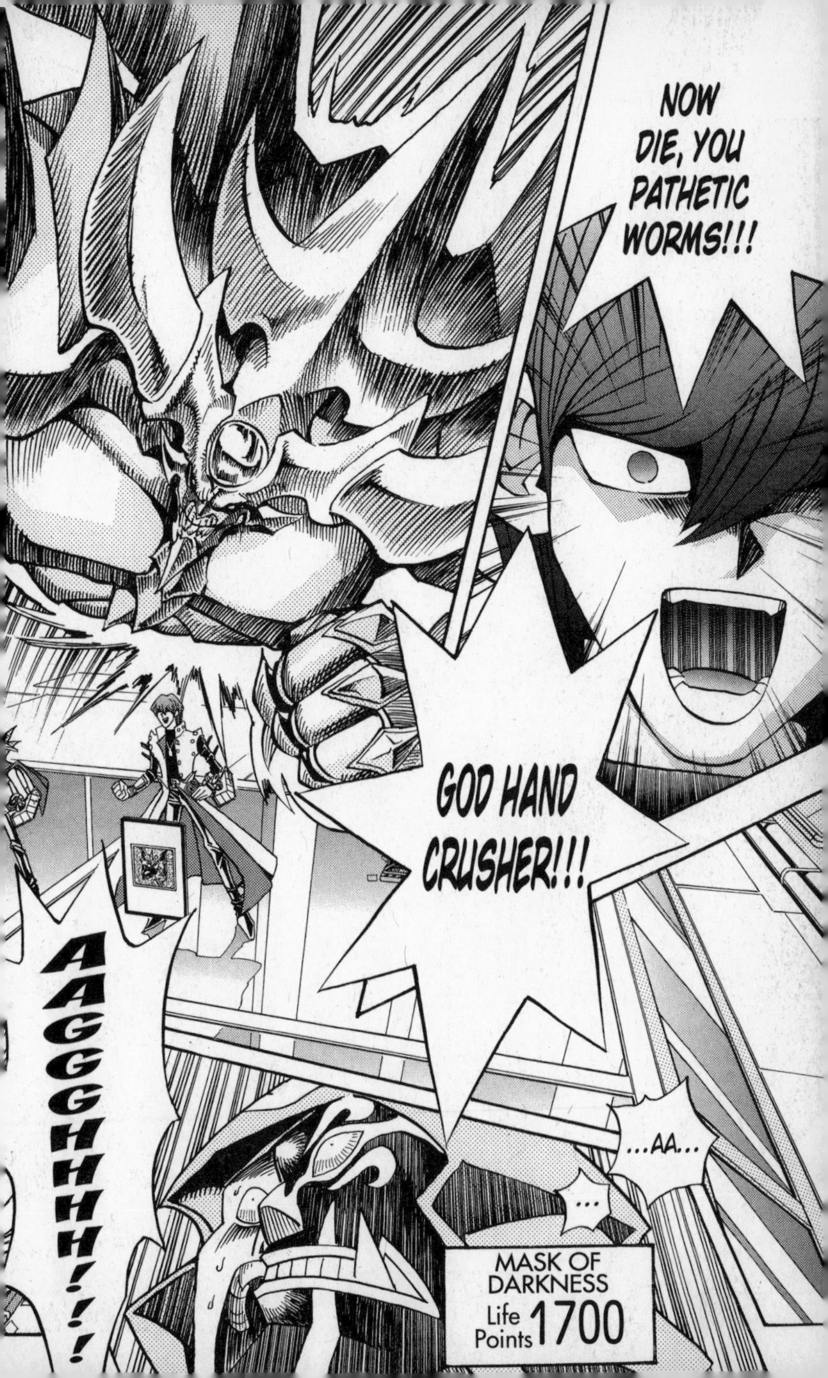
NOW DIE, YOU PATHETIC WORMS!!!
GOD HAND CRUSHER!!!
AAGGGHHHH!!!
...AA...
...
MASK OF DARKNESS Life Points 1700

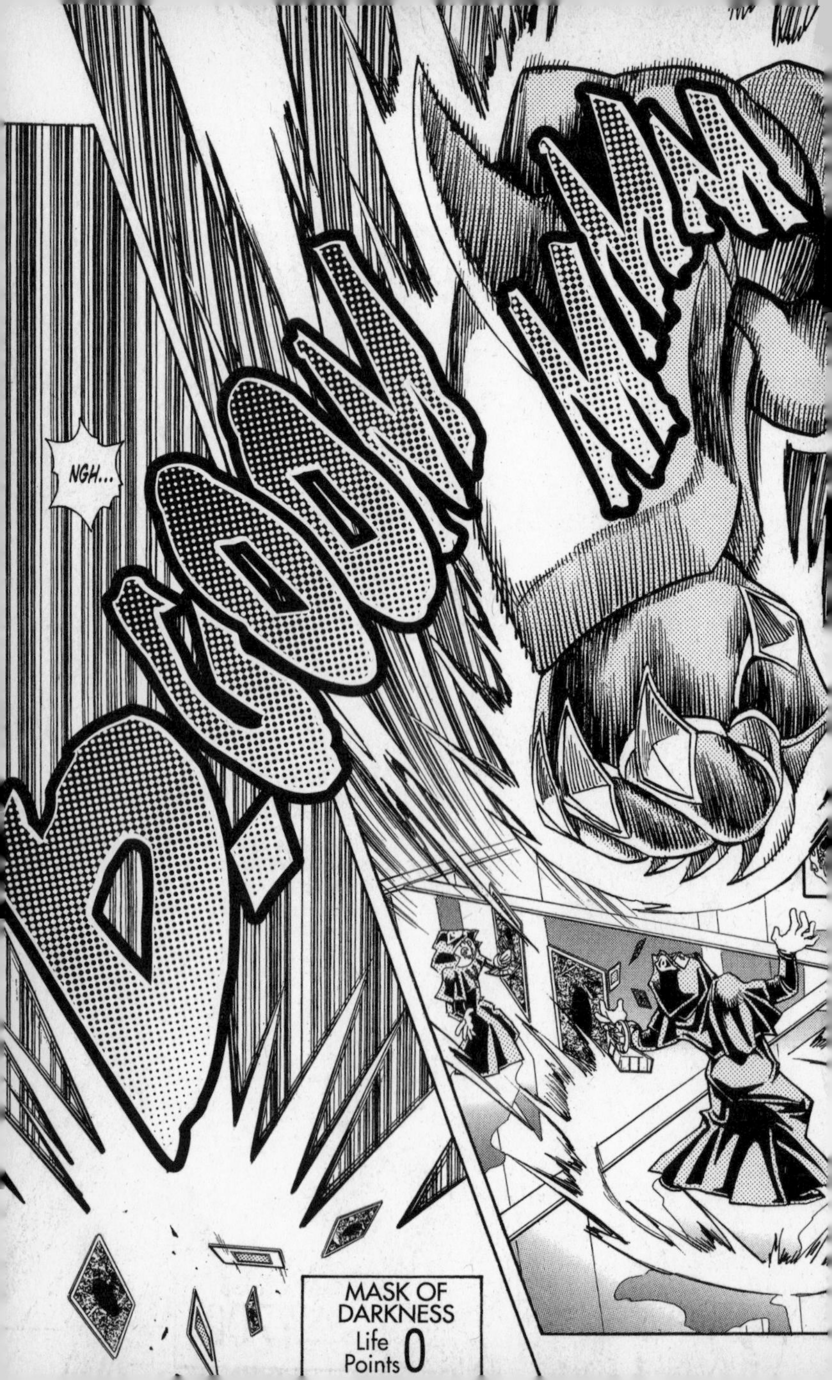
NGH...
MASK OF DARKNESS
Life Points 0

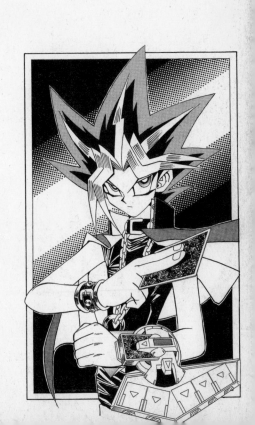

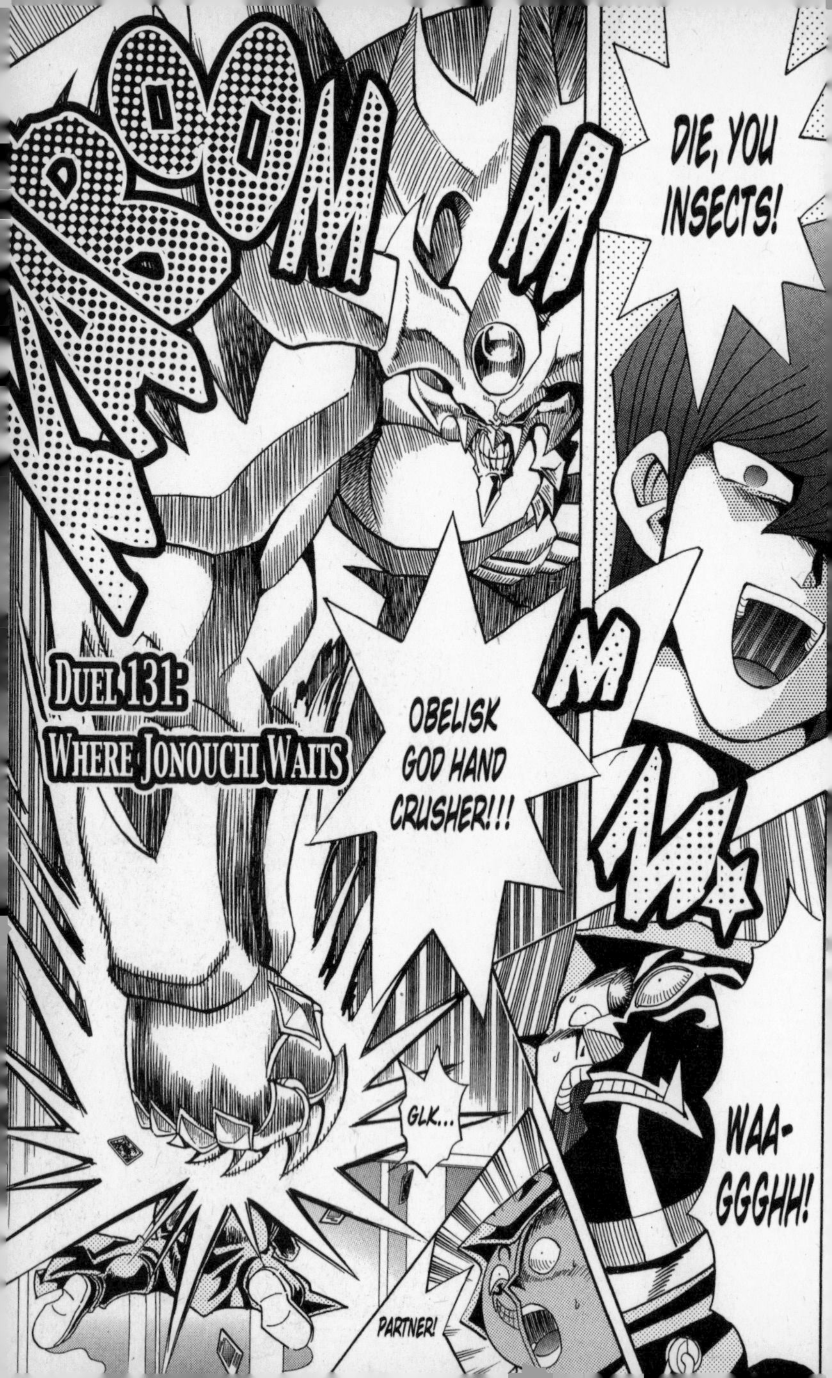
DIE, YOU INSECTS!
DUEL 131: WHERE JONOUCHI WAITS
OBELISK GOD HAND CRUSHER!!!
WAA-GGGHH!
GLK...
PARTNER!

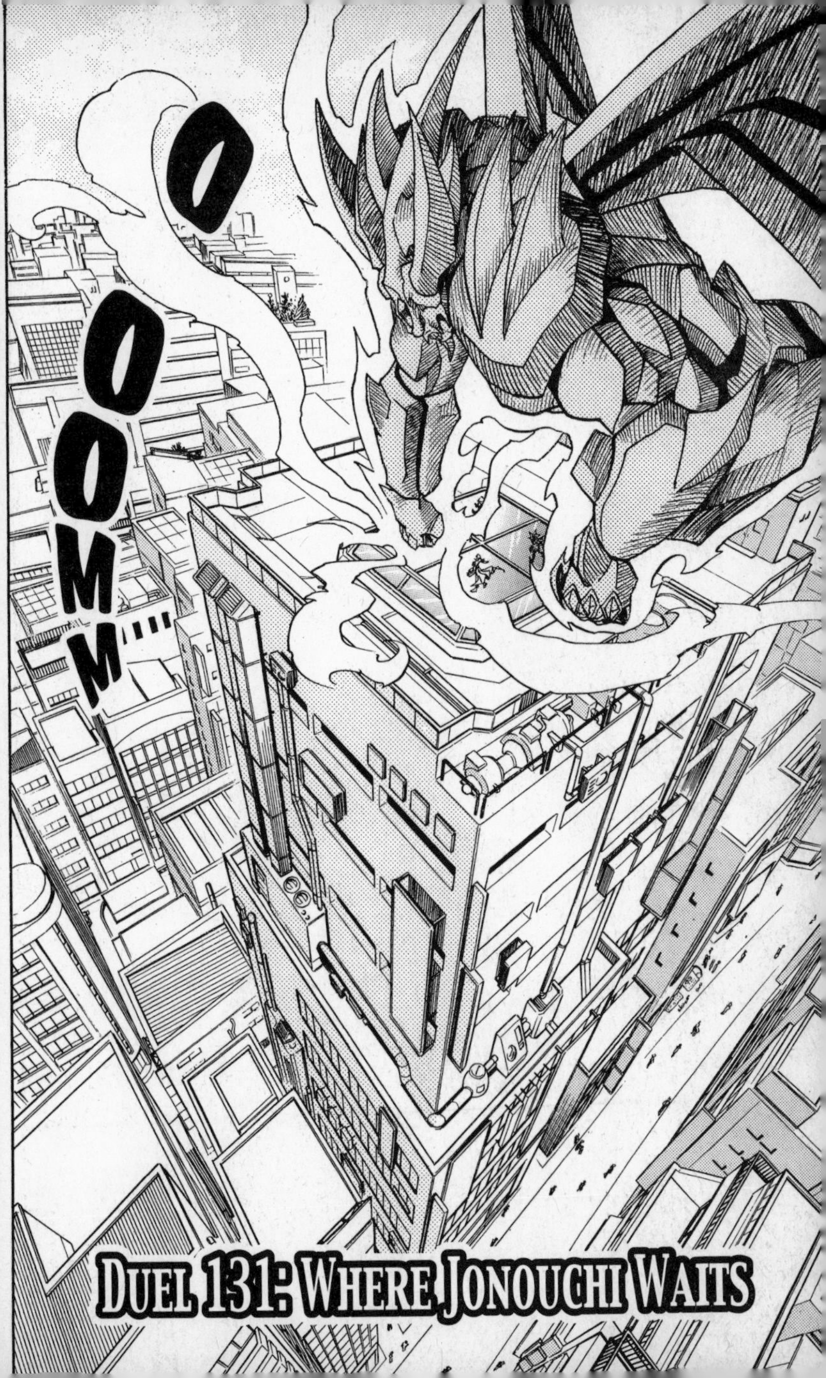
OOOOMM.....
Duel 131: Where Jonouchi Waits

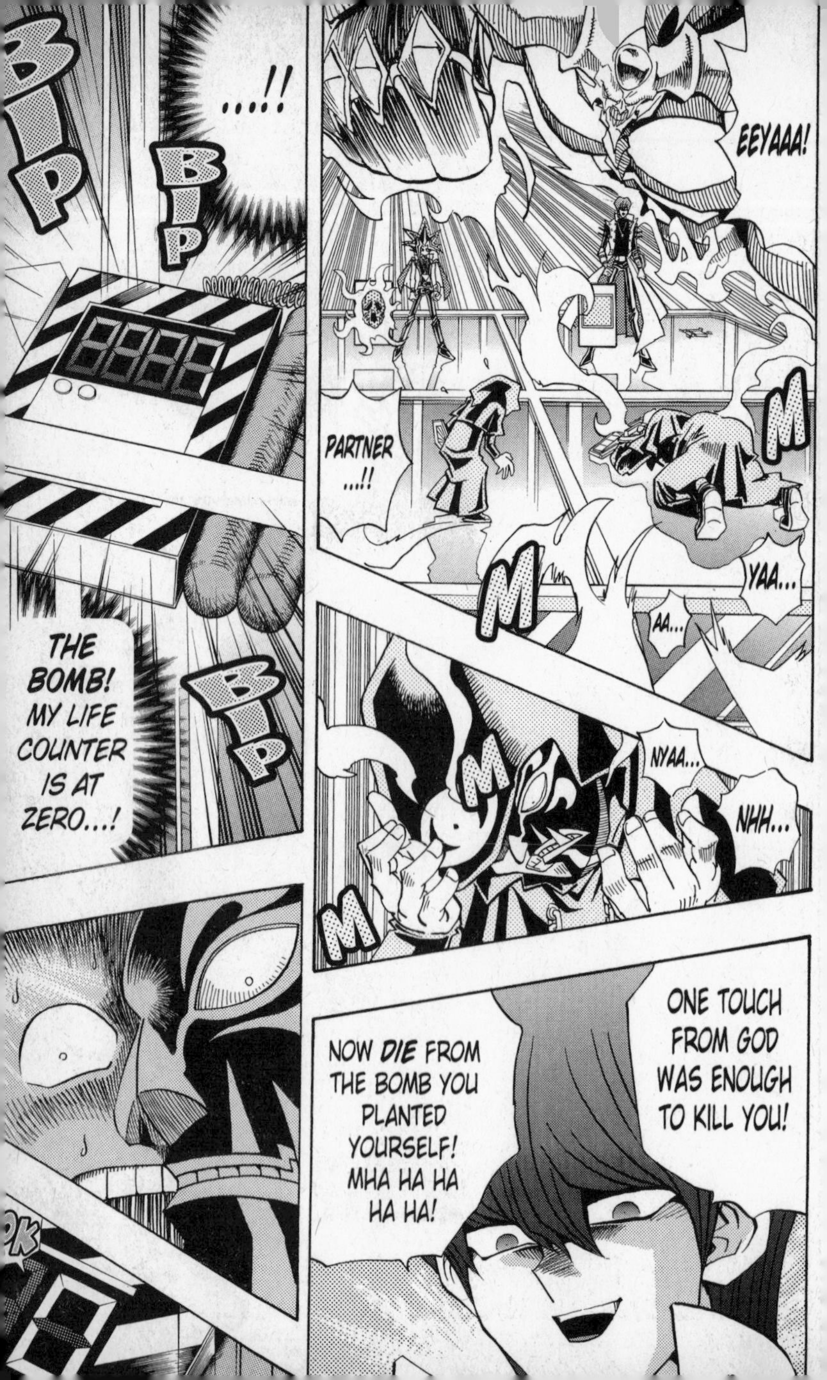
EEYAAA!
M
PARTNER ...!!
YAA...
M
...!!
BIP
BIP
AA...
NYAA...
NHH...
M
M
M
THE BOMB! MY LIFE COUNTER IS AT ZERO...!
BIP
ONE TOUCH FROM GOD WAS ENOUGH TO KILL YOU!
NOW *DIE* FROM THE BOMB YOU PLANTED YOURSELF! MHA HA HA HA HA!

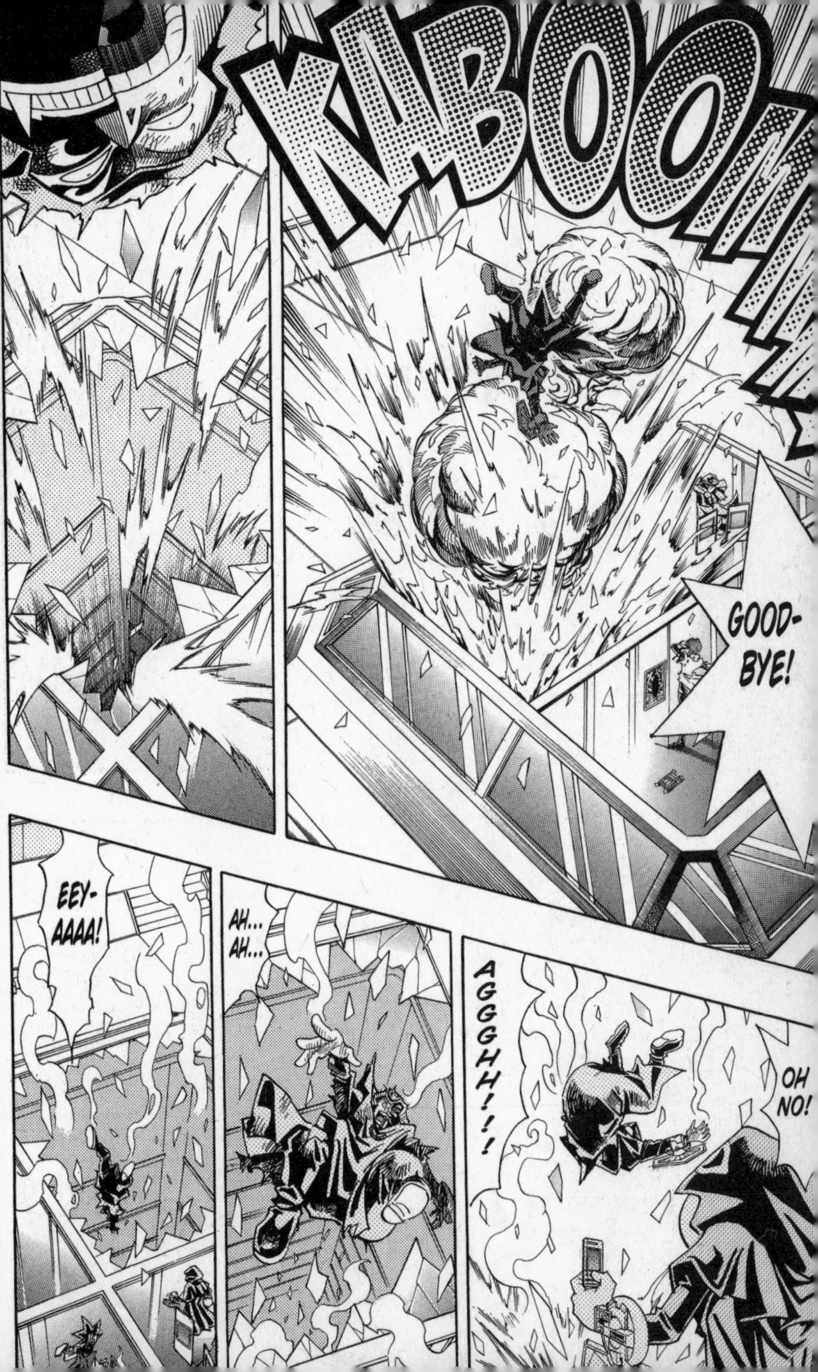
KABOOM
GOOD-BYE!
AGGGHH!!!
OH NO!
AH... AH...
EEY-AAAA!

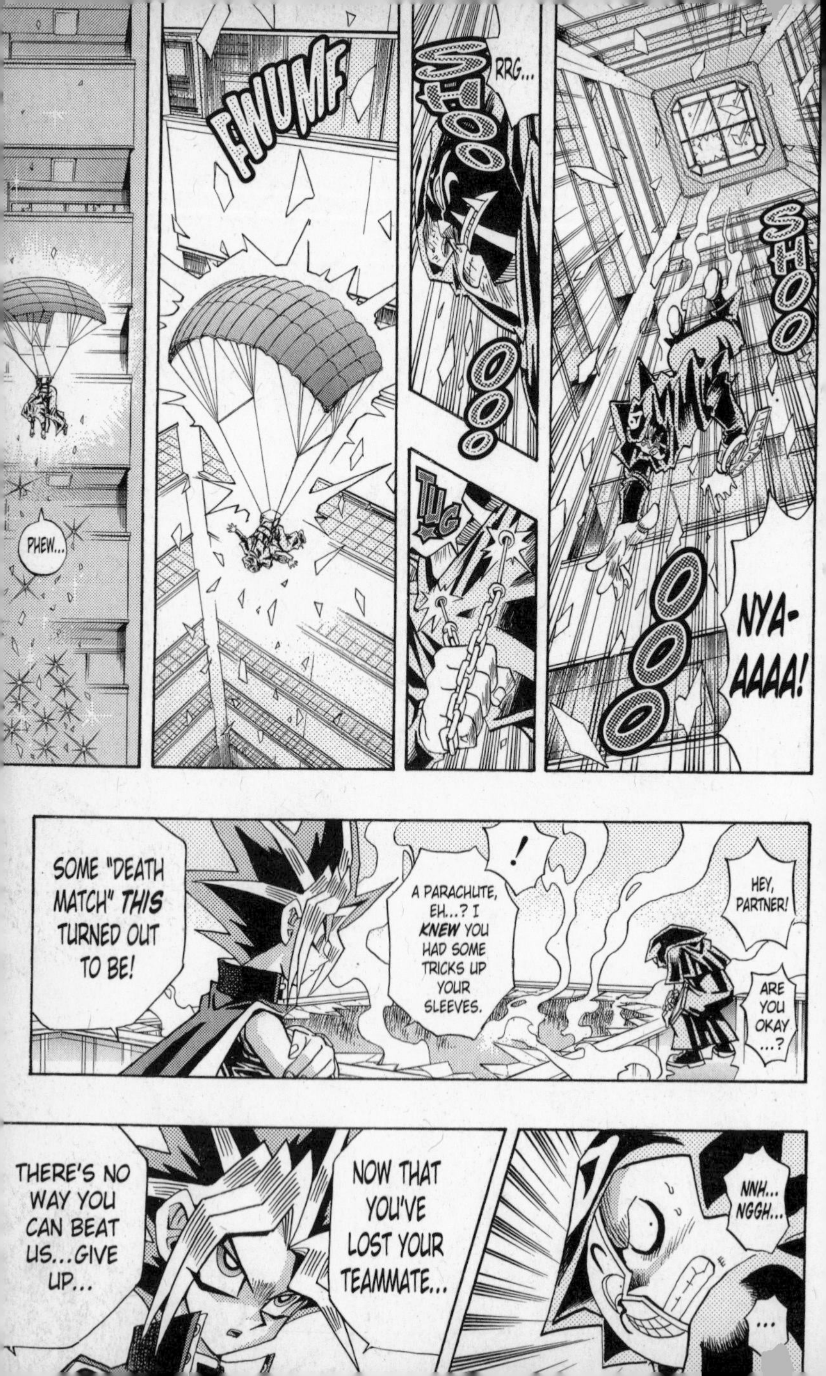
SHOOOO
OOOOO
NYA-AAAA!
RRG...
SHOOOOOOOO
TUG
FWUMF
PHEW...
HEY, PARTNER!
ARE YOU OKAY...?
!
A PARACHUTE, EH...? I *KNEW* YOU HAD SOME TRICKS UP YOUR SLEEVES.
SOME "DEATH MATCH" *THIS* TURNED OUT TO BE!
NNH... NGGH...
...
NOW THAT YOU'VE LOST YOUR TEAMMATE...
THERE'S NO WAY YOU CAN BEAT US...GIVE UP...

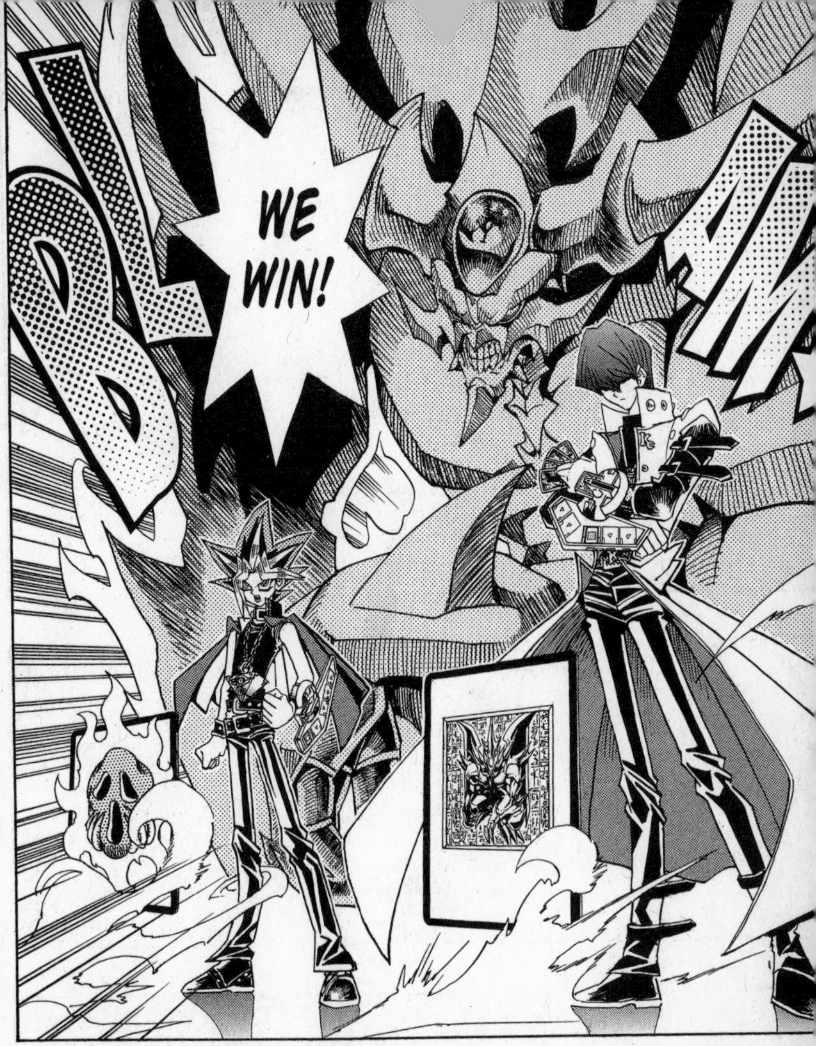
WE WIN!

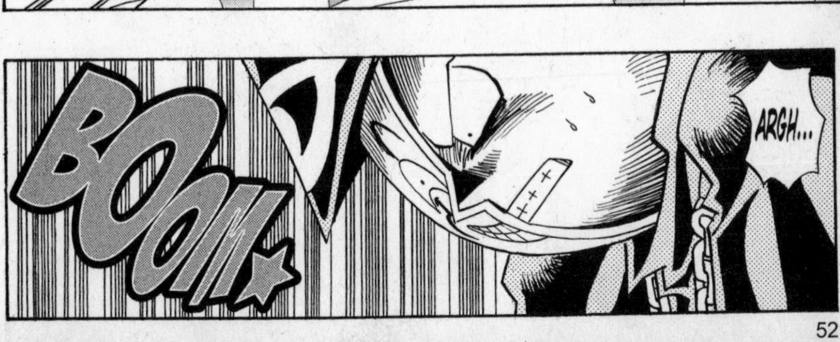
ARGH...
BOOM★

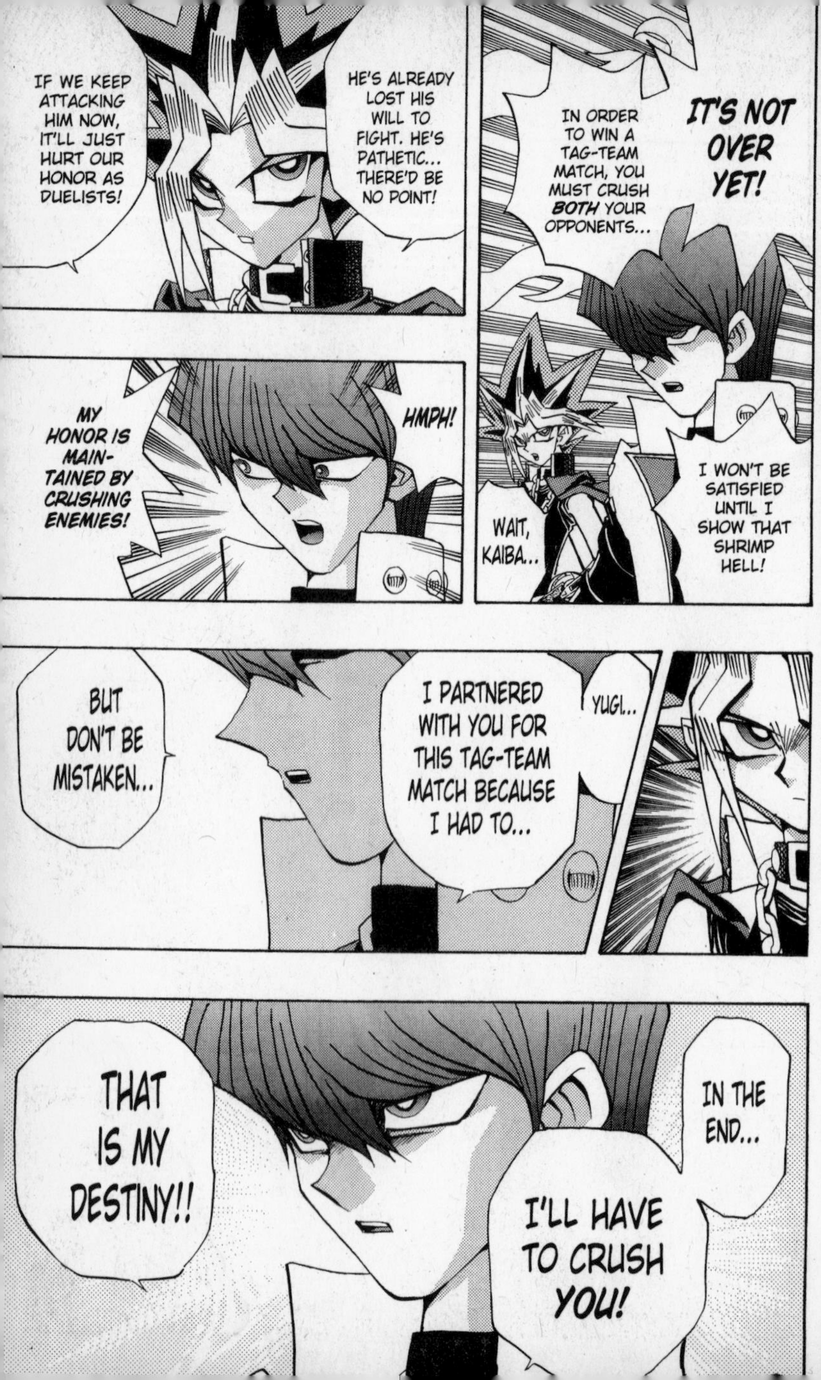
IT'S NOT OVER YET!
IN ORDER TO WIN A TAG-TEAM MATCH, YOU MUST CRUSH BOTH YOUR OPPONENTS...
I WON'T BE SATISFIED UNTIL I SHOW THAT SHRIMP HELL!
WAIT, KAIBA...
HE'S ALREADY LOST HIS WILL TO FIGHT. HE'S PATHETIC... THERE'D BE NO POINT!
IF WE KEEP ATTACKING HIM NOW, IT'LL JUST HURT OUR HONOR AS DUELISTS!
HMPH!
MY HONOR IS MAIN-TAINED BY CRUSHING ENEMIES!
YUGI...
I PARTNERED WITH YOU FOR THIS TAG-TEAM MATCH BECAUSE I HAD TO...
BUT DON'T BE MISTAKEN...
IN THE END...
I'LL HAVE TO CRUSH YOU!
THAT IS MY DESTINY!!

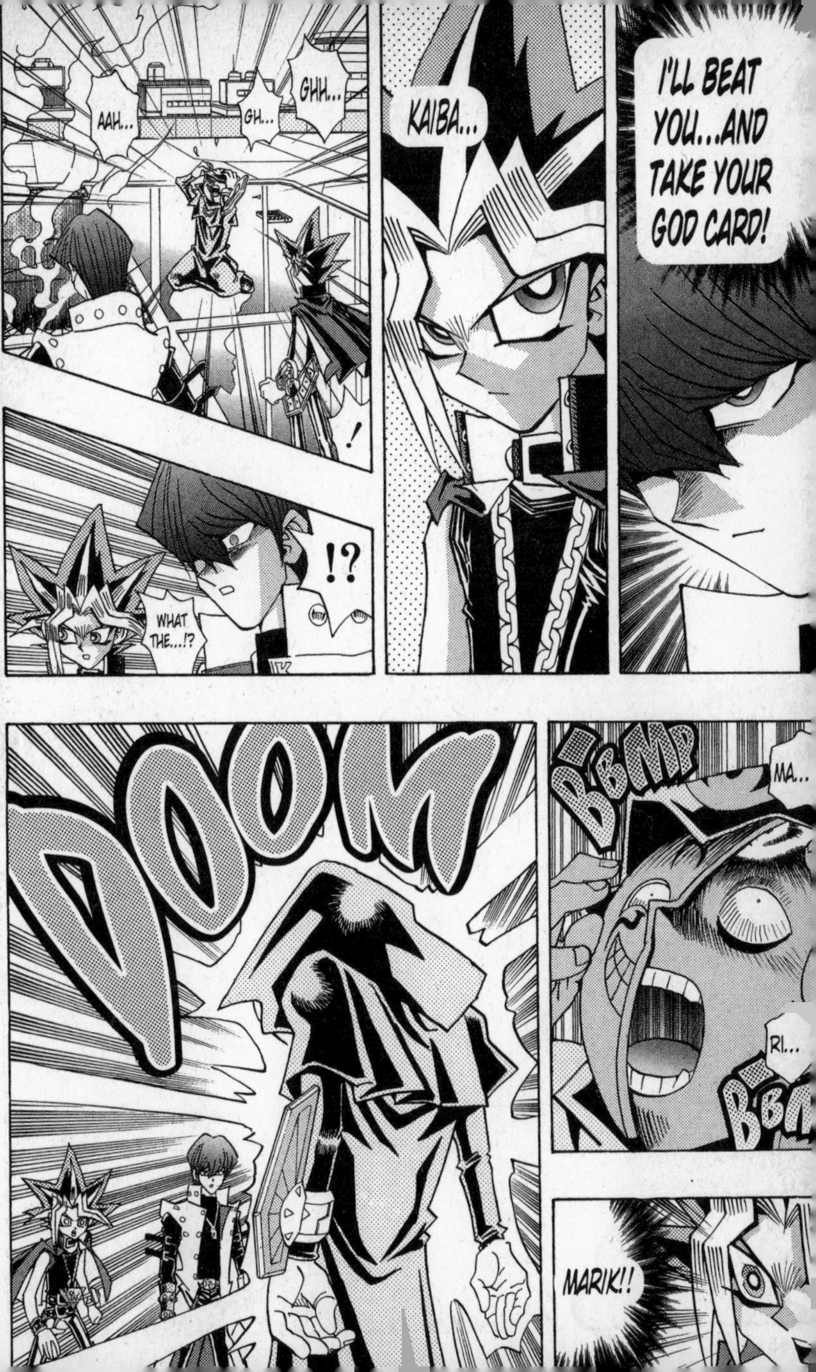

I'LL BEAT YOU...AND TAKE YOUR GOD CARD!
KAIBA...
GHH...
GH...
AAH...
!
!?
WHAT THE...!?
MA...
BBMP
RI...
MARIK!!
DOOM

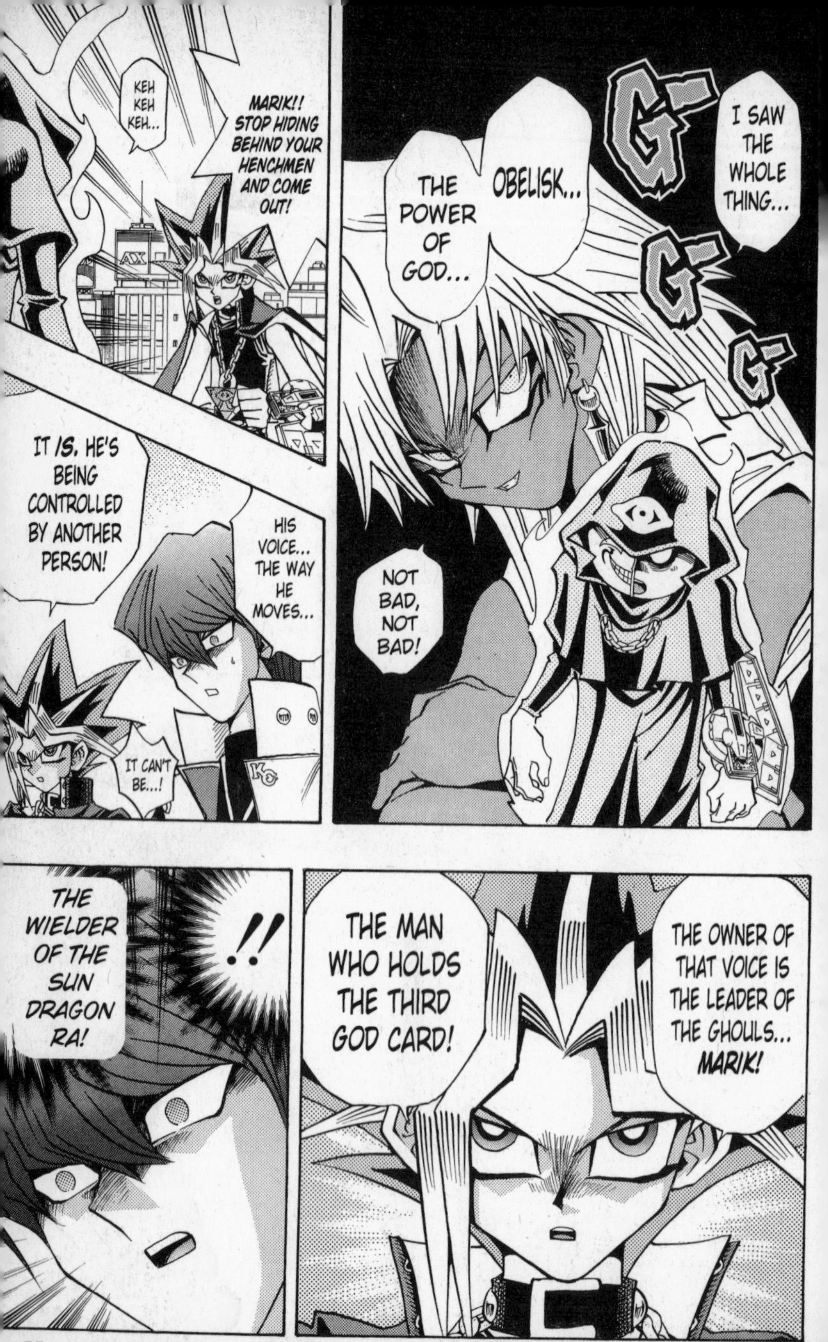
I SAW THE WHOLE THING...
G- G- G-
OBELISK...
THE POWER OF GOD...
NOT BAD, NOT BAD!
MARIK!! STOP HIDING BEHIND YOUR HENCHMEN AND COME OUT!
KEH KEH KEH...
HIS VOICE... THE WAY HE MOVES...
IT IS. HE'S BEING CONTROLLED BY ANOTHER PERSON!
IT CAN'T BE...!
THE OWNER OF THAT VOICE IS THE LEADER OF THE GHOULS... MARIK!
THE MAN WHO HOLDS THE THIRD GOD CARD!
!!
THE WIELDER OF THE SUN DRAGON RA!

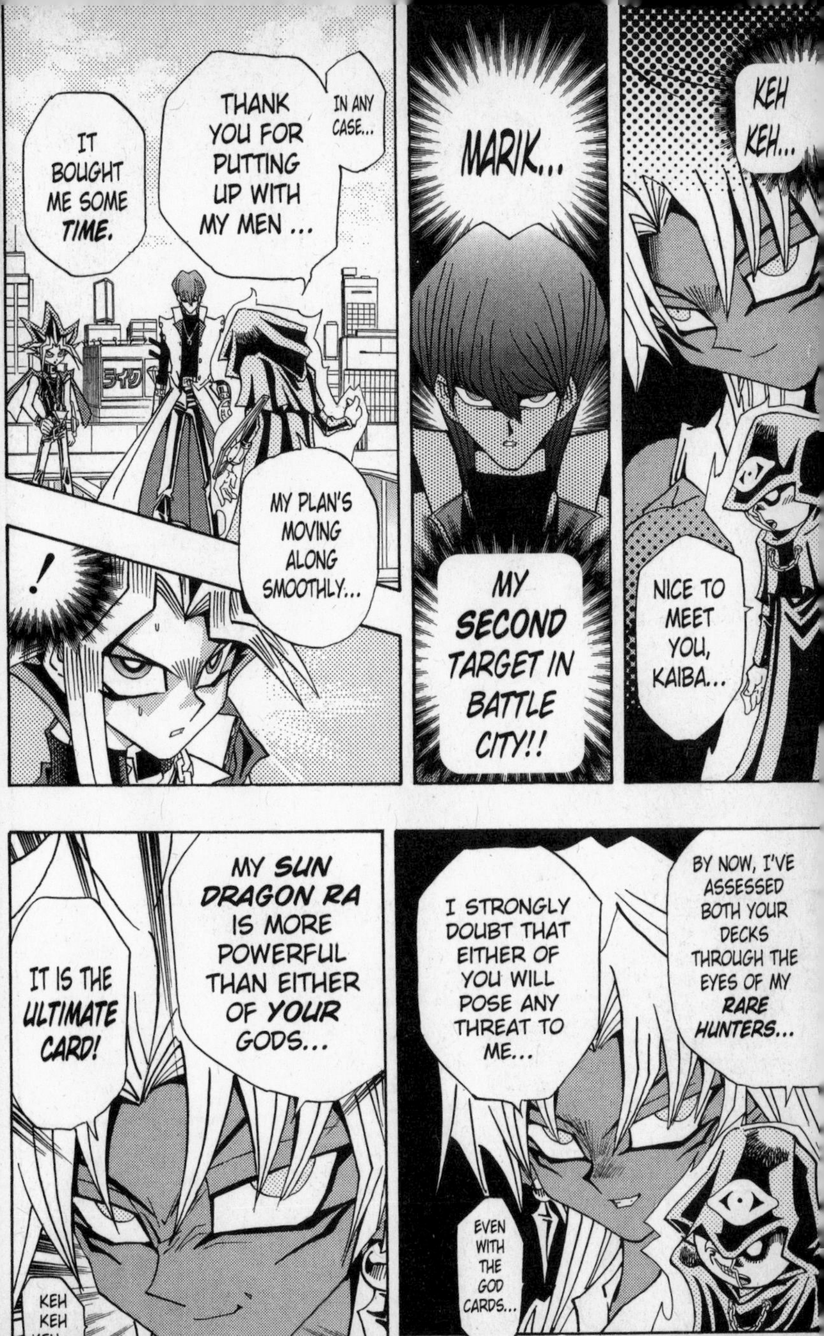
KEH KEH...
NICE TO MEET YOU, KAIBA...
MARIK...
MY SECOND TARGET IN BATTLE CITY!!
IN ANY CASE...
THANK YOU FOR PUTTING UP WITH MY MEN ...
IT BOUGHT ME SOME TIME.
MY PLAN'S MOVING ALONG SMOOTHLY...
!
BY NOW, I'VE ASSESSED BOTH YOUR DECKS THROUGH THE EYES OF MY RARE HUNTERS...
I STRONGLY DOUBT THAT EITHER OF YOU WILL POSE ANY THREAT TO ME...
EVEN WITH THE GOD CARDS...
MY SUN DRAGON RA IS MORE POWERFUL THAN EITHER OF YOUR GODS...
IT IS THE ULTIMATE CARD!
KEH KEH KEH...

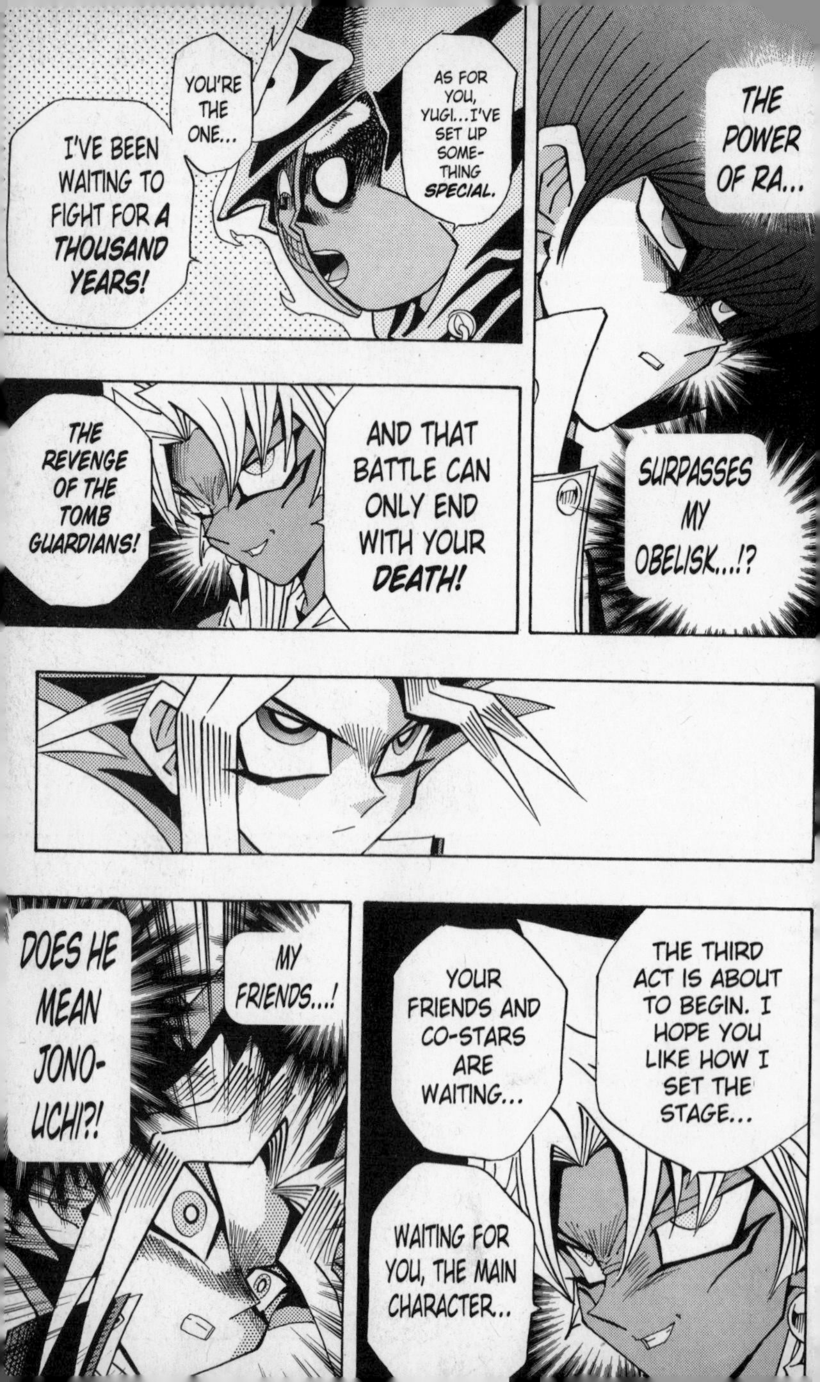

THE POWER OF RA...
SURPASSES MY OBELISK...!?
AS FOR YOU, YUGI...I'VE SET UP SOMETHING SPECIAL.
YOU'RE THE ONE...
I'VE BEEN WAITING TO FIGHT FOR A THOUSAND YEARS!
AND THAT BATTLE CAN ONLY END WITH YOUR DEATH!
THE REVENGE OF THE TOMB GUARDIANS!
THE THIRD ACT IS ABOUT TO BEGIN. I HOPE YOU LIKE HOW I SET THE STAGE...
YOUR FRIENDS AND CO-STARS ARE WAITING...
WAITING FOR YOU, THE MAIN CHARACTER...
MY FRIENDS...!
DOES HE MEAN JONO-UCHI?!

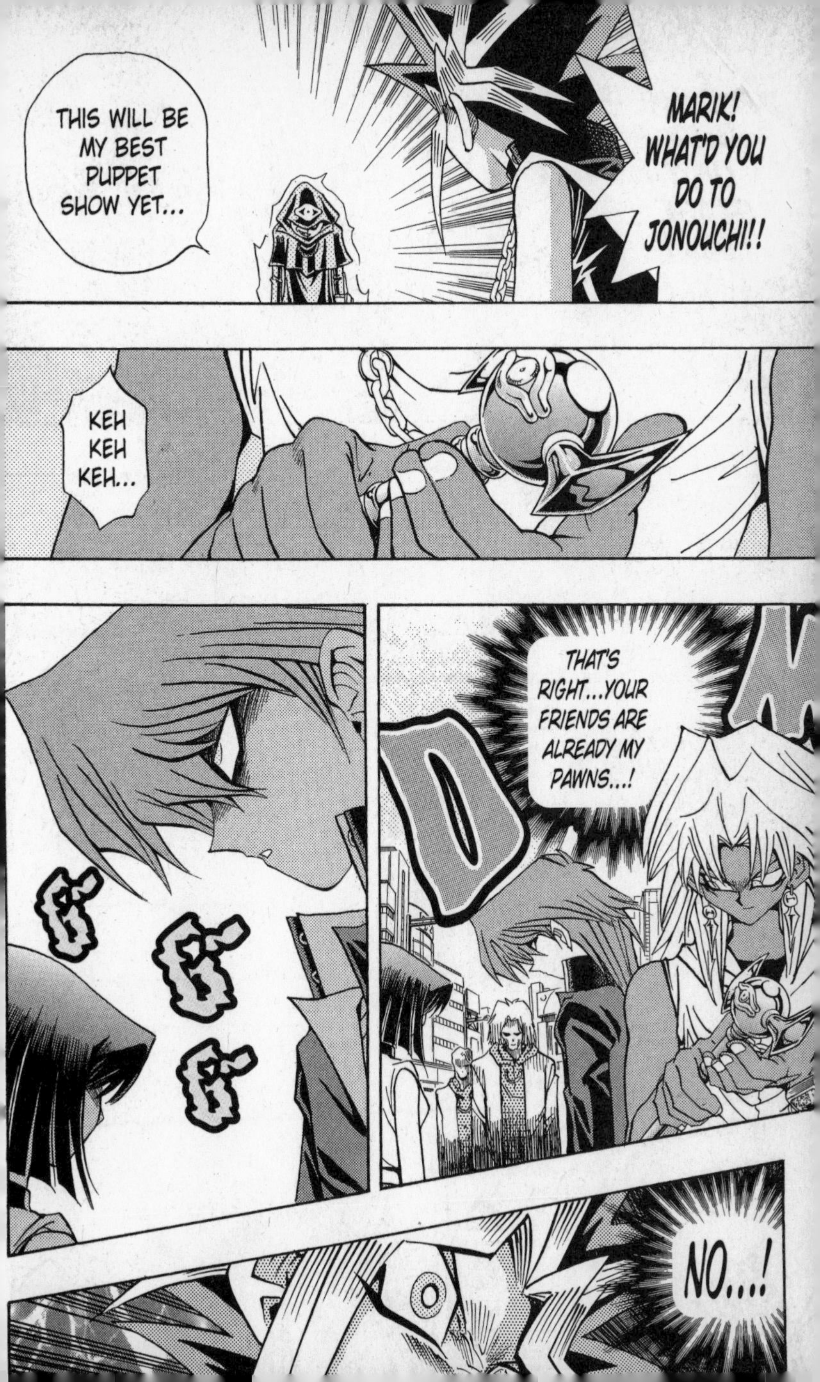
MARIK! WHAT'D YOU DO TO JONOUCHI!!
THIS WILL BE MY BEST PUPPET SHOW YET...
KEH KEH KEH...
THAT'S RIGHT...YOUR FRIENDS ARE ALREADY MY PAWNS...!
NO...!

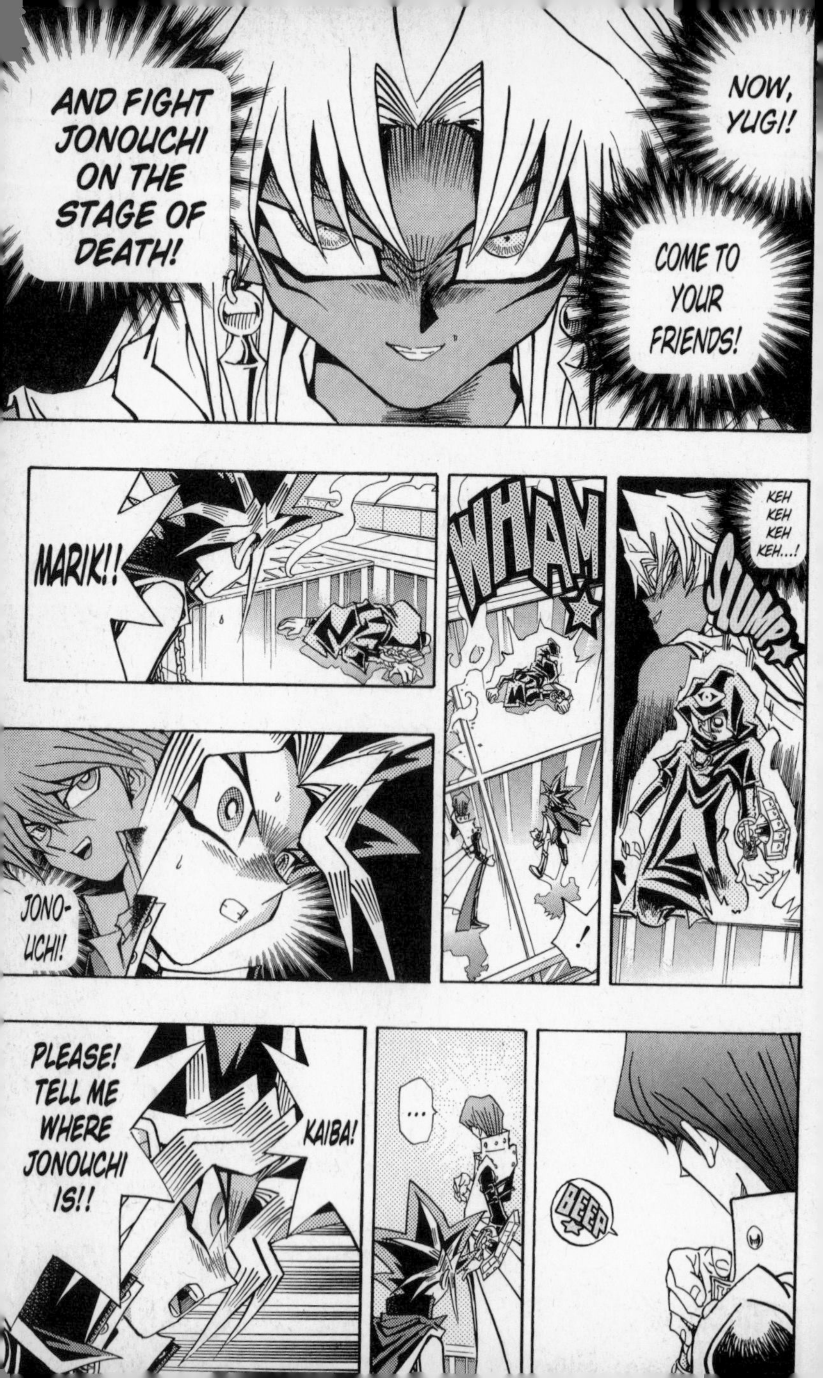
NOW, YUGI!
COME TO YOUR FRIENDS!
AND FIGHT JONOUCHI ON THE STAGE OF DEATH!
KEH KEH KEH KEH...!
SLUMP
WHAM
!
MARIK!!
JONO-UCHI!
BEEP
KAIBA!
...
PLEASE! TELL ME WHERE JONOUCHI IS!!

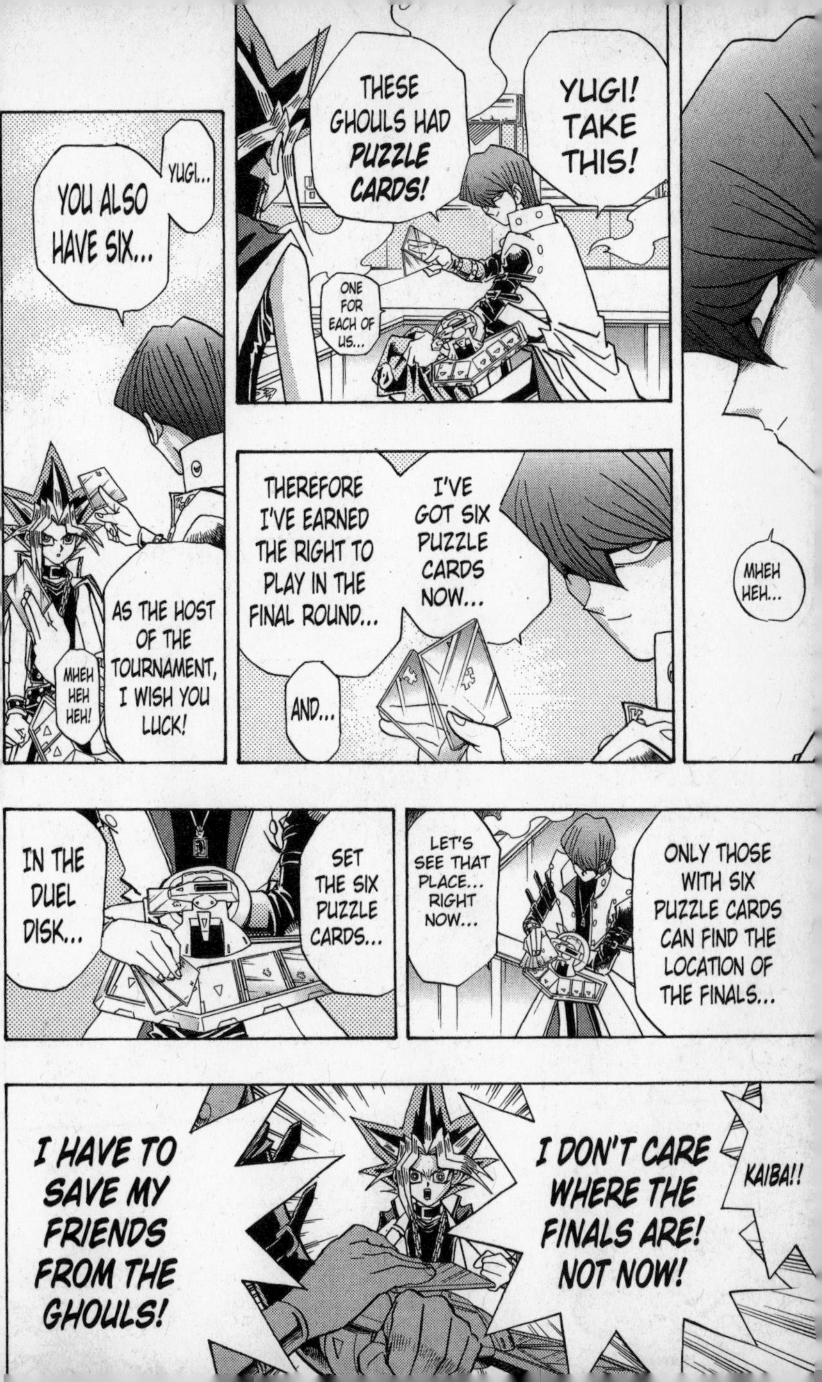
MHEH HEH...
YUGI! TAKE THIS!
THESE GHOULS HAD PUZZLE CARDS!
ONE FOR EACH OF US...
I'VE GOT SIX PUZZLE CARDS NOW...
THEREFORE I'VE EARNED THE RIGHT TO PLAY IN THE FINAL ROUND...
AND...
YUGI...
YOU ALSO HAVE SIX...
AS THE HOST OF THE TOURNAMENT, I WISH YOU LUCK!
MHEH HEH HEH!
ONLY THOSE WITH SIX PUZZLE CARDS CAN FIND THE LOCATION OF THE FINALS...
LET'S SEE THAT PLACE... RIGHT NOW...
SET THE SIX PUZZLE CARDS...
IN THE DUEL DISK...
KAIBA!!
I DON'T CARE WHERE THE FINALS ARE! NOT NOW!
I HAVE TO SAVE MY FRIENDS FROM THE GHOULS!

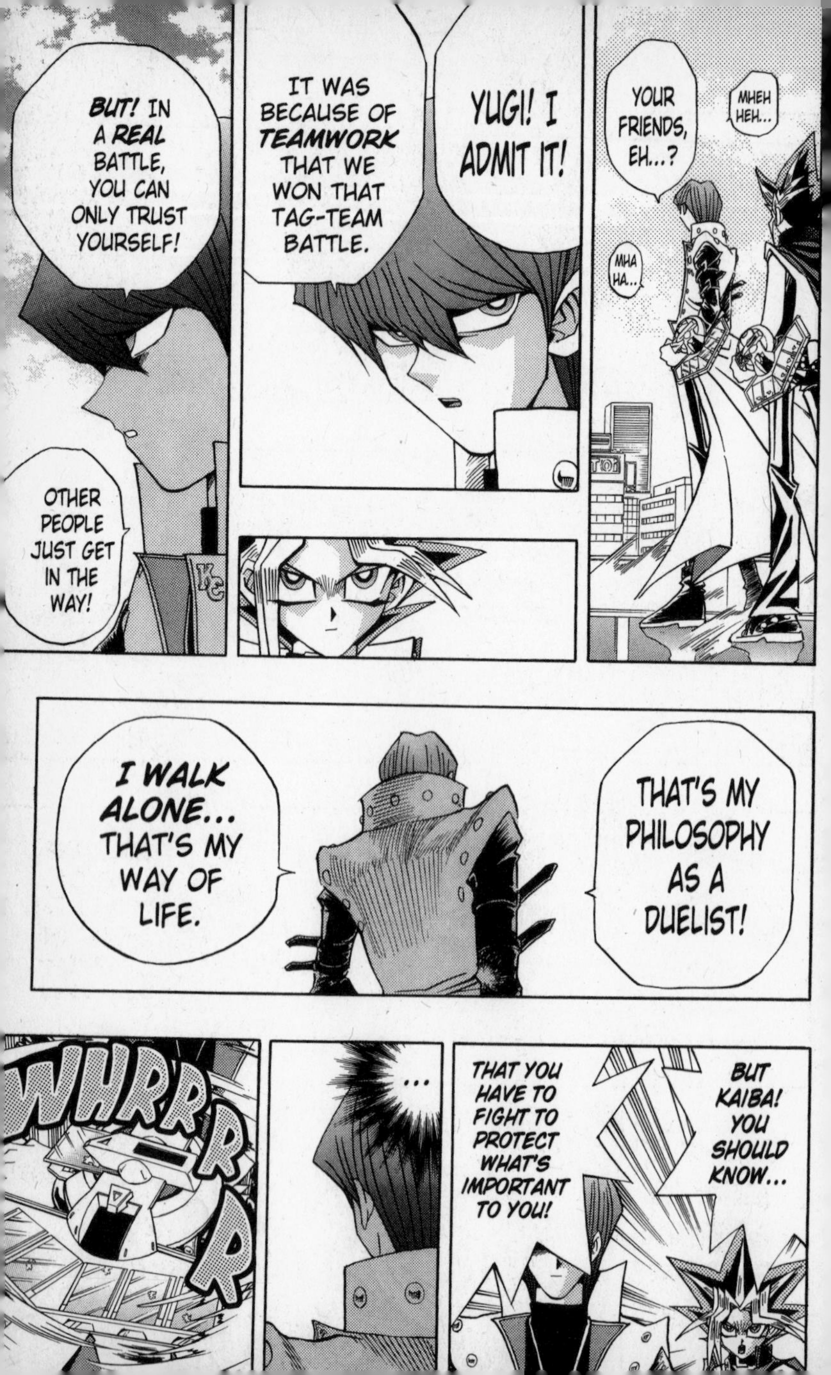
MHEH HEH...
YOUR FRIENDS, EH...?
MHA HA...
YUGI! I ADMIT IT!
IT WAS BECAUSE OF TEAMWORK THAT WE WON THAT TAG-TEAM BATTLE.
BUT! IN A REAL BATTLE, YOU CAN ONLY TRUST YOURSELF!
OTHER PEOPLE JUST GET IN THE WAY!
THAT'S MY PHILOSOPHY AS A DUELIST!
I WALK ALONE... THAT'S MY WAY OF LIFE.
BUT KAIBA! YOU SHOULD KNOW...
THAT YOU HAVE TO FIGHT TO PROTECT WHAT'S IMPORTANT TO YOU!
...
WHRRRR

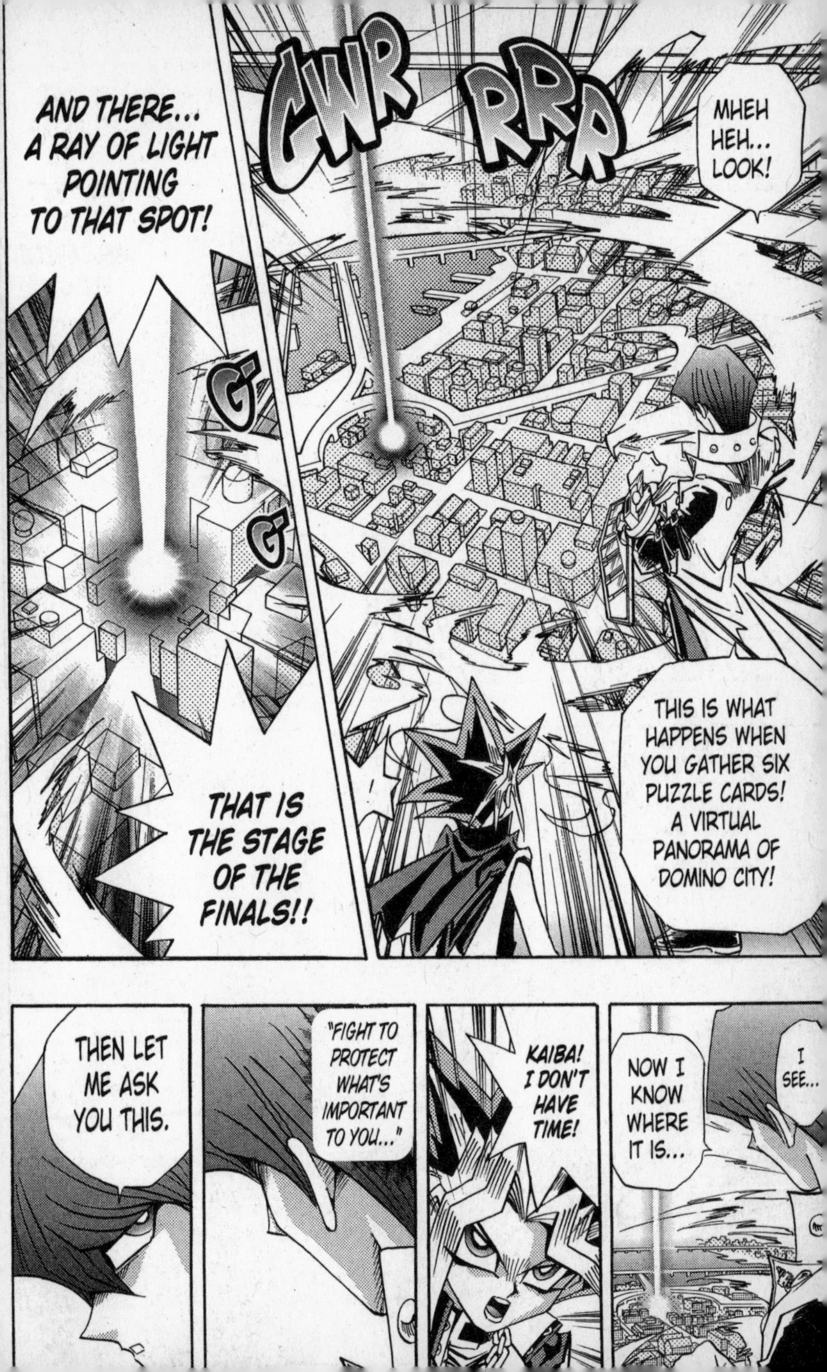
GWR RRR
MHEH HEH... LOOK!
THIS IS WHAT HAPPENS WHEN YOU GATHER SIX PUZZLE CARDS! A VIRTUAL PANORAMA OF DOMINO CITY!
AND THERE... A RAY OF LIGHT POINTING TO THAT SPOT!
G
G
THAT IS THE STAGE OF THE FINALS!!
I SEE...
NOW I KNOW WHERE IT IS...
KAIBA! I DON'T HAVE TIME!
"FIGHT TO PROTECT WHAT'S IMPORTANT TO YOU..."
THEN LET ME ASK YOU THIS.

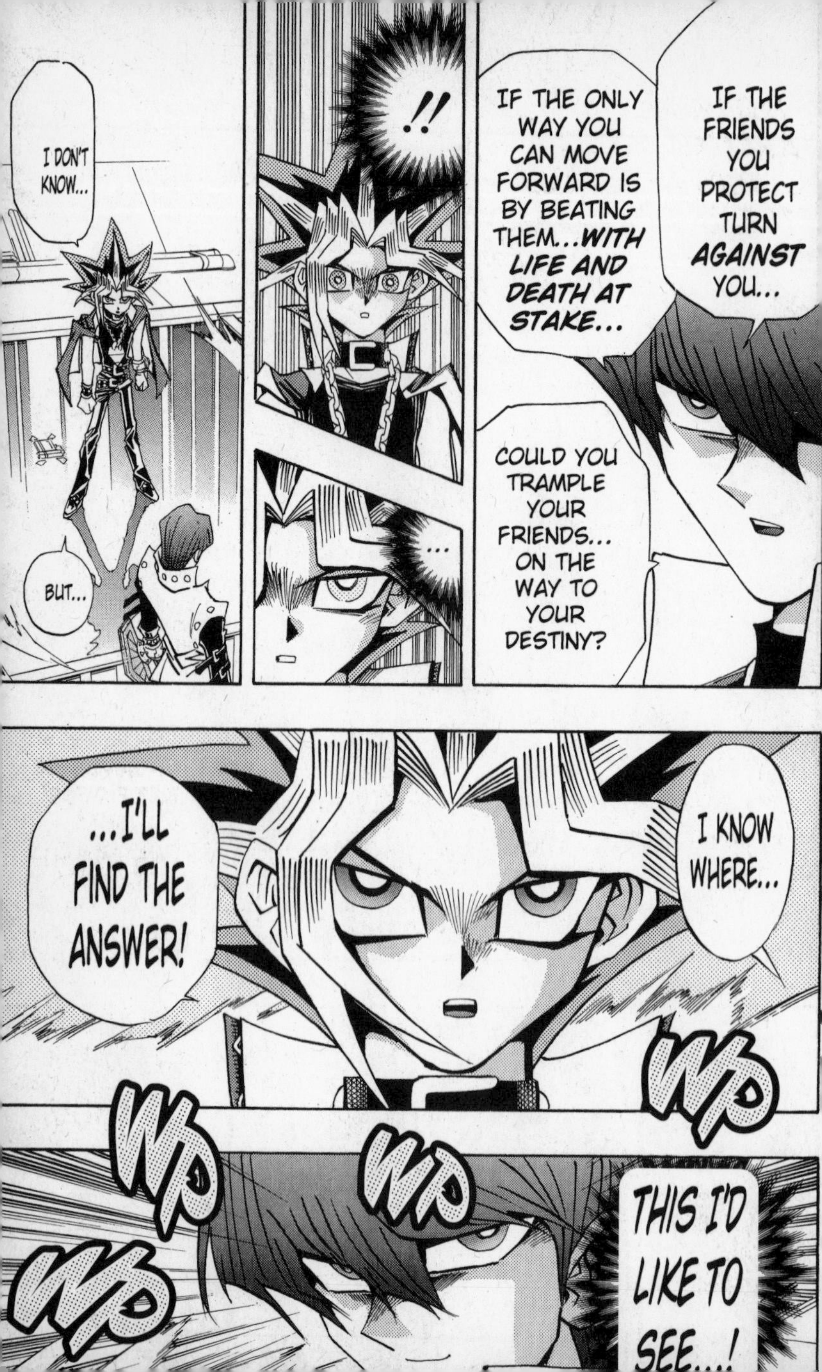

IF THE FRIENDS YOU PROTECT TURN *AGAINST* YOU...
IF THE ONLY WAY YOU CAN MOVE FORWARD IS BY BEATING THEM... *WITH LIFE AND DEATH AT STAKE...*
COULD YOU TRAMPLE YOUR FRIENDS... ON THE WAY TO YOUR DESTINY?
!!
...
I DON'T KNOW...
BUT...
I KNOW WHERE...
...I'LL FIND THE ANSWER!
WP
WP
WP
WP
THIS I'D LIKE TO SEE...!

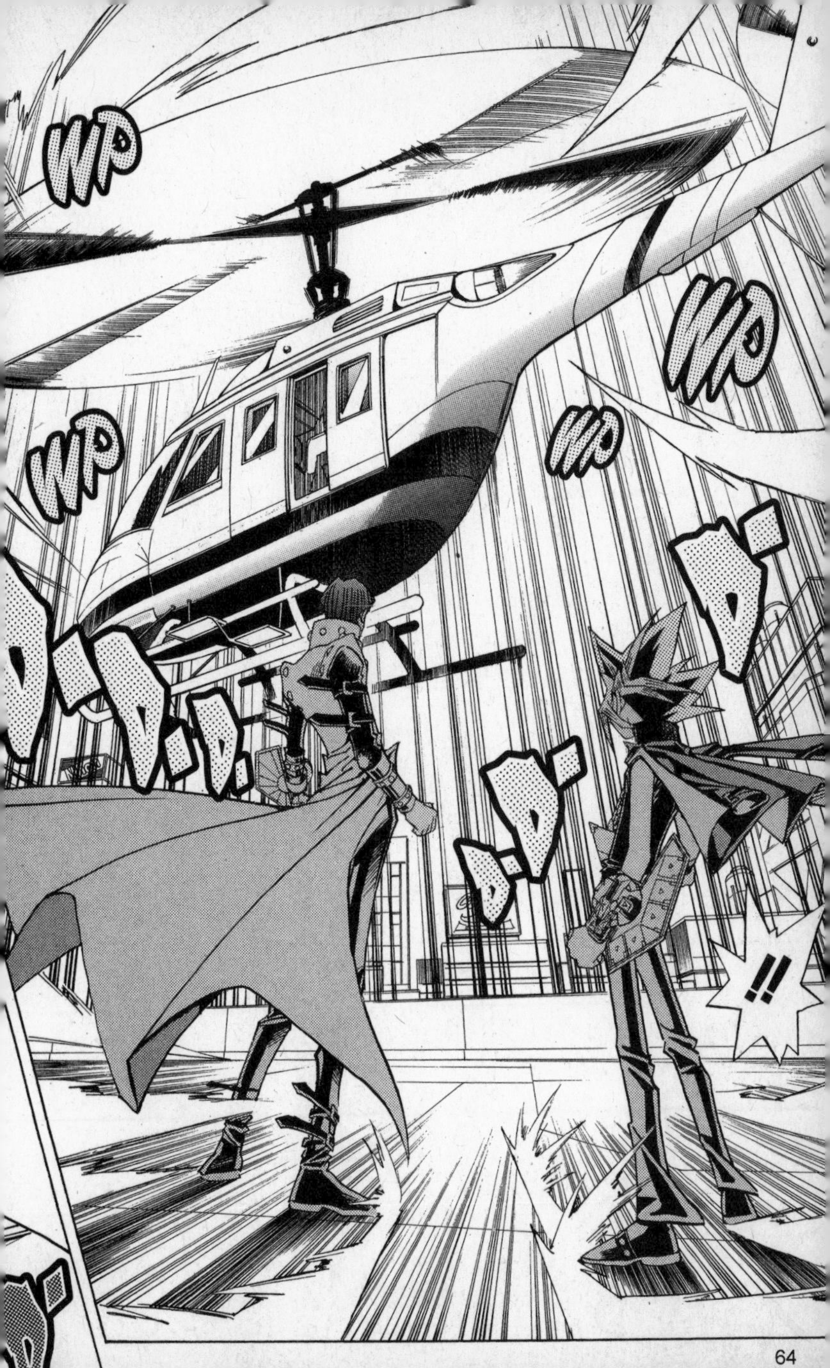
WIP
WIP
WIP
WIP
D
D..D..
!!
D..D..D..

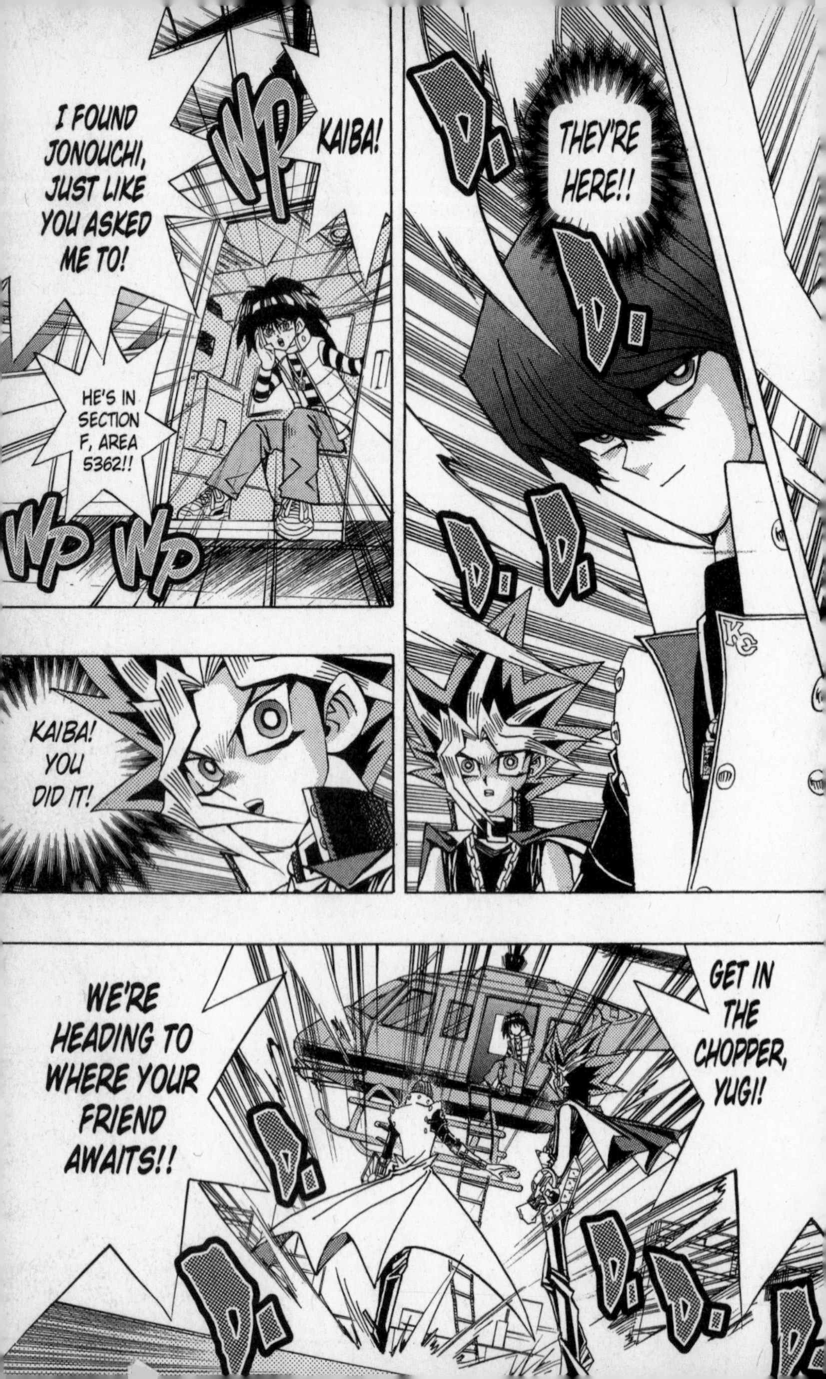
D.
THEY'RE HERE!!
D.
D. D.
KAIBA!
WP
I FOUND JONOUCHI, JUST LIKE YOU ASKED ME TO!
HE'S IN SECTION F, AREA 5362!!
WP WP
KAIBA! YOU DID IT!
GET IN THE CHOPPER, YUGI!
WE'RE HEADING TO WHERE YOUR FRIEND AWAITS!!
D.
D. D.
D.
D.

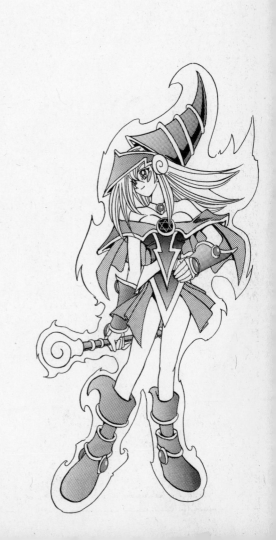

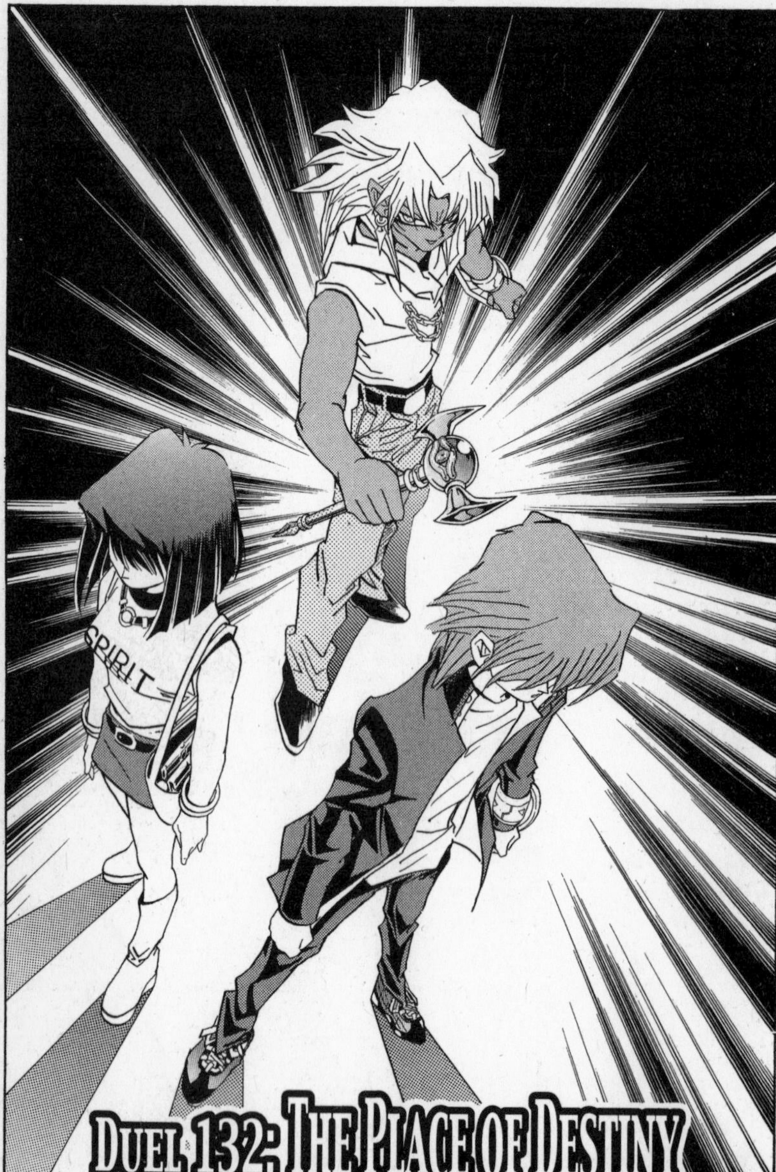
SPIRIT
DUEL 132: THE PLACE OF DESTINY

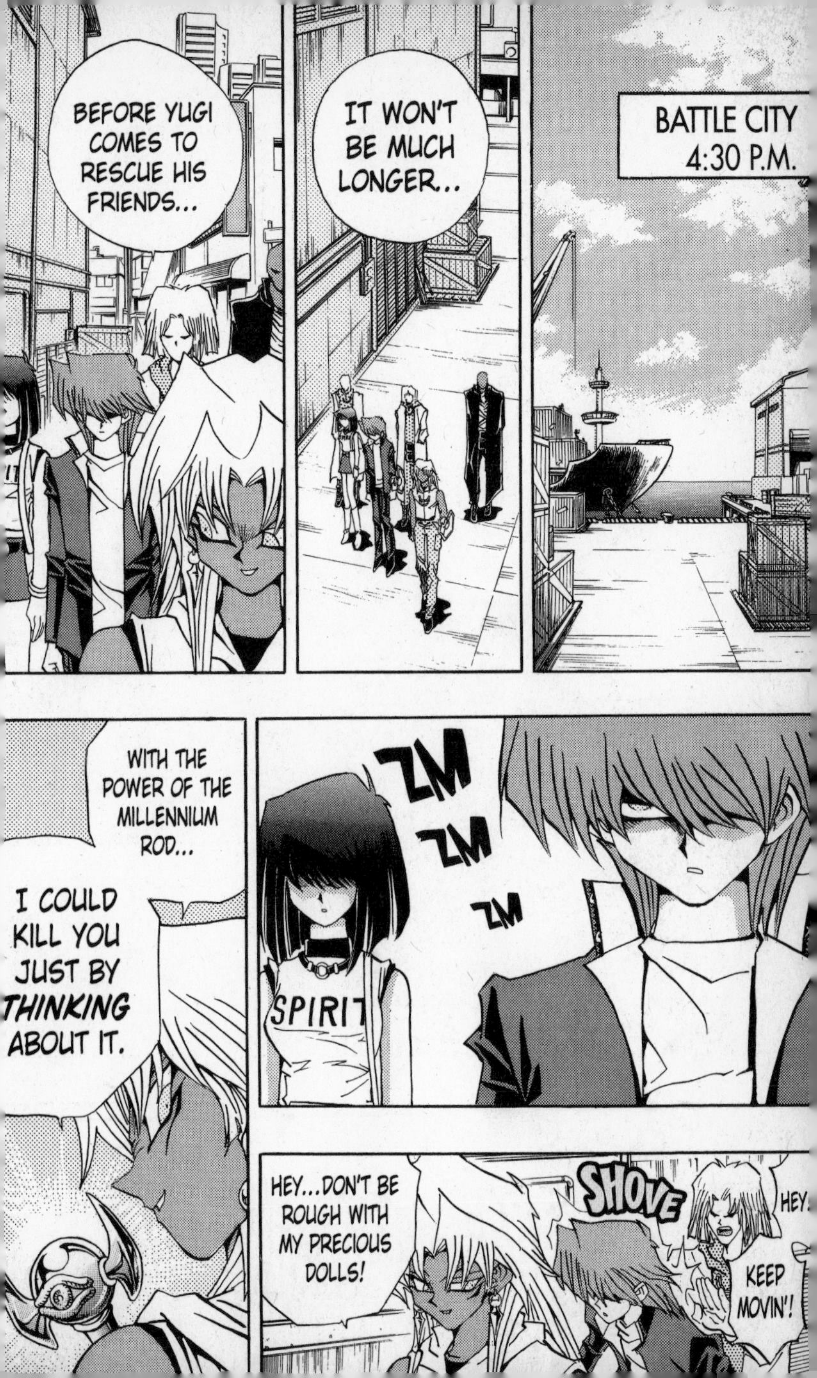
BATTLE CITY 4:30 P.M.
IT WON'T BE MUCH LONGER...
BEFORE YUGI COMES TO RESCUE HIS FRIENDS...
ZM
ZM
ZM
SPIRIT
HEY.
SHOVE
KEEP MOVIN'!
HEY...DON'T BE ROUGH WITH MY PRECIOUS DOLLS!
WITH THE POWER OF THE MILLENNIUM ROD...
I COULD KILL YOU JUST BY *THINKING* ABOUT IT.

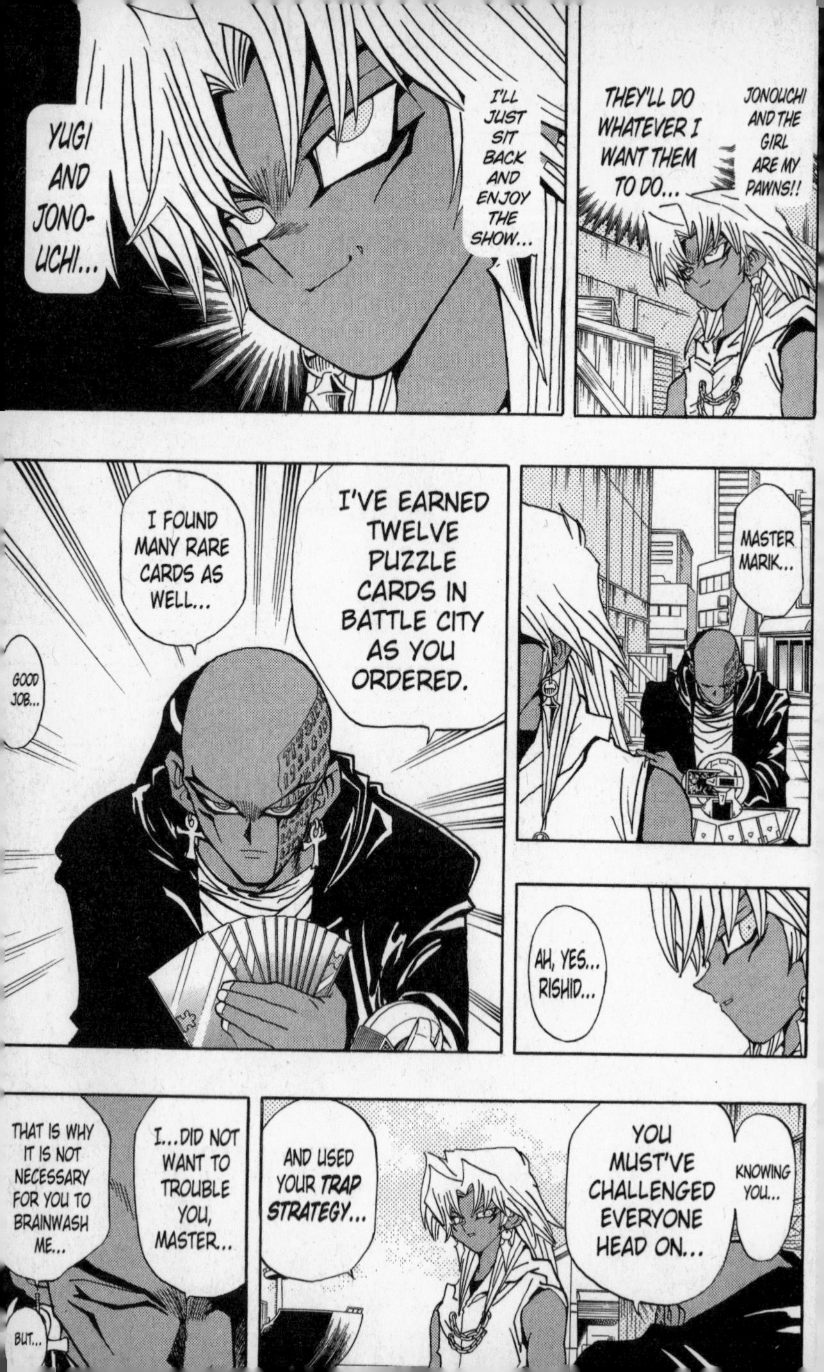
JONOUCHI AND THE GIRL ARE MY PAWNS!!
THEY'LL DO WHATEVER I WANT THEM TO DO...
I'LL JUST SIT BACK AND ENJOY THE SHOW...
YUGI AND JONO-UCHI...
MASTER MARIK...
AH, YES... RISHID...
I'VE EARNED TWELVE PUZZLE CARDS IN BATTLE CITY AS YOU ORDERED.
I FOUND MANY RARE CARDS AS WELL...
GOOD JOB...
KNOWING YOU...
YOU MUST'VE CHALLENGED EVERYONE HEAD ON...
AND USED YOUR *TRAP STRATEGY*...
I...DID NOT WANT TO TROUBLE YOU, MASTER...
THAT IS WHY IT IS NOT NECESSARY FOR YOU TO BRAINWASH ME...
BUT...

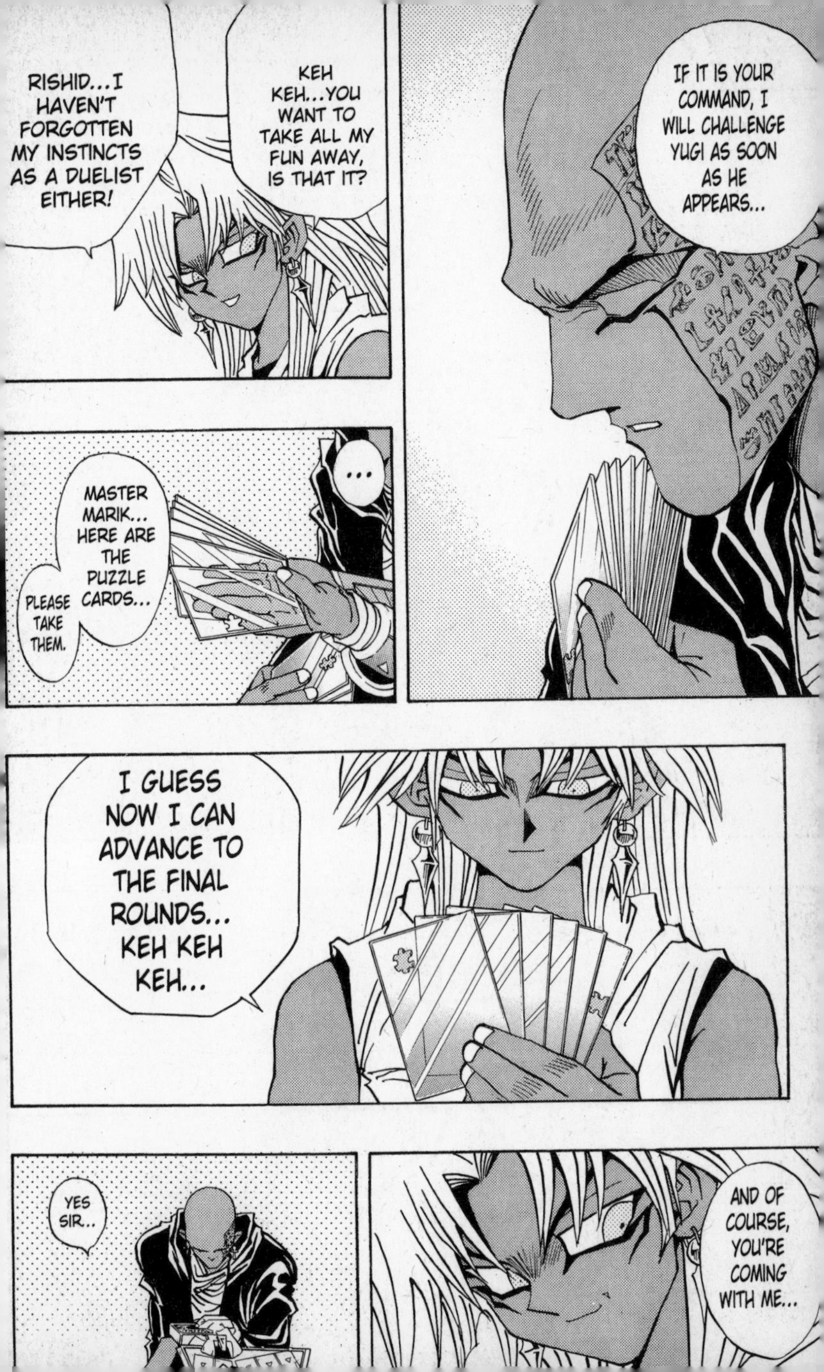

IF IT IS YOUR COMMAND, I WILL CHALLENGE YUGI AS SOON AS HE APPEARS...
KEH KEH...YOU WANT TO TAKE ALL MY FUN AWAY, IS THAT IT?
RISHID...I HAVEN'T FORGOTTEN MY INSTINCTS AS A DUELIST EITHER!
...
MASTER MARIK... HERE ARE THE PUZZLE CARDS...
PLEASE TAKE THEM.
I GUESS NOW I CAN ADVANCE TO THE FINAL ROUNDS... KEH KEH KEH...
AND OF COURSE, YOU'RE COMING WITH ME...
YES SIR..

READ THIS WAY

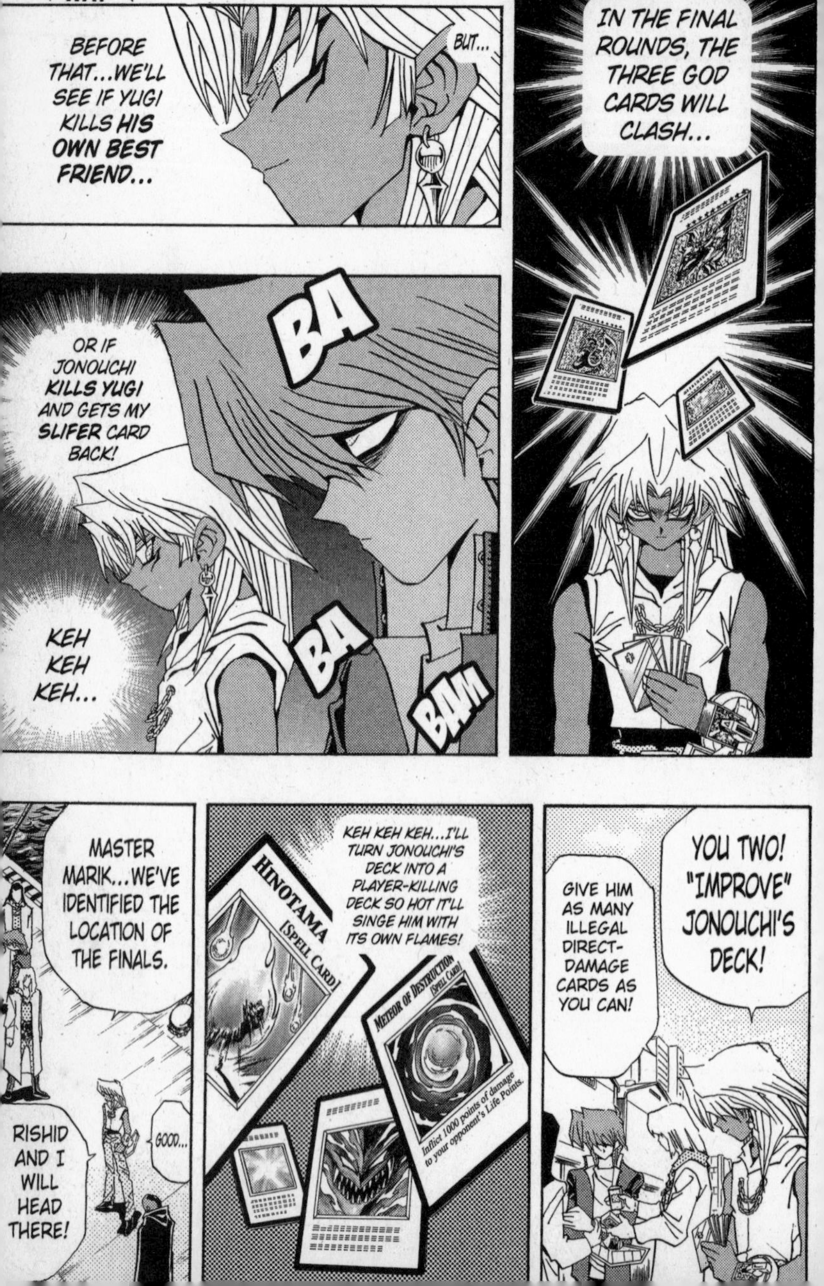
IN THE FINAL ROUNDS, THE THREE GOD CARDS WILL CLASH...
BUT...
BEFORE THAT...WE'LL SEE IF YUGI KILLS HIS OWN BEST FRIEND...
BA
OR IF JONOUCHI KILLS YUGI AND GETS MY SLIFER CARD BACK!
BA
BAM
KEH KEH KEH...
YOU TWO! "IMPROVE" JONOUCHI'S DECK!
GIVE HIM AS MANY ILLEGAL DIRECT-DAMAGE CARDS AS YOU CAN!
KEH KEH KEH...I'LL TURN JONOUCHI'S DECK INTO A PLAYER-KILLING DECK SO HOT IT'LL SINGE HIM WITH ITS OWN FLAMES!
HINOTAMA
[SPELL CARD]
METEOR OF DESTRUCTION
[SPELL CARD]
Inflict 1000 points of damage to your opponent's Life Points.
MASTER MARIK...WE'VE IDENTIFIED THE LOCATION OF THE FINALS.
GOOD...
RISHID AND I WILL HEAD THERE!

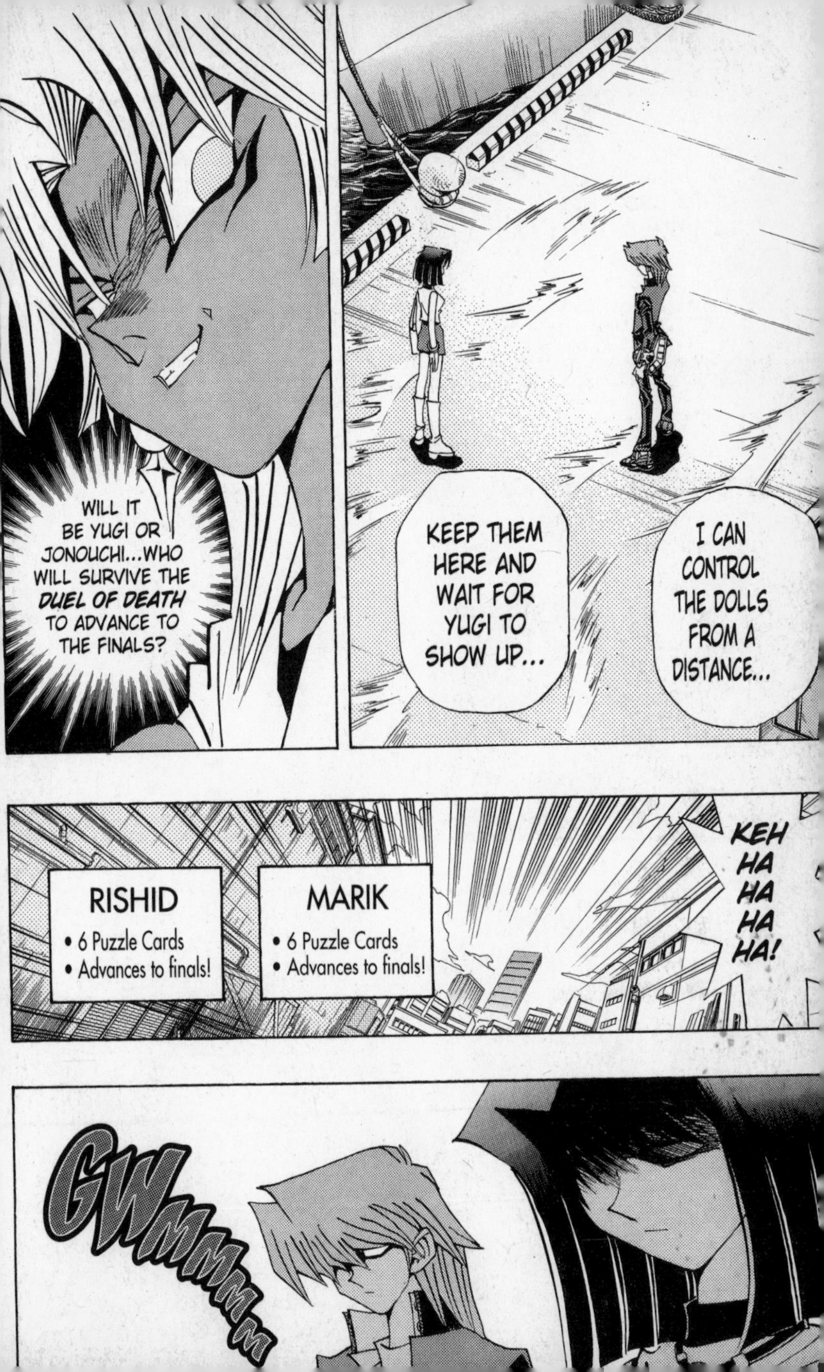
I CAN CONTROL THE DOLLS FROM A DISTANCE...
KEEP THEM HERE AND WAIT FOR YUGI TO SHOW UP...
WILL IT BE YUGI OR JONOUCHI...WHO WILL SURVIVE THE *DUEL OF DEATH* TO ADVANCE TO THE FINALS?
KEH HA HA HA HA!
MARIK
• 6 Puzzle Cards
• Advances to finals!
RISHID
• 6 Puzzle Cards
• Advances to finals!
GWMMMmm

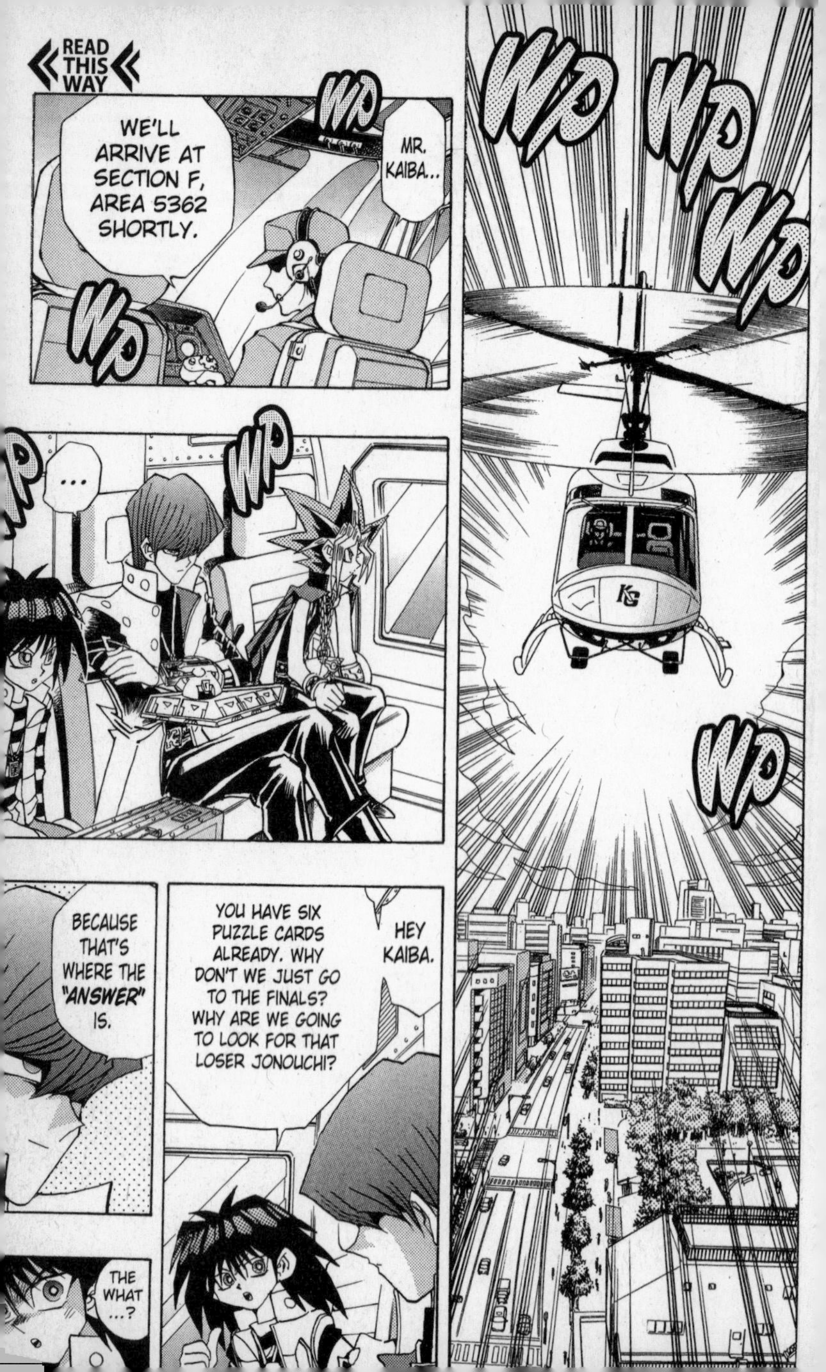
READ THIS WAY
WP WP
WP
WP
WP
WP
MR. KAIBA...
WE'LL ARRIVE AT SECTION F, AREA 5362 SHORTLY.
WP
WP
...
WP
HEY KAIBA.
YOU HAVE SIX PUZZLE CARDS ALREADY. WHY DON'T WE JUST GO TO THE FINALS? WHY ARE WE GOING TO LOOK FOR THAT LOSER JONOUCHI?
BECAUSE THAT'S WHERE THE "ANSWER" IS.
THE WHAT ...?

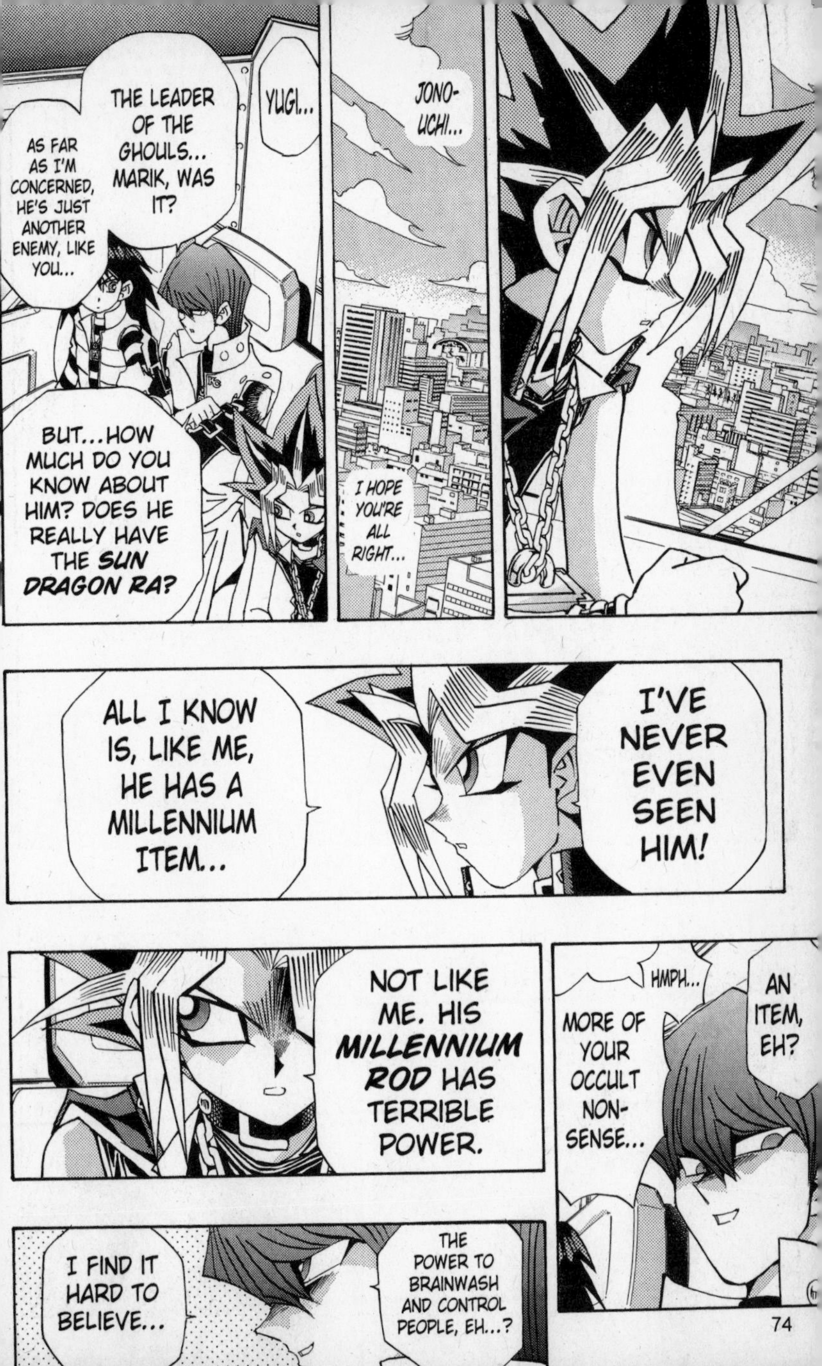
JONO-UCHI...
I HOPE YOU'RE ALL RIGHT...
YUGI...
THE LEADER OF THE GHOULS... MARIK, WAS IT?
AS FAR AS I'M CONCERNED, HE'S JUST ANOTHER ENEMY, LIKE YOU...
BUT...HOW MUCH DO YOU KNOW ABOUT HIM? DOES HE REALLY HAVE THE SUN DRAGON RA?
I'VE NEVER EVEN SEEN HIM!
ALL I KNOW IS, LIKE ME, HE HAS A MILLENNIUM ITEM...
AN ITEM, EH?
HMPH...
MORE OF YOUR OCCULT NON-SENSE...
NOT LIKE ME. HIS MILLENNIUM ROD HAS TERRIBLE POWER.
THE POWER TO BRAINWASH AND CONTROL PEOPLE, EH...?
I FIND IT HARD TO BELIEVE...

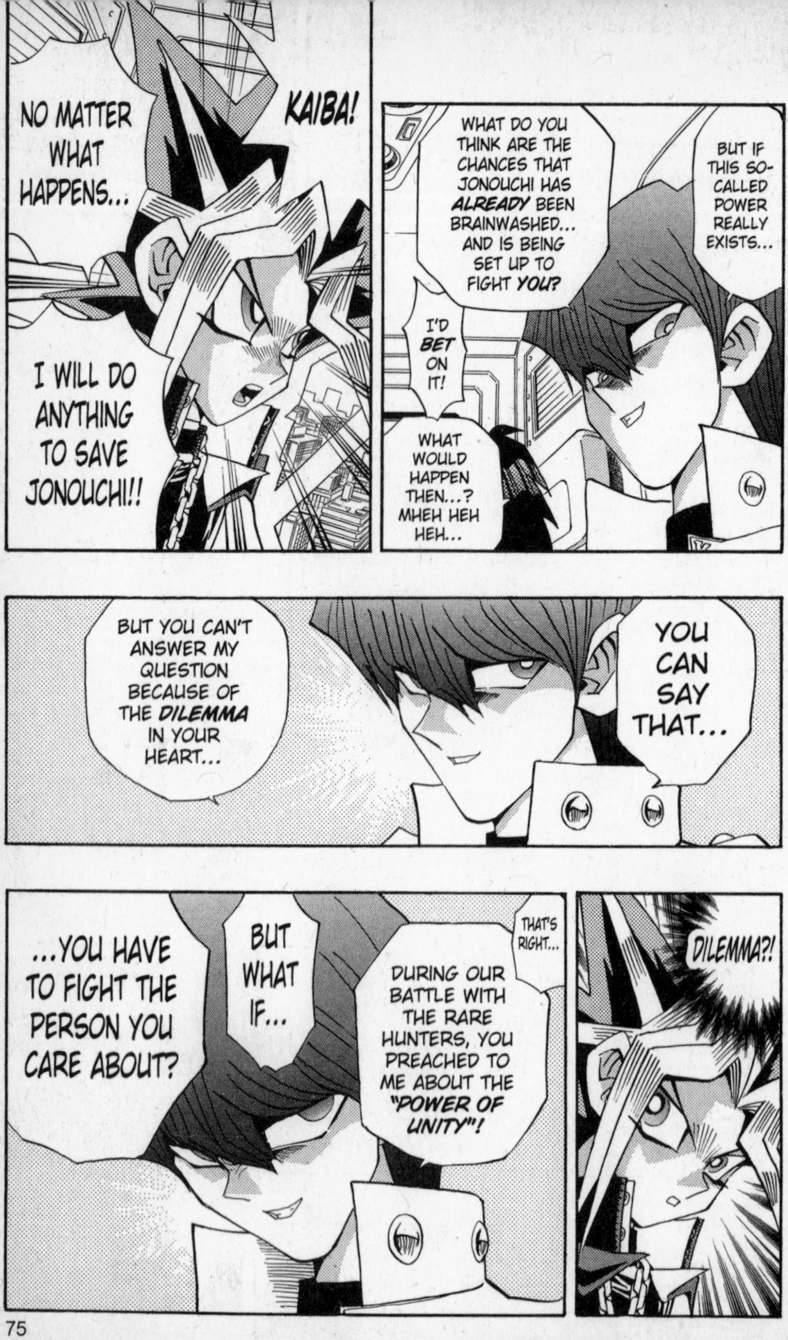
BUT IF THIS SO-CALLED POWER REALLY EXISTS...
WHAT DO YOU THINK ARE THE CHANCES THAT JONOUCHI HAS ALREADY BEEN BRAINWASHED... AND IS BEING SET UP TO FIGHT YOU?
I'D BET ON IT!
WHAT WOULD HAPPEN THEN...? MHEH HEH HEH...
KAIBA!
NO MATTER WHAT HAPPENS...
I WILL DO ANYTHING TO SAVE JONOUCHI!!
YOU CAN SAY THAT...
BUT YOU CAN'T ANSWER MY QUESTION BECAUSE OF THE DILEMMA IN YOUR HEART...
DILEMMA?!
THAT'S RIGHT...
DURING OUR BATTLE WITH THE RARE HUNTERS, YOU PREACHED TO ME ABOUT THE "POWER OF UNITY"!
BUT WHAT IF...
...YOU HAVE TO FIGHT THE PERSON YOU CARE ABOUT?

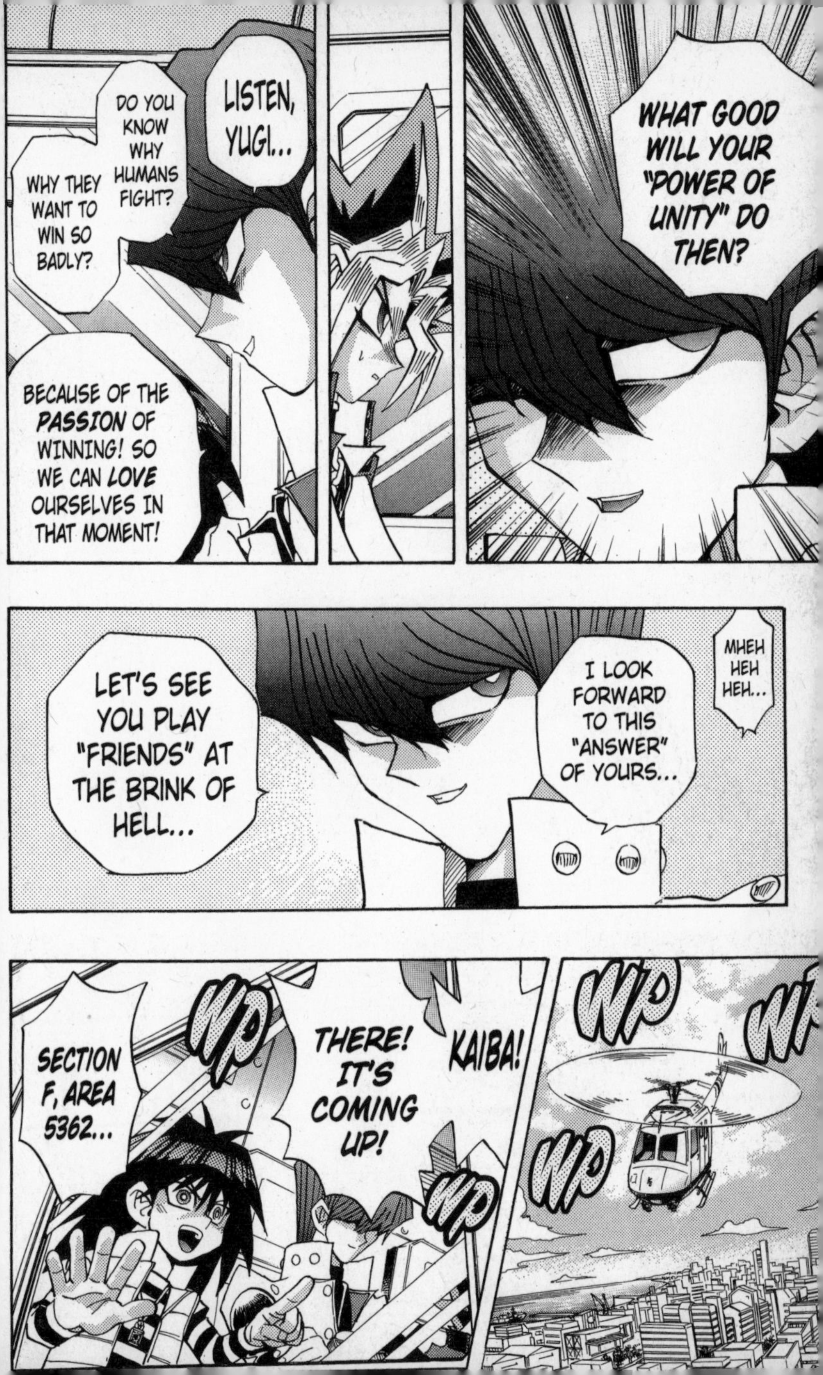
WHAT GOOD WILL YOUR "POWER OF UNITY" DO THEN?
LISTEN, YUGI...
DO YOU KNOW WHY HUMANS FIGHT?
WHY THEY WANT TO WIN SO BADLY?
BECAUSE OF THE PASSION OF WINNING! SO WE CAN LOVE OURSELVES IN THAT MOMENT!
MHEH HEH HEH...
I LOOK FORWARD TO THIS "ANSWER" OF YOURS...
LET'S SEE YOU PLAY "FRIENDS" AT THE BRINK OF HELL...
WIP
WIP
KAIBA!
THERE! IT'S COMING UP!
WIP
WIP
SECTION F, AREA 5362...

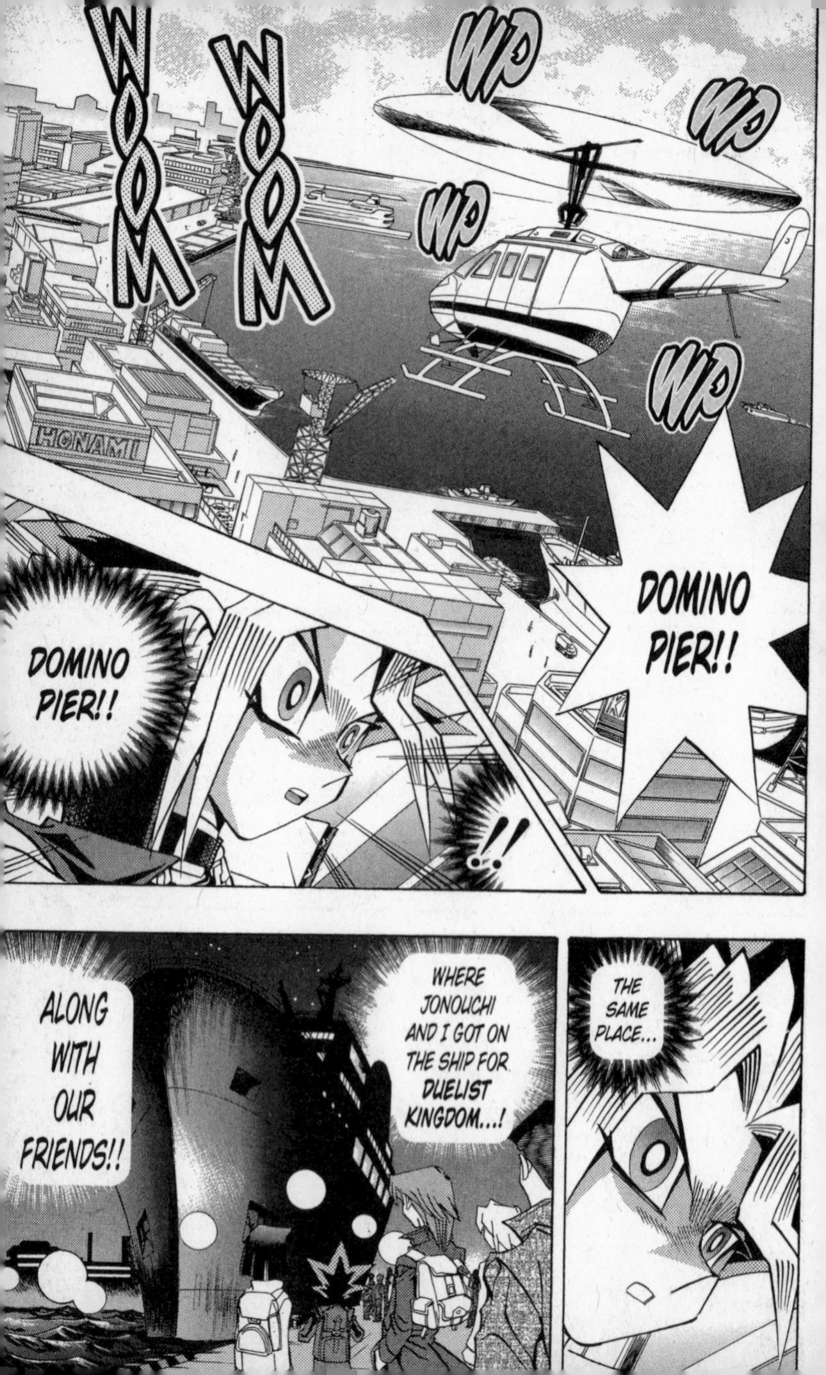
WP
WP
WP
WP
WOOM
WOOM
HONAMI
DOMINO PIER!!
DOMINO PIER!!
!!
THE SAME PLACE...
WHERE JONOUCHI AND I GOT ON THE SHIP FOR DUELIST KINGDOM...!
ALONG WITH OUR FRIENDS!!

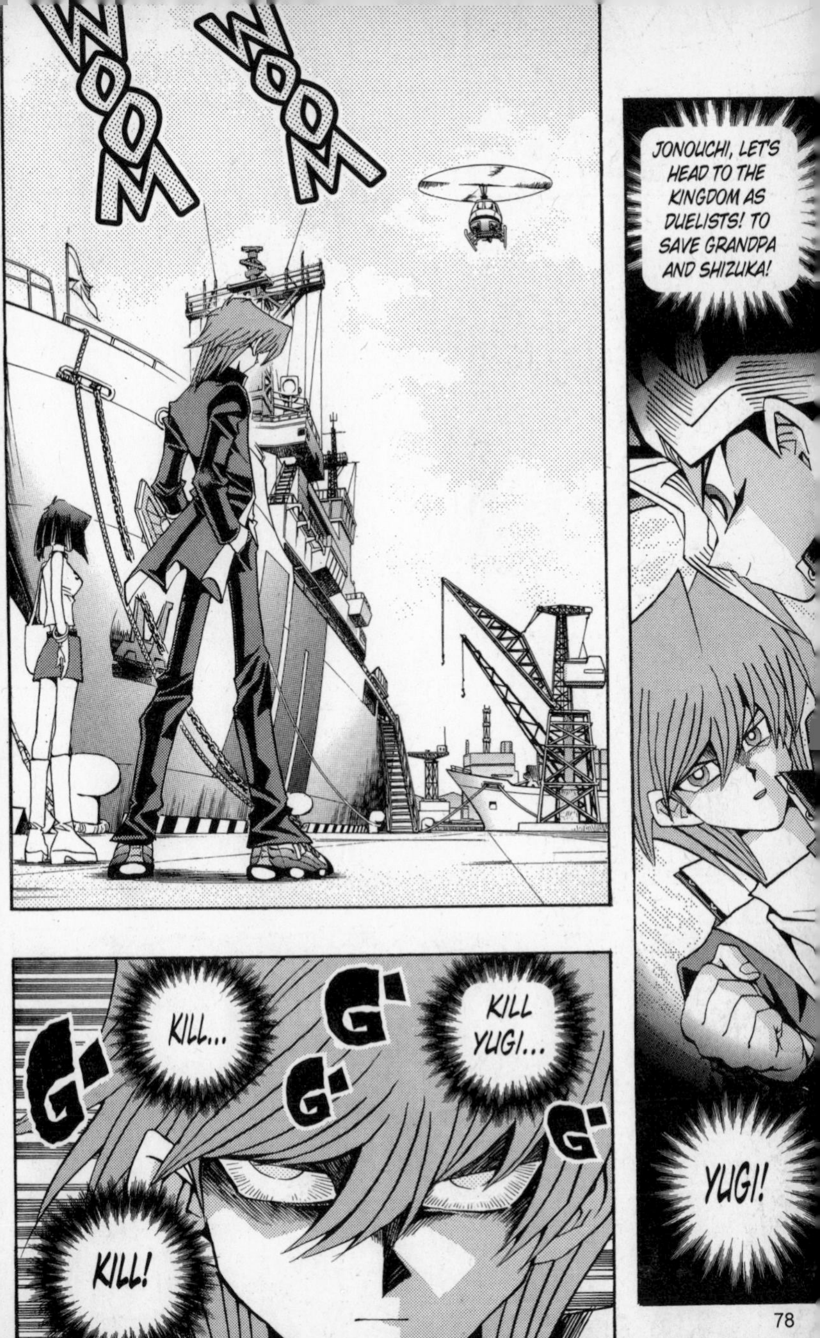
JONOUCHI, LET'S HEAD TO THE KINGDOM AS DUELISTS! TO SAVE GRANDPA AND SHIZUKA!
YUGI!
WOOM
WOOM
KILL YUGI...
G'
G'
G'
KILL...
G'
KILL!

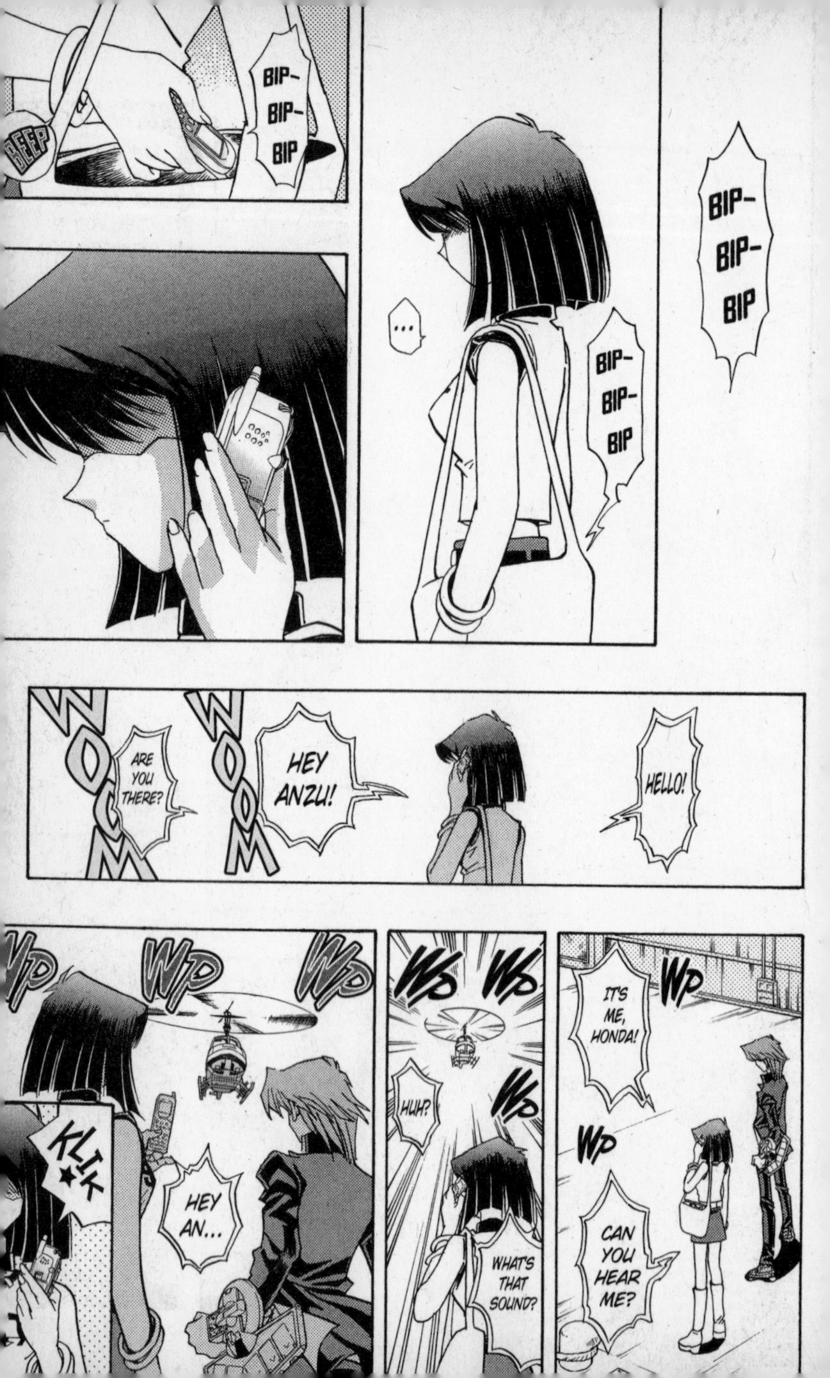
BIP-
BIP-
BIP
BIP-
BIP-
BIP
...
BIP-
BIP-
BIP
BEEP
HELLO!
HEY ANZU!
WOOM
ARE YOU THERE?
WOOM
IT'S ME, HONDA!
WP
WP
CAN YOU HEAR ME?
WP
WP
HUH?
WP
WHAT'S THAT SOUND?
WP
WP
WP
KLIK★K
HEY AN...

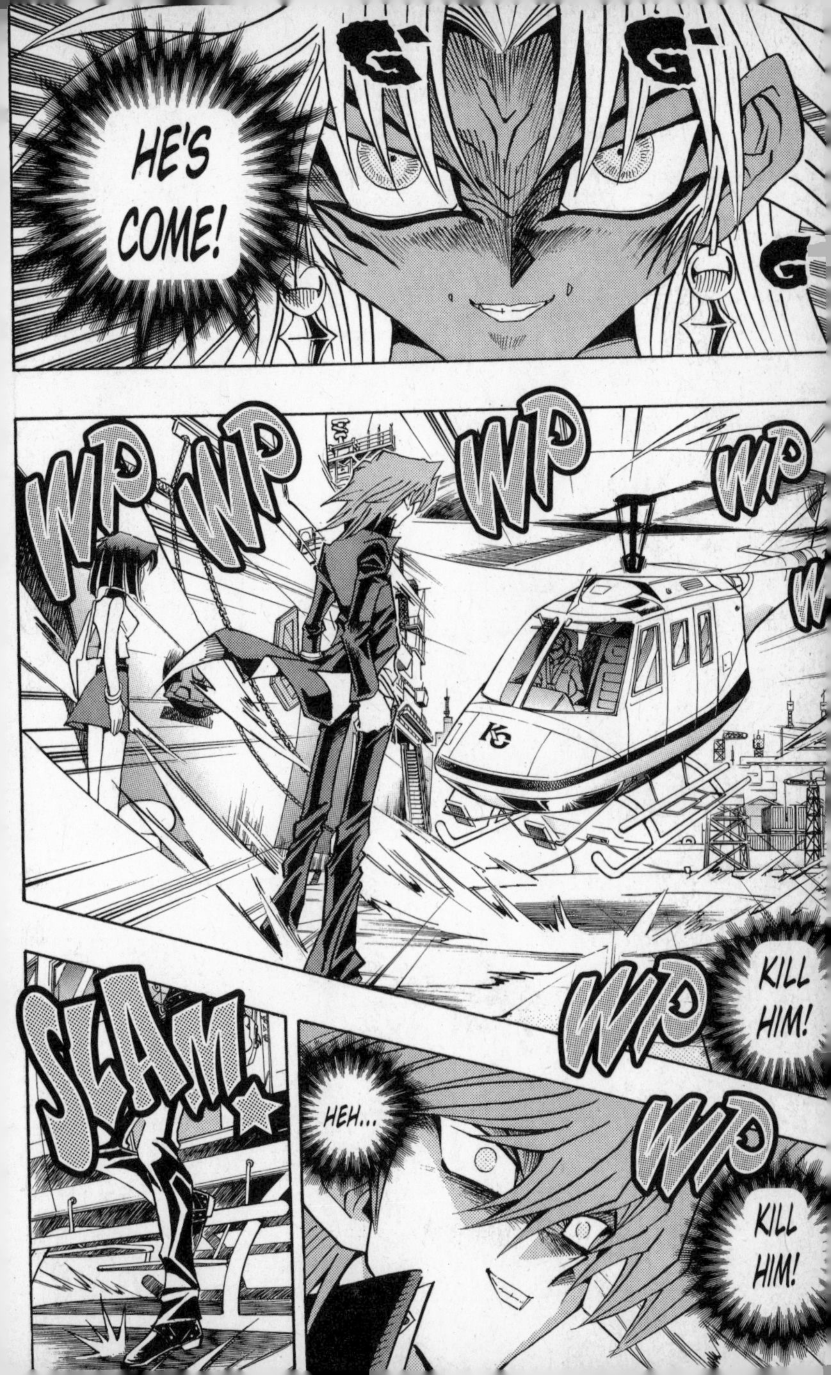
G-
G-
G
HE'S COME!
WP
WP
WP
WP
KILL HIM!
WP
WP
HEH...
KILL HIM!
SLAM

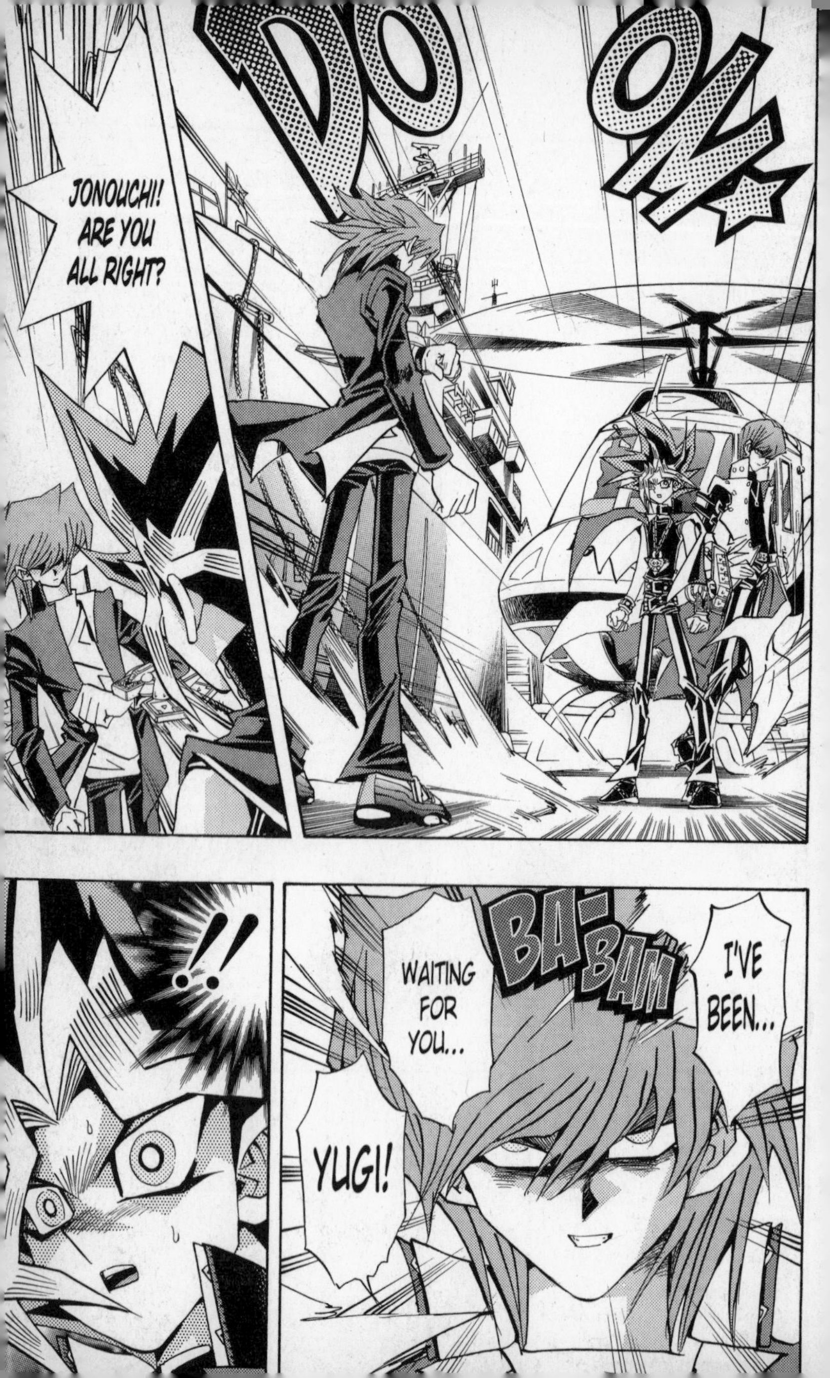
DOOM
JONOUCHI! ARE YOU ALL RIGHT?
I'VE BEEN...
BA-BAM
WAITING FOR YOU...
YUGI!
!!

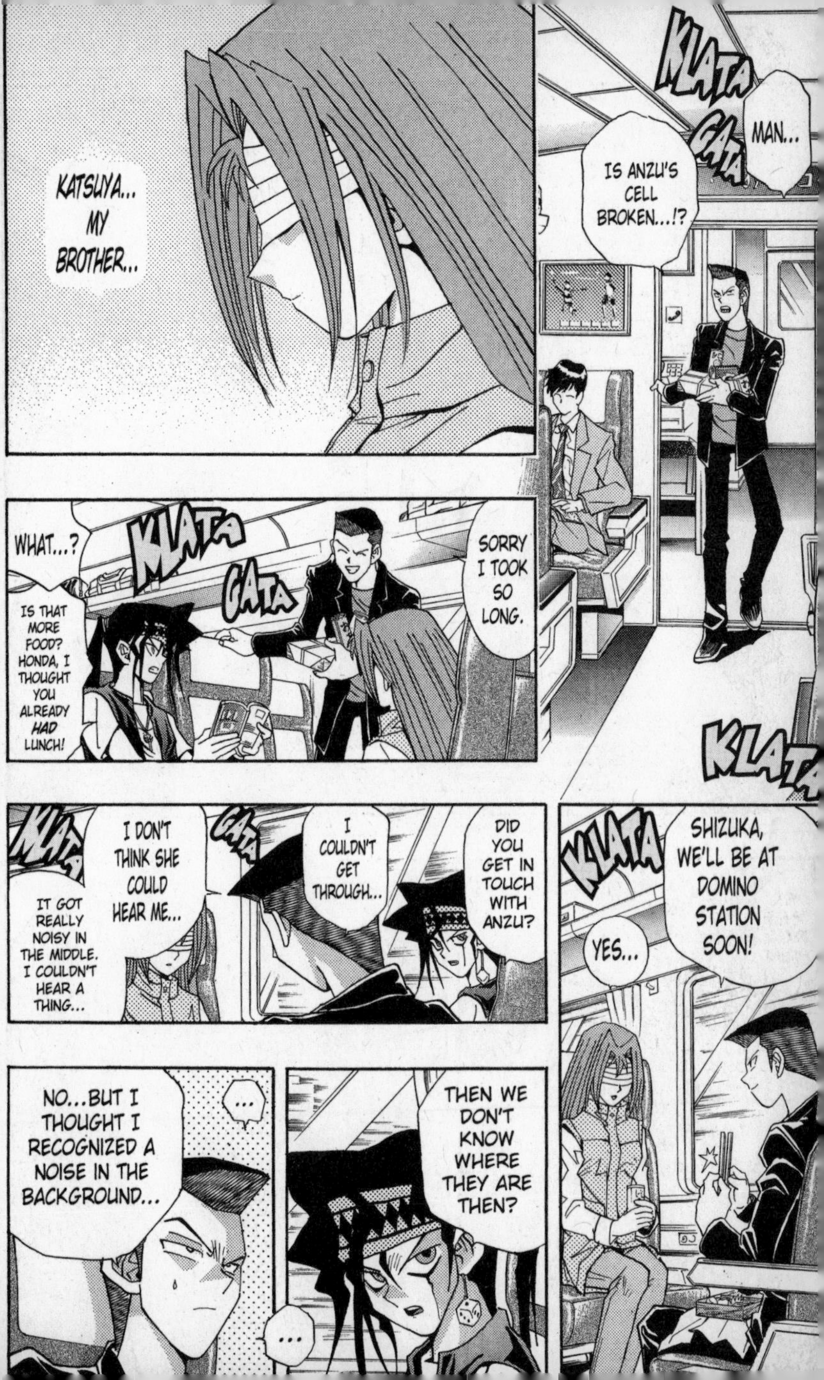
KLATA
GATA
MAN...
IS ANZU'S CELL BROKEN...!?
KLATA
KATSUYA... MY BROTHER...
SORRY I TOOK SO LONG.
KLATA
GATA
WHAT...?
IS THAT MORE FOOD? HONDA, I THOUGHT YOU ALREADY *HAD* LUNCH!
KLATA
SHIZUKA, WE'LL BE AT DOMINO STATION SOON!
YES...
DID YOU GET IN TOUCH WITH ANZU?
I COULDN'T GET THROUGH...
GATA
I DON'T THINK SHE COULD HEAR ME...
KLATA
IT GOT REALLY NOISY IN THE MIDDLE. I COULDN'T HEAR A THING...
THEN WE DON'T KNOW WHERE THEY ARE THEN?
...
...
NO...BUT I THOUGHT I RECOGNIZED A NOISE IN THE BACKGROUND...

READ THIS WAY

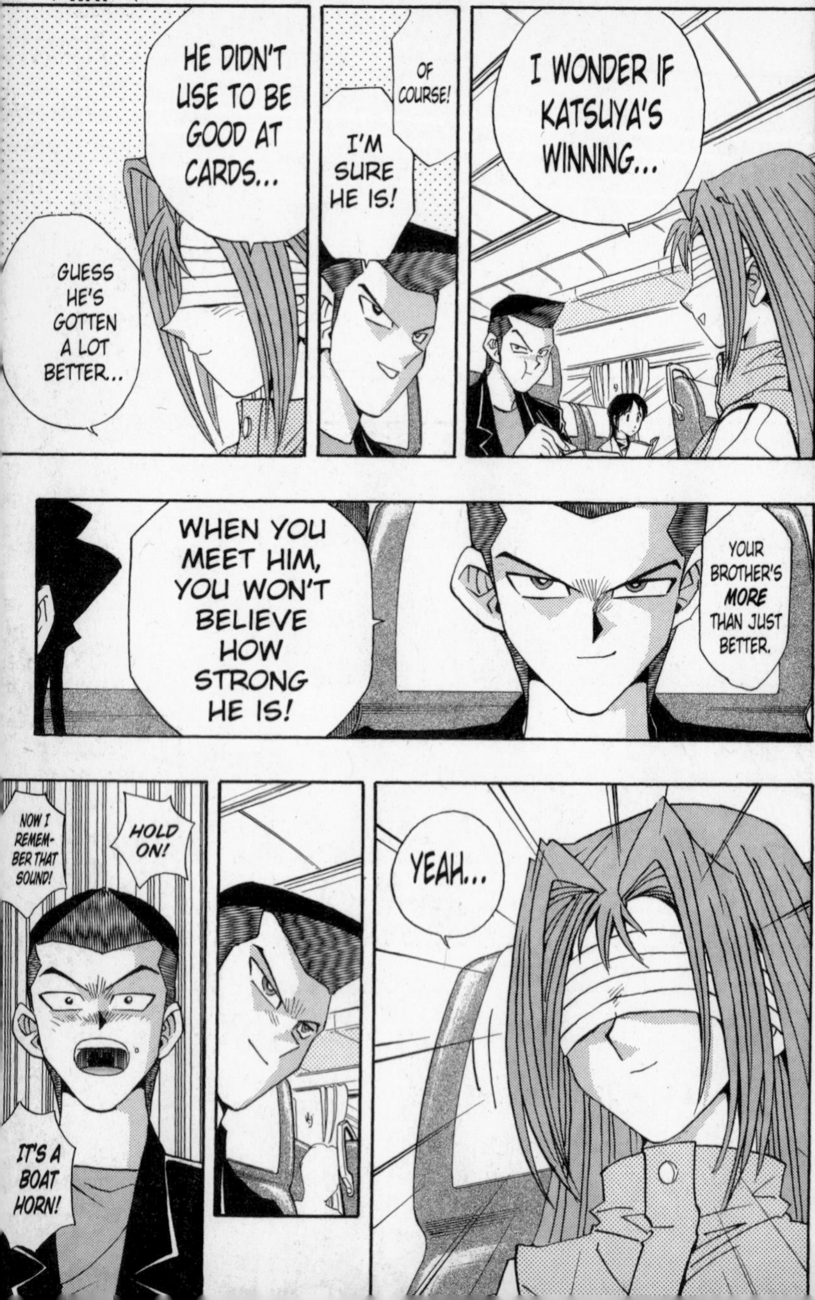
I WONDER IF KATSUYA'S WINNING...
OF COURSE!
I'M SURE HE IS!
HE DIDN'T USE TO BE GOOD AT CARDS...
GUESS HE'S GOTTEN A LOT BETTER...
YOUR BROTHER'S MORE THAN JUST BETTER.
WHEN YOU MEET HIM, YOU WON'T BELIEVE HOW STRONG HE IS!
YEAH...
HOLD ON!
NOW I REMEMBER THAT SOUND!
IT'S A BOAT HORN!

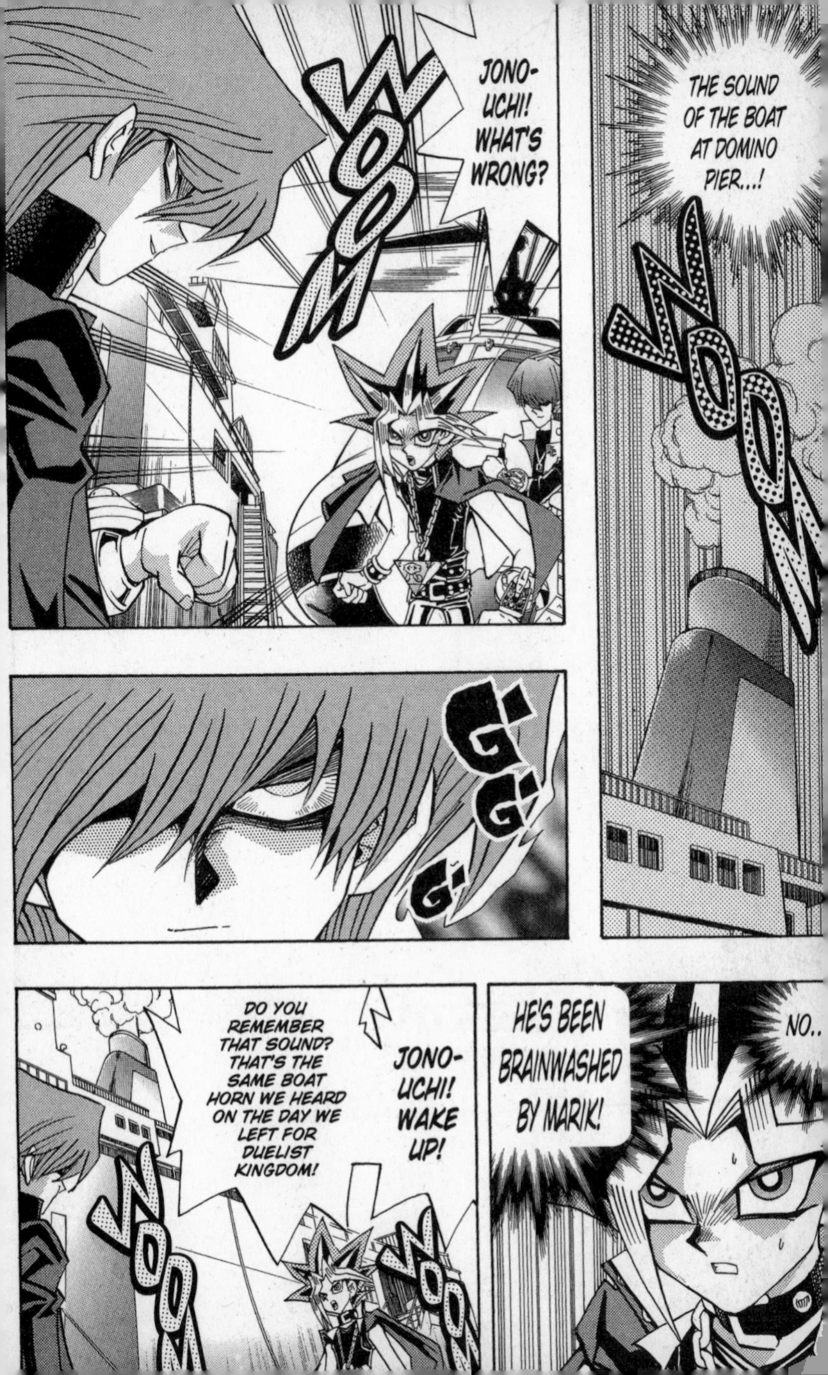
THE SOUND OF THE BOAT AT DOMINO PIER...!
WOOOM
JONO-UCHI! WHAT'S WRONG?
WOOOM
G G G
NO..
HE'S BEEN BRAINWASHED BY MARIK!
JONO-UCHI! WAKE UP!
DO YOU REMEMBER THAT SOUND? THAT'S THE SAME BOAT HORN WE HEARD ON THE DAY WE LEFT FOR DUELIST KINGDOM!
WOOOM
WOOOM

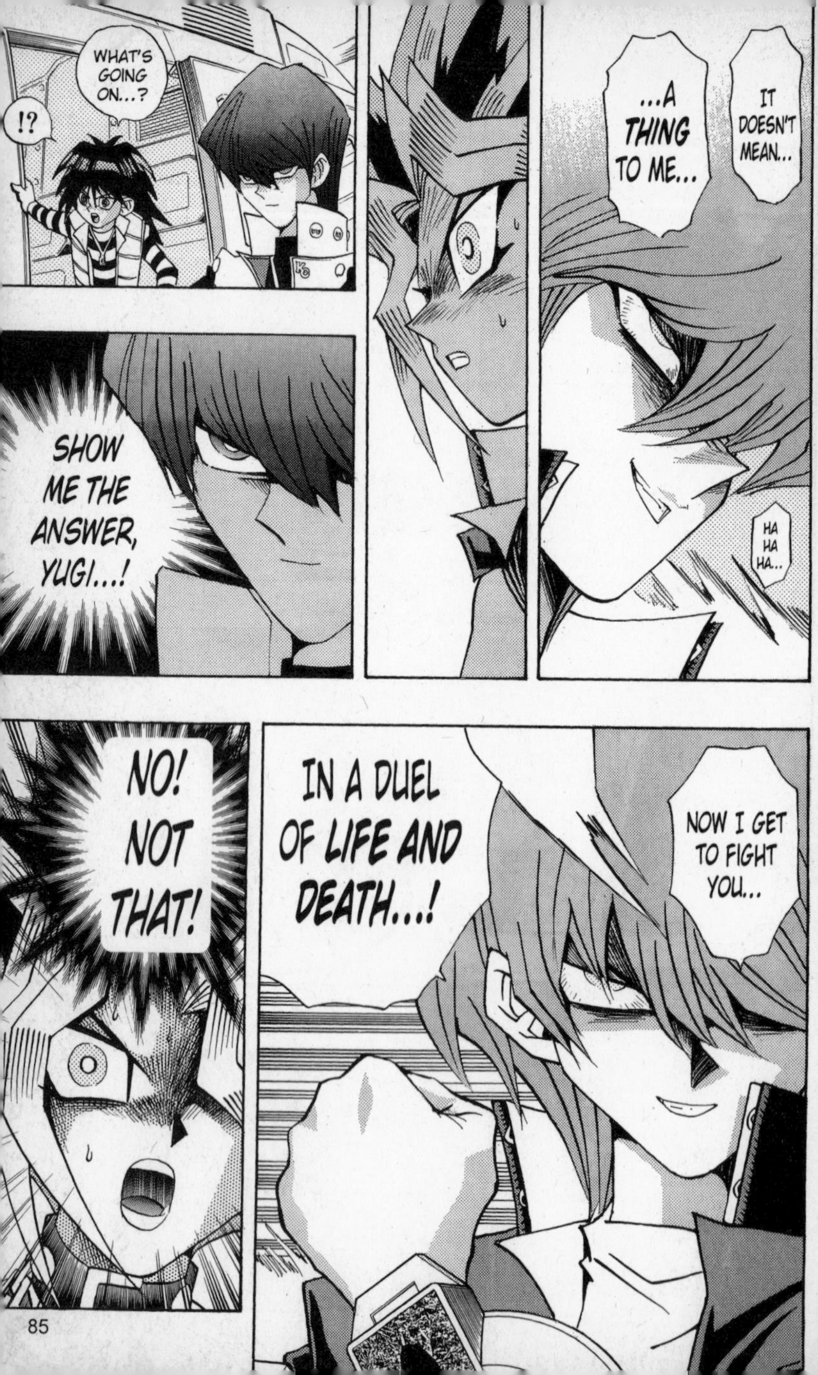
IT DOESN'T MEAN...
...A THING TO ME...
HA HA HA...
WHAT'S GOING ON...?
!?
SHOW ME THE ANSWER, YUGI...!
NOW I GET TO FIGHT YOU...
IN A DUEL OF LIFE AND DEATH...!
NO! NOT THAT!

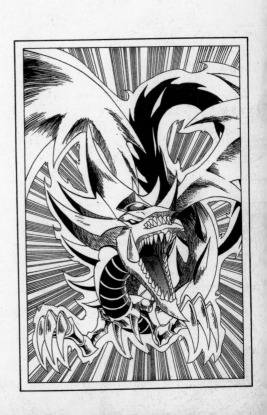

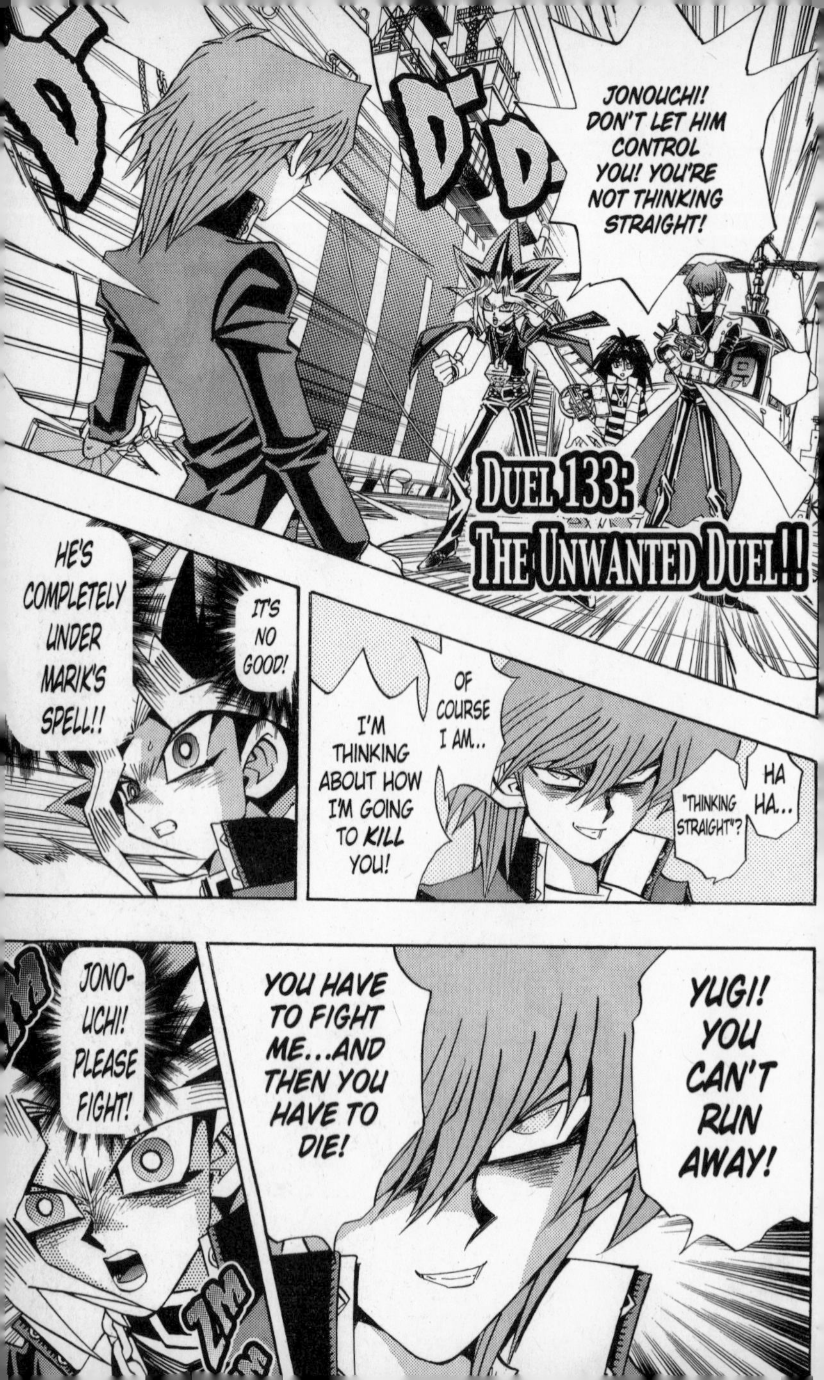
JONOUCHI! DON'T LET HIM CONTROL YOU! YOU'RE NOT THINKING STRAIGHT!
DUEL 133: THE UNWANTED DUEL!!
HA HA...
"THINKING STRAIGHT"?
OF COURSE I AM...
I'M THINKING ABOUT HOW I'M GOING TO KILL YOU!
IT'S NO GOOD!
HE'S COMPLETELY UNDER MARIK'S SPELL!!
YUGI! YOU CAN'T RUN AWAY!
YOU HAVE TO FIGHT ME...AND THEN YOU HAVE TO DIE!
JONO-UCHI! PLEASE FIGHT!

Duel 133: The Unwanted Duel!!

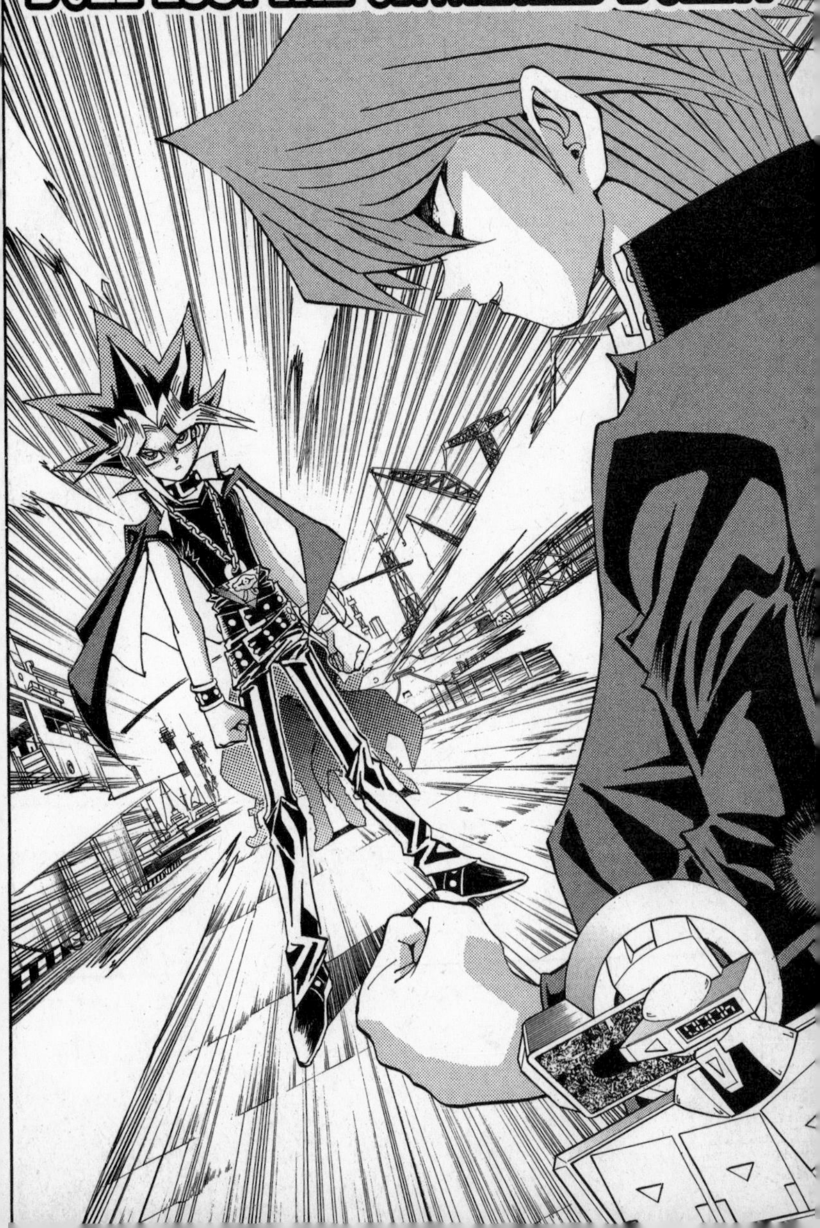

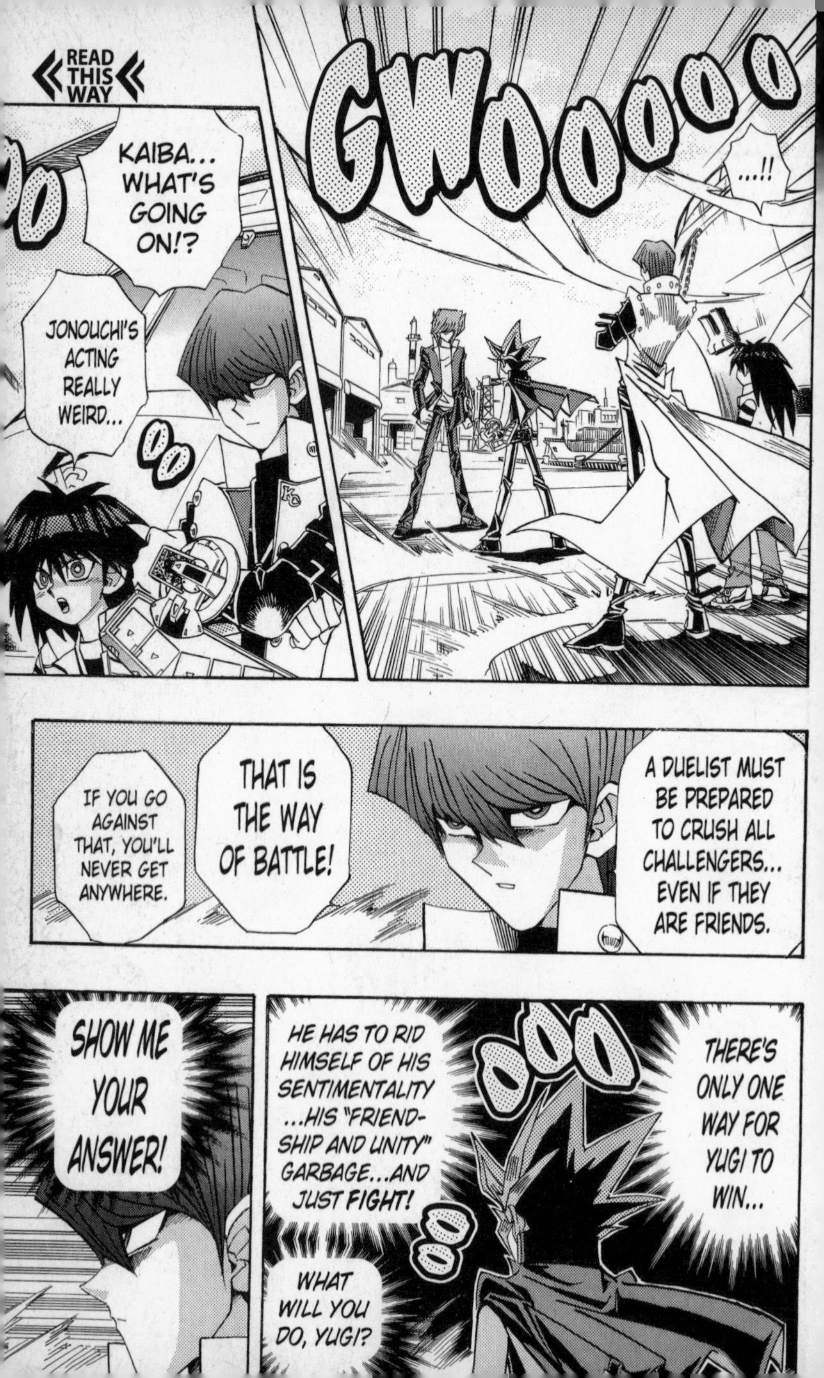
READ THIS WAY
GWOOOOOO
...!!
KAIBA... WHAT'S GOING ON!?
JONOUCHI'S ACTING REALLY WEIRD...
A DUELIST MUST BE PREPARED TO CRUSH ALL CHALLENGERS... EVEN IF THEY ARE FRIENDS.
THAT IS THE WAY OF BATTLE!
IF YOU GO AGAINST THAT, YOU'LL NEVER GET ANYWHERE.
THERE'S ONLY ONE WAY FOR YUGI TO WIN...
HE HAS TO RID HIMSELF OF HIS SENTIMENTALITY ...HIS "FRIEND-SHIP AND UNITY" GARBAGE...AND JUST FIGHT!
WHAT WILL YOU DO, YUGI?
SHOW ME YOUR ANSWER!

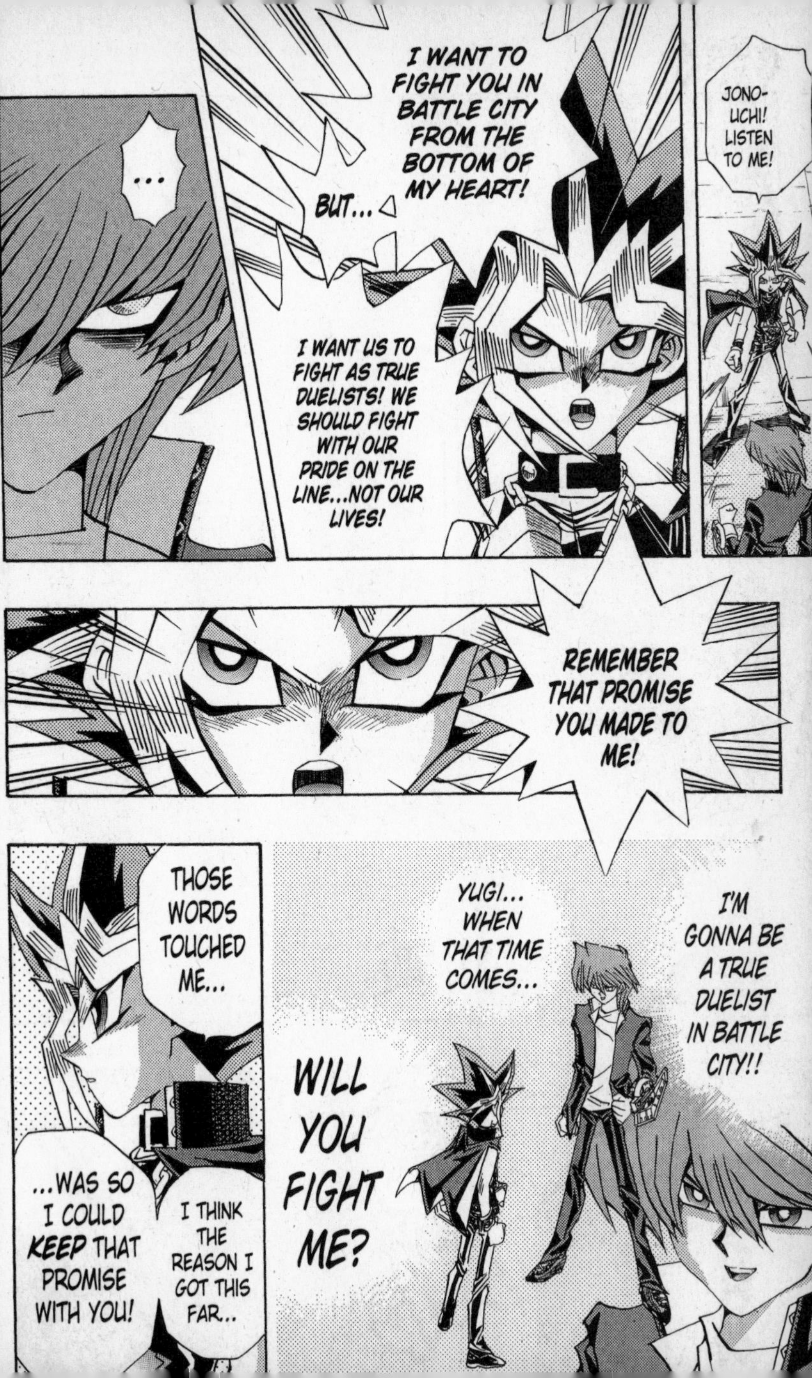
JONO-UCHI! LISTEN TO ME!
I WANT TO FIGHT YOU IN BATTLE CITY FROM THE BOTTOM OF MY HEART!
BUT...
I WANT US TO FIGHT AS TRUE DUELISTS! WE SHOULD FIGHT WITH OUR PRIDE ON THE LINE...NOT OUR LIVES!
...
REMEMBER THAT PROMISE YOU MADE TO ME!
I'M GONNA BE A TRUE DUELIST IN BATTLE CITY!!
YUGI... WHEN THAT TIME COMES...
WILL YOU FIGHT ME?
THOSE WORDS TOUCHED ME...
I THINK THE REASON I GOT THIS FAR..
...WAS SO I COULD **KEEP** THAT PROMISE WITH YOU!

READ THIS WAY

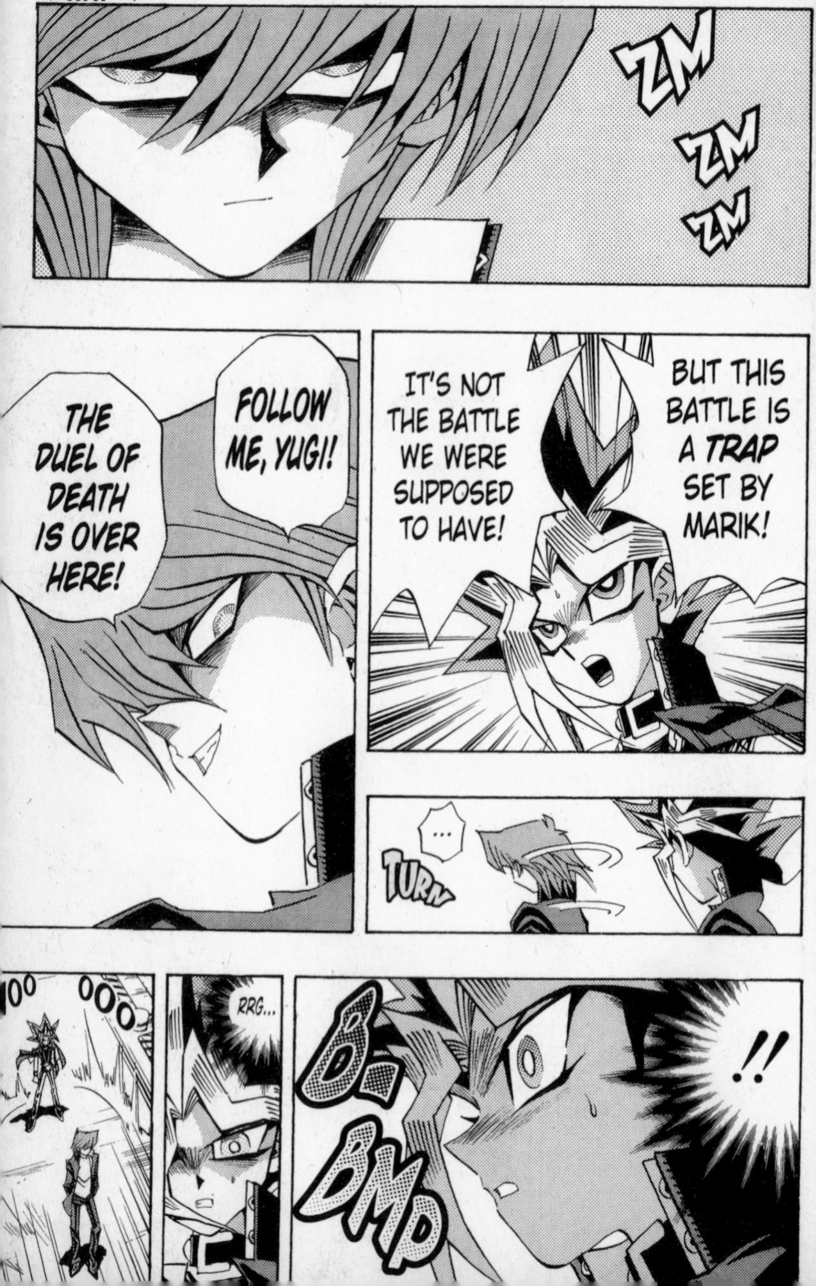
ZM
ZM
ZM
BUT THIS BATTLE IS A TRAP SET BY MARIK!
IT'S NOT THE BATTLE WE WERE SUPPOSED TO HAVE!
...
TURN
FOLLOW ME, YUGI!
THE DUEL OF DEATH IS OVER HERE!
!!
B-BMP
RRG...
OOO
OOO

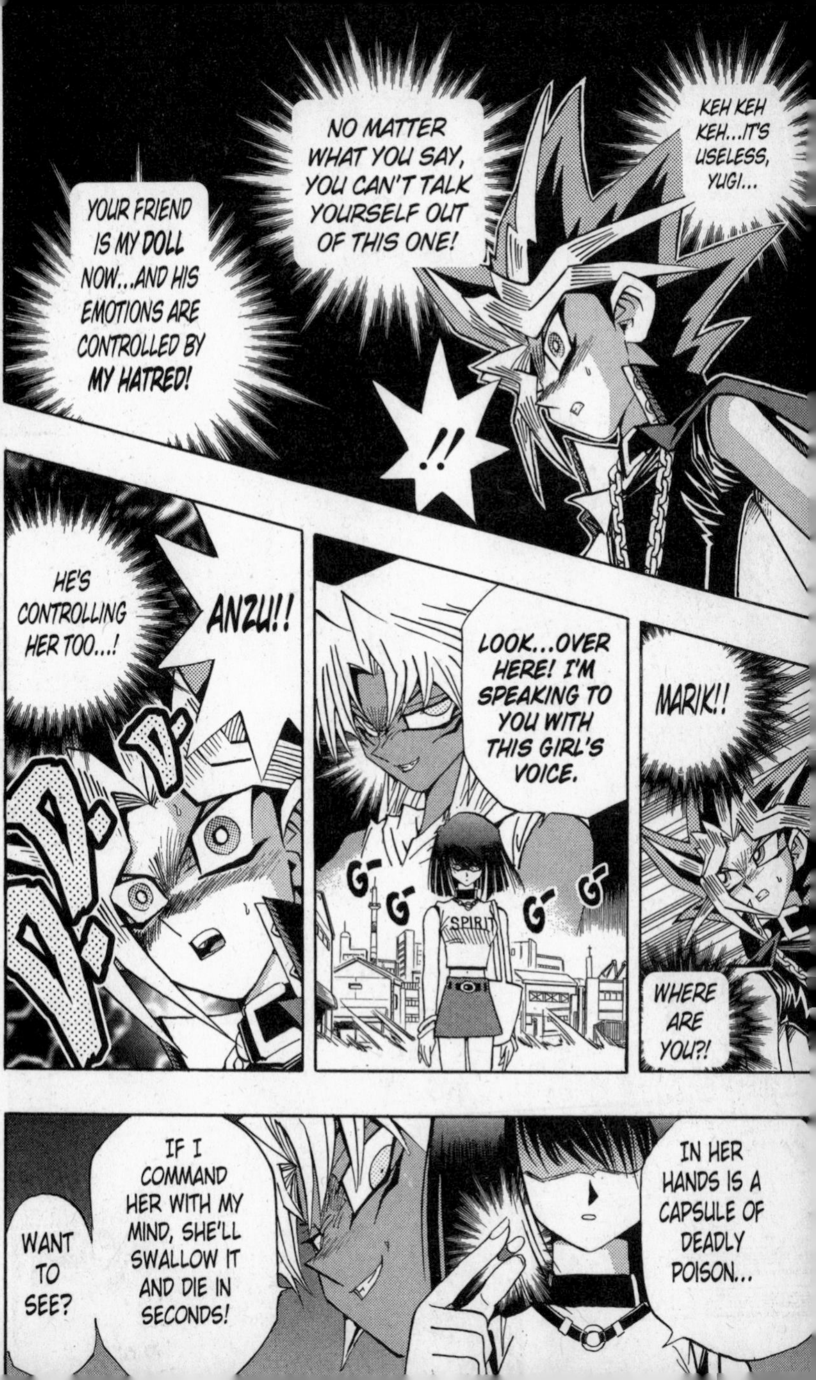
KEH KEH KEH...IT'S USELESS, YUGI...
NO MATTER WHAT YOU SAY, YOU CAN'T TALK YOURSELF OUT OF THIS ONE!
YOUR FRIEND IS MY DOLL NOW...AND HIS EMOTIONS ARE CONTROLLED BY MY HATRED!
!!
MARIK!!
WHERE ARE YOU?!
LOOK...OVER HERE! I'M SPEAKING TO YOU WITH THIS GIRL'S VOICE.
G- G- G- G-
SPIRIT
ANZU!!
HE'S CONTROLLING HER TOO...!
IN HER HANDS IS A CAPSULE OF DEADLY POISON...
IF I COMMAND HER WITH MY MIND, SHE'LL SWALLOW IT AND DIE IN SECONDS!
WANT TO SEE?

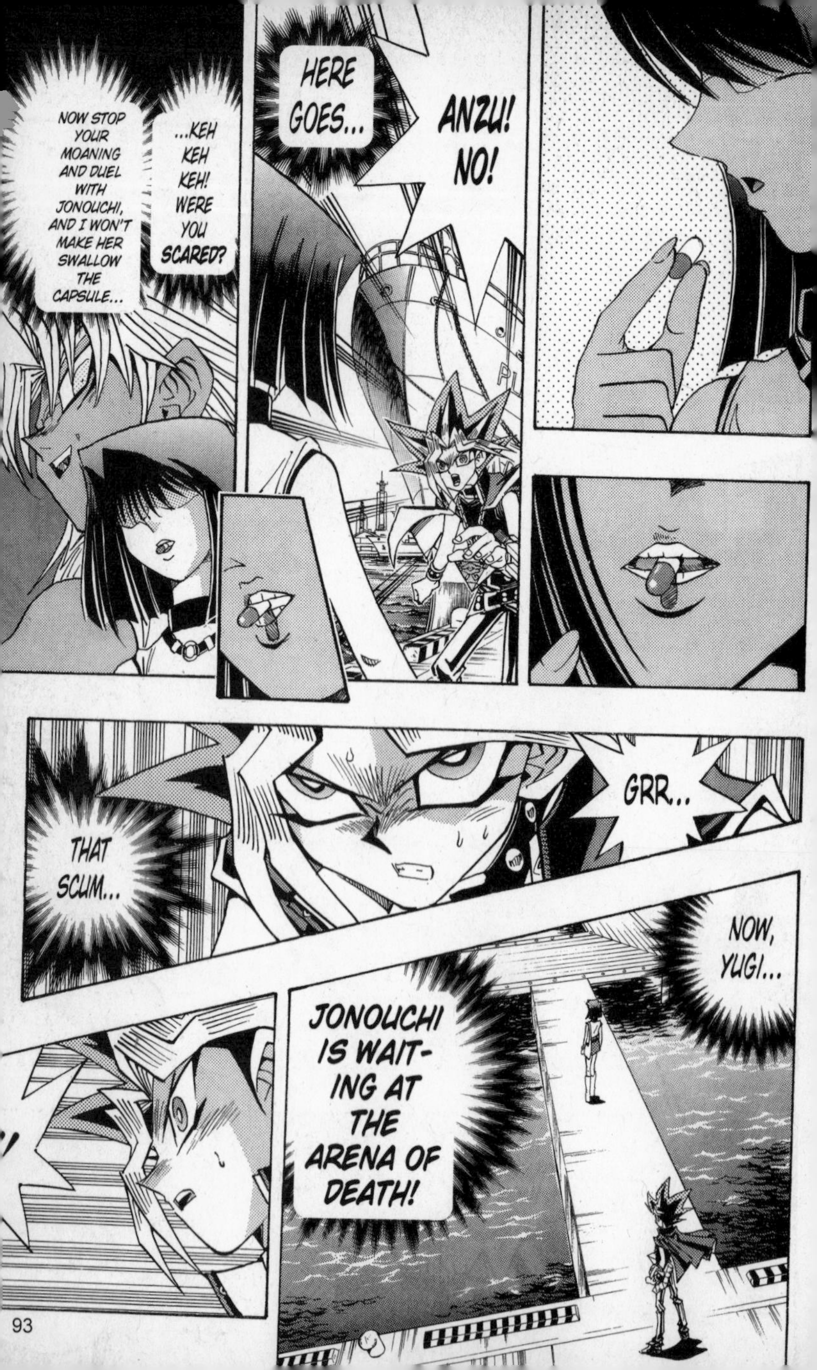
HERE GOES...
ANZU! NO!
...KEH KEH KEH! WERE YOU SCARED?
NOW STOP YOUR MOANING AND DUEL WITH JONOUCHI, AND I WON'T MAKE HER SWALLOW THE CAPSULE...
GRR...
THAT SCUM...
NOW, YUGI...
JONOUCHI IS WAIT-ING AT THE ARENA OF DEATH!

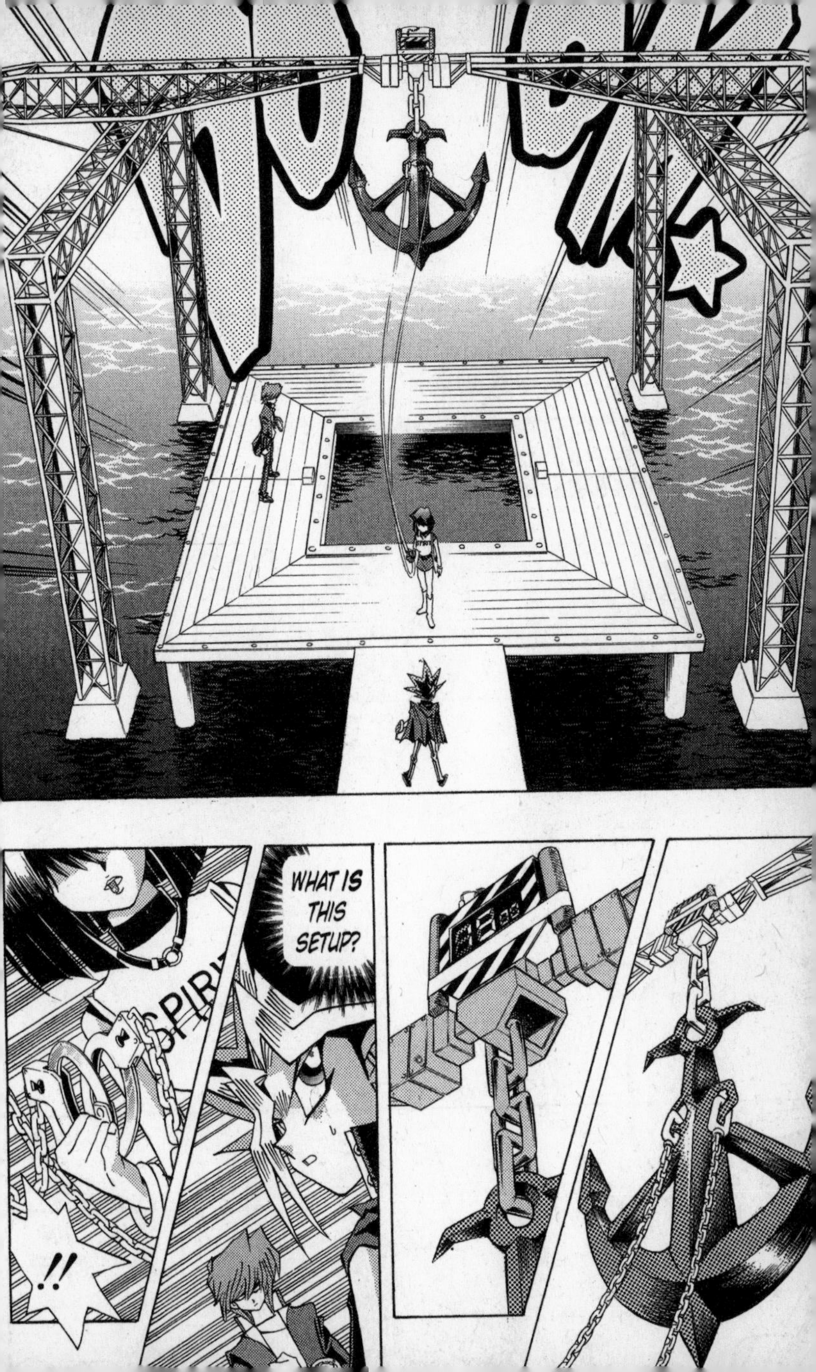
WHAT IS THIS SETUP?
!!

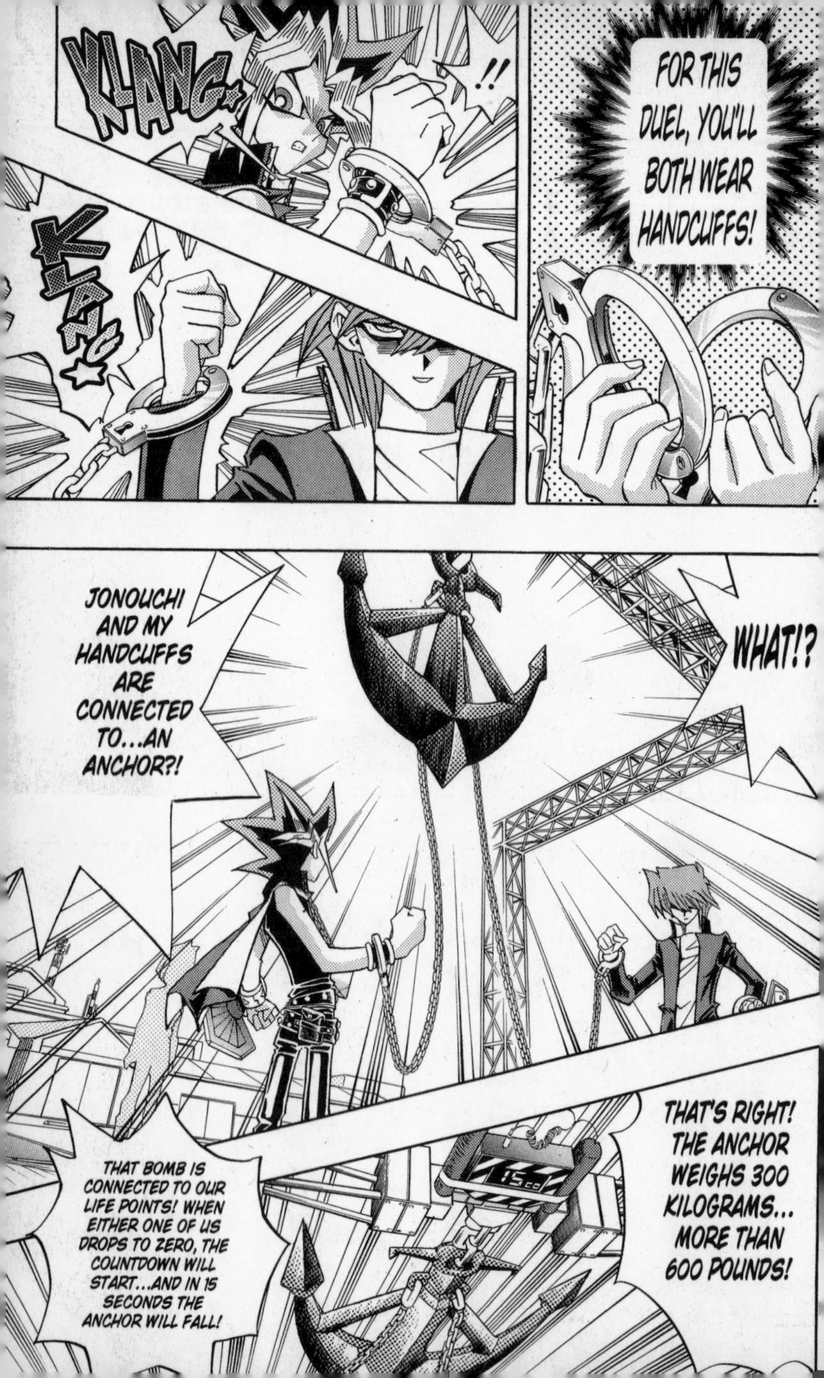
FOR THIS DUEL, YOU'LL BOTH WEAR HANDCUFFS!
KLANG
!!
KLANG
WHAT!?
JONOUCHI AND MY HANDCUFFS ARE CONNECTED TO...AN ANCHOR?!
THAT'S RIGHT! THE ANCHOR WEIGHS 300 KILOGRAMS... MORE THAN 600 POUNDS!
THAT BOMB IS CONNECTED TO OUR LIFE POINTS! WHEN EITHER ONE OF US DROPS TO ZERO, THE COUNTDOWN WILL START...AND IN 15 SECONDS THE ANCHOR WILL FALL!

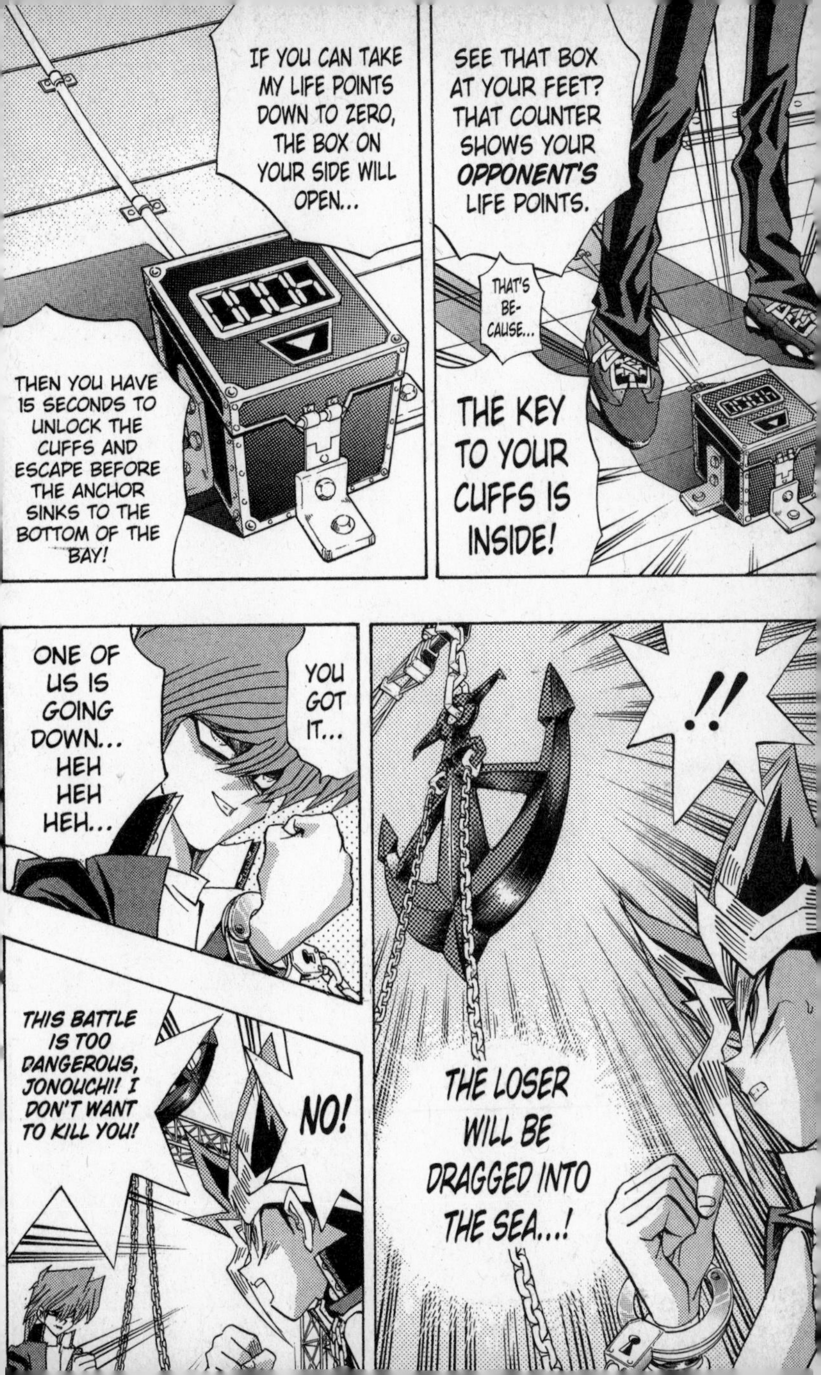
SEE THAT BOX AT YOUR FEET? THAT COUNTER SHOWS YOUR *OPPONENT'S* LIFE POINTS.
THAT'S BE-CAUSE...
THE KEY TO YOUR CUFFS IS INSIDE!
IF YOU CAN TAKE MY LIFE POINTS DOWN TO ZERO, THE BOX ON YOUR SIDE WILL OPEN...
THEN YOU HAVE 15 SECONDS TO UNLOCK THE CUFFS AND ESCAPE BEFORE THE ANCHOR SINKS TO THE BOTTOM OF THE BAY!
!!
THE LOSER WILL BE DRAGGED INTO THE SEA...!
YOU GOT IT...
ONE OF US IS GOING DOWN... HEH HEH HEH...
NO!
THIS BATTLE IS TOO DANGEROUS, JONOUCHI! I DON'T WANT TO KILL YOU!

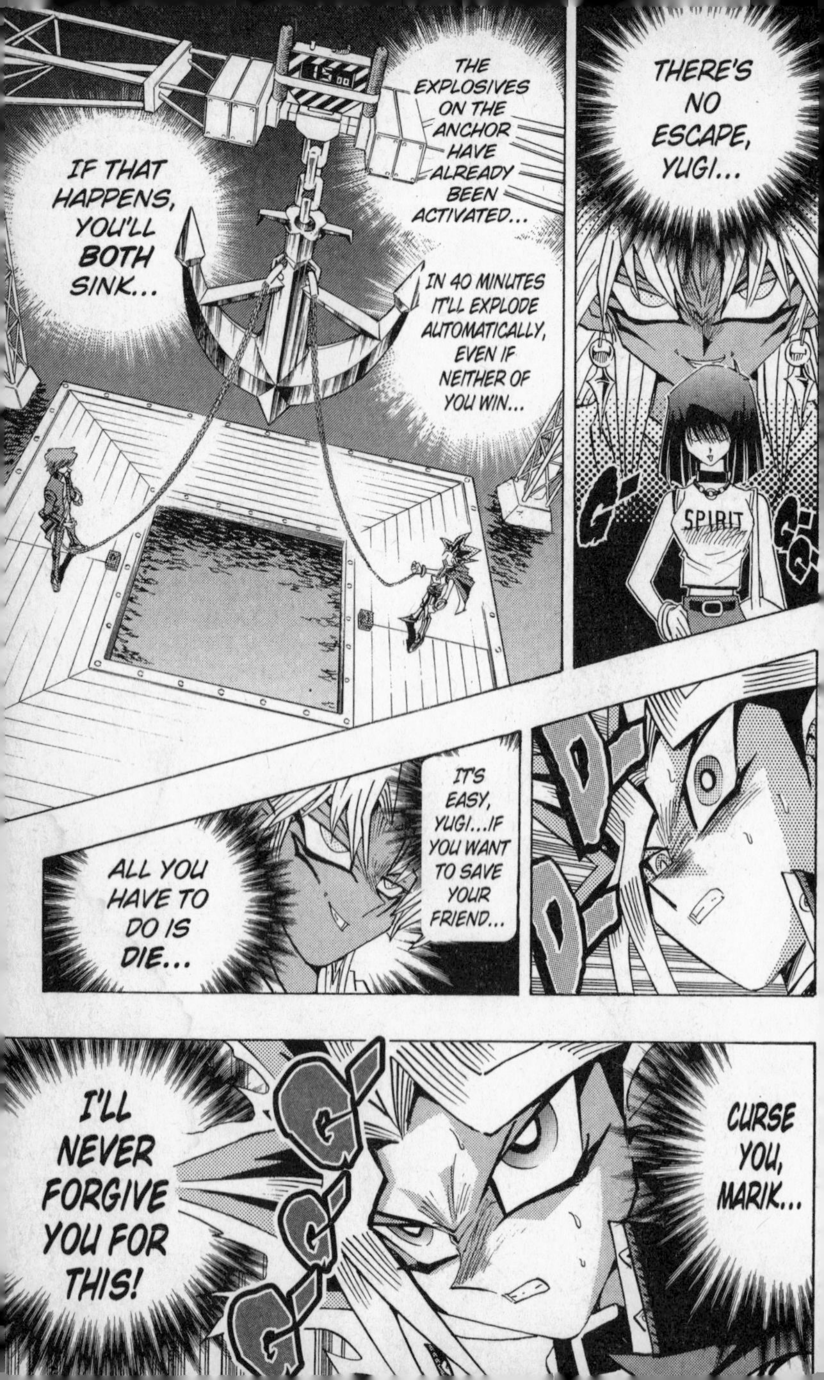
THERE'S NO ESCAPE, YUGI...
THE EXPLOSIVES ON THE ANCHOR HAVE ALREADY BEEN ACTIVATED...
IN 40 MINUTES IT'LL EXPLODE AUTOMATICALLY, EVEN IF NEITHER OF YOU WIN...
IF THAT HAPPENS, YOU'LL BOTH SINK...
SPIRIT
IT'S EASY, YUGI...IF YOU WANT TO SAVE YOUR FRIEND...
ALL YOU HAVE TO DO IS DIE...
CURSE YOU, MARIK...
I'LL NEVER FORGIVE YOU FOR THIS!

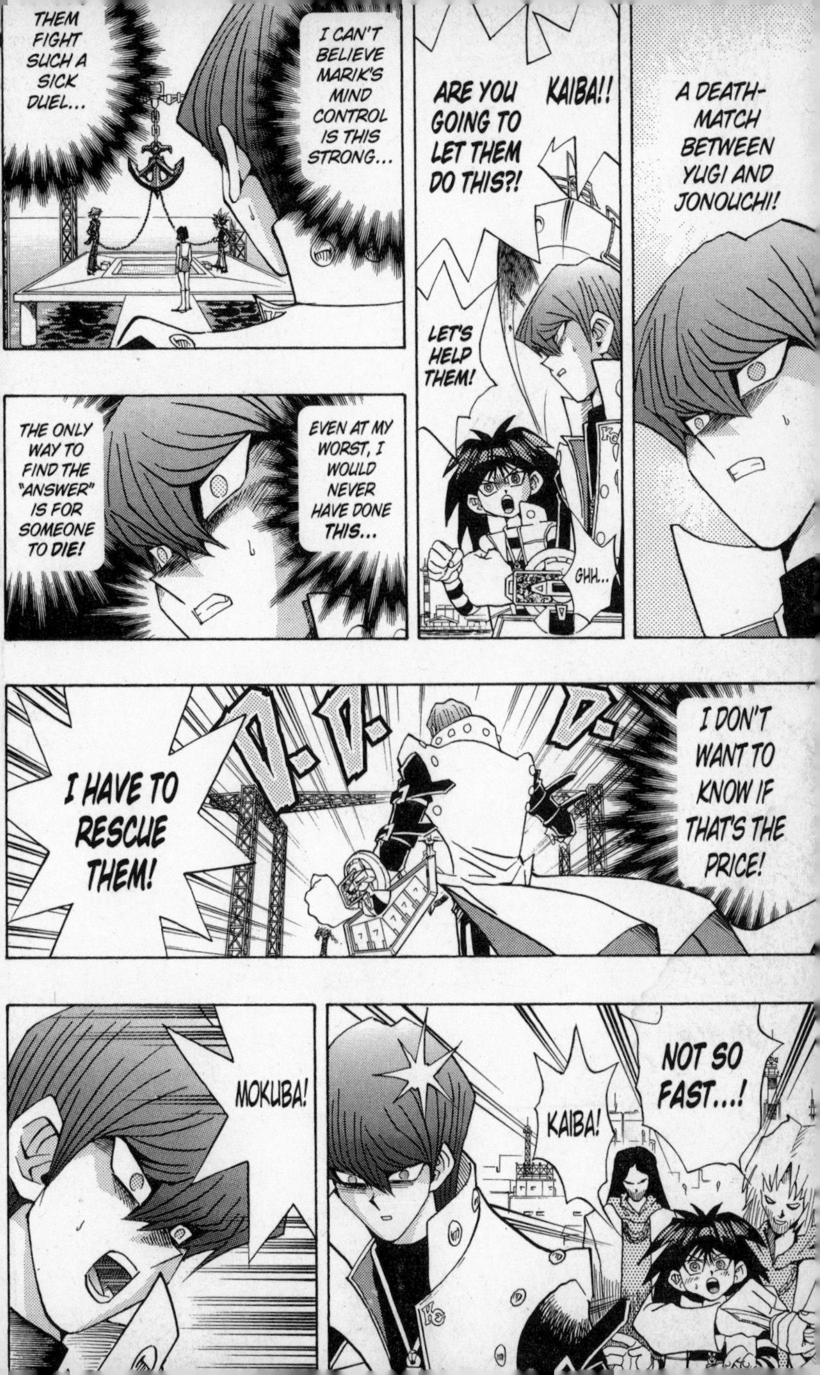
A DEATH-MATCH BETWEEN YUGI AND JONOUCHI!
KAIBA!!
ARE YOU GOING TO LET THEM DO THIS?!
LET'S HELP THEM!
GHH...
I CAN'T BELIEVE MARIK'S MIND CONTROL IS THIS STRONG...
THEM FIGHT SUCH A SICK DUEL...
EVEN AT MY WORST, I WOULD NEVER HAVE DONE THIS...
THE ONLY WAY TO FIND THE "ANSWER" IS FOR SOMEONE TO DIE!
I DON'T WANT TO KNOW IF THAT'S THE PRICE!
I HAVE TO RESCUE THEM!
NOT SO FAST...!
KAIBA!
MOKUBA!

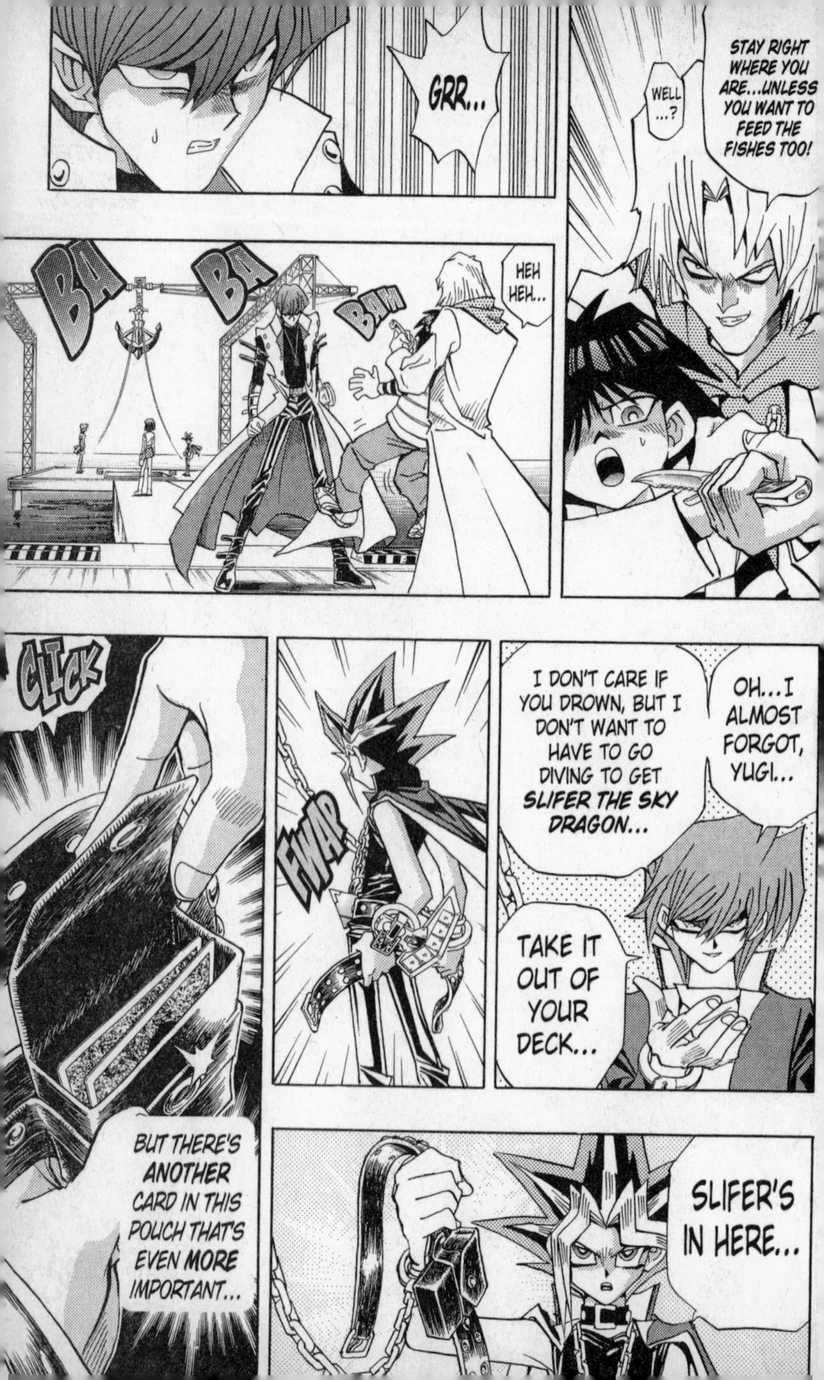
STAY RIGHT WHERE YOU ARE...UNLESS YOU WANT TO FEED THE FISHES TOO!
WELL ...?
GRR...
HEH HEH...
BAM
BA
BA
OH...I ALMOST FORGOT, YUGI...
I DON'T CARE IF YOU DROWN, BUT I DON'T WANT TO HAVE TO GO DIVING TO GET **SLIFER THE SKY DRAGON...**
TAKE IT OUT OF YOUR DECK...
FWAP
SLIFER'S IN HERE...
CLICK
BUT THERE'S **ANOTHER** CARD IN THIS POUCH THAT'S EVEN **MORE** IMPORTANT...

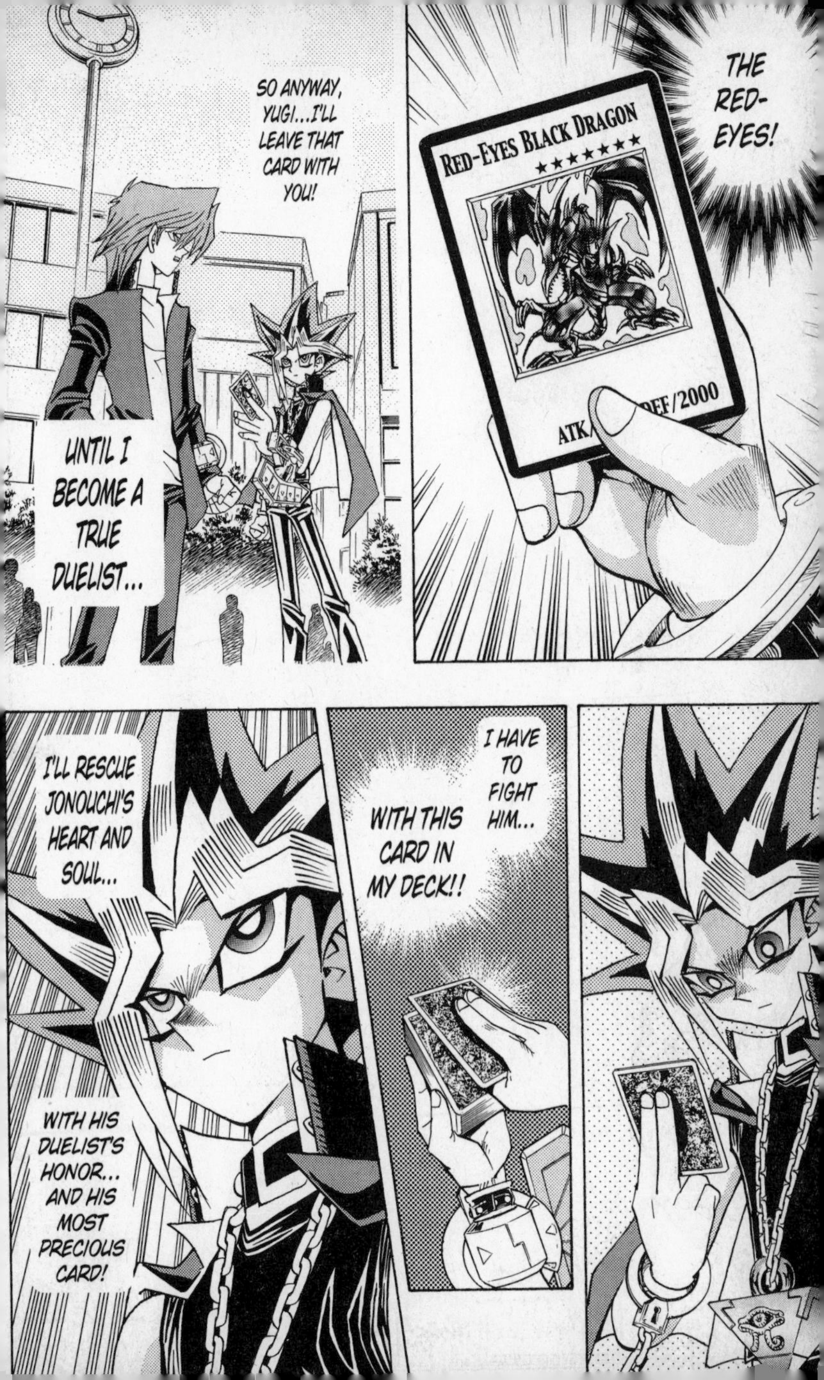
THE RED-EYES!
RED-EYES BLACK DRAGON
ATK/
DEF/2000
SO ANYWAY, YUGI...I'LL LEAVE THAT CARD WITH YOU!
UNTIL I BECOME A TRUE DUELIST...
I HAVE TO FIGHT HIM...
WITH THIS CARD IN MY DECK!!
I'LL RESCUE JONOUCHI'S HEART AND SOUL...
WITH HIS DUELIST'S HONOR... AND HIS MOST PRECIOUS CARD!

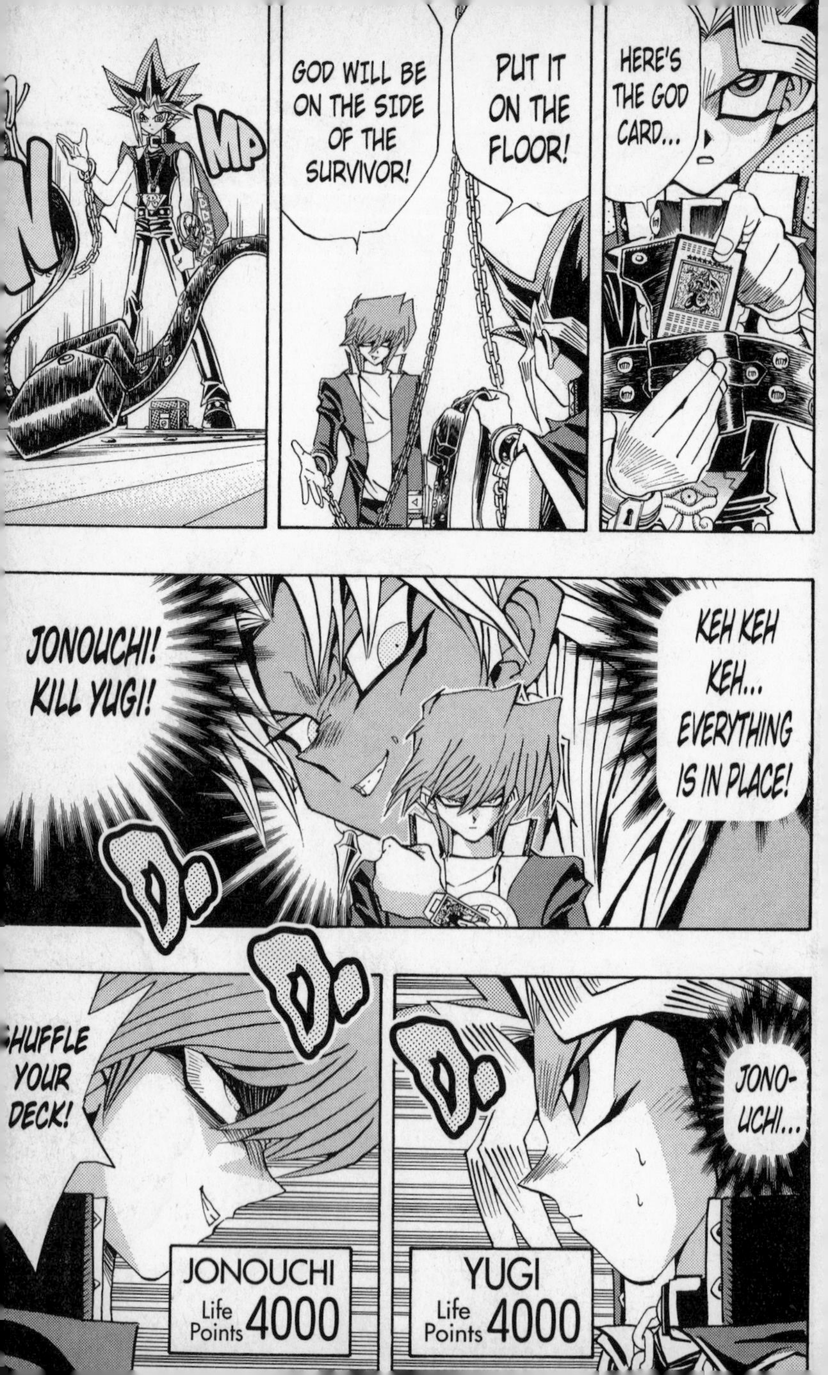
HERE'S THE GOD CARD...
PUT IT ON THE FLOOR!
GOD WILL BE ON THE SIDE OF THE SURVIVOR!
KEH KEH KEH... EVERYTHING IS IN PLACE!
JONOUCHI! KILL YUGI!
D
D
D
JONO-UCHI...
YUGI
Life Points 4000
HUFFLE YOUR DECK!
JONOUCHI
Life Points 4000

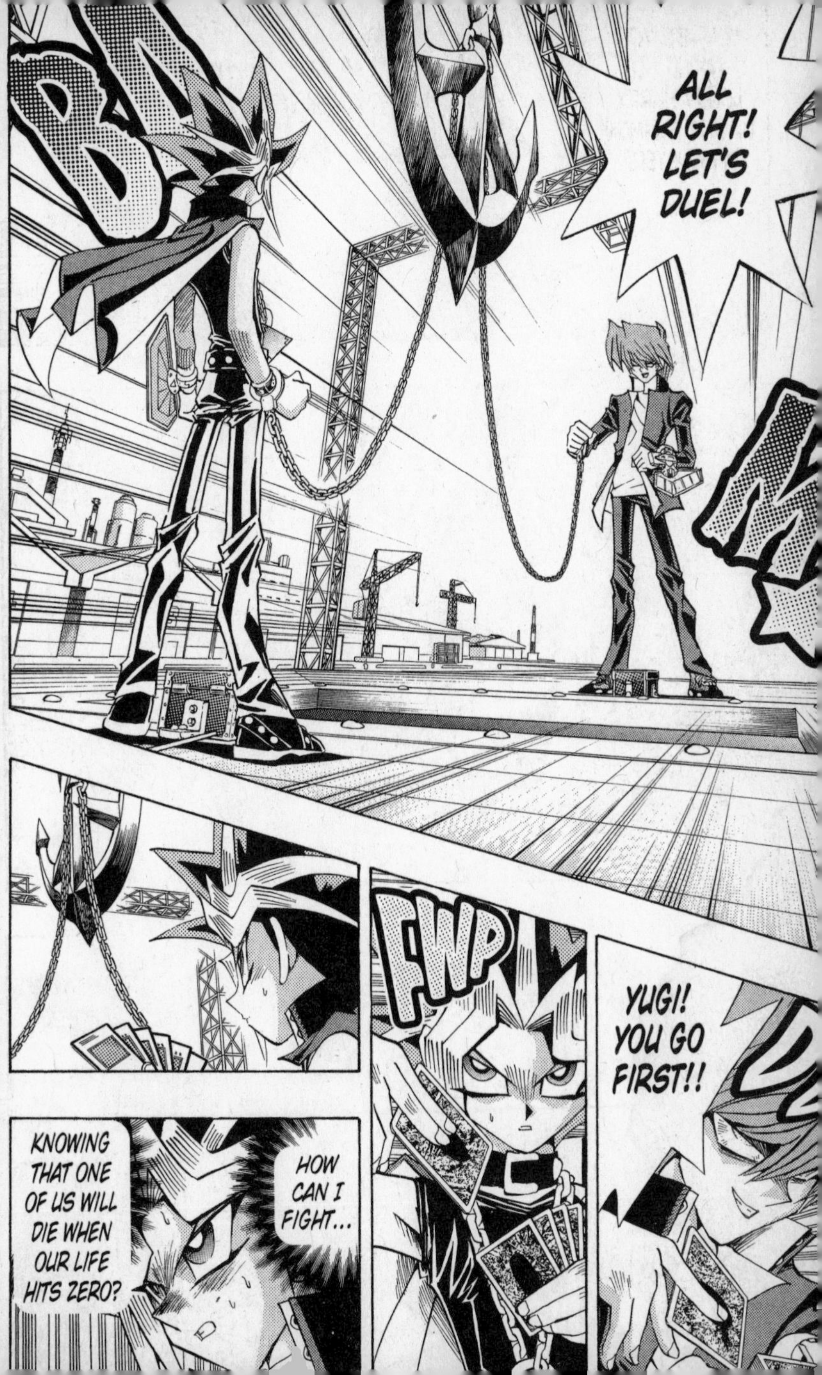

ALL RIGHT! LET'S DUEL!
YUGI! YOU GO FIRST!!
FWP
HOW CAN I FIGHT...
KNOWING THAT ONE OF US WILL DIE WHEN OUR LIFE HITS ZERO?

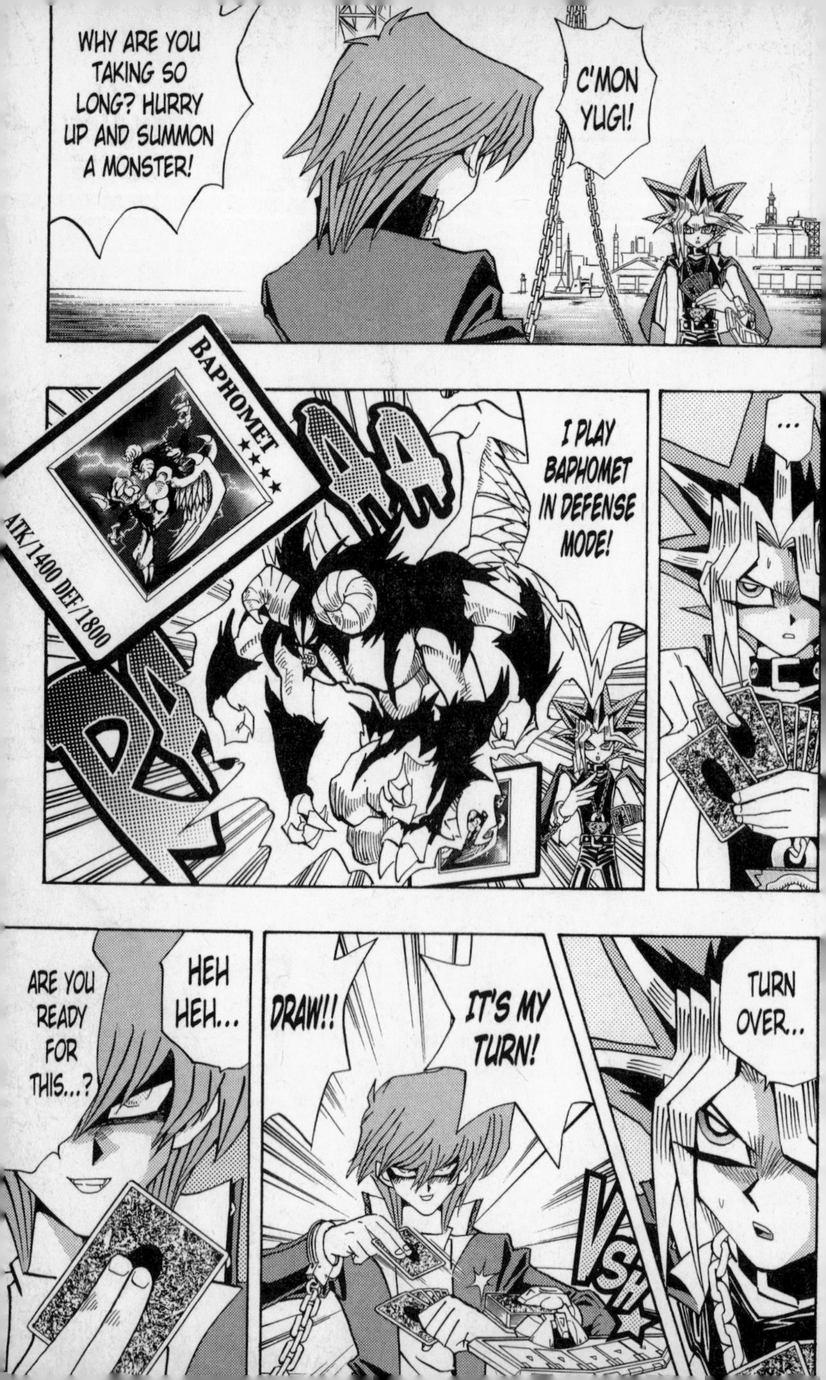
C'MON YUGI!
WHY ARE YOU TAKING SO LONG? HURRY UP AND SUMMON A MONSTER!
...
I PLAY BAPHOMET IN DEFENSE MODE!
BAPHOMET
ATK/1400 DEF/1800
TURN OVER...
VSH
IT'S MY TURN!
DRAW!!
HEH HEH...
ARE YOU READY FOR THIS...?

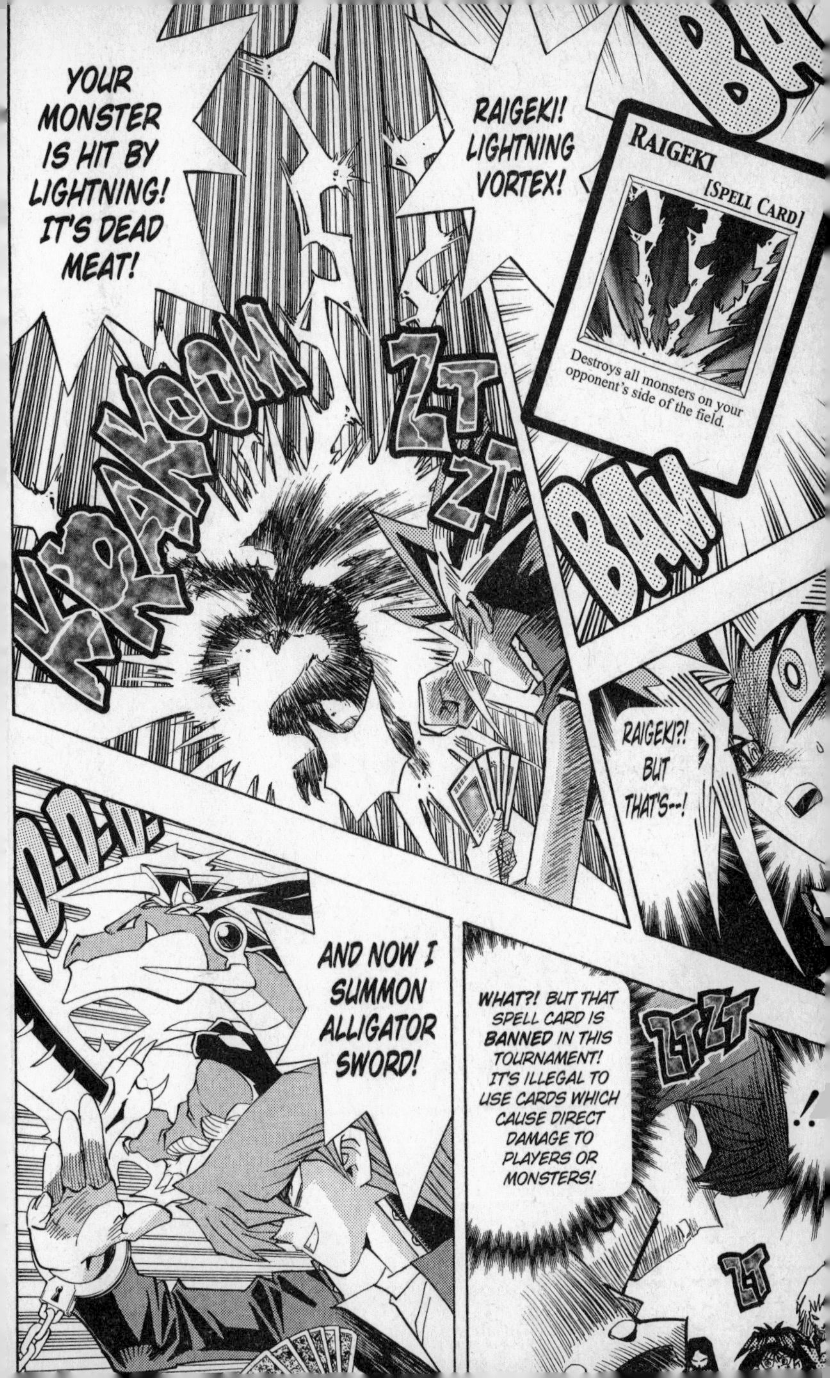
BA
RAIGEKI
[SPELL CARD]
Destroys all monsters on your opponent's side of the field.
RAIGEKI! LIGHTNING VORTEX!
YOUR MONSTER IS HIT BY LIGHTNING! IT'S DEAD MEAT!
ZT
ZT!
BAM!
KRAKOOM
RAIGEKI!?! BUT THAT'S--!
WHAT?! BUT THAT SPELL CARD IS BANNED IN THIS TOURNAMENT! IT'S ILLEGAL TO USE CARDS WHICH CAUSE DIRECT DAMAGE TO PLAYERS OR MONSTERS!
ZTZT
ZT
AND NOW I SUMMON ALLIGATOR SWORD!

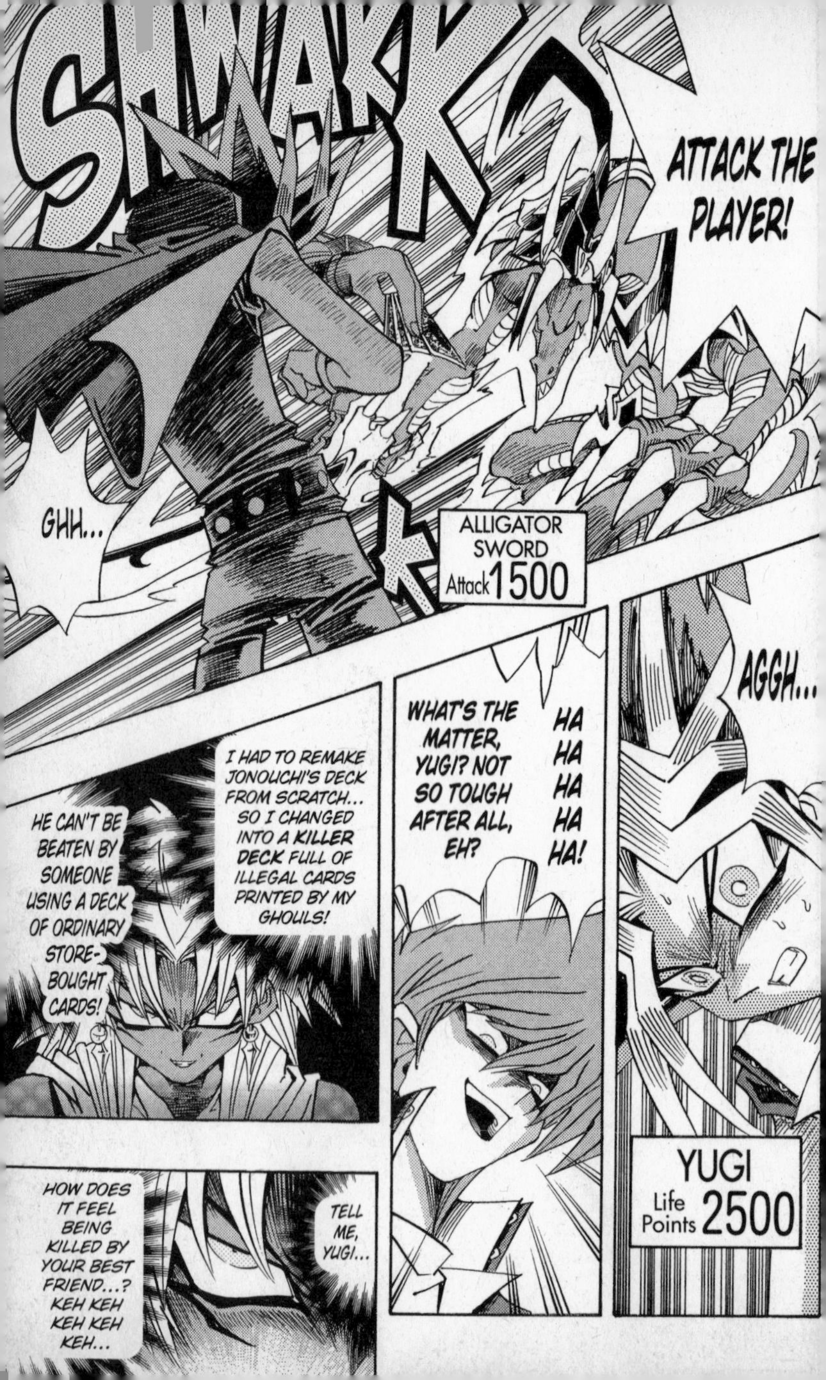
SHWAK
ATTACK THE PLAYER!
ALLIGATOR SWORD Attack 1500
GHH...
AGGH...
YUGI Life Points 2500
WHAT'S THE MATTER, YUGI? NOT SO TOUGH AFTER ALL, EH?
HA HA HA HA HA!
I HAD TO REMAKE JONOUCHI'S DECK FROM SCRATCH... SO I CHANGED INTO A KILLER DECK FULL OF ILLEGAL CARDS PRINTED BY MY GHOULS!
HE CAN'T BE BEATEN BY SOMEONE USING A DECK OF ORDINARY STORE-BOUGHT CARDS!
TELL ME, YUGI...
HOW DOES IT FEEL BEING KILLED BY YOUR BEST FRIEND...? KEH KEH KEH KEH KEH...

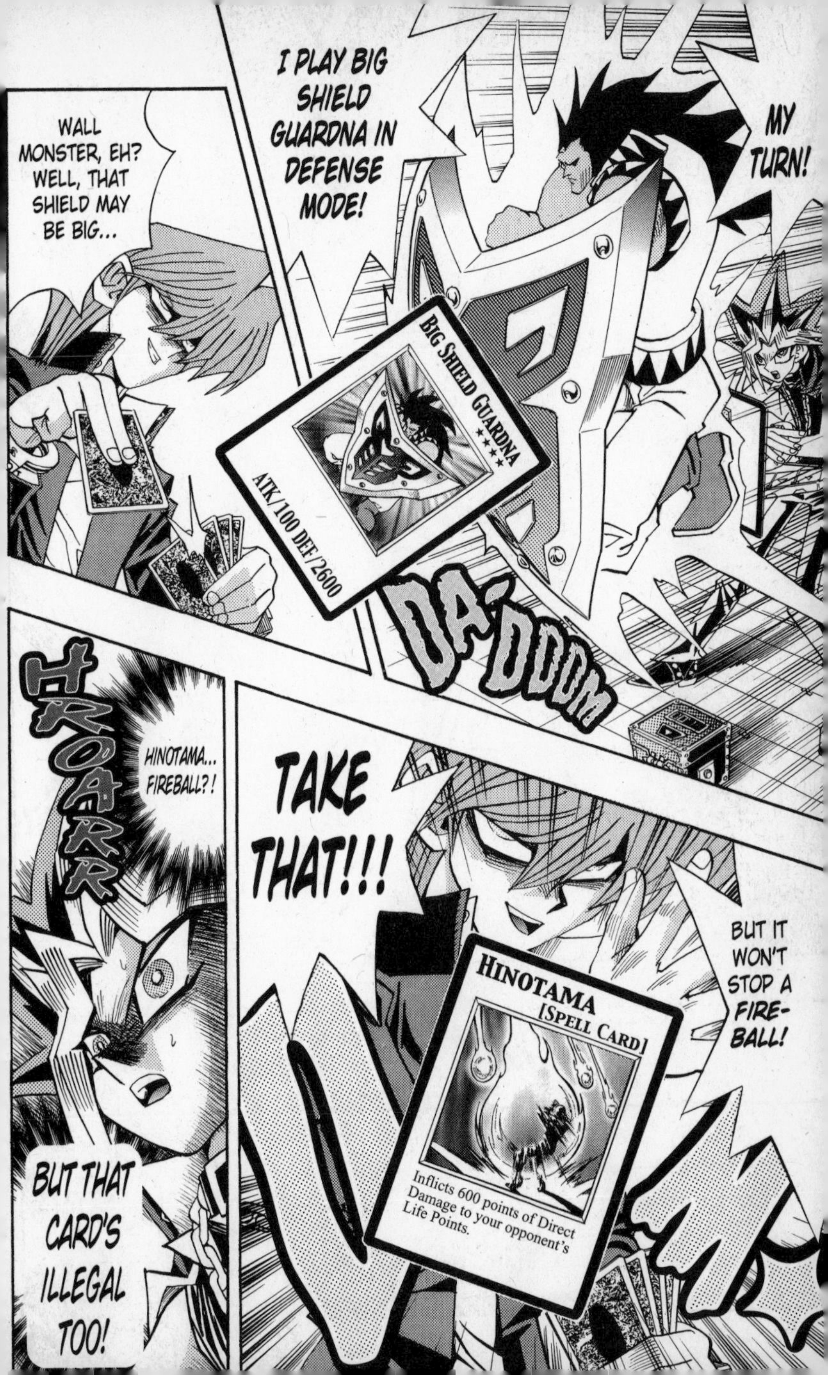
MY TURN!
I PLAY BIG SHIELD GUARDNA IN DEFENSE MODE!
BIG SHIELD GUARDNA
ATK/100 DEF/2600
DA-DOOM
WALL MONSTER, EH? WELL, THAT SHIELD MAY BE BIG...
BUT IT WON'T STOP A FIRE-BALL!
TAKE THAT!!!
HINOTAMA
[SPELL CARD]
Inflicts 600 points of Direct Damage to your opponent's Life Points.
HROARR
HINOTAMA... FIREBALL?!
BUT THAT CARD'S ILLEGAL TOO!

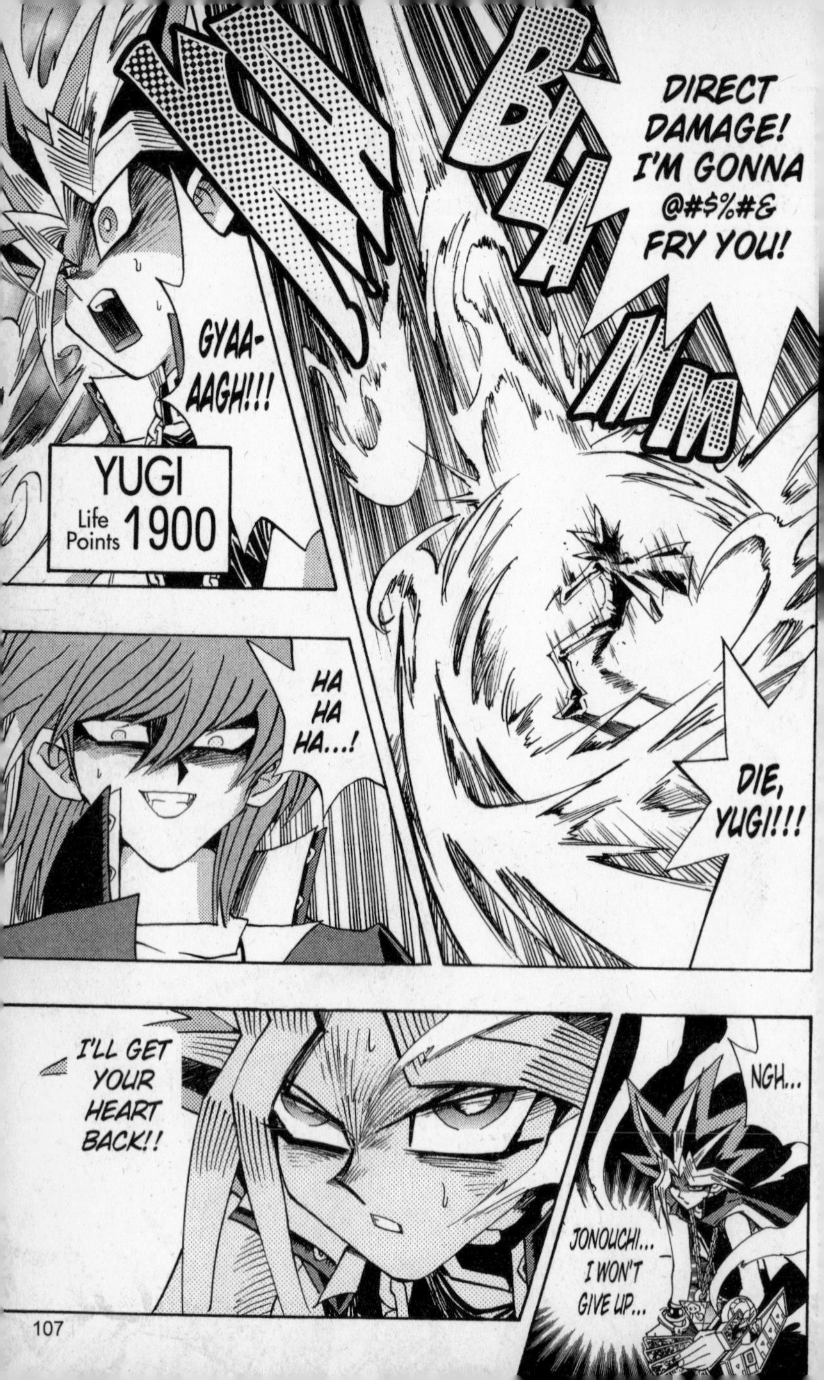
DIRECT DAMAGE! I'M GONNA @#$%#& FRY YOU!
DIE, YUGI!!!
GYAA-AAGH!!!
YUGI
Life Points 1900
HA HA HA...!
NGH...
JONOUCHI... I WON'T GIVE UP...
I'LL GET YOUR HEART BACK!!

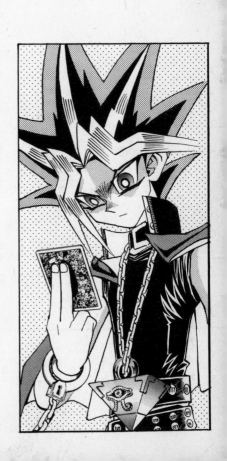

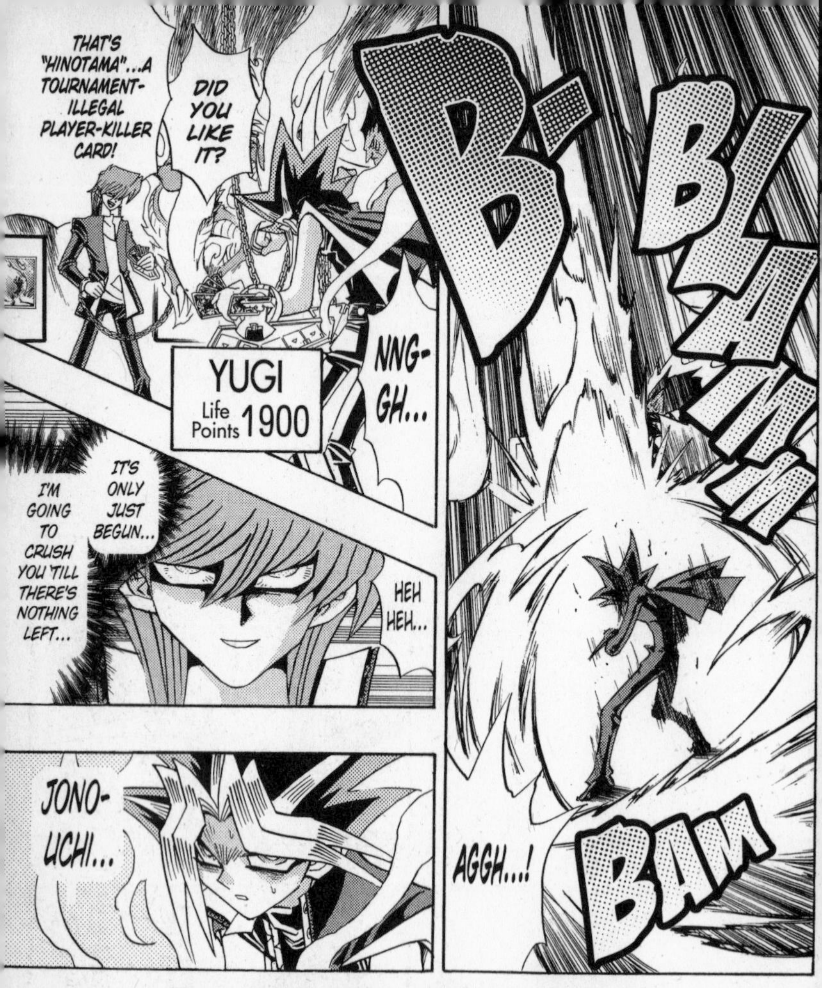
B-BLAMM
AGGH...!
BAM
DID YOU LIKE IT?
THAT'S "HINOTAMA"...A TOURNAMENT-ILLEGAL PLAYER-KILLER CARD!
NNG-GH...
YUGI Life Points 1900
IT'S ONLY JUST BEGUN...
I'M GOING TO CRUSH YOU 'TILL THERE'S NOTHING LEFT...
HEH HEH...
JONO-UCHI...

DUEL 134: HEART ATTACK!!

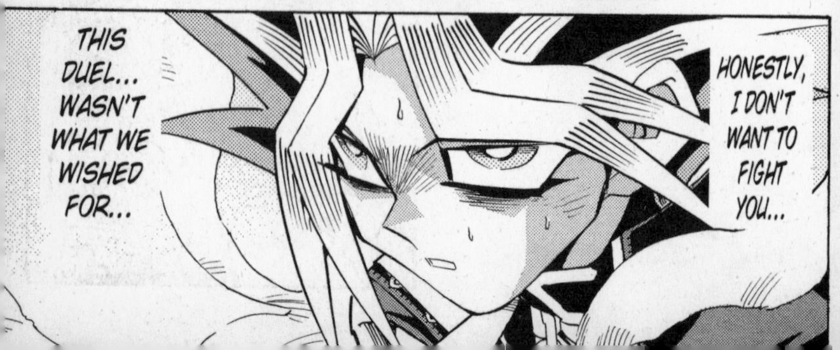
HONESTLY, I DON'T WANT TO FIGHT YOU...
THIS DUEL... WASN'T WHAT WE WISHED FOR...

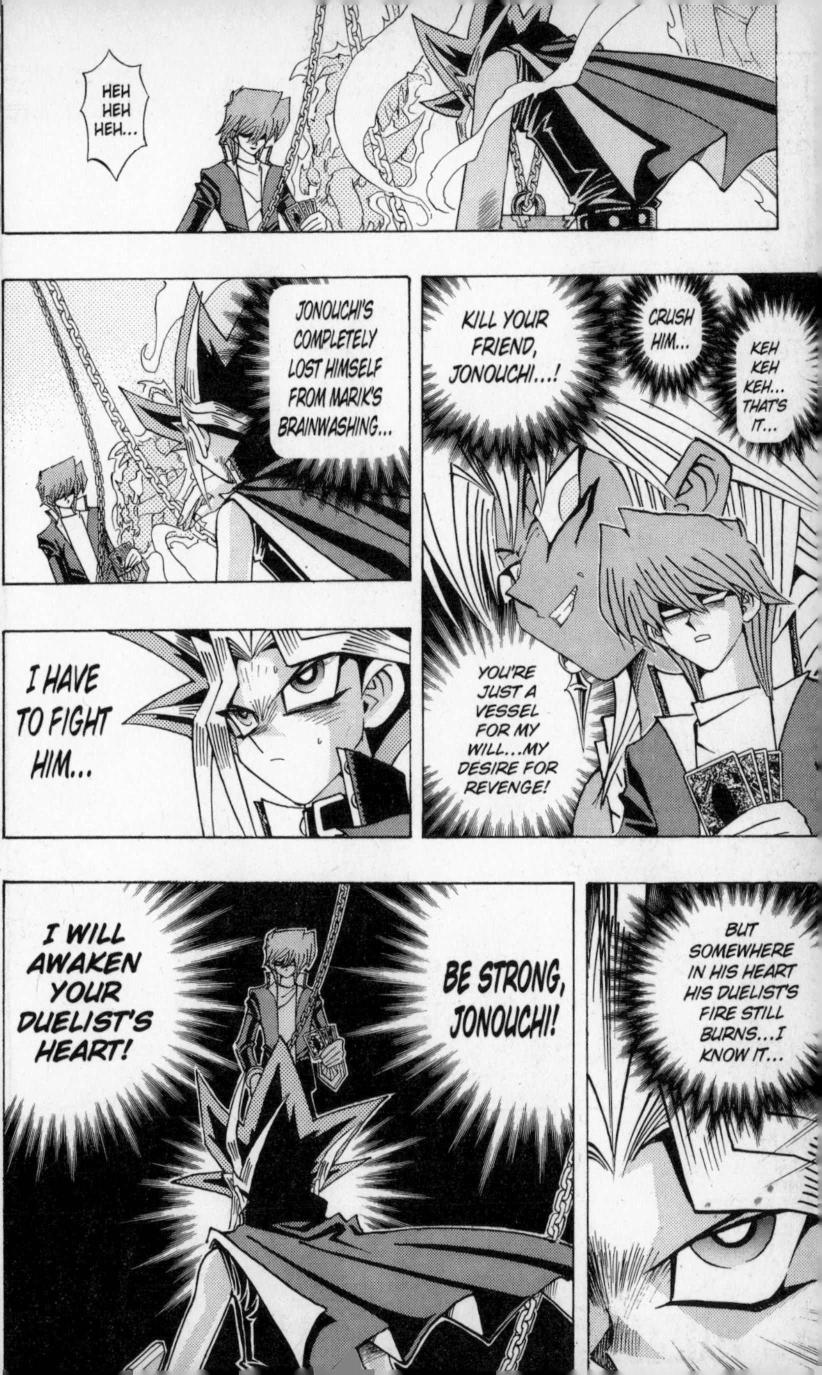
HEH HEH HEH...
KEH KEH KEH... THAT'S IT...
CRUSH HIM...
KILL YOUR FRIEND, JONOUCHI...!
YOU'RE JUST A VESSEL FOR MY WILL...MY DESIRE FOR REVENGE!
JONOUCHI'S COMPLETELY LOST HIMSELF FROM MARIK'S BRAINWASHING...
I HAVE TO FIGHT HIM...
BUT SOMEWHERE IN HIS HEART HIS DUELIST'S FIRE STILL BURNS...I KNOW IT...
BE STRONG, JONOUCHI!
I WILL AWAKEN YOUR DUELIST'S HEART!

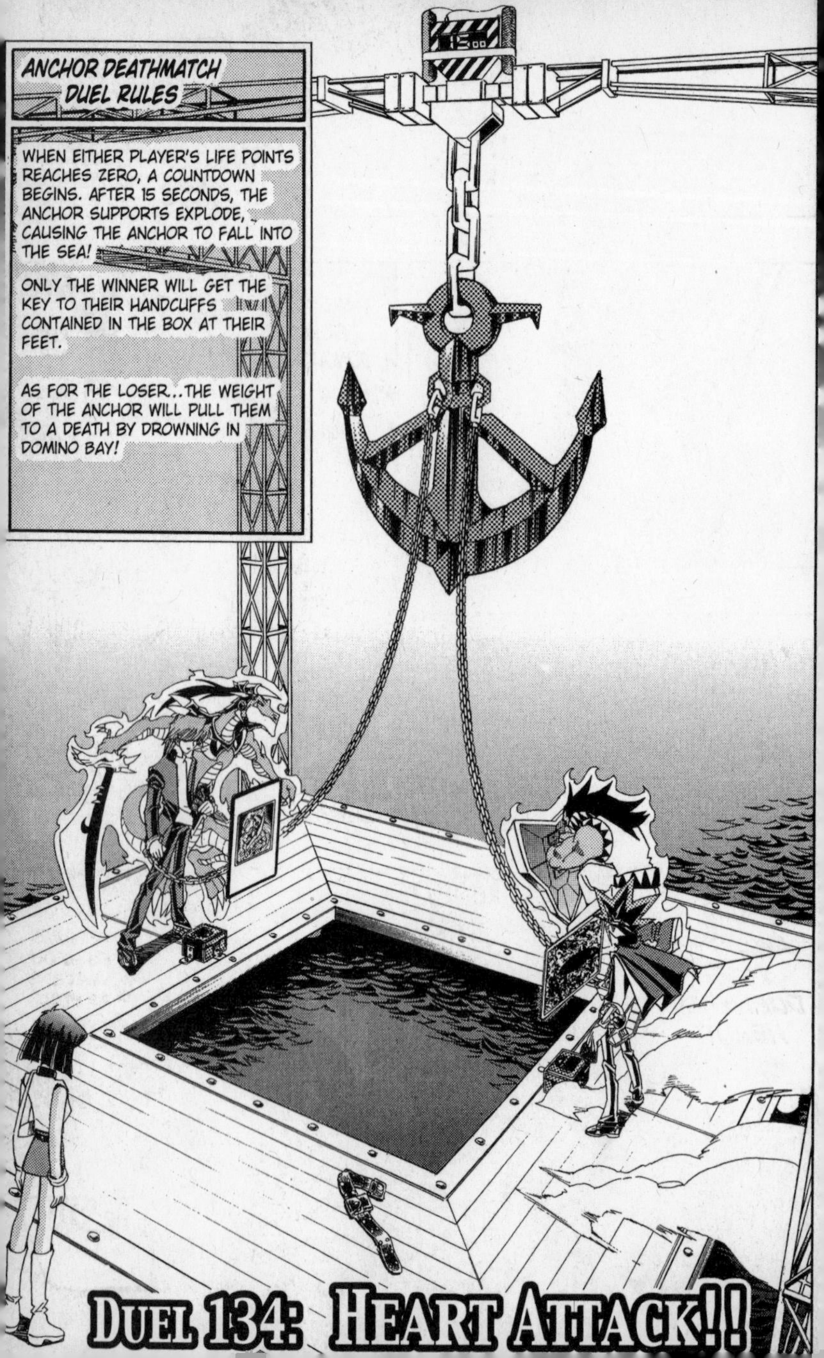
ANCHOR DEATHMATCH DUEL RULES
WHEN EITHER PLAYER'S LIFE POINTS REACHES ZERO, A COUNTDOWN BEGINS. AFTER 15 SECONDS, THE ANCHOR SUPPORTS EXPLODE, CAUSING THE ANCHOR TO FALL INTO THE SEA!
ONLY THE WINNER WILL GET THE KEY TO THEIR HANDCUFFS CONTAINED IN THE BOX AT THEIR FEET.
AS FOR THE LOSER...THE WEIGHT OF THE ANCHOR WILL PULL THEM TO A DEATH BY DROWNING IN DOMINO BAY!
DUEL 134: HEART ATTACK!!

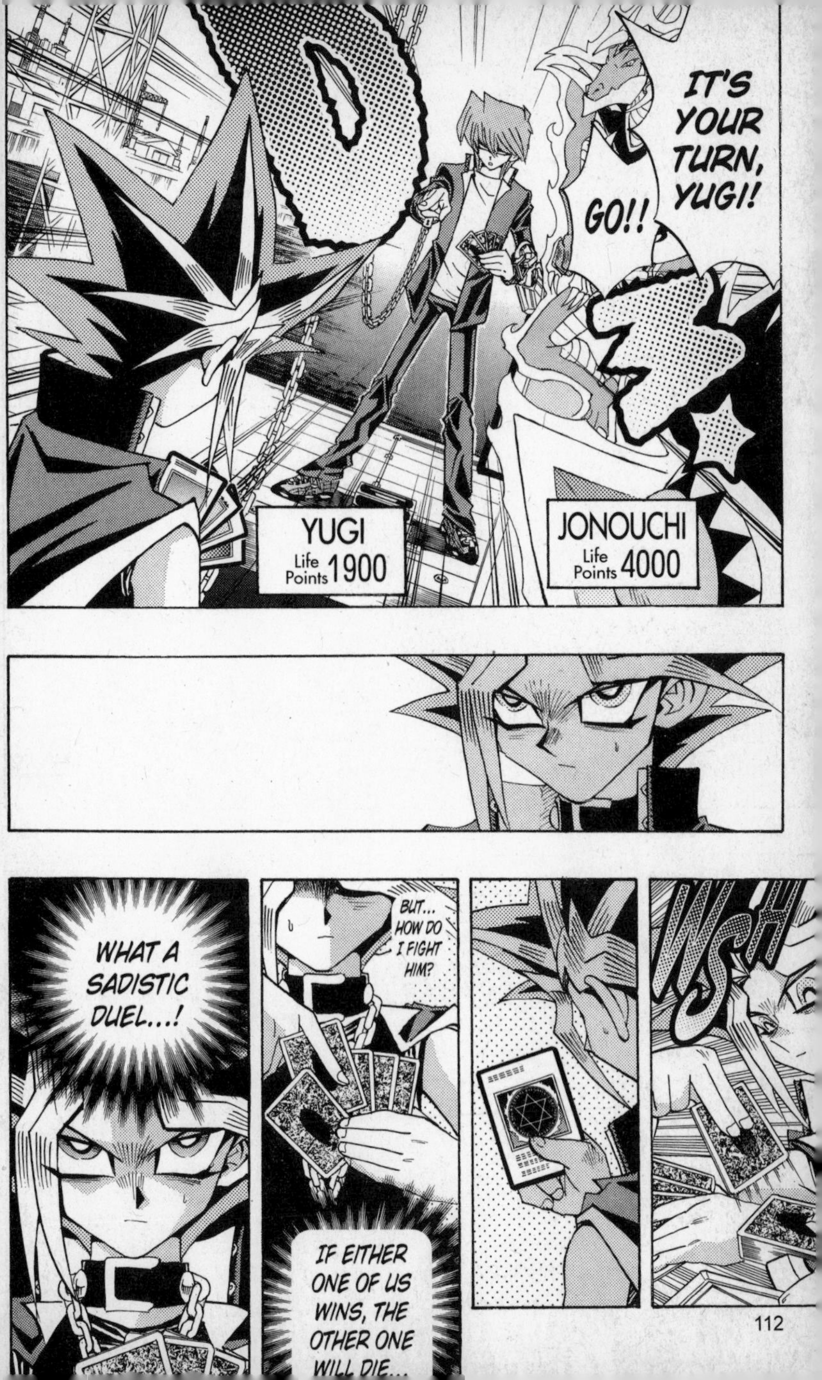
IT'S YOUR TURN, YUGI!
GO!!
JONOUCHI Life Points 4000
YUGI Life Points 1900
BUT... HOW DO I FIGHT HIM?
IF EITHER ONE OF US WINS, THE OTHER ONE WILL DIE...
WHAT A SADISTIC DUEL...!

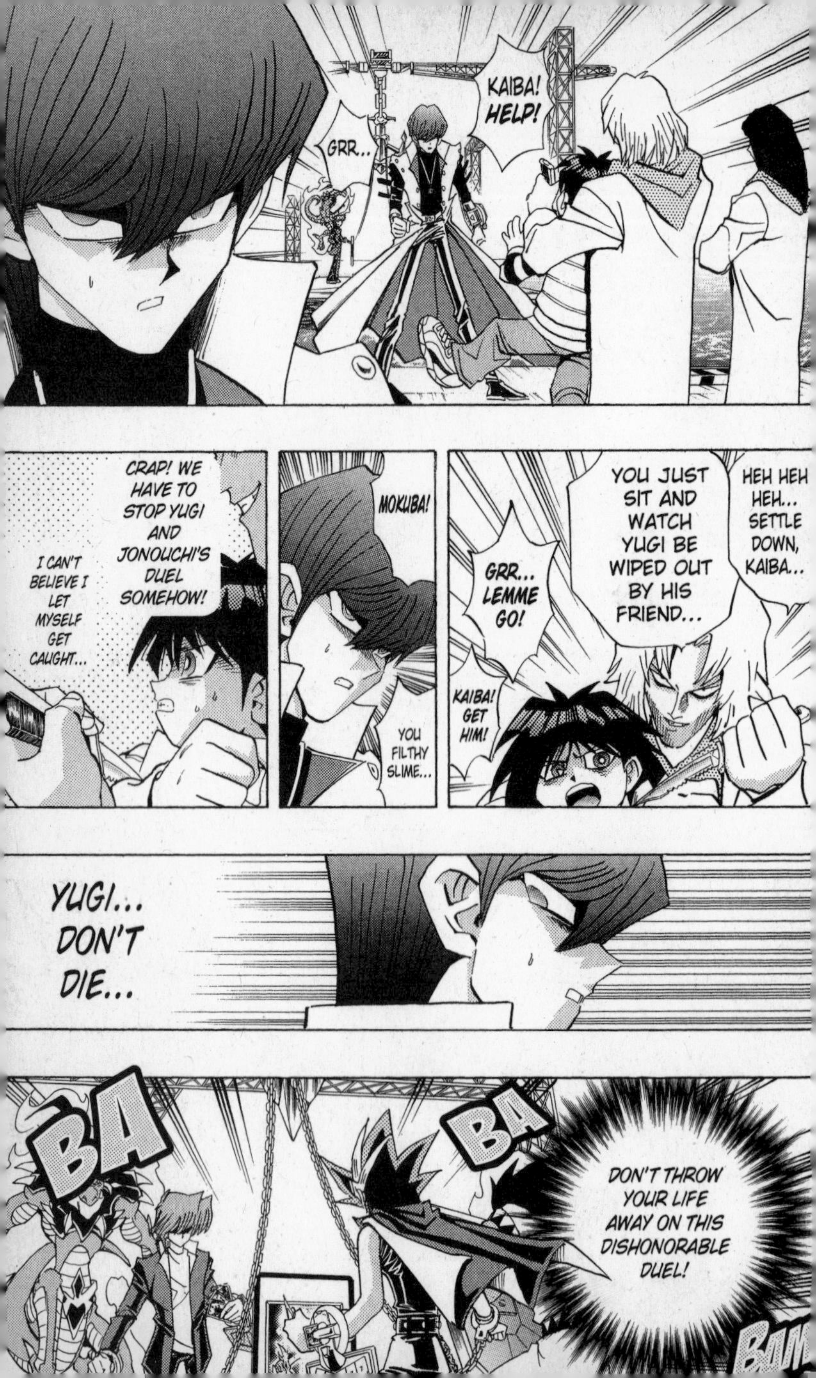
KAIBA! HELP!
GRR...
HEH HEH HEH... SETTLE DOWN, KAIBA...
YOU JUST SIT AND WATCH YUGI BE WIPED OUT BY HIS FRIEND...
GRR... LEMME GO!
KAIBA! GET HIM!
MOKUBA!
YOU FILTHY SLIME...
CRAP! WE HAVE TO STOP YUGI AND JONOUCHI'S DUEL SOMEHOW!
I CAN'T BELIEVE I LET MYSELF GET CAUGHT...
YUGI... DON'T DIE...
DON'T THROW YOUR LIFE AWAY ON THIS DISHONORABLE DUEL!
BA
BA
BAM

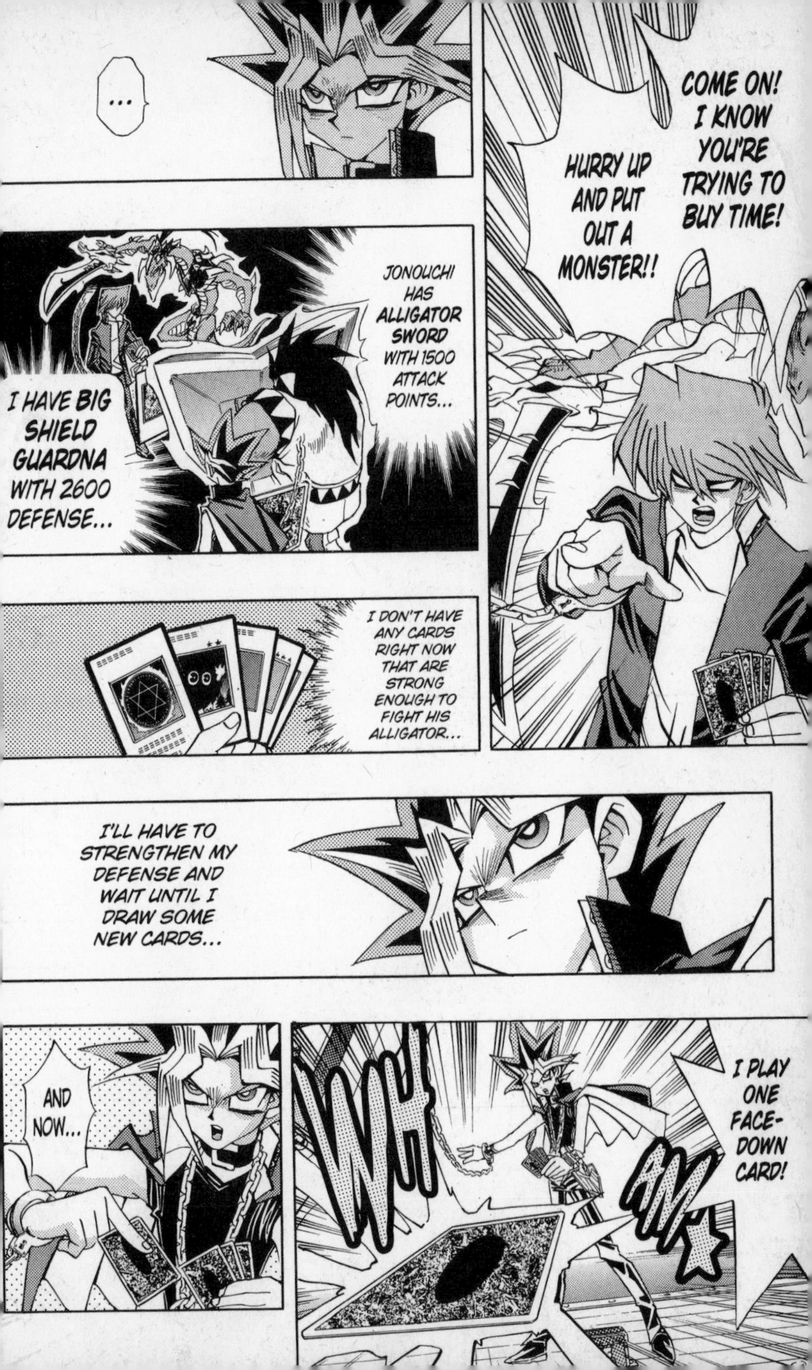
COME ON! I KNOW YOU'RE TRYING TO BUY TIME!
HURRY UP AND PUT OUT A MONSTER!!
...
JONOUCHI HAS ALLIGATOR SWORD WITH 1500 ATTACK POINTS...
I HAVE BIG SHIELD GUARDNA WITH 2600 DEFENSE...
I DON'T HAVE ANY CARDS RIGHT NOW THAT ARE STRONG ENOUGH TO FIGHT HIS ALLIGATOR...
I'LL HAVE TO STRENGTHEN MY DEFENSE AND WAIT UNTIL I DRAW SOME NEW CARDS...
I PLAY ONE FACE-DOWN CARD!
WH
AM
AND NOW...

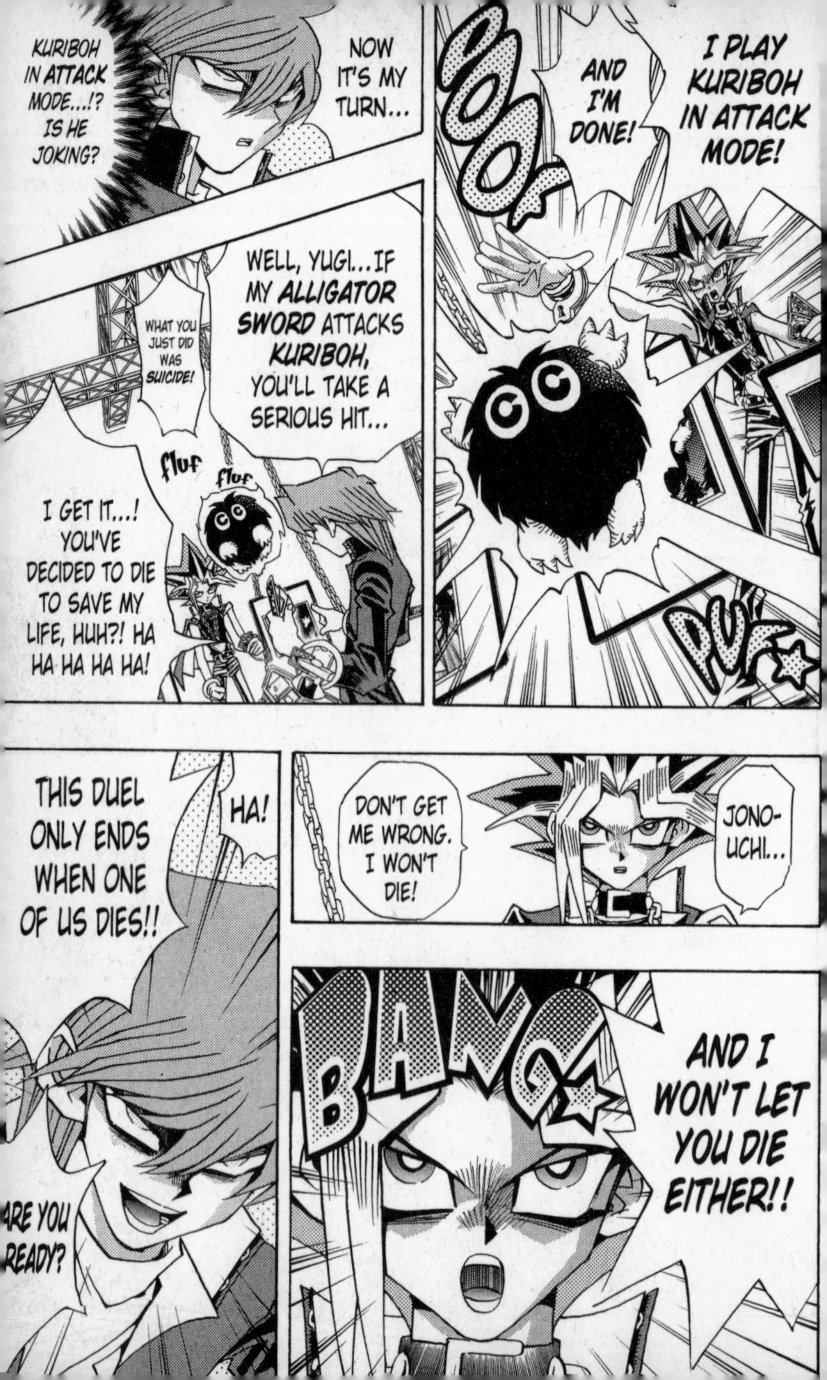
I PLAY KURIBOH IN ATTACK MODE!
AND I'M DONE!
PUF
NOW IT'S MY TURN...
KURIBOH IN ATTACK MODE...!? IS HE JOKING?
WELL, YUGI...IF MY ALLIGATOR SWORD ATTACKS KURIBOH, YOU'LL TAKE A SERIOUS HIT...
WHAT YOU JUST DID WAS SUICIDE!
fluf
fluf
I GET IT...! YOU'VE DECIDED TO DIE TO SAVE MY LIFE, HUH?! HA HA HA HA HA!
JONO-UCHI...
DON'T GET ME WRONG. I WON'T DIE!
BANG
AND I WON'T LET YOU DIE EITHER!!
HA!
THIS DUEL ONLY ENDS WHEN ONE OF US DIES!!
ARE YOU READY?

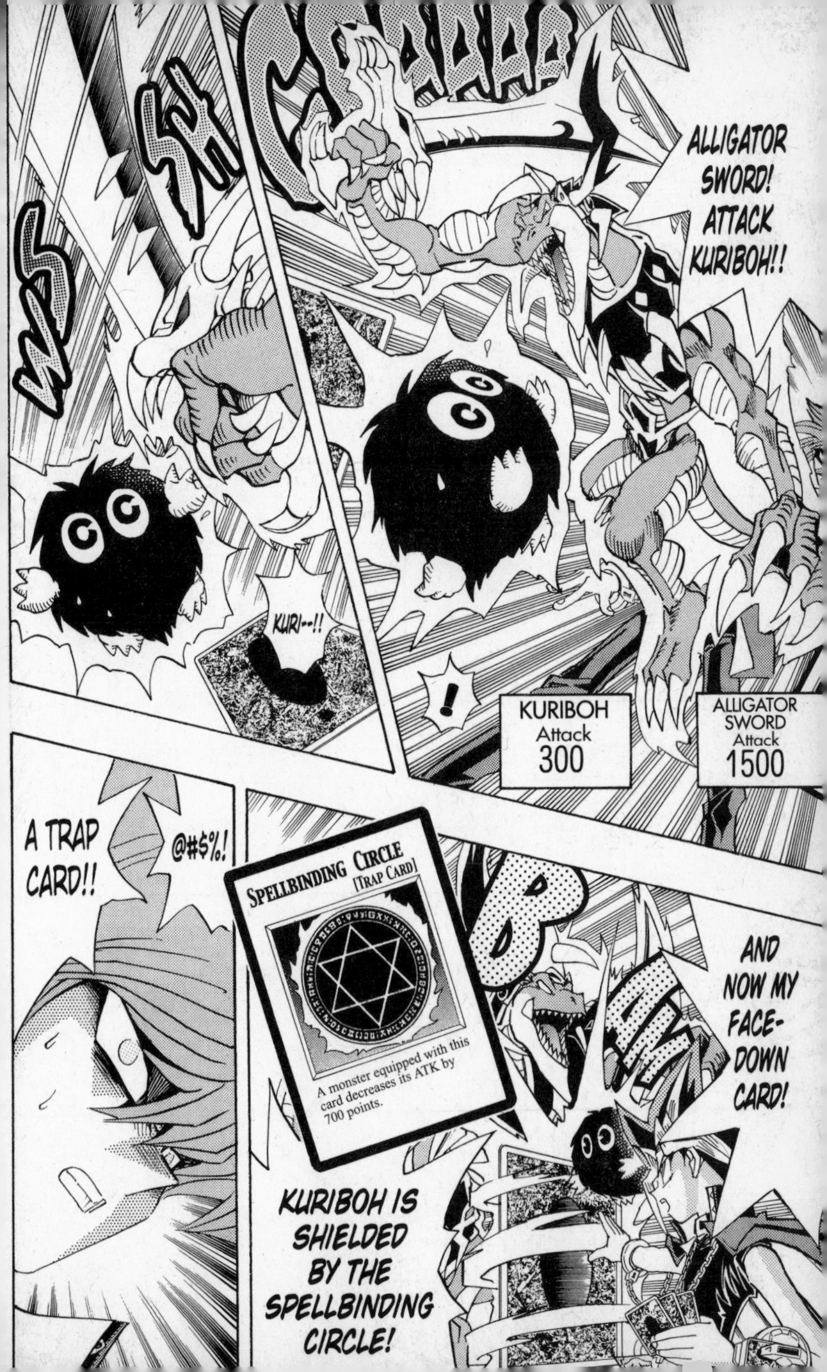
ALLIGATOR SWORD! ATTACK KURIBOH!!
KURIBOH
Attack
300
ALLIGATOR SWORD
Attack
1500
!
KURI--!!
AND NOW MY FACE-DOWN CARD!
SPELLBINDING CIRCLE
[TRAP CARD]
A monster equipped with this card decreases its ATK by 700 points.
KURIBOH IS SHIELDED BY THE SPELLBINDING CIRCLE!
@#$%!
A TRAP CARD!!

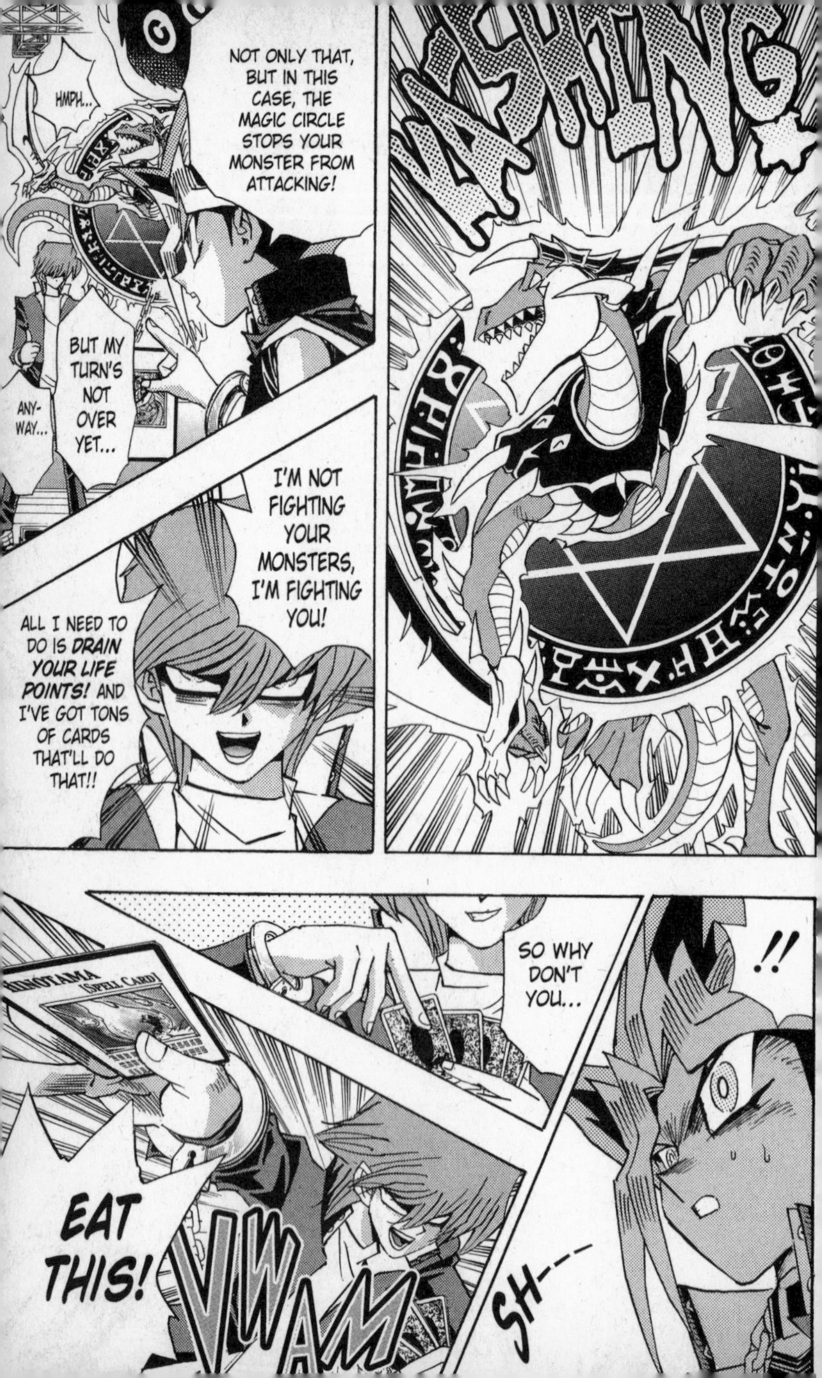
NOT ONLY THAT, BUT IN THIS CASE, THE MAGIC CIRCLE STOPS YOUR MONSTER FROM ATTACKING!
HMPH...
BUT MY TURN'S NOT OVER YET...
ANY-WAY...
I'M NOT FIGHTING YOUR MONSTERS, I'M FIGHTING YOU!
ALL I NEED TO DO IS *DRAIN YOUR LIFE POINTS!* AND I'VE GOT TONS OF CARDS THAT'LL DO THAT!!
SO WHY DON'T YOU...
!!
SH---
HINOTAMA [SPELL CARD]
EAT THIS!
VWAM

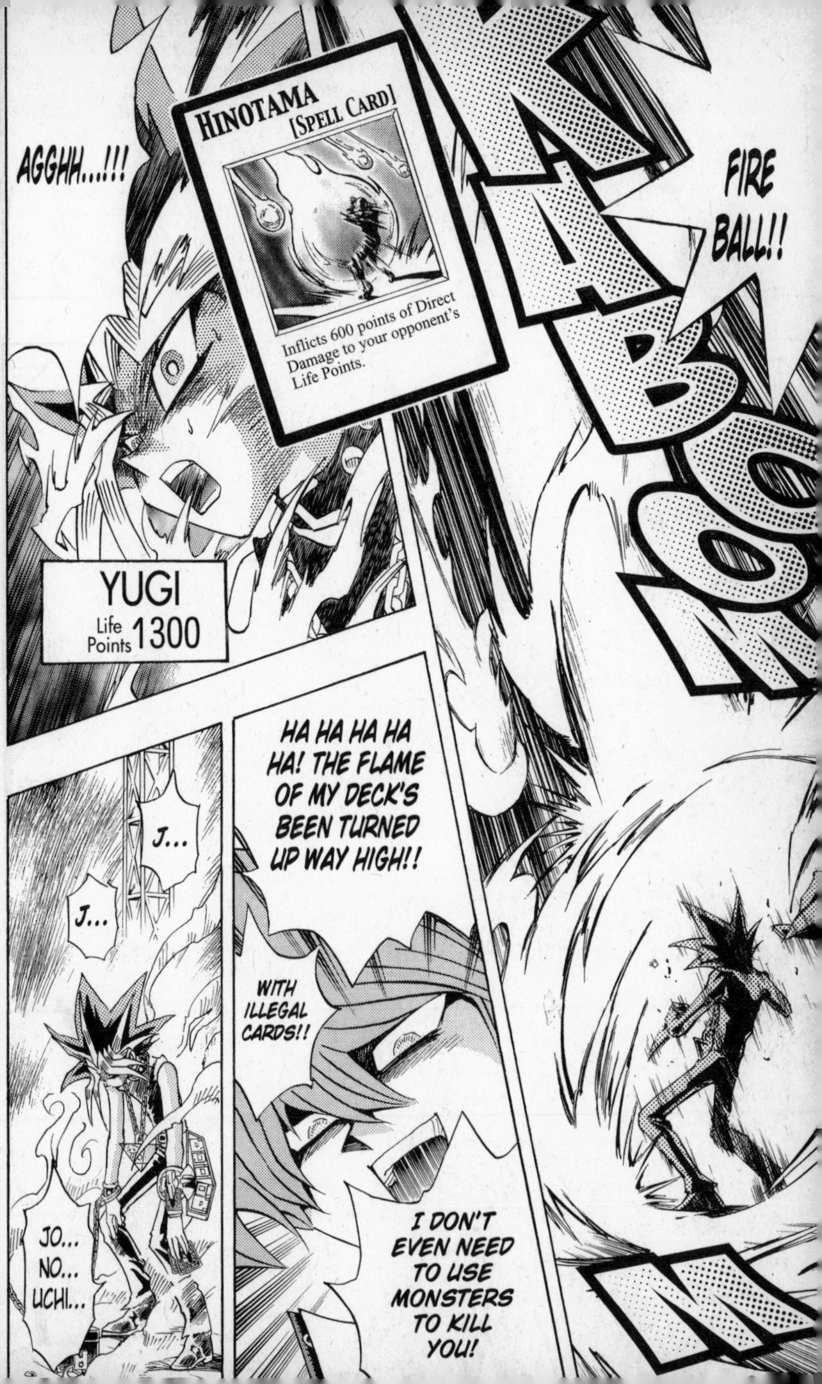

FIRE BALL!!
HINOTAMA
[SPELL CARD]
Inflicts 600 points of Direct Damage to your opponent's Life Points.
AGGHH...!!!
YUGI
Life Points 1300
HA HA HA HA HA! THE FLAME OF MY DECK'S BEEN TURNED UP WAY HIGH!!
WITH ILLEGAL CARDS!!
I DON'T EVEN NEED TO USE MONSTERS TO KILL YOU!
J...
J...
JO... NO... UCHI...

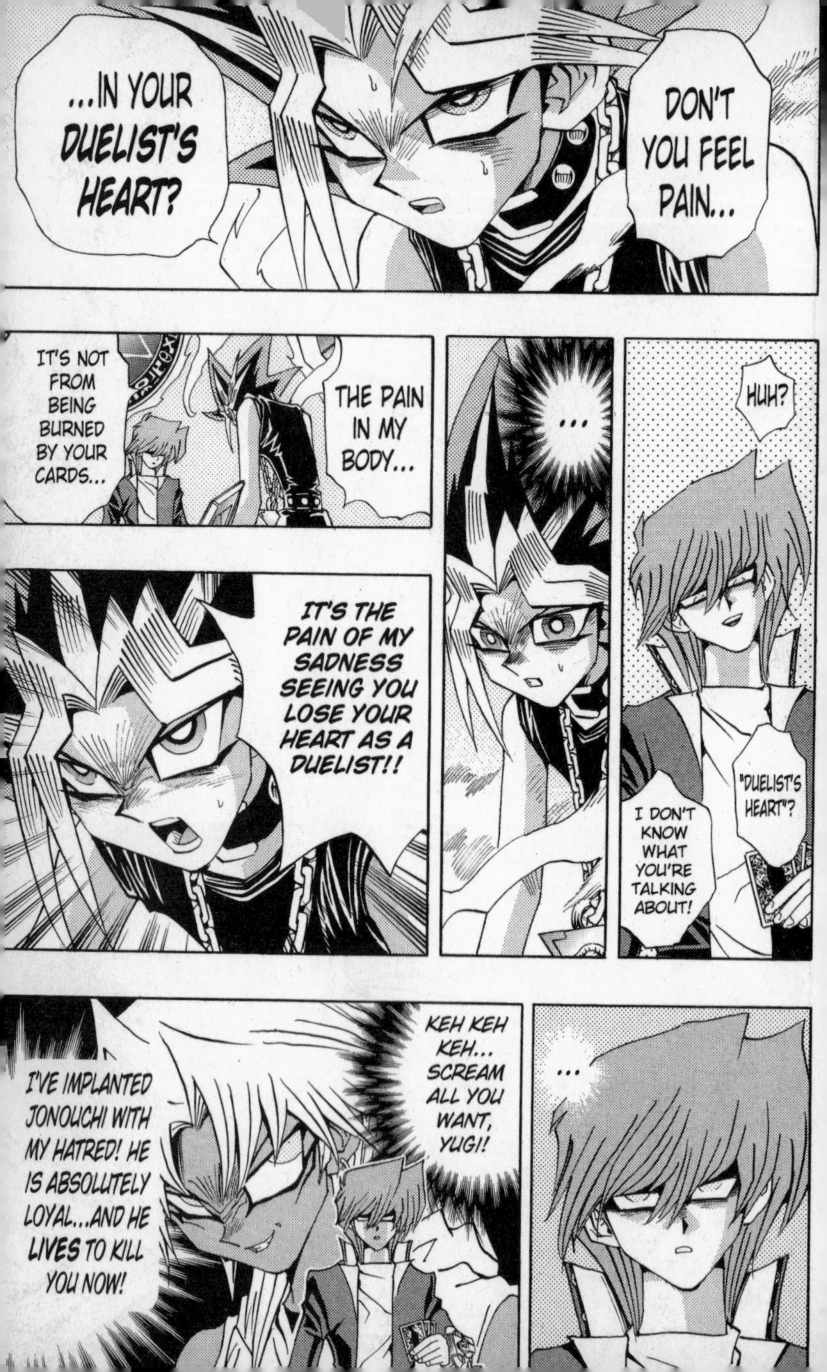
DON'T YOU FEEL PAIN...
...IN YOUR DUELIST'S HEART?
HUH?
"DUELIST'S HEART"?
I DON'T KNOW WHAT YOU'RE TALKING ABOUT!
...
THE PAIN IN MY BODY...
IT'S NOT FROM BEING BURNED BY YOUR CARDS...
IT'S THE PAIN OF MY SADNESS SEEING YOU LOSE YOUR HEART AS A DUELIST!!
...
KEH KEH KEH... SCREAM ALL YOU WANT, YUGI!
I'VE IMPLANTED JONOUCHI WITH MY HATRED! HE IS ABSOLUTELY LOYAL...AND HE LIVES TO KILL YOU NOW!

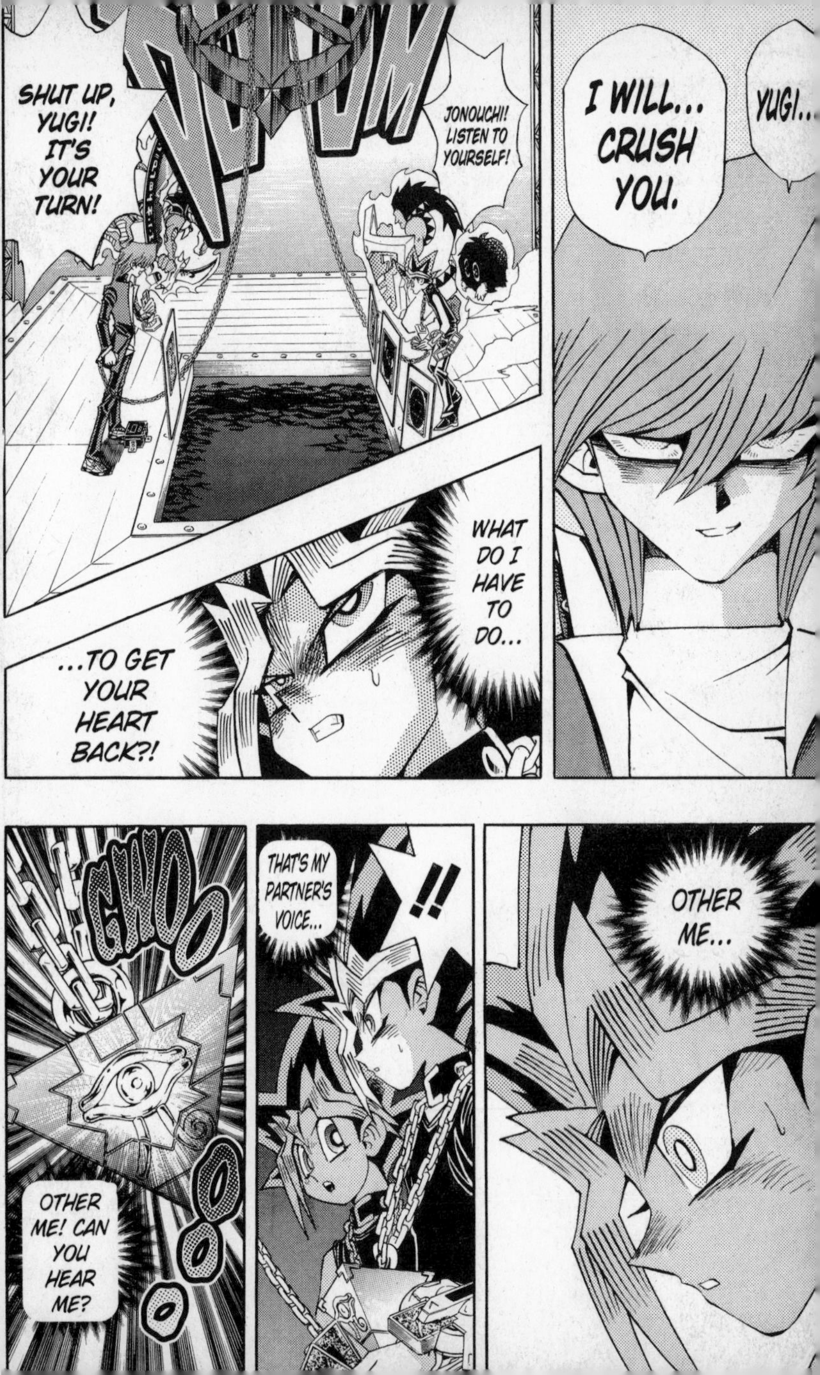
YUGI...
I WILL... CRUSH YOU.
JONOUCHI! LISTEN TO YOURSELF!
SHUT UP, YUGI! IT'S YOUR TURN!
WHAT DO I HAVE TO DO...
...TO GET YOUR HEART BACK?!
OTHER ME...
!!
THAT'S MY PARTNER'S VOICE...
OTHER ME! CAN YOU HEAR ME?

READ THIS WAY

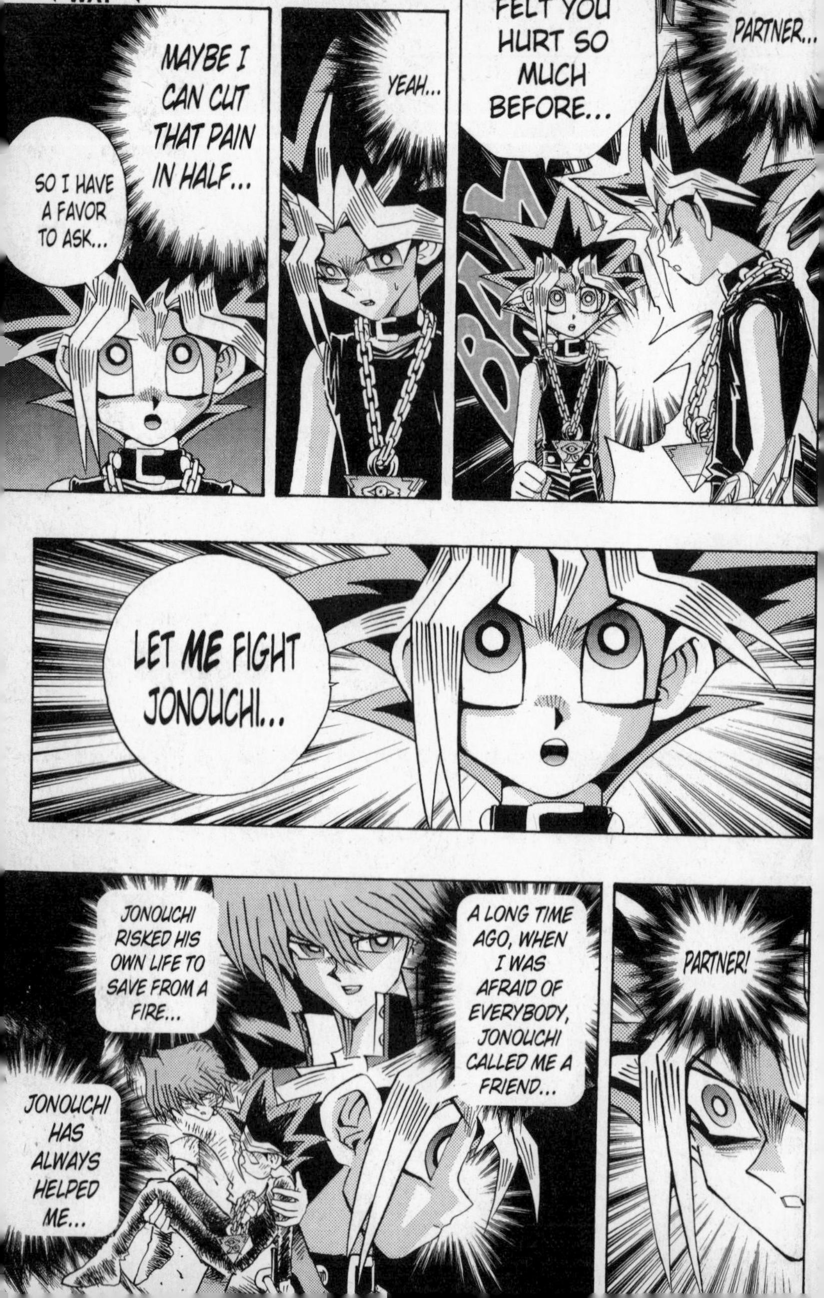

I'VE NEVER FELT YOU HURT SO MUCH BEFORE...
PARTNER...
YEAH...
MAYBE I CAN CUT THAT PAIN IN HALF...
SO I HAVE A FAVOR TO ASK...
LET ME FIGHT JONOUCHI...
PARTNER!
A LONG TIME AGO, WHEN I WAS AFRAID OF EVERYBODY, JONOUCHI CALLED ME A FRIEND...
JONOUCHI RISKED HIS OWN LIFE TO SAVE FROM A FIRE...
JONOUCHI HAS ALWAYS HELPED ME...

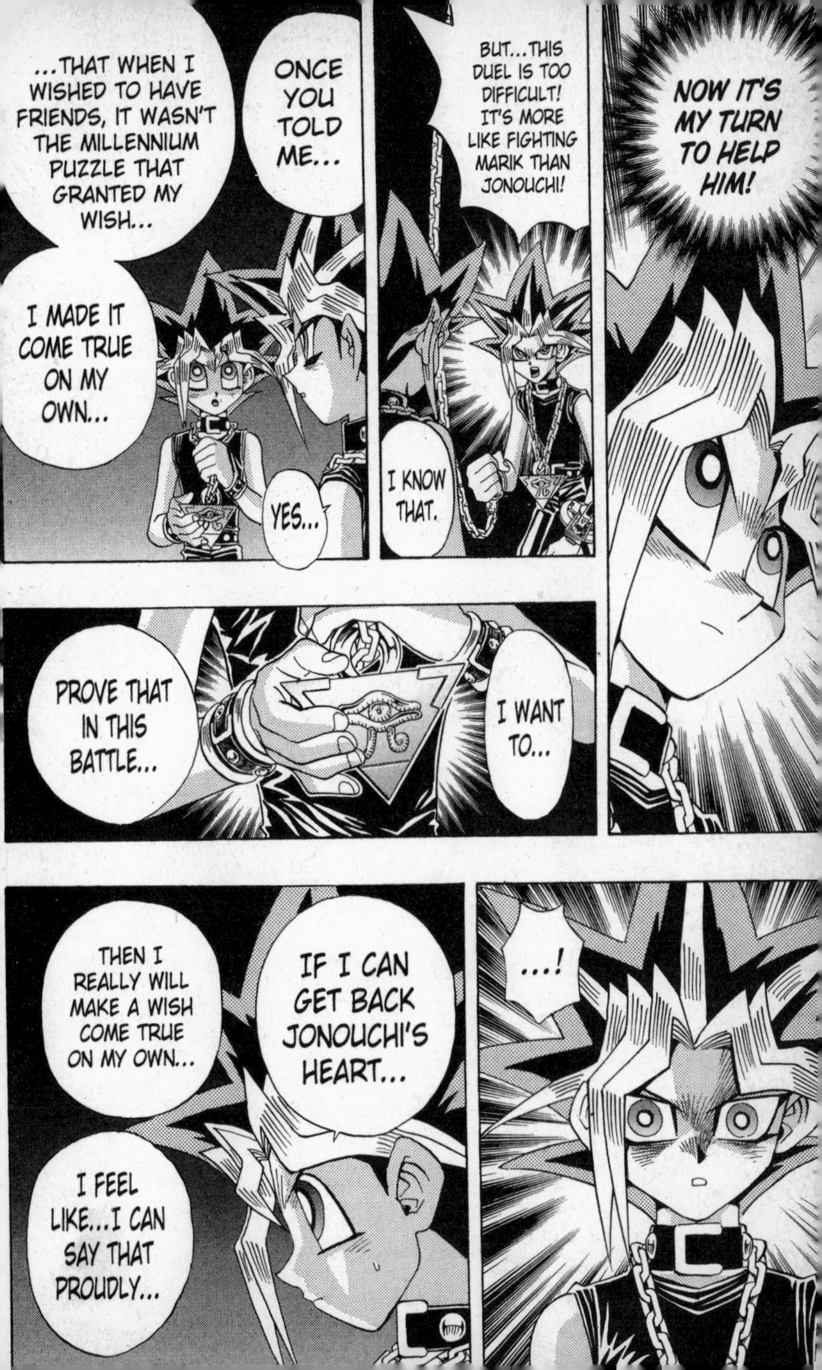
NOW IT'S MY TURN TO HELP HIM!
BUT... THIS DUEL IS TOO DIFFICULT! IT'S MORE LIKE FIGHTING MARIK THAN JONOUCHI!
I KNOW THAT.
ONCE YOU TOLD ME...
...THAT WHEN I WISHED TO HAVE FRIENDS, IT WASN'T THE MILLENNIUM PUZZLE THAT GRANTED MY WISH...
I MADE IT COME TRUE ON MY OWN...
YES...
I WANT TO...
PROVE THAT IN THIS BATTLE...
...!
IF I CAN GET BACK JONOUCHI'S HEART...
THEN I REALLY WILL MAKE A WISH COME TRUE ON MY OWN...
I FEEL LIKE...I CAN SAY THAT PROUDLY...

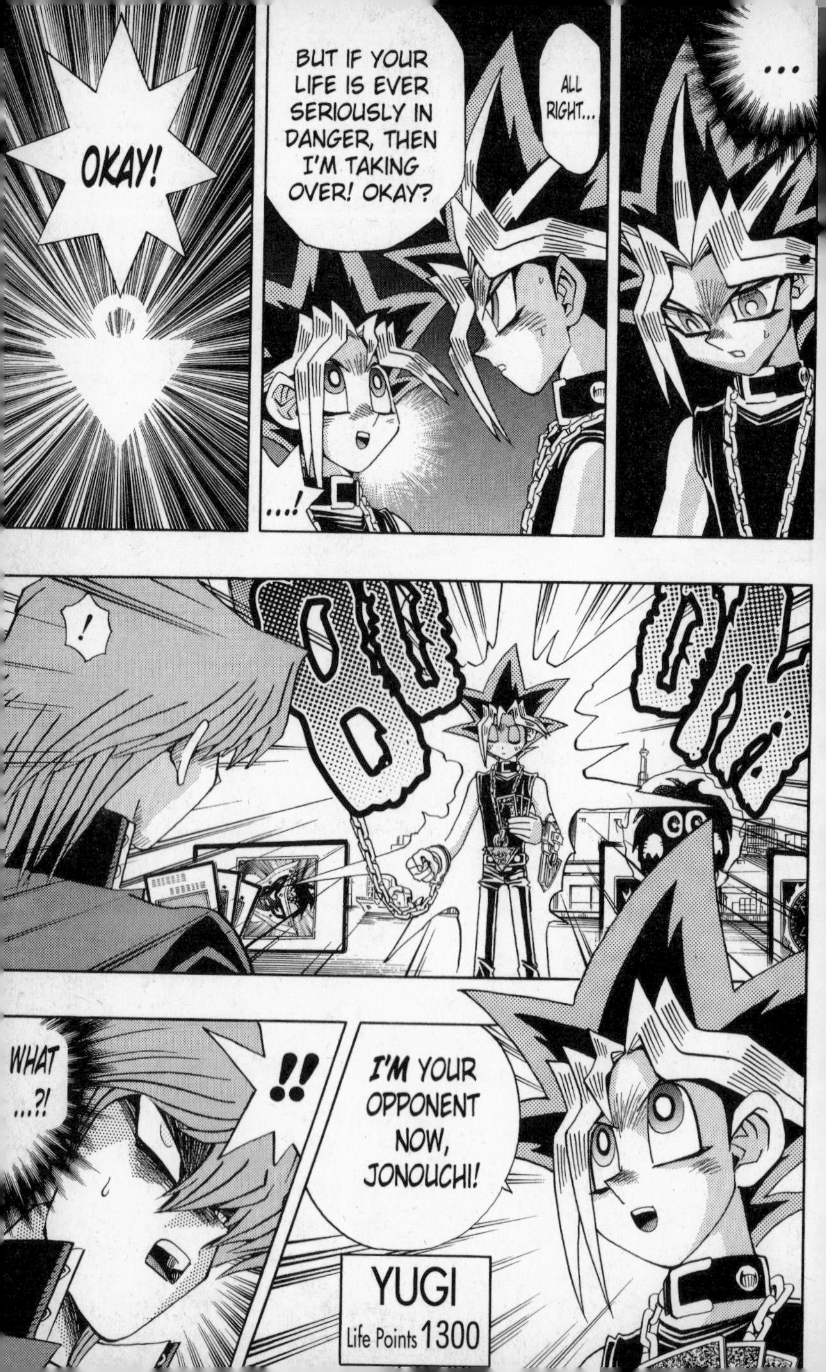
...
ALL RIGHT...
BUT IF YOUR LIFE IS EVER SERIOUSLY IN DANGER, THEN I'M TAKING OVER! OKAY?
...!
OKAY!
!
I'M YOUR OPPONENT NOW, JONOUCHI!
YUGI
Life Points 1300
!!
WHAT ...?!

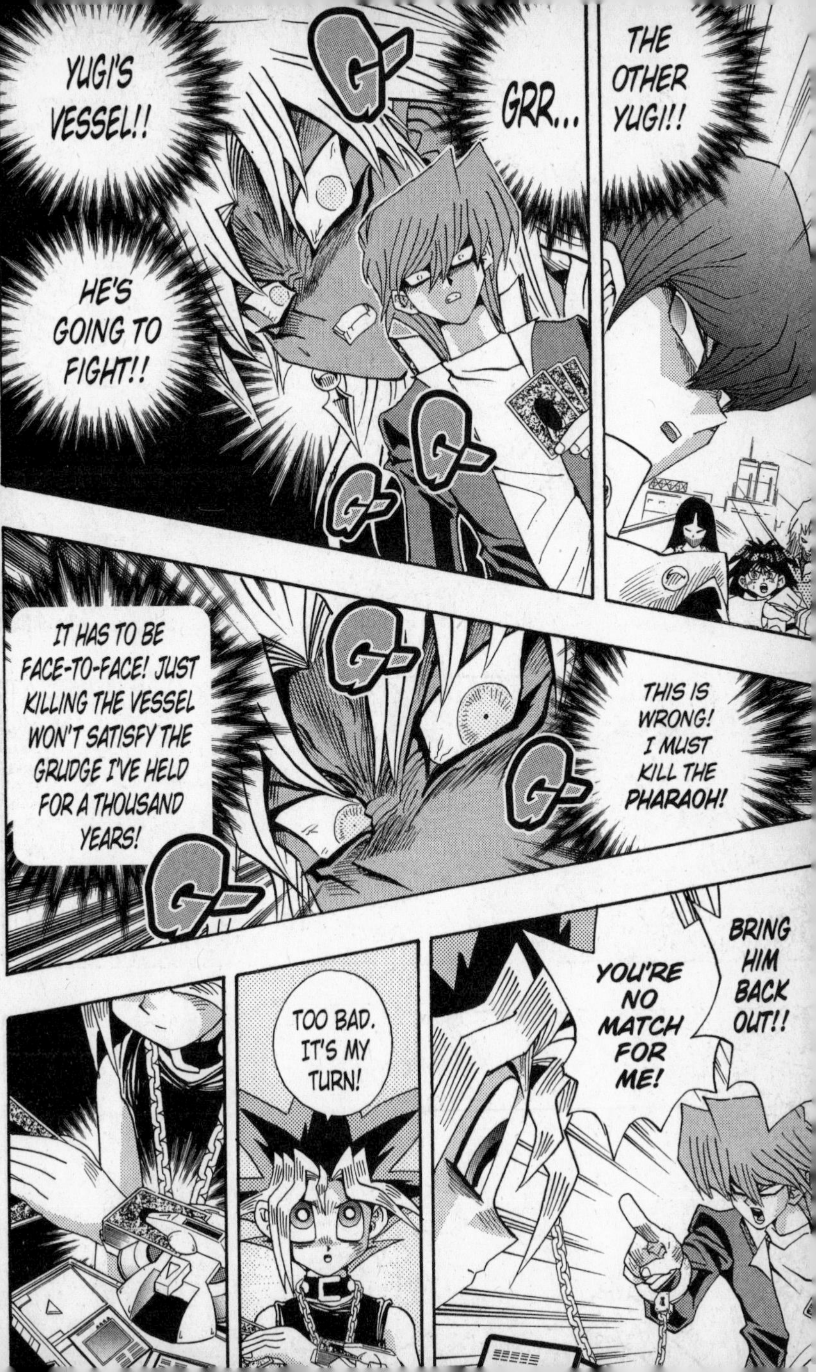
THE OTHER YUGI!!
GRR...
G-
YUGI'S VESSEL!!
HE'S GOING TO FIGHT!!
G-
G-
THIS IS WRONG! I MUST KILL THE PHARAOH!
G-
G-
IT HAS TO BE FACE-TO-FACE! JUST KILLING THE VESSEL WON'T SATISFY THE GRUDGE I'VE HELD FOR A THOUSAND YEARS!
G-
BRING HIM BACK OUT!!
YOU'RE NO MATCH FOR ME!
TOO BAD. IT'S MY TURN!

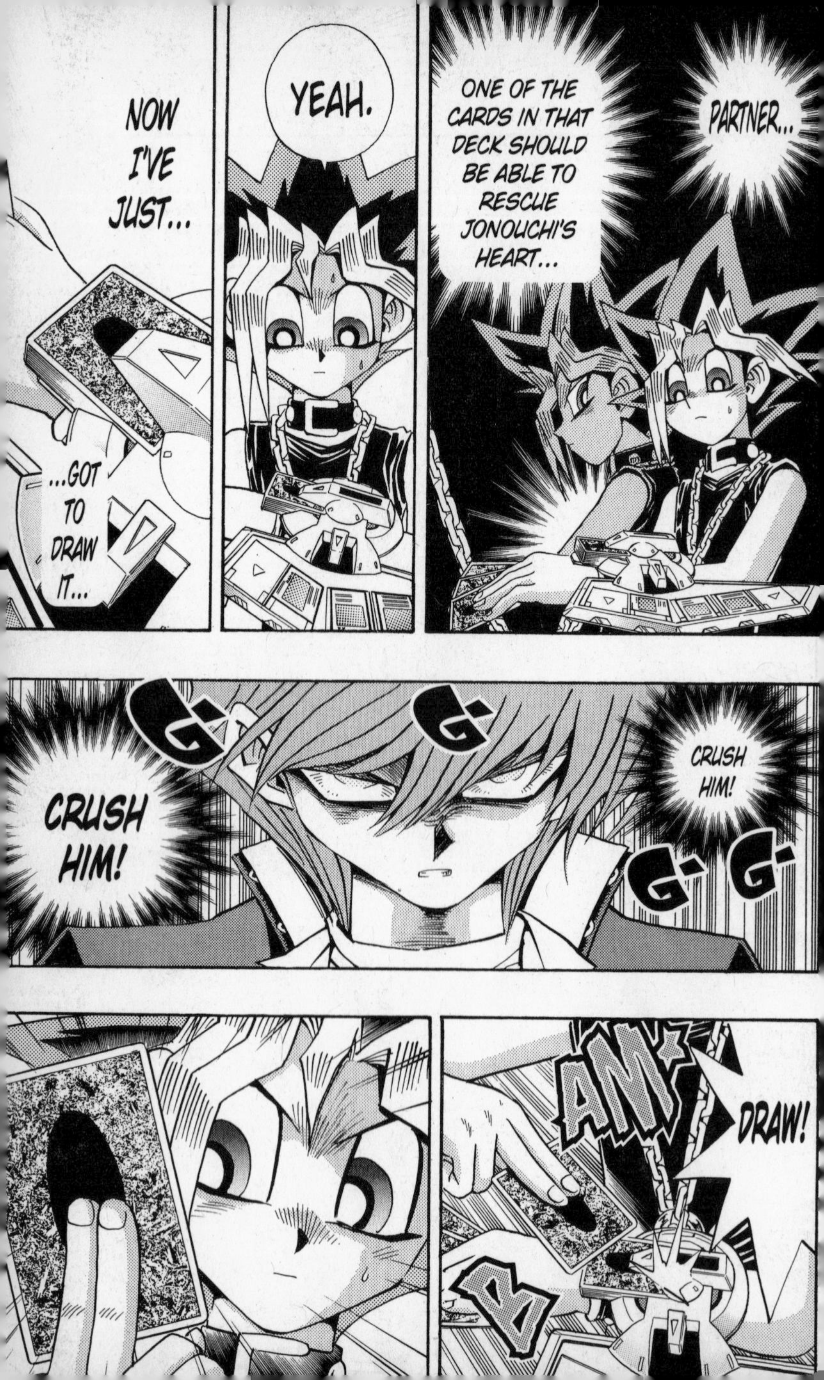
PARTNER...
ONE OF THE CARDS IN THAT DECK SHOULD BE ABLE TO RESCUE JONOUCHI'S HEART...
YEAH.
NOW I'VE JUST...
...GOT TO DRAW IT...
CRUSH HIM!
CRUSH HIM!
DRAW!

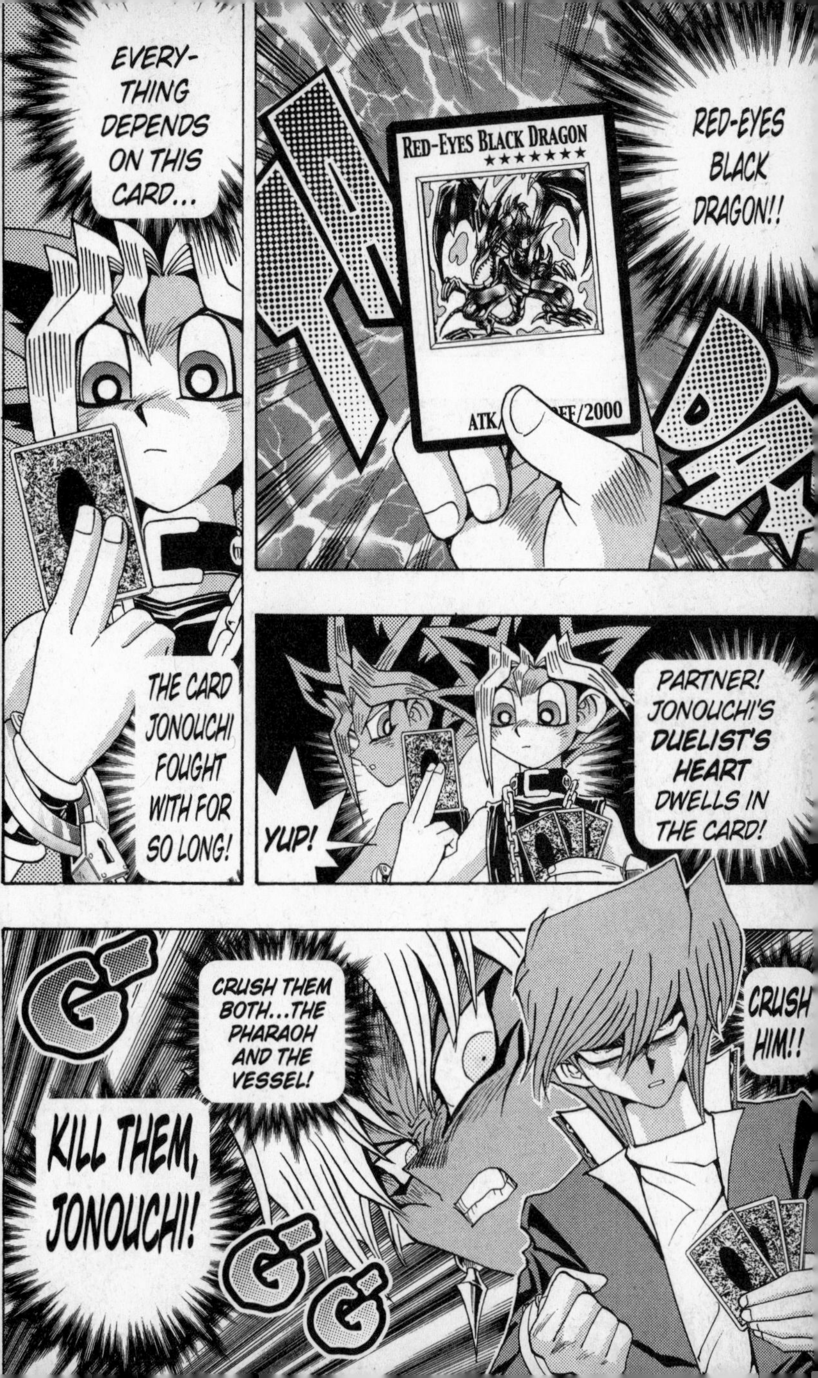
RED-EYES BLACK DRAGON
DEF/2000
RED-EYES BLACK DRAGON!!
PARTNER! JONOUCHI'S DUELIST'S HEART DWELLS IN THE CARD!
YUP!
EVERY-THING DEPENDS ON THIS CARD...
THE CARD JONOUCHI FOUGHT WITH FOR SO LONG!
CRUSH HIM!!
CRUSH THEM BOTH...THE PHARAOH AND THE VESSEL!
KILL THEM, JONOUCHI!
G
G
G

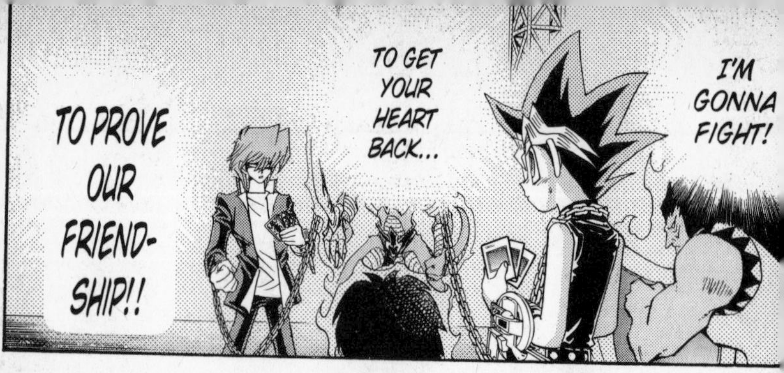
I'M GONNA FIGHT!
TO GET YOUR HEART BACK...
TO PROVE OUR FRIEND-SHIP!!

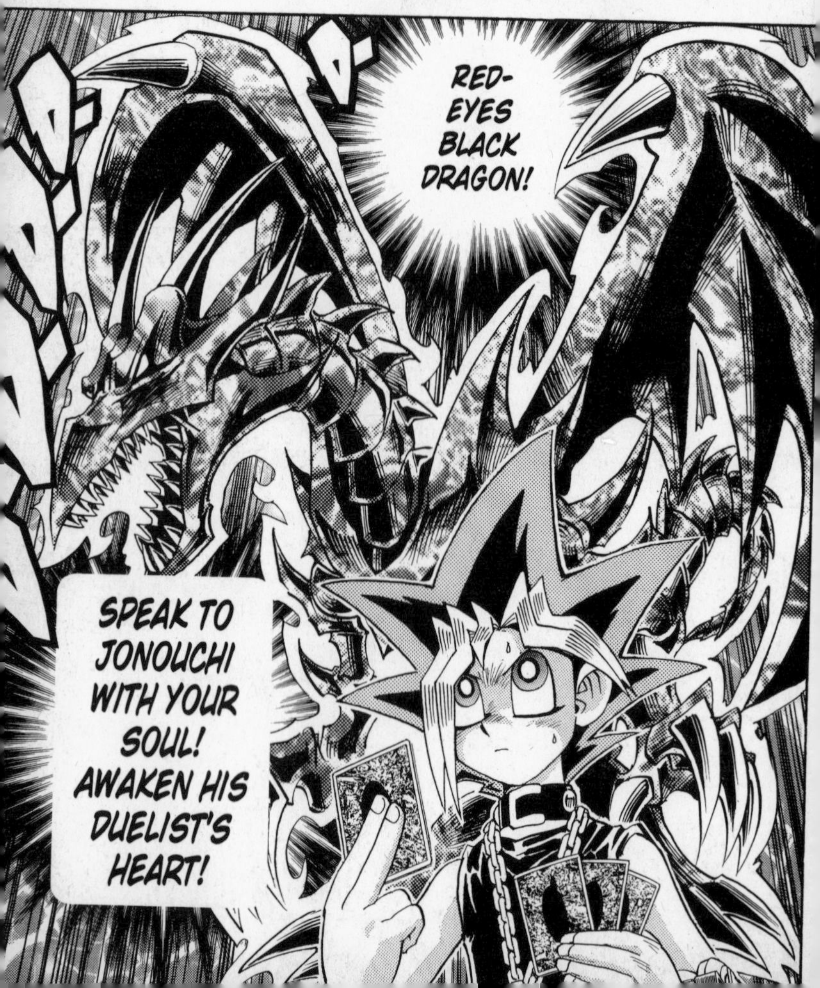
RED-EYES BLACK DRAGON!
SPEAK TO JONOUCHI WITH YOUR SOUL! AWAKEN HIS DUELIST'S HEART!

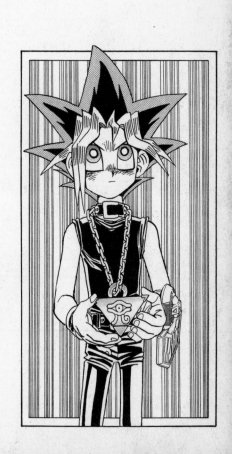

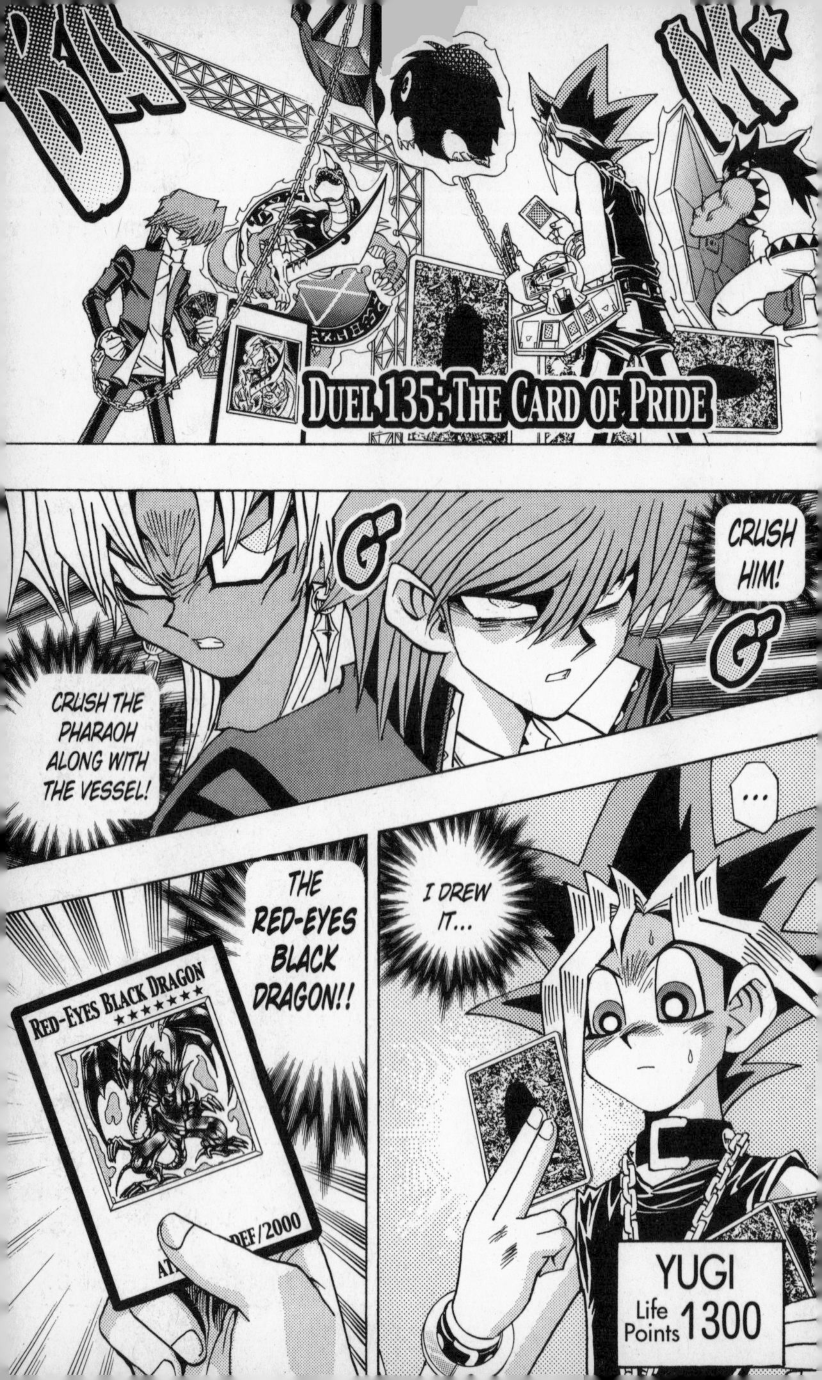
BAM!
DUEL 135: THE CARD OF PRIDE
CRUSH HIM!
G
G
CRUSH THE PHARAOH ALONG WITH THE VESSEL!
...
I DREW IT...
YUGI
Life Points 1300
THE RED-EYES BLACK DRAGON!!
RED-EYES BLACK DRAGON
DEF/2000

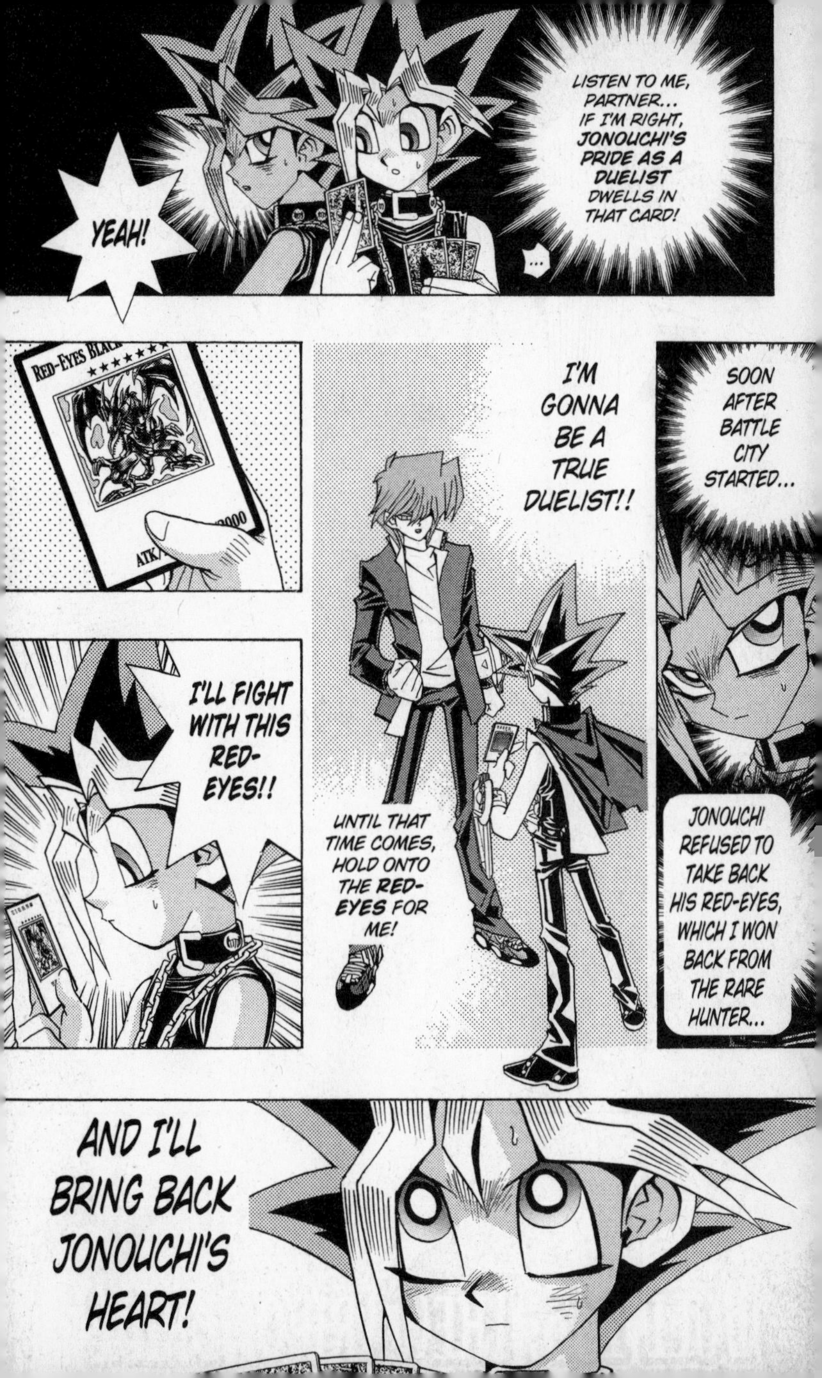
LISTEN TO ME, PARTNER... IF I'M RIGHT, JONOUCHI'S PRIDE AS A DUELIST DWELLS IN THAT CARD!
...
YEAH!
SOON AFTER BATTLE CITY STARTED...
JONOUCHI REFUSED TO TAKE BACK HIS RED-EYES, WHICH I WON BACK FROM THE RARE HUNTER...
I'M GONNA BE A TRUE DUELIST!!
UNTIL THAT TIME COMES, HOLD ONTO THE RED-EYES FOR ME!
RED-EYES BLACK
I'LL FIGHT WITH THIS RED-EYES!!
AND I'LL BRING BACK JONOUCHI'S HEART!

DUEL 135: THE CARD OF PRIDE

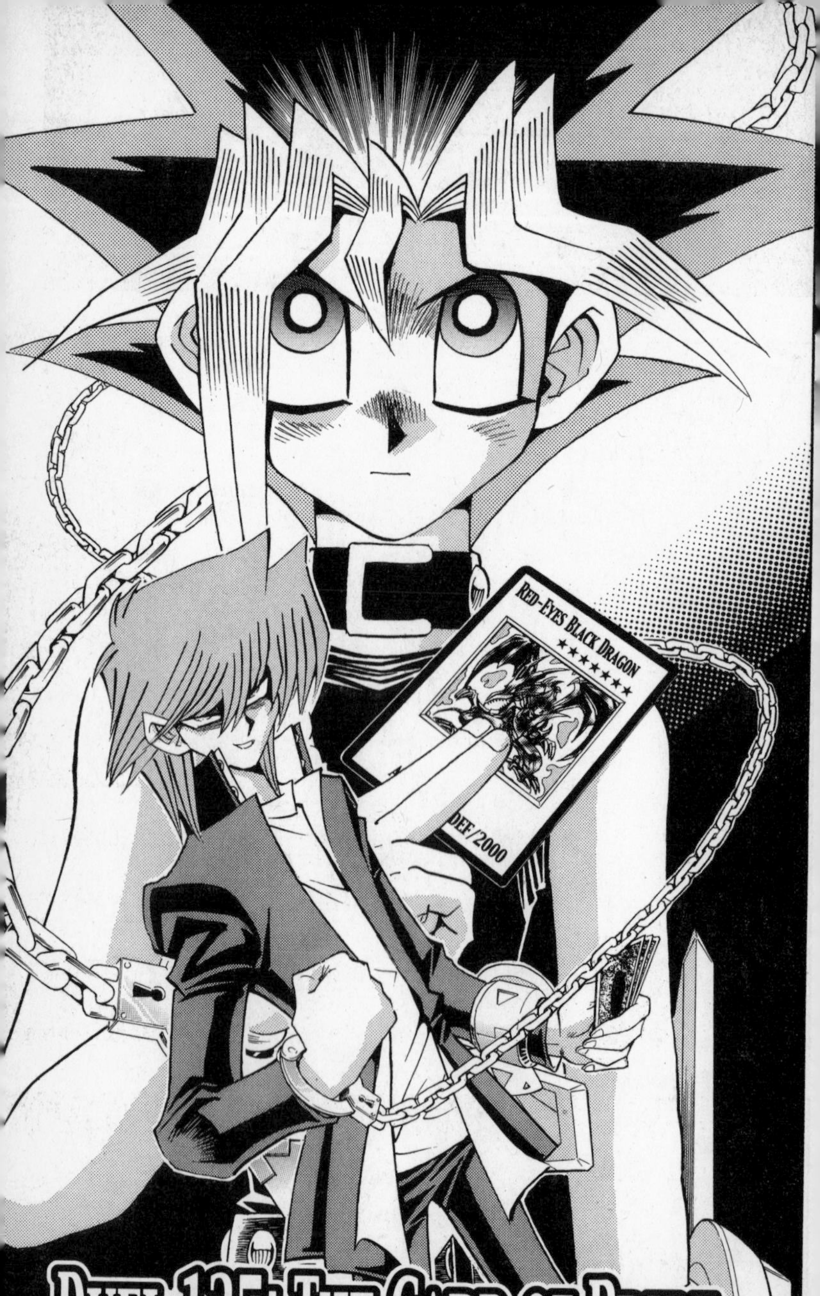
RED-EYES BLACK DRAGON
DEF/2000

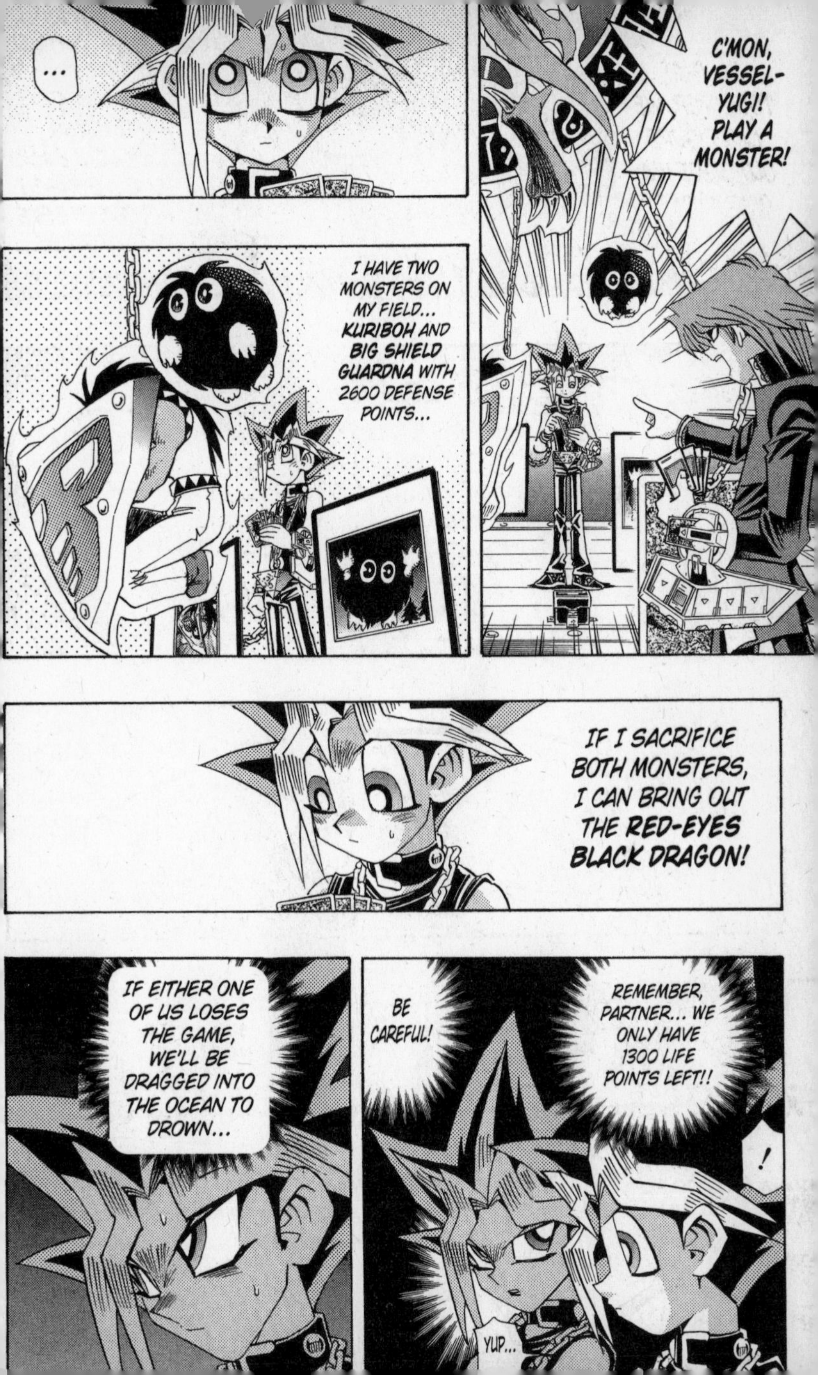
C'MON, VESSEL-YUGI! PLAY A MONSTER!
...
I HAVE TWO MONSTERS ON MY FIELD... KURIBOH AND BIG SHIELD GUARDNA WITH 2600 DEFENSE POINTS...
IF I SACRIFICE BOTH MONSTERS, I CAN BRING OUT THE RED-EYES BLACK DRAGON!
REMEMBER, PARTNER... WE ONLY HAVE 1300 LIFE POINTS LEFT!!
BE CAREFUL!
!
YUP...
IF EITHER ONE OF US LOSES THE GAME, WE'LL BE DRAGGED INTO THE OCEAN TO DROWN...

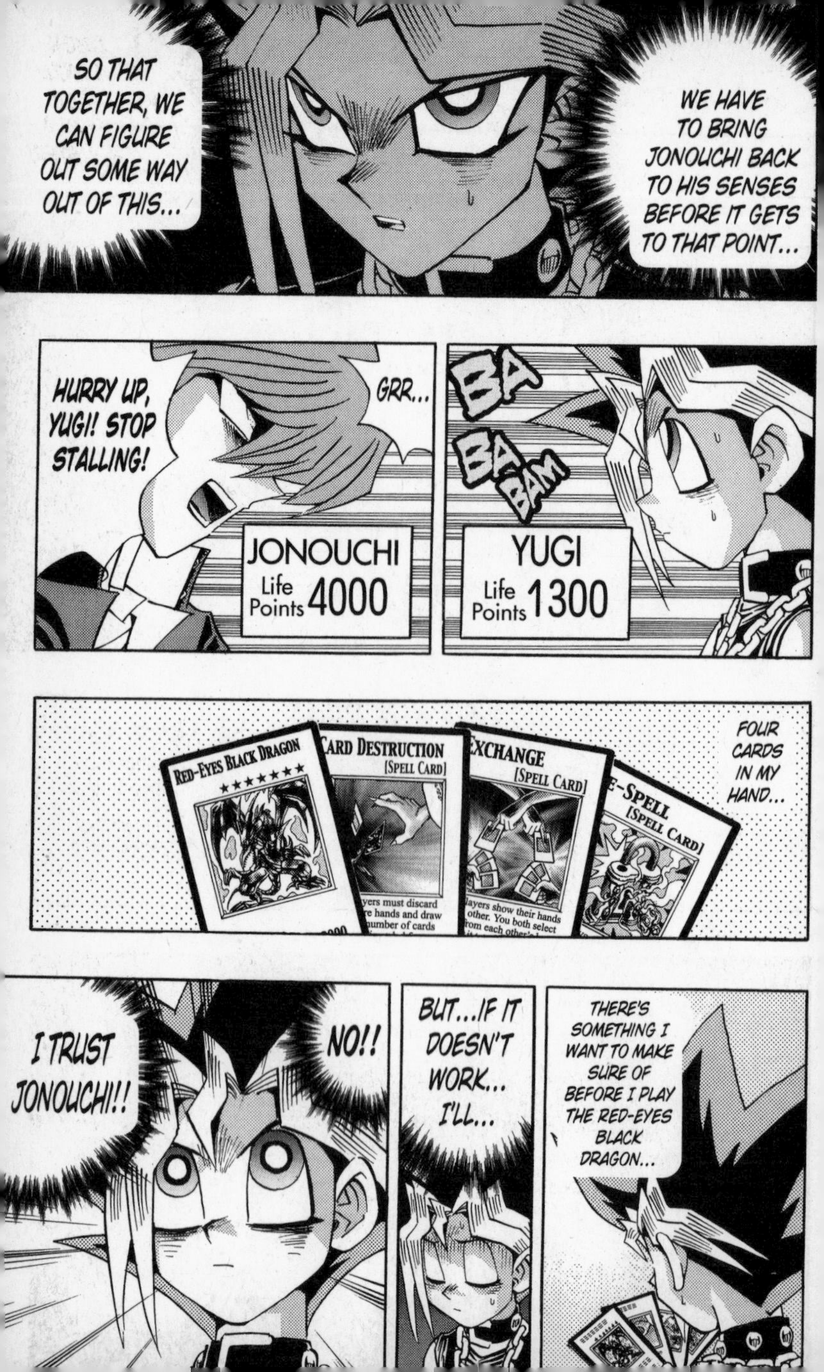
WE HAVE TO BRING JONOUCHI BACK TO HIS SENSES BEFORE IT GETS TO THAT POINT...
SO THAT TOGETHER, WE CAN FIGURE OUT SOME WAY OUT OF THIS...
BA
BA
BAM
YUGI
Life Points 1300
GRR...
HURRY UP, YUGI! STOP STALLING!
JONOUCHI
Life Points 4000
FOUR CARDS IN MY HAND...
E-SPELL
[SPELL CARD]
EXCHANGE
[SPELL CARD]
CARD DESTRUCTION
[SPELL CARD]
RED-EYES BLACK DRAGON
THERE'S SOMETHING I WANT TO MAKE SURE OF BEFORE I PLAY THE RED-EYES BLACK DRAGON...
BUT...IF IT DOESN'T WORK... I'LL...
NO!!
I TRUST JONOUCHI!!

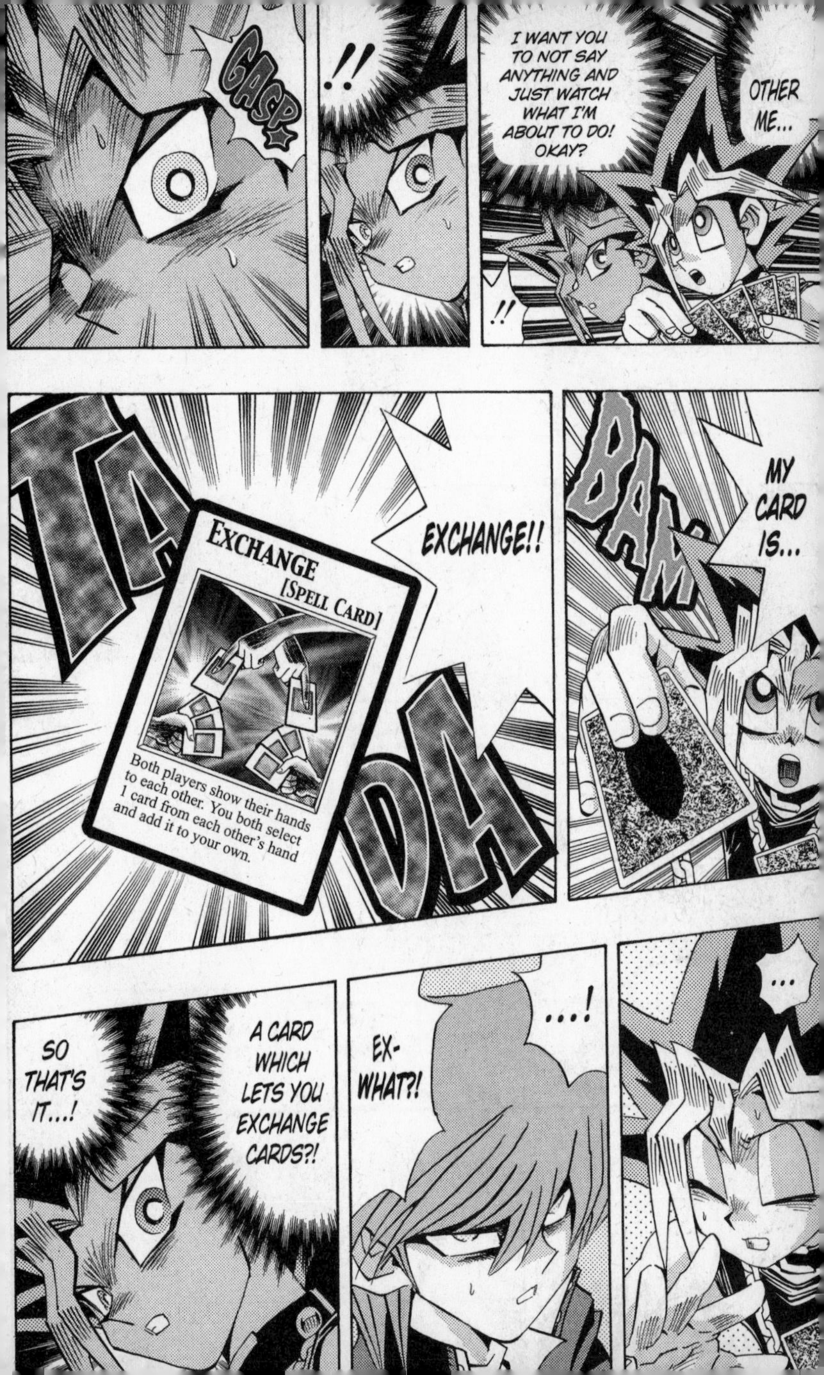
OTHER ME...
I WANT YOU TO NOT SAY ANYTHING AND JUST WATCH WHAT I'M ABOUT TO DO! OKAY?
!!
!!
GASP
MY CARD IS...
BAM
EXCHANGE!!
EXCHANGE
[SPELL CARD]
Both players show their hands to each other. You both select 1 card from each other's hand and add it to your own.
TA
DA
...
...!
EX-WHAT?!
A CARD WHICH LETS YOU EXCHANGE CARDS?!
SO THAT'S IT...!

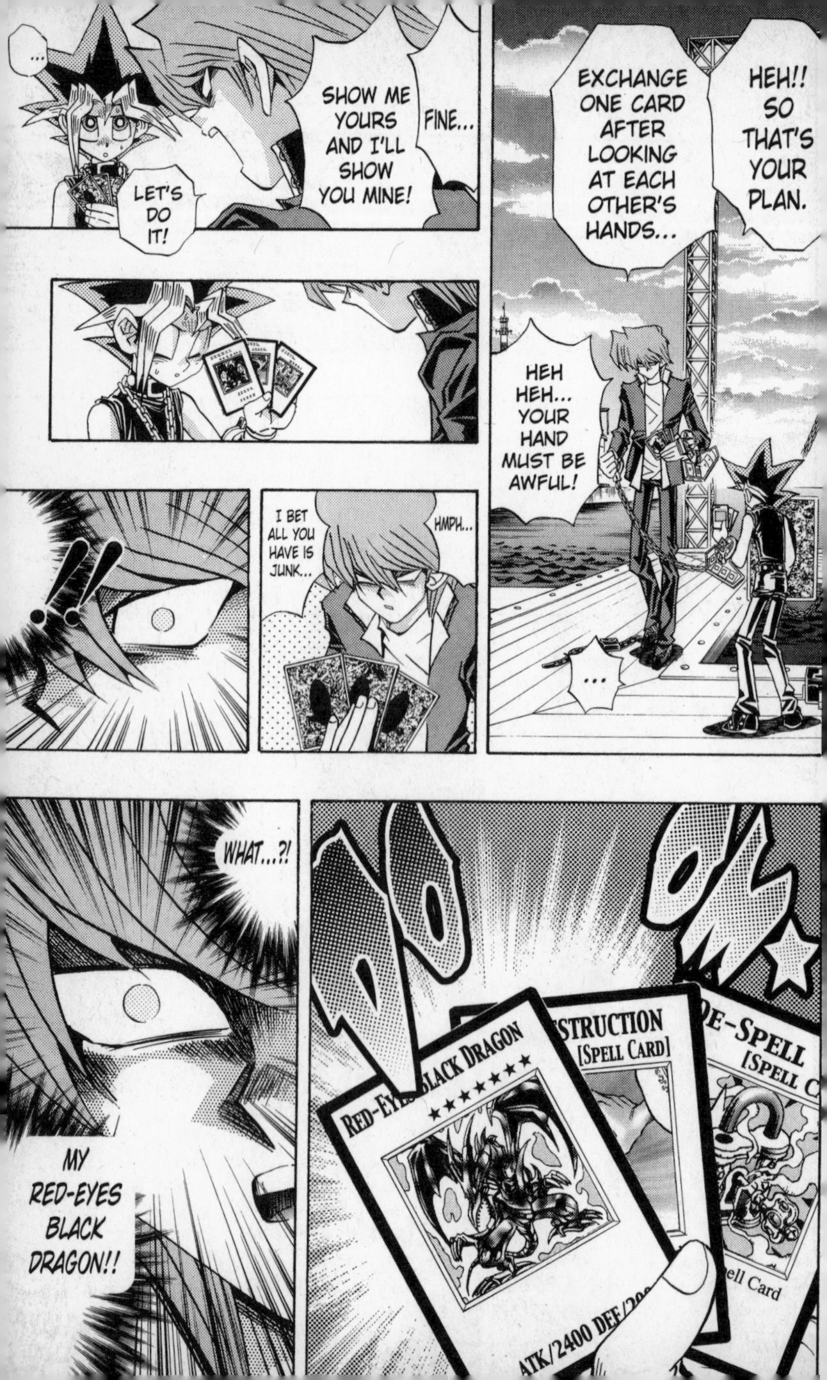
HEH!! SO THAT'S YOUR PLAN.
EXCHANGE ONE CARD AFTER LOOKING AT EACH OTHER'S HANDS...
HEH HEH... YOUR HAND MUST BE AWFUL!
...
FINE...
SHOW ME YOURS AND I'LL SHOW YOU MINE!
...
LET'S DO IT!
HMPH...
I BET ALL YOU HAVE IS JUNK...
!!
[SPELL CARD]
WHAT...?!
MY RED-EYES BLACK DRAGON!!

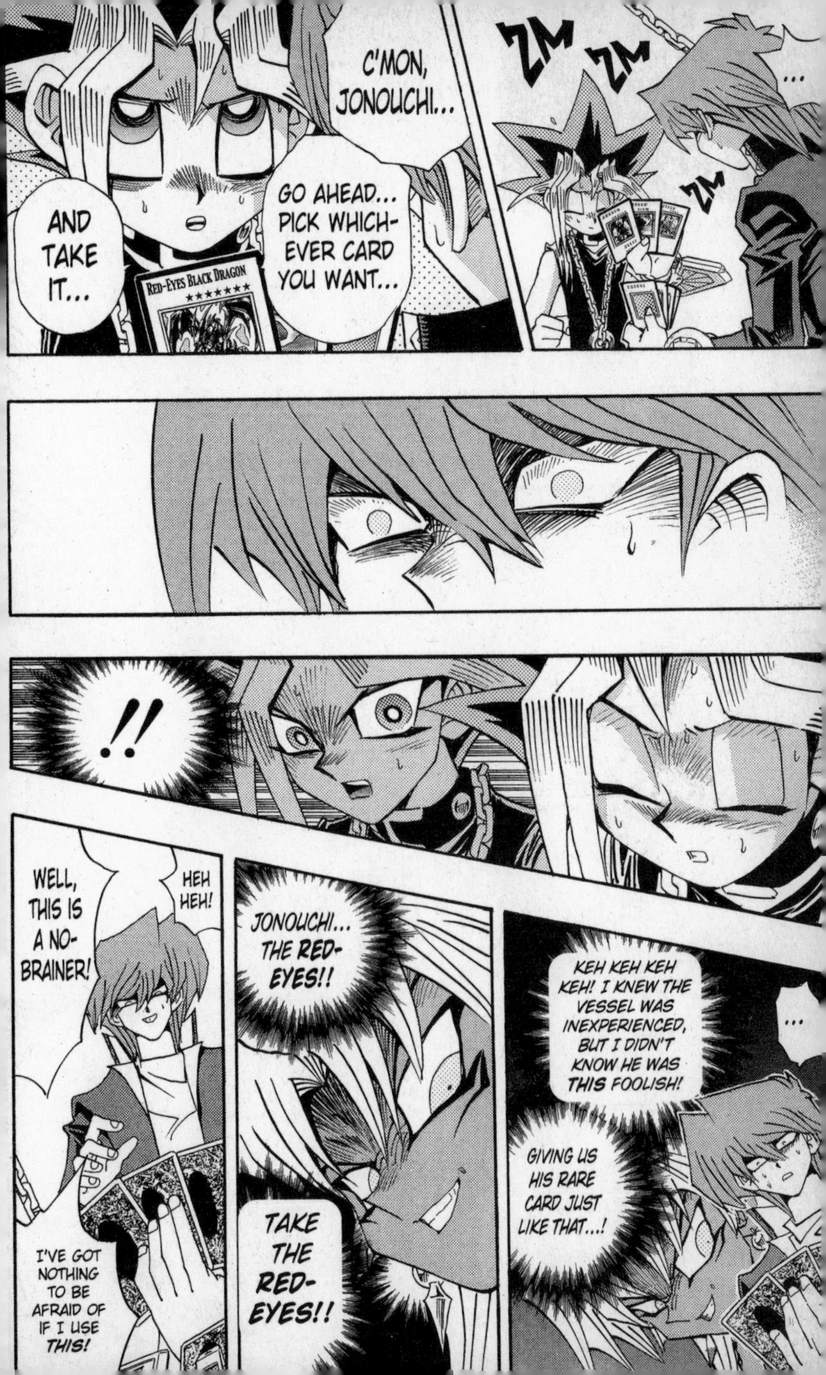
ZM
ZM
ZM
...
C'MON, JONOUCHI...
GO AHEAD... PICK WHICH-EVER CARD YOU WANT...
AND TAKE IT...
RED-EYES BLACK DRAGON
!!
KEH KEH KEH KEH! I KNEW THE VESSEL WAS INEXPERIENCED, BUT I DIDN'T KNOW HE WAS THIS FOOLISH!
...
GIVING US HIS RARE CARD JUST LIKE THAT...!
JONOUCHI... THE RED-EYES!!
TAKE THE RED-EYES!!
HEH HEH!
WELL, THIS IS A NO-BRAINER!
I'VE GOT NOTHING TO BE AFRAID OF IF I USE THIS!

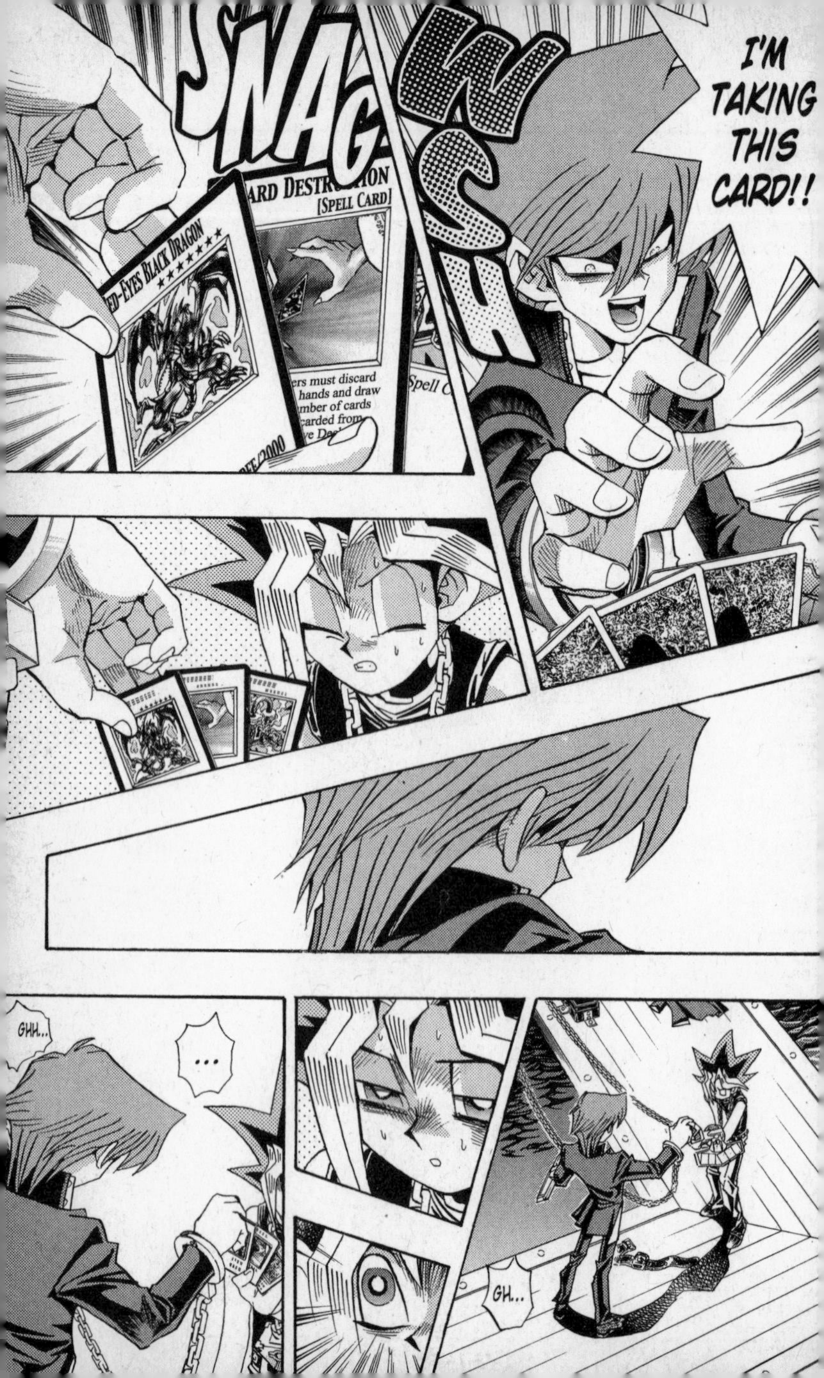
I'M TAKING THIS CARD!!
SNAG
[SPELL CARD]
GH...
GHH...
...

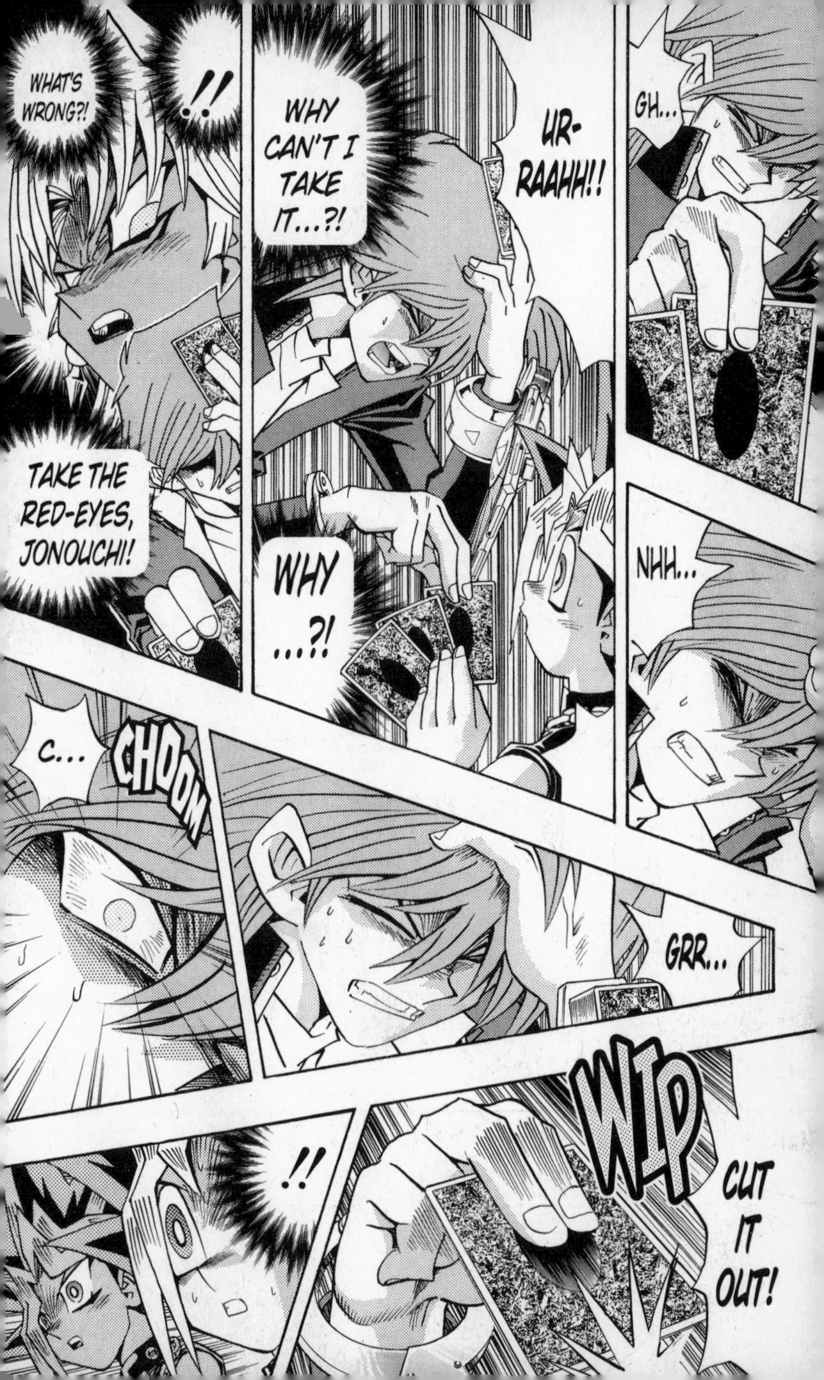
GH...
NHH...
UR-RAAHH!!
WHY CAN'T I TAKE IT...?!
WHY ...?!
!!
WHAT'S WRONG?!
TAKE THE RED-EYES, JONOUCHI!
GRR...
C...
CHOOM
WIP
CUT IT OUT!
!!

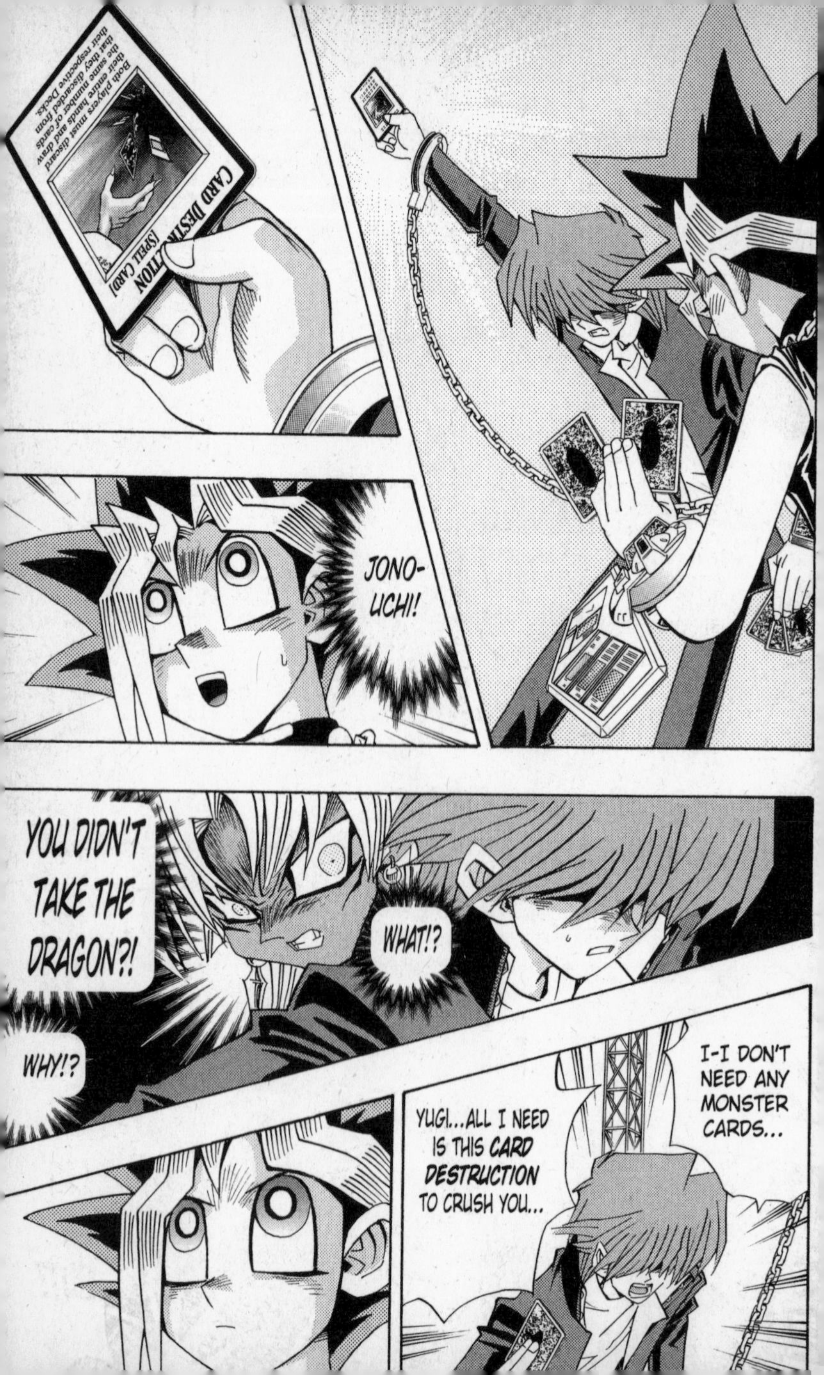

[SPELL CARD]
Both players must discard their entire hands of cards and draw the same number of cards that they discarded from their respective Decks.
JONO-UCHI!
WHAT!?
YOU DIDN'T TAKE THE DRAGON?!
WHY!?
I-I DON'T NEED ANY MONSTER CARDS...
YUGI...ALL I NEED IS THIS CARD DESTRUCTION TO CRUSH YOU...

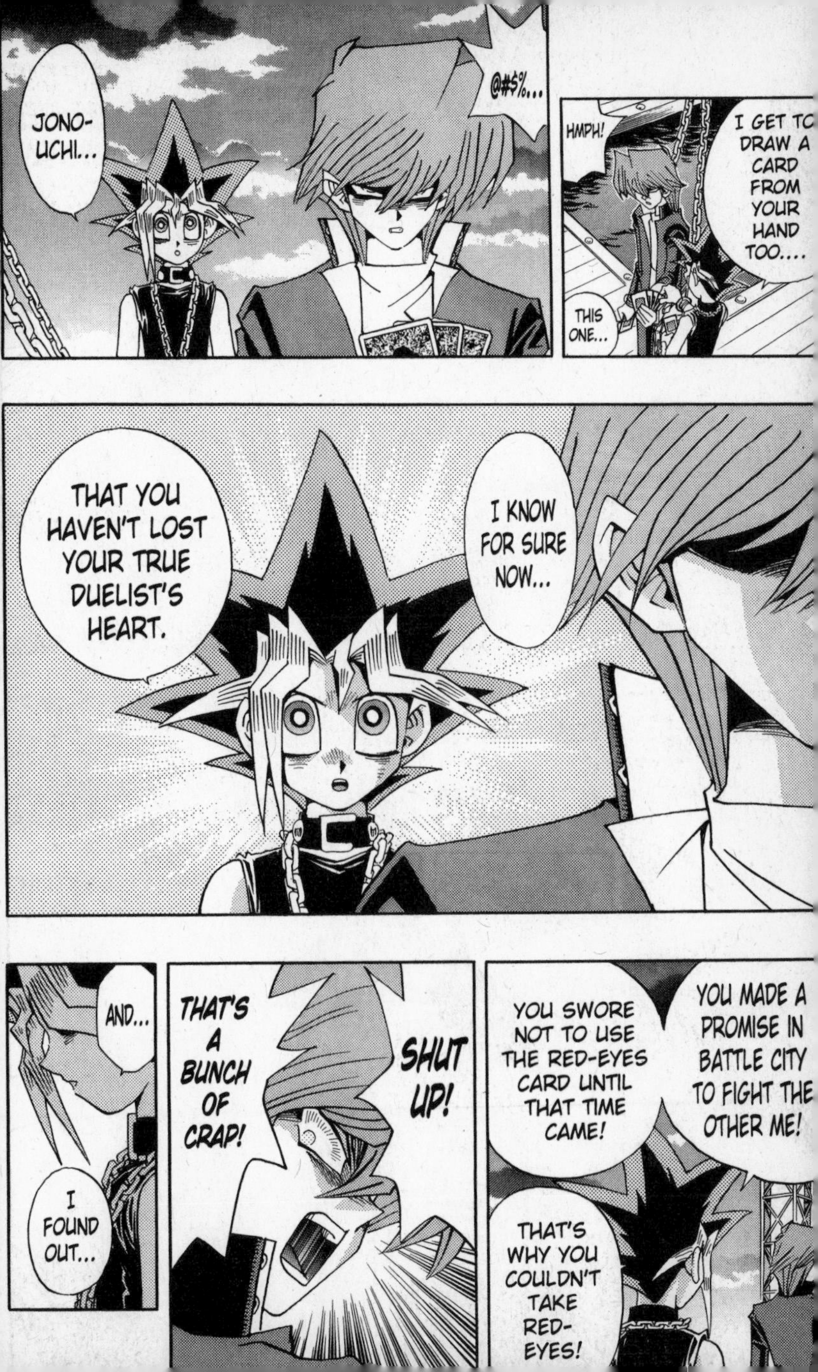
I GET TO DRAW A CARD FROM YOUR HAND TOO....
HMPH!
THIS ONE...
@#$%...
JONO-UCHI...
I KNOW FOR SURE NOW...
THAT YOU HAVEN'T LOST YOUR TRUE DUELIST'S HEART.
YOU MADE A PROMISE IN BATTLE CITY TO FIGHT THE OTHER ME!
YOU SWORE NOT TO USE THE RED-EYES CARD UNTIL THAT TIME CAME!
THAT'S WHY YOU COULDN'T TAKE RED-EYES!
SHUT UP!
THAT'S A BUNCH OF CRAP!
AND...
I FOUND OUT...

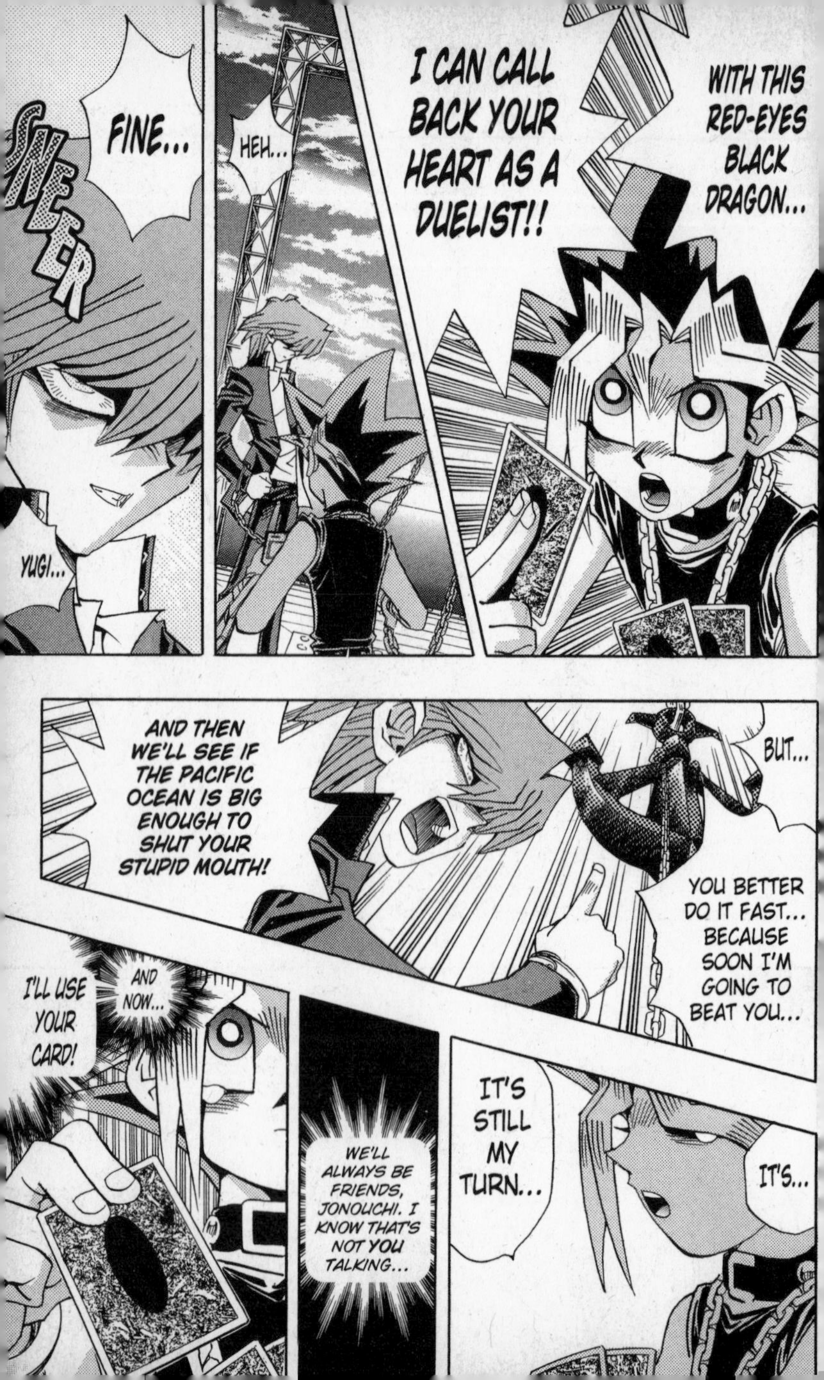
WITH THIS RED-EYES BLACK DRAGON...
I CAN CALL BACK YOUR HEART AS A DUELIST!!
HEH...
FINE...
SNEER
YUGI...
BUT...
YOU BETTER DO IT FAST... BECAUSE SOON I'M GOING TO BEAT YOU...
AND THEN WE'LL SEE IF THE PACIFIC OCEAN IS BIG ENOUGH TO SHUT YOUR STUPID MOUTH!
IT'S...
IT'S STILL MY TURN...
WE'LL ALWAYS BE FRIENDS, JONOUCHI. I KNOW THAT'S NOT YOU TALKING...
AND NOW...
I'LL USE YOUR CARD!

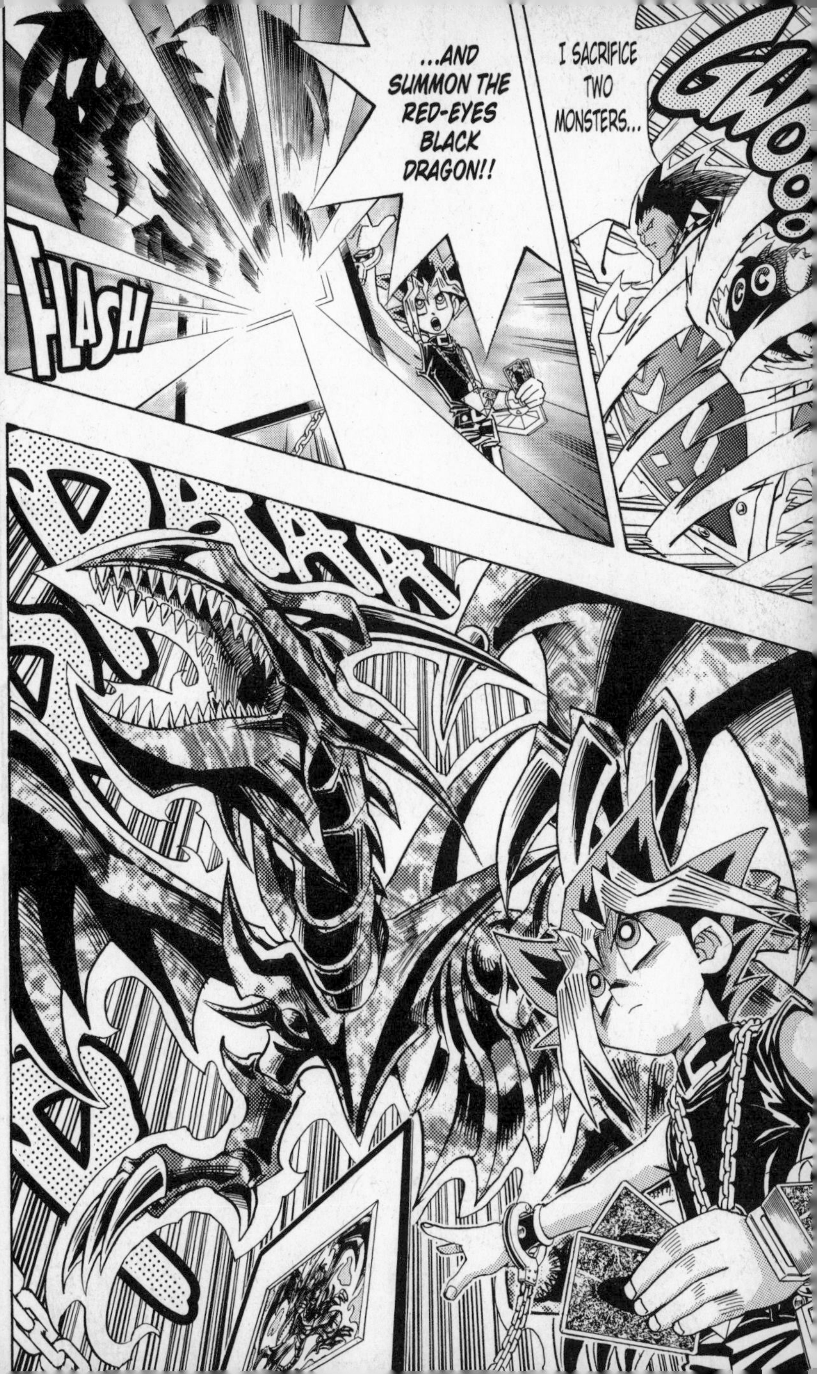
I SACRIFICE TWO MONSTERS...
...AND SUMMON THE RED-EYES BLACK DRAGON!!
FLASH

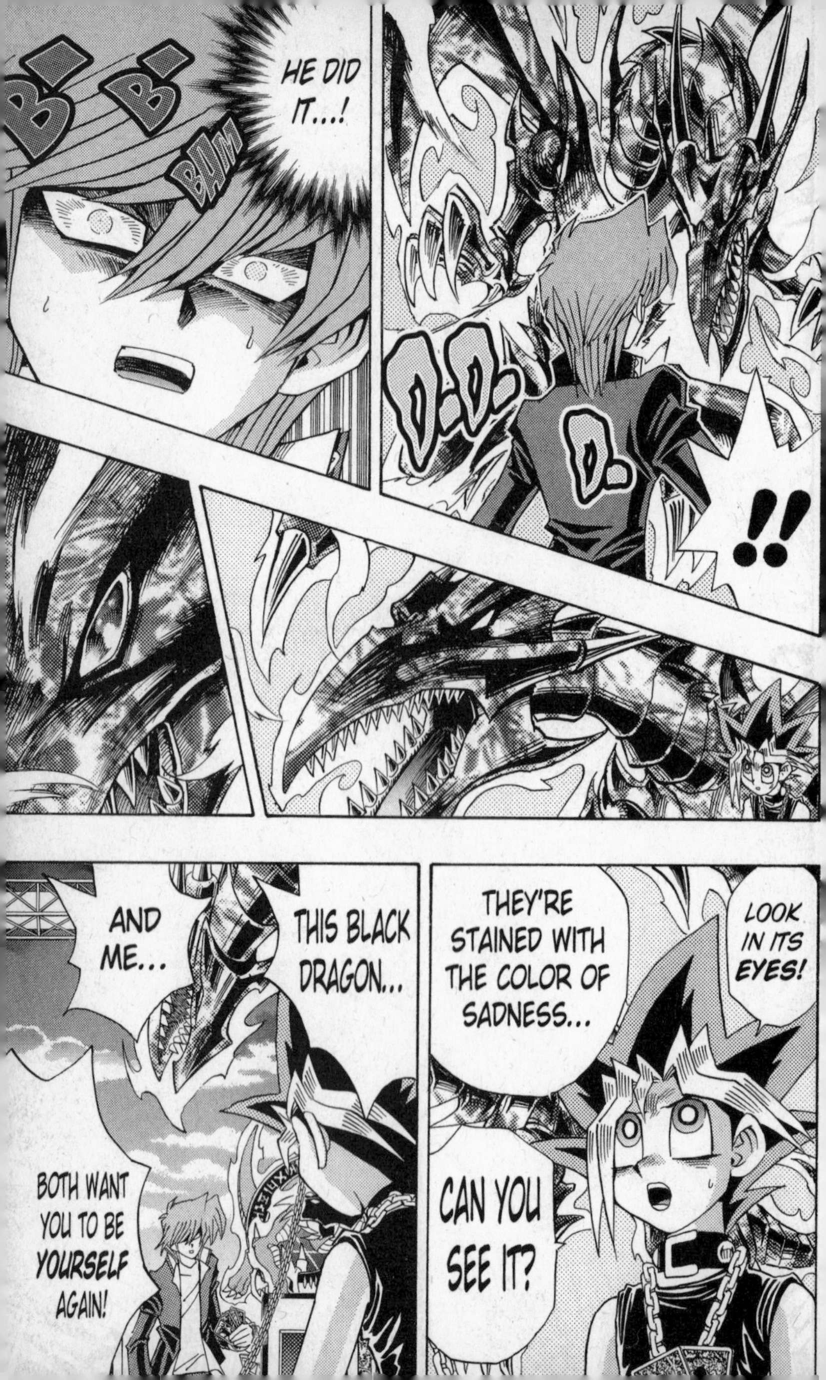
D. D.
D.
!!
B B BAM
HE DID IT...!
LOOK IN ITS EYES!
THEY'RE STAINED WITH THE COLOR OF SADNESS...
CAN YOU SEE IT?
THIS BLACK DRAGON...
AND ME...
BOTH WANT YOU TO BE YOURSELF AGAIN!

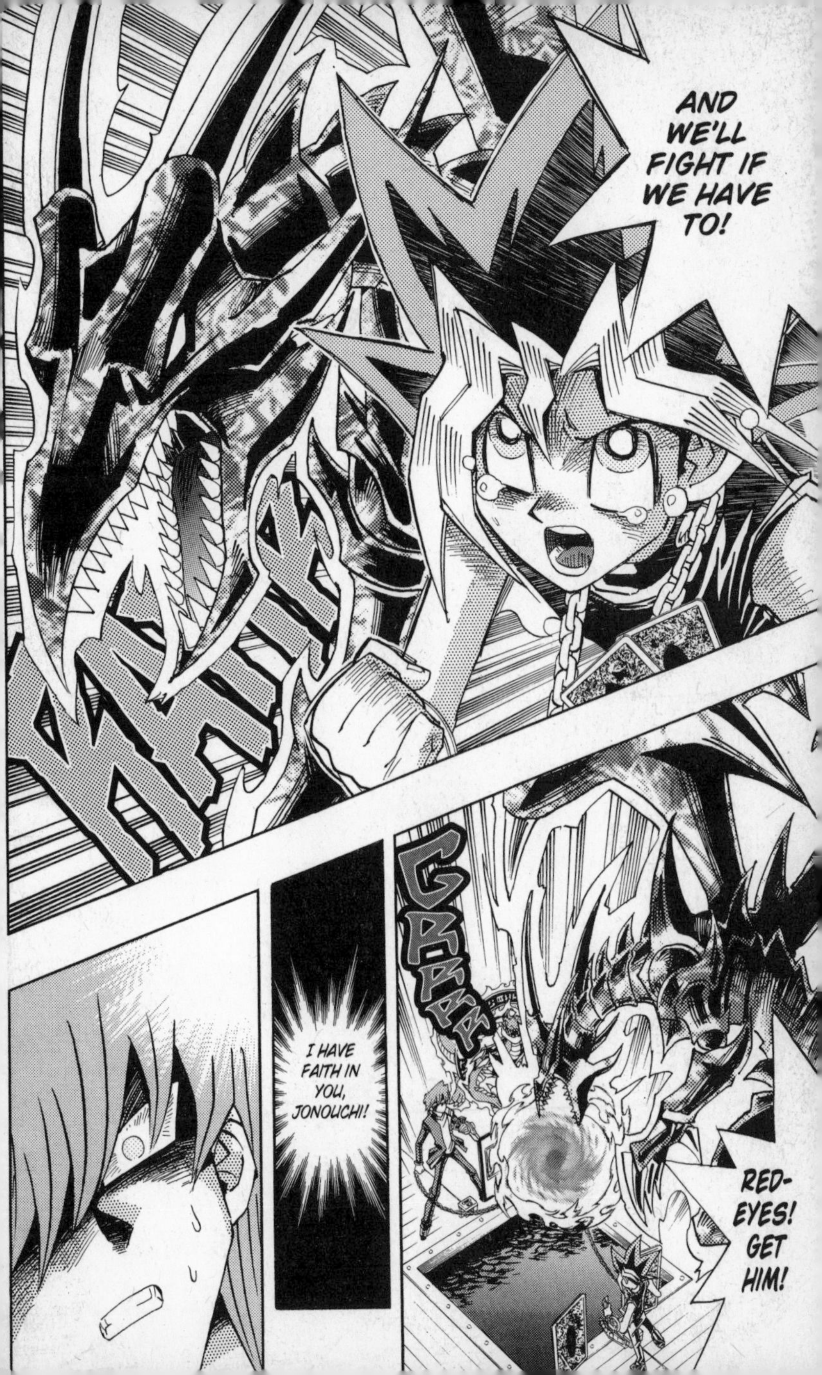
AND WE'LL FIGHT IF WE HAVE TO!
RED-EYES! GET HIM!
GRRRR
I HAVE FAITH IN YOU, JONOUCHI!

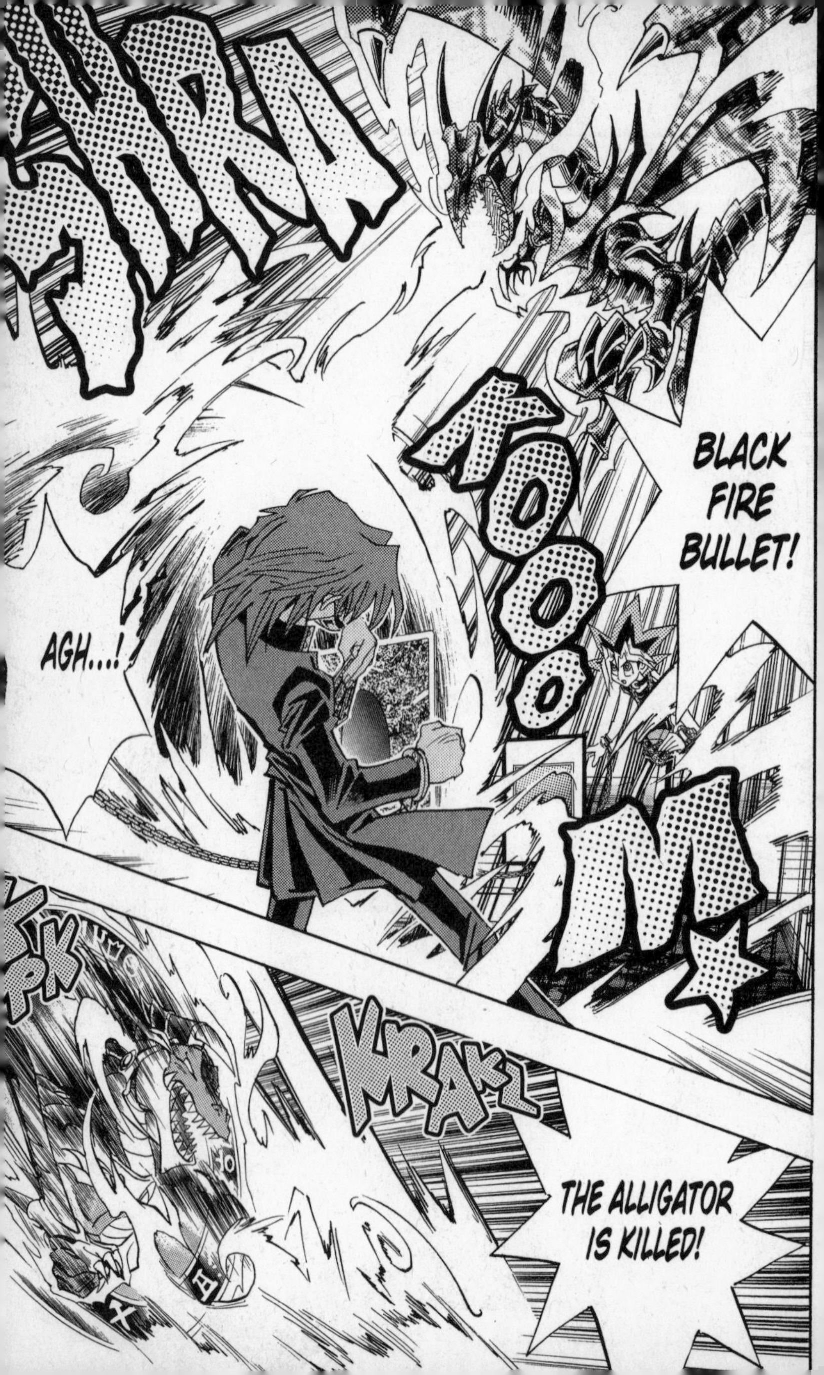
BLACK FIRE BULLET!
KOOOOM
AGH...!
THE ALLIGATOR IS KILLED!
KRAK

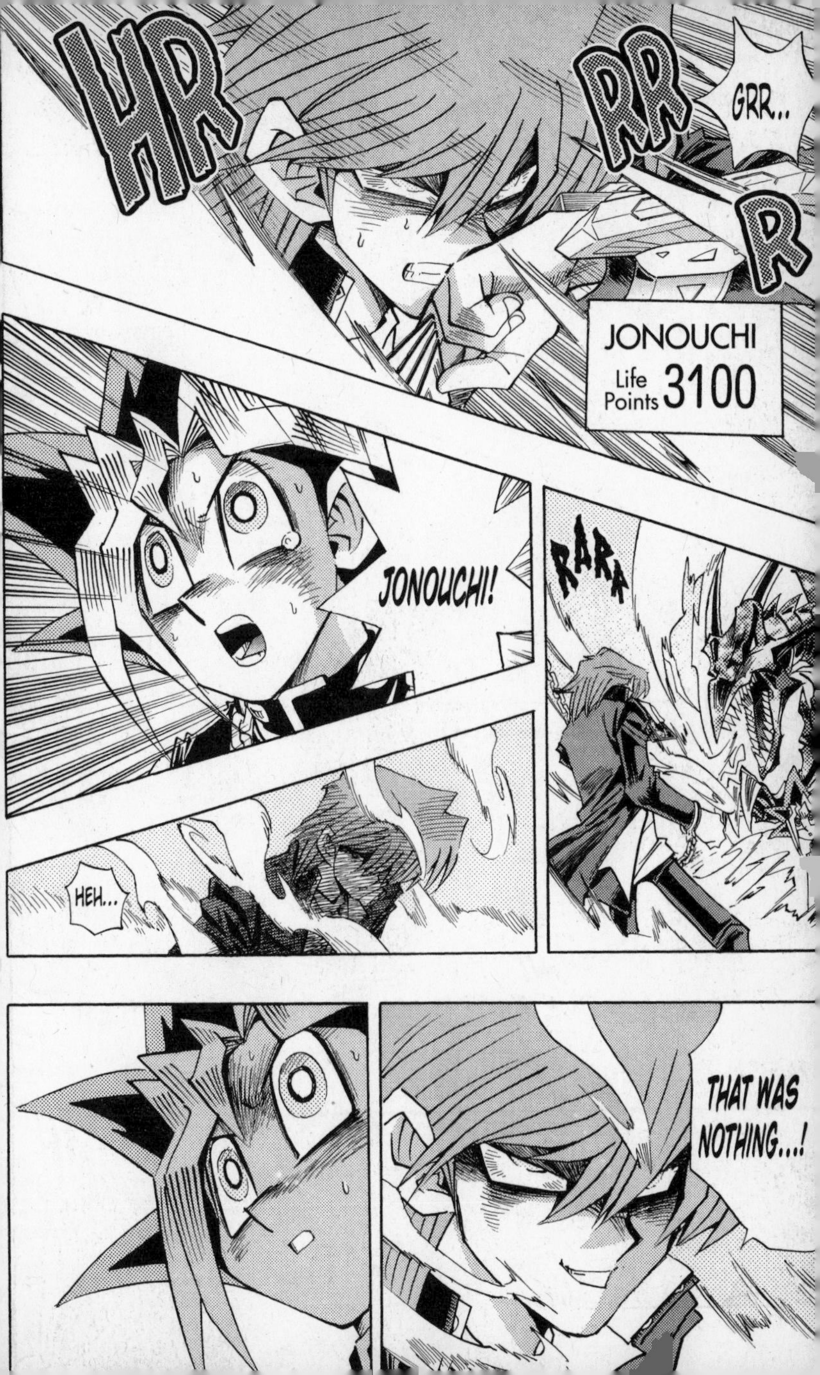
GRR...
HR
RR
R
JONOUCHI
Life Points 3100
RARA
JONOUCHI!
HEH...
THAT WAS NOTHING...!

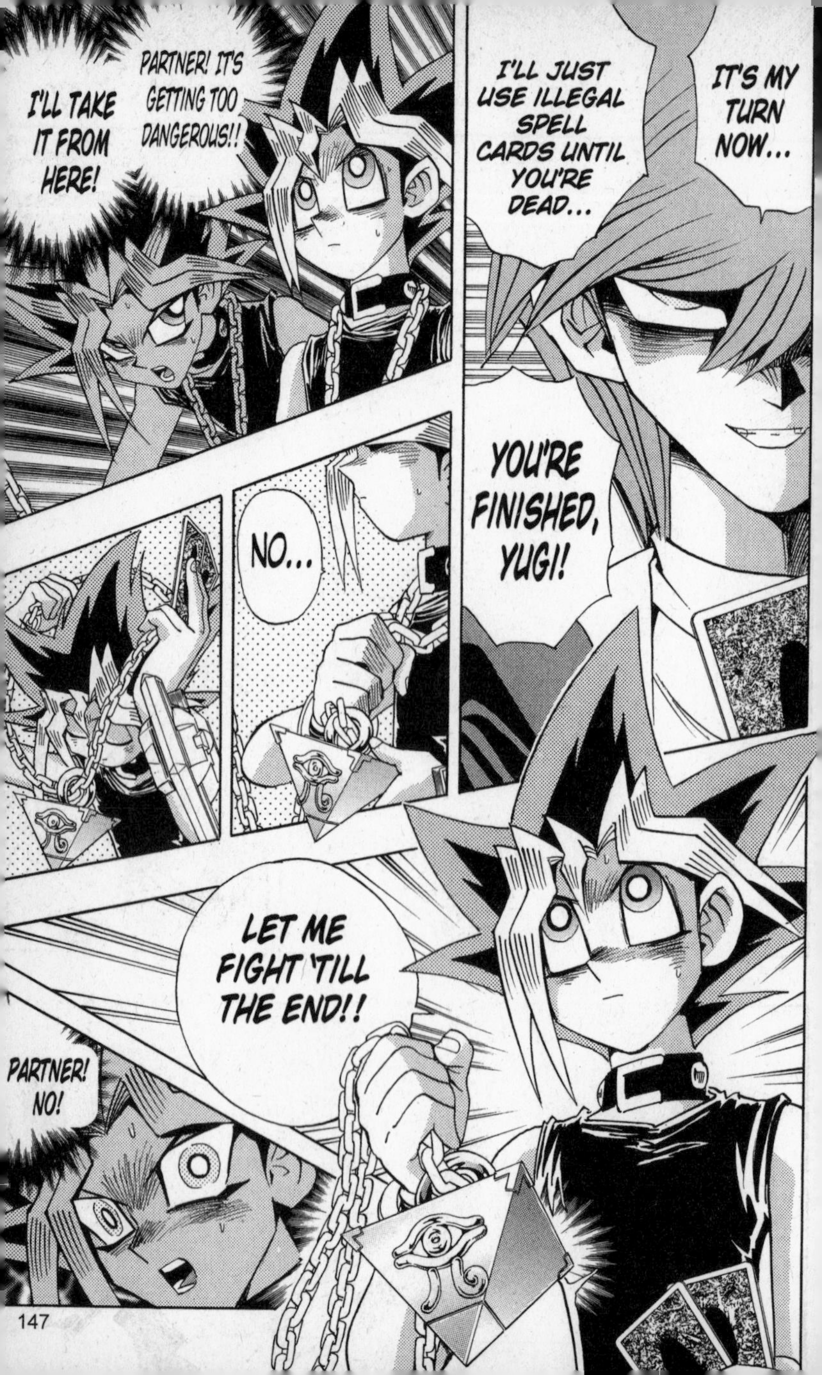
IT'S MY TURN NOW...
I'LL JUST USE ILLEGAL SPELL CARDS UNTIL YOU'RE DEAD...
YOU'RE FINISHED, YUGI!
PARTNER! IT'S GETTING TOO DANGEROUS!!
I'LL TAKE IT FROM HERE!
NO...
LET ME FIGHT 'TILL THE END!!
PARTNER! NO!

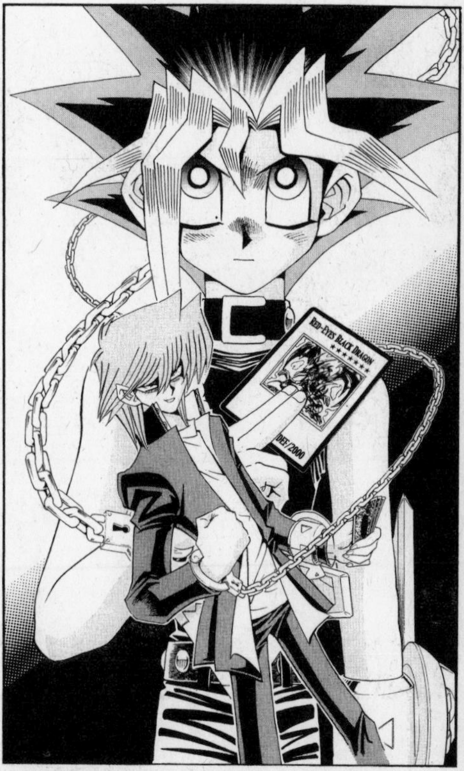
RED-EYES BLACK DRAGON
DEF/2000

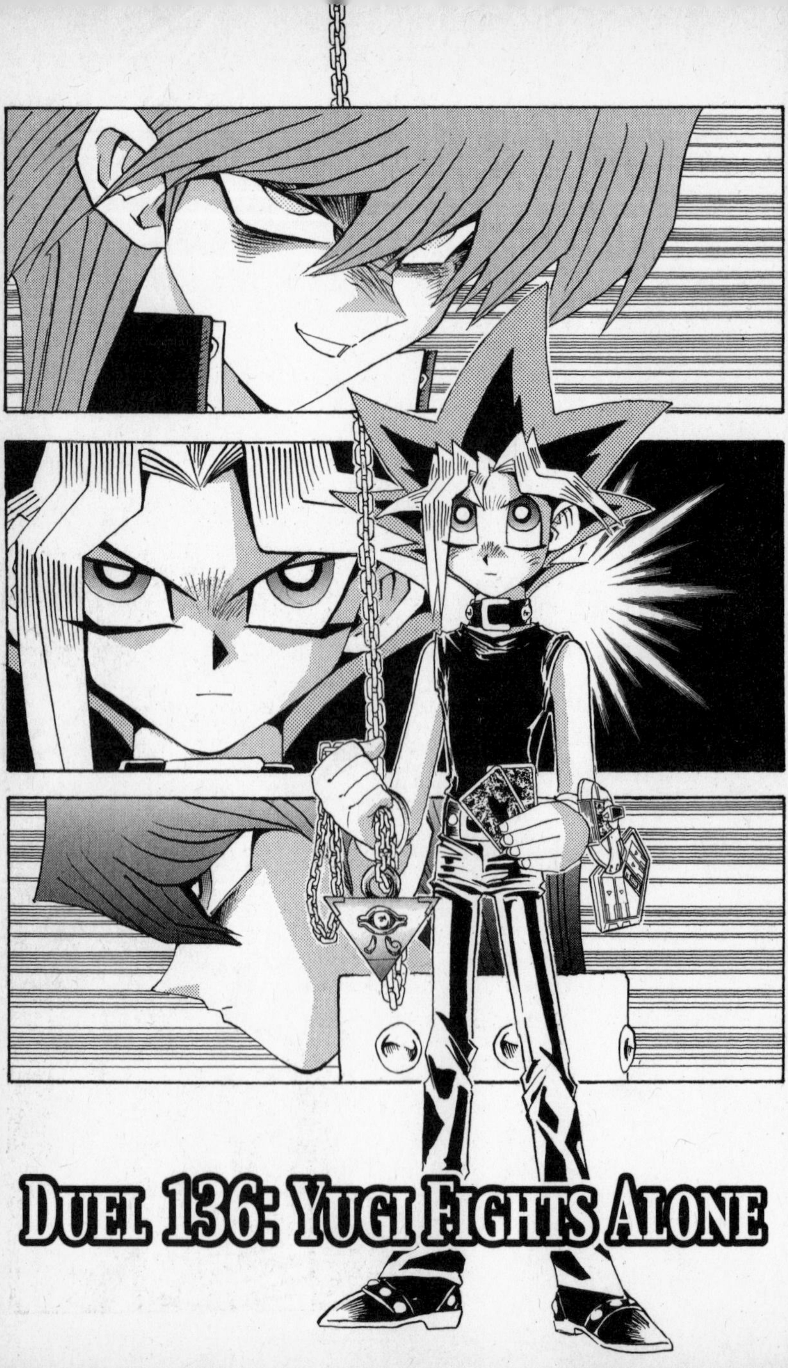
DUEL 136: YUGI FIGHTS ALONE

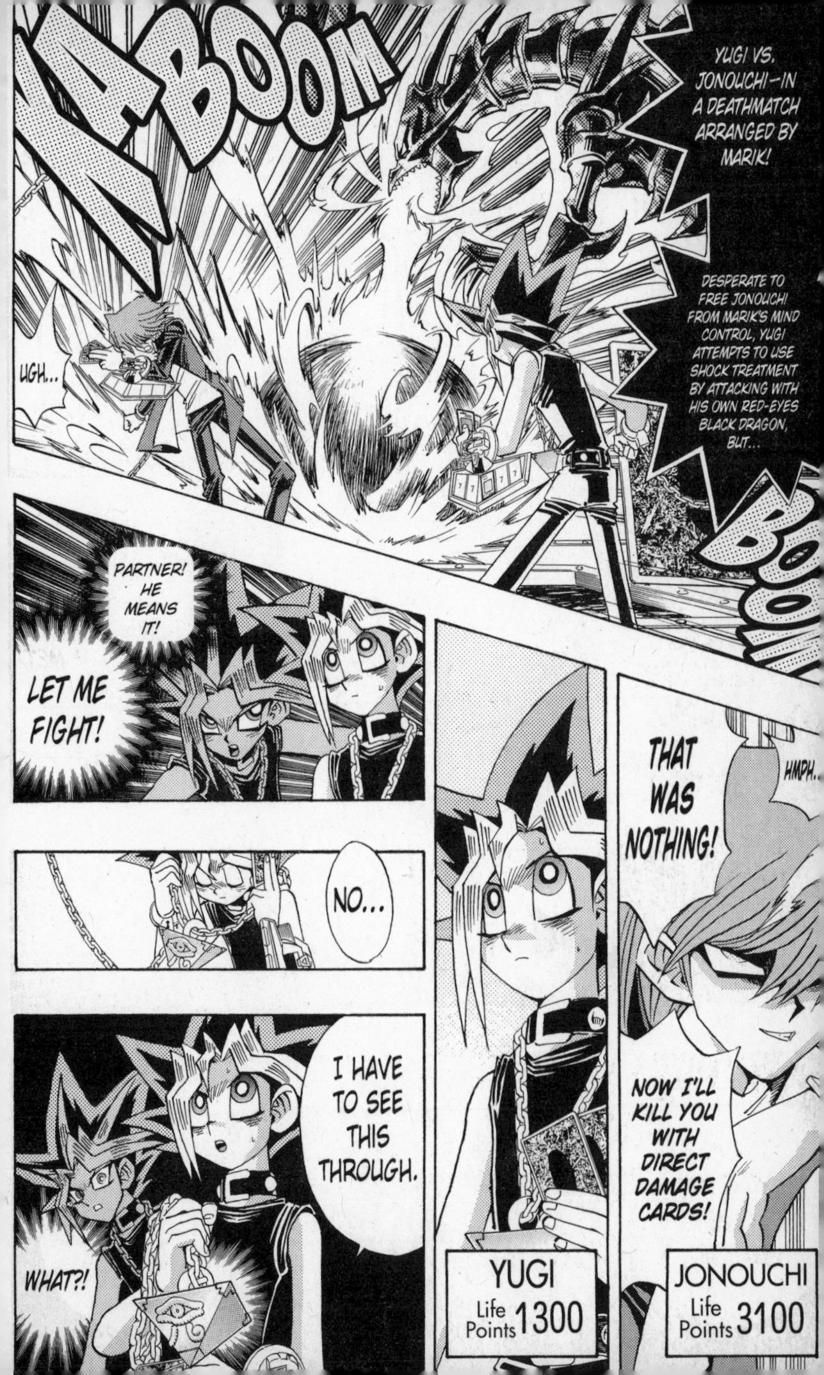
YUGI VS. JONOUCHI—IN A DEATHMATCH ARRANGED BY MARIK!
DESPERATE TO FREE JONOUCHI FROM MARIK'S MIND CONTROL, YUGI ATTEMPTS TO USE SHOCK TREATMENT BY ATTACKING WITH HIS OWN RED-EYES BLACK DRAGON, BUT...
BOOM
KA-BOOM
UGH...
HMPH.
THAT WAS NOTHING!
NOW I'LL KILL YOU WITH DIRECT DAMAGE CARDS!
JONOUCHI Life Points 3100
YUGI Life Points 1300
PARTNER! HE MEANS IT!
LET ME FIGHT!
NO...
I HAVE TO SEE THIS THROUGH.
WHAT?!

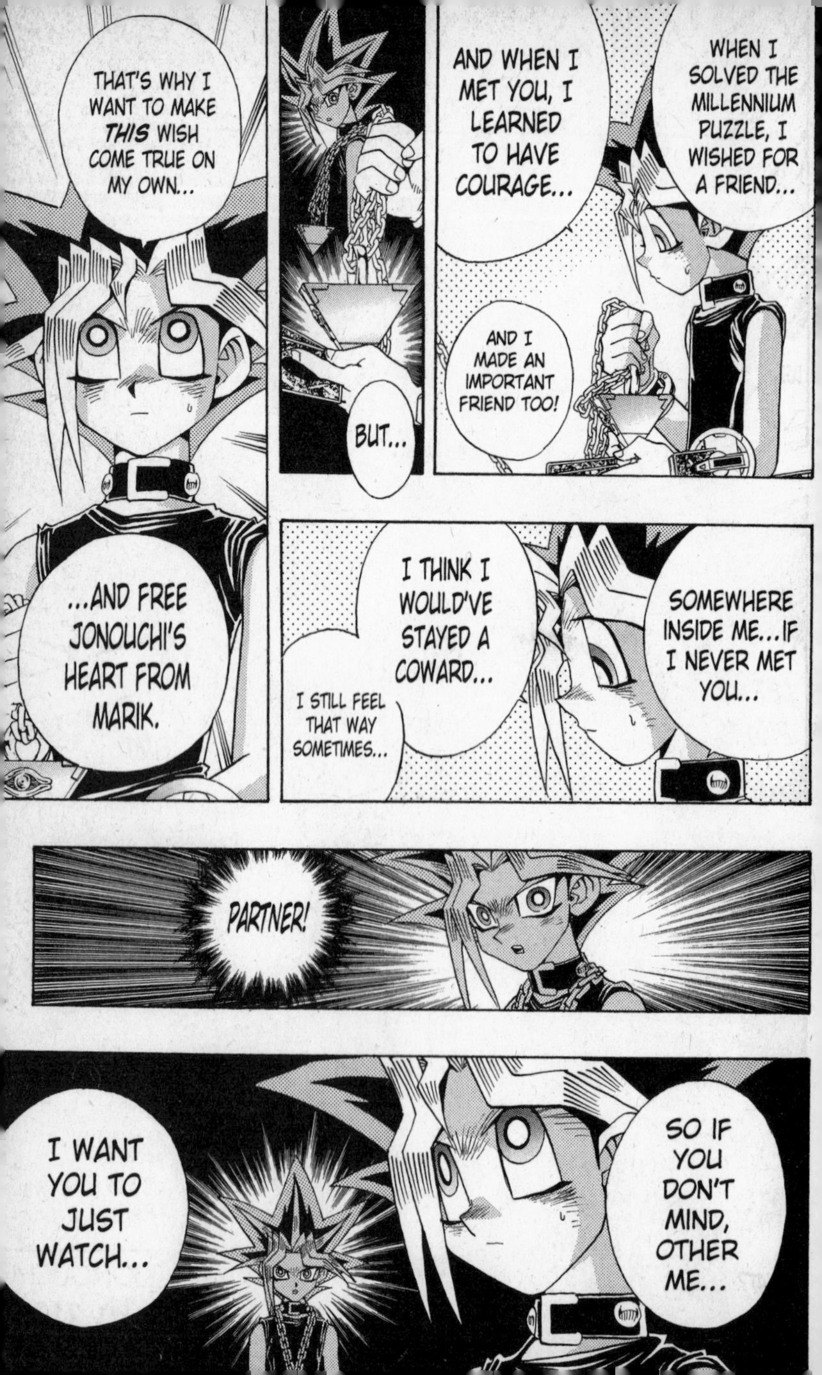
WHEN I SOLVED THE MILLENNIUM PUZZLE, I WISHED FOR A FRIEND...
AND WHEN I MET YOU, I LEARNED TO HAVE COURAGE...
AND I MADE AN IMPORTANT FRIEND TOO!
BUT...
SOMEWHERE INSIDE ME...IF I NEVER MET YOU...
I THINK I WOULD'VE STAYED A COWARD...
I STILL FEEL THAT WAY SOMETIMES...
THAT'S WHY I WANT TO MAKE *THIS* WISH COME TRUE ON MY OWN...
...AND FREE JONOUCHI'S HEART FROM MARIK.
PARTNER!
SO IF YOU DON'T MIND, OTHER ME...
I WANT YOU TO JUST WATCH...

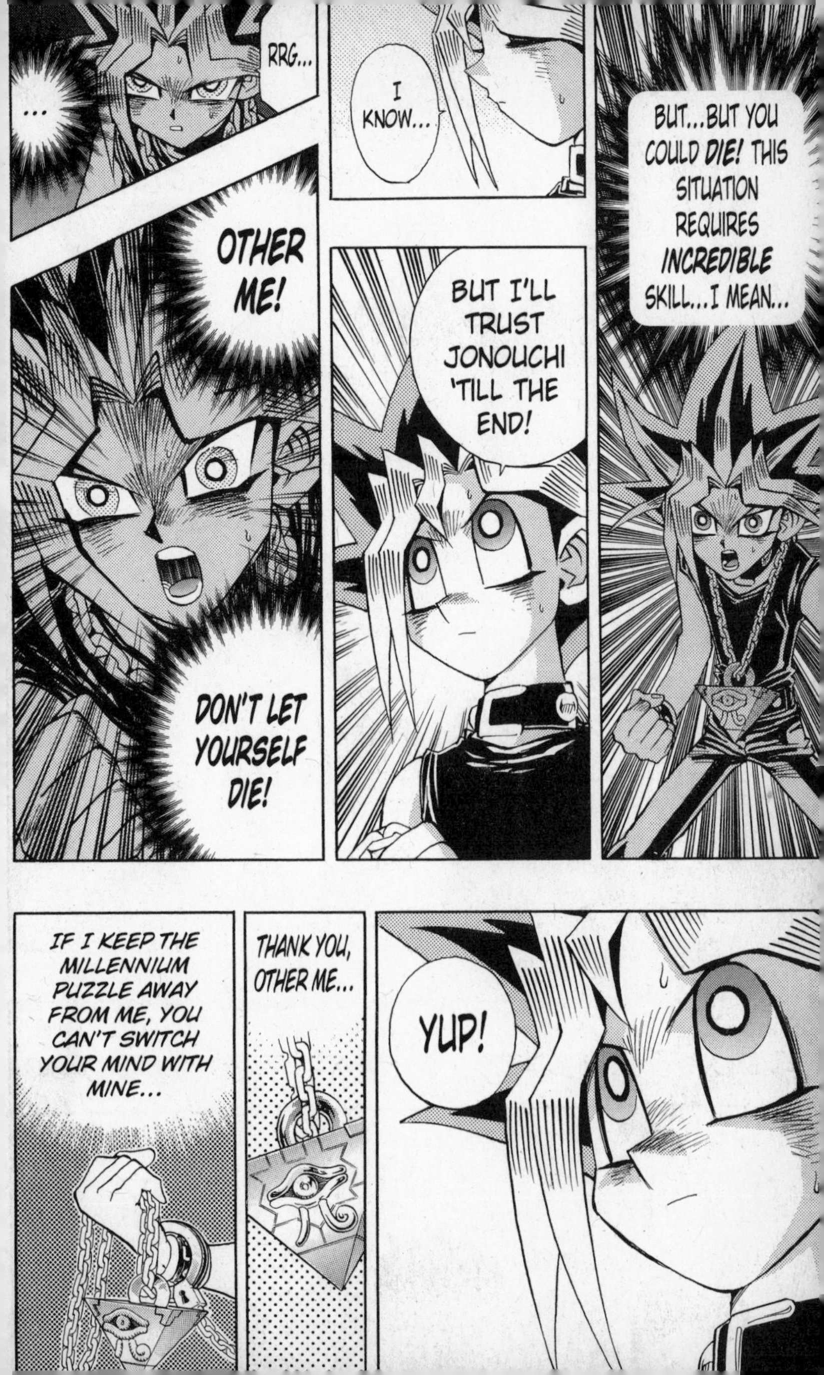
BUT...BUT YOU COULD DIE! THIS SITUATION REQUIRES INCREDIBLE SKILL...I MEAN...
I KNOW...
BUT I'LL TRUST JONOUCHI 'TILL THE END!
RRG...
...
OTHER ME!
DON'T LET YOURSELF DIE!
YUP!
THANK YOU, OTHER ME...
IF I KEEP THE MILLENNIUM PUZZLE AWAY FROM ME, YOU CAN'T SWITCH YOUR MIND WITH MINE...

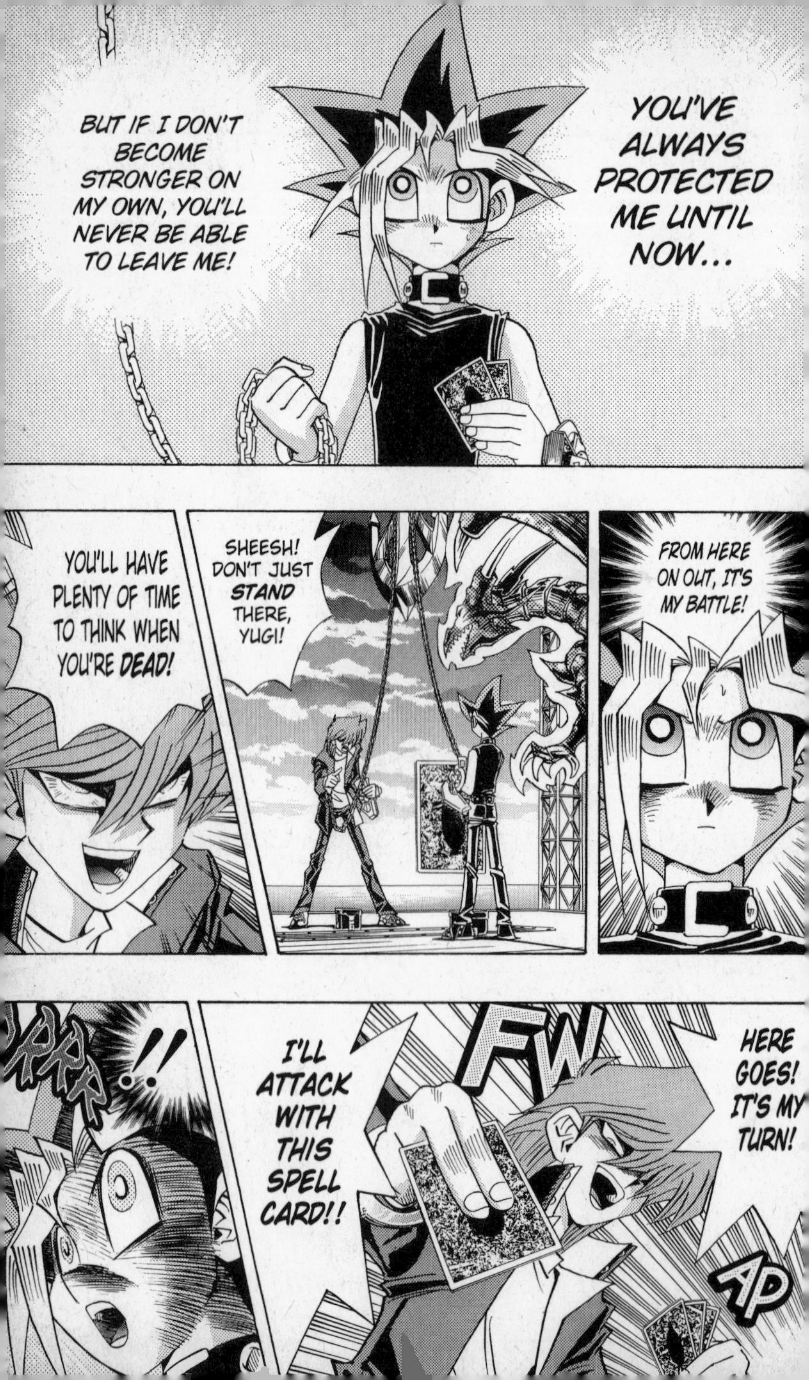
YOU'VE ALWAYS PROTECTED ME UNTIL NOW...
BUT IF I DON'T BECOME STRONGER ON MY OWN, YOU'LL NEVER BE ABLE TO LEAVE ME!
FROM HERE ON OUT, IT'S MY BATTLE!
SHEESH! DON'T JUST **STAND** THERE, YUGI!
YOU'LL HAVE PLENTY OF TIME TO THINK WHEN YOU'RE **DEAD!**
HERE GOES! IT'S MY TURN!
FW
AP
I'LL ATTACK WITH THIS SPELL CARD!!
!!

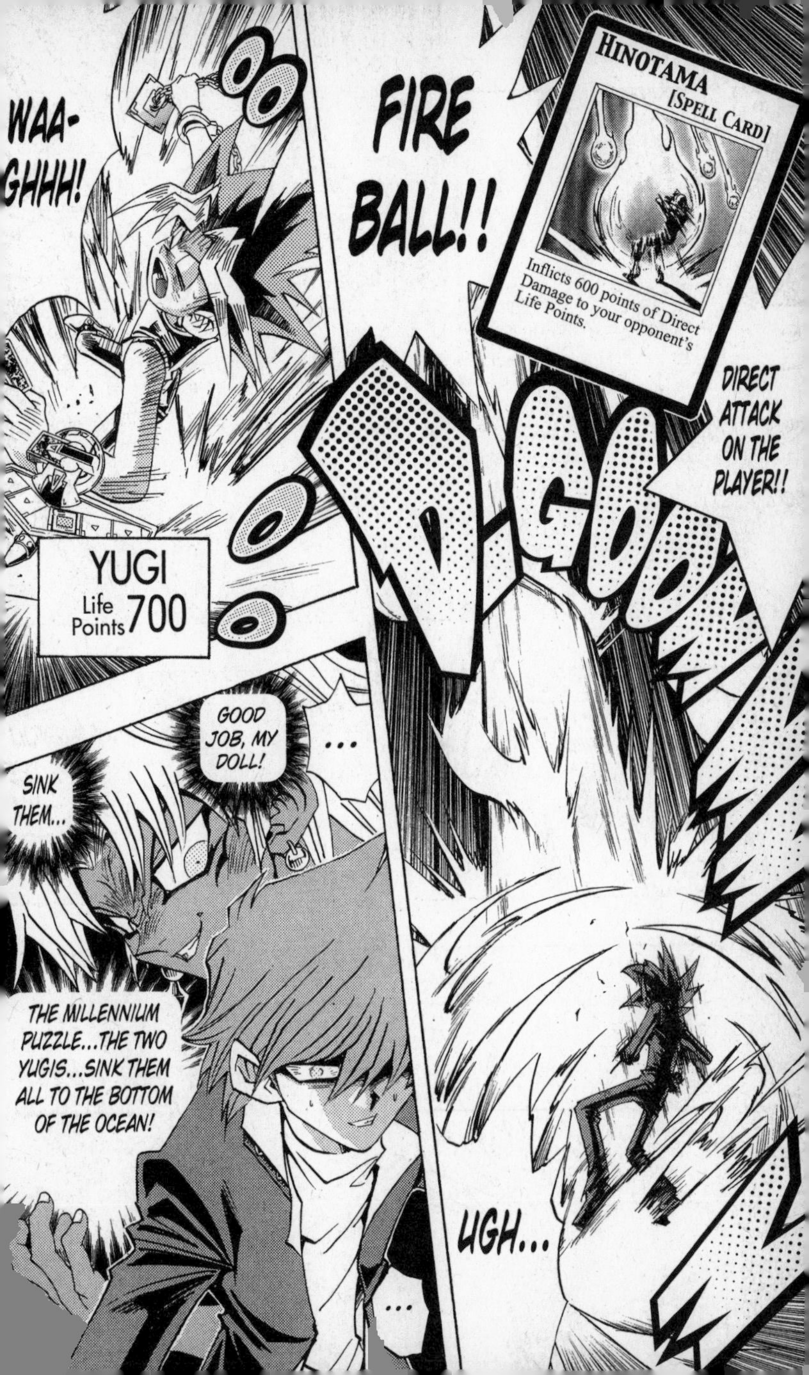
HINOTAMA
[SPELL CARD]
Inflicts 600 points of Direct Damage to your opponent's Life Points.
FIRE BALL!!
DIRECT ATTACK ON THE PLAYER!!
D-GOOM
WAA-GHHH!
YUGI
Life Points 700
UGH...
...
GOOD JOB, MY DOLL!
SINK THEM...
THE MILLENNIUM PUZZLE...THE TWO YUGIS...SINK THEM ALL TO THE BOTTOM OF THE OCEAN!
...

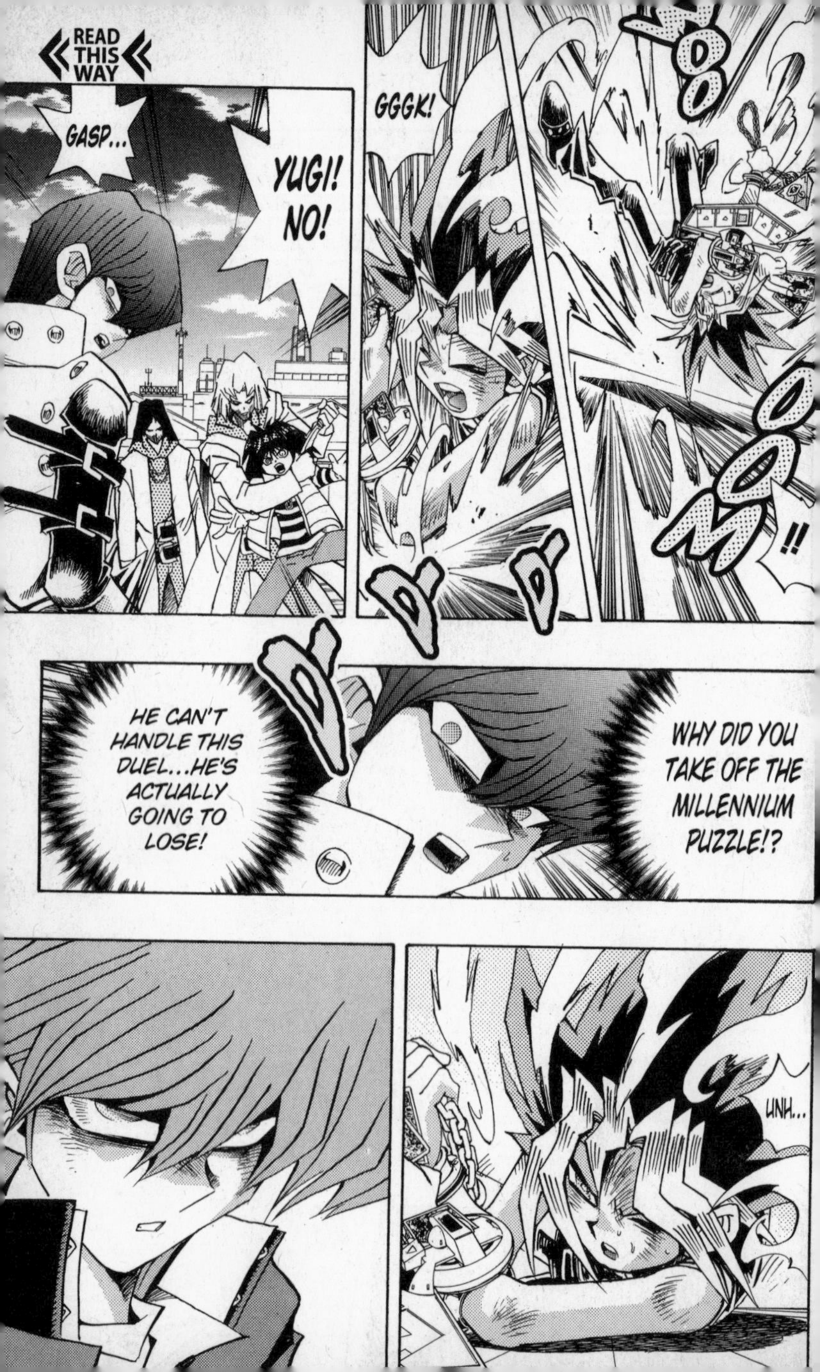
READ THIS WAY
DO
OOOM!!
GGGK!
GASP...
YUGI! NO!
WHY DID YOU TAKE OFF THE MILLENNIUM PUZZLE!?
HE CAN'T HANDLE THIS DUEL...HE'S ACTUALLY GOING TO LOSE!
UNH...

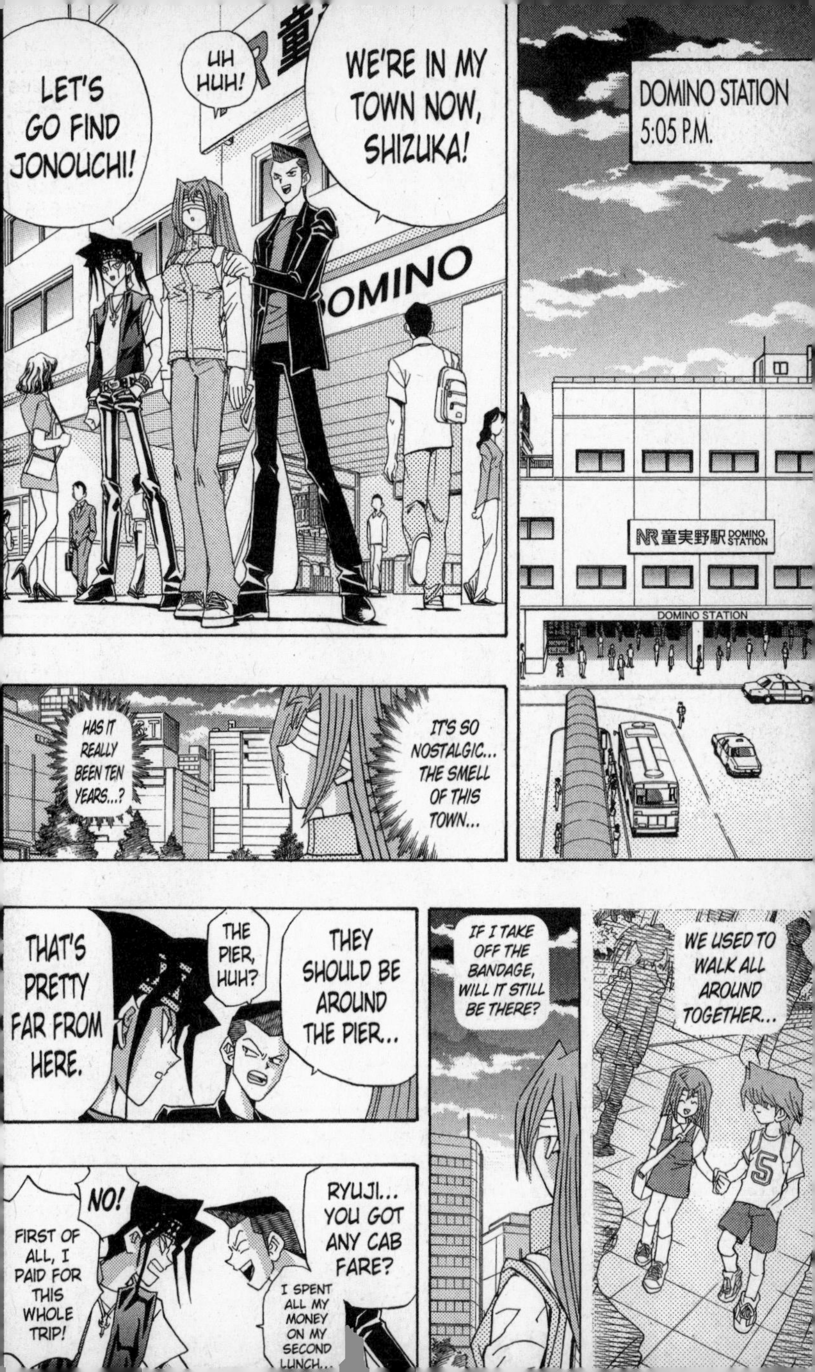
DOMINO STATION
5:05 P.M.
NR 童実野駅 DOMINO STATION
DOMINO STATION
WE'RE IN MY TOWN NOW, SHIZUKA!
UH HUH!
LET'S GO FIND JONOUCHI!
DOMINO
IT'S SO NOSTALGIC... THE SMELL OF THIS TOWN...
HAS IT REALLY BEEN TEN YEARS...?
WE USED TO WALK ALL AROUND TOGETHER...
IF I TAKE OFF THE BANDAGE, WILL IT STILL BE THERE?
THEY SHOULD BE AROUND THE PIER...
THE PIER, HUH?
THAT'S PRETTY FAR FROM HERE.
RYUJI... YOU GOT ANY CAB FARE?
I SPENT ALL MY MONEY ON MY SECOND LUNCH...
NO!
FIRST OF ALL, I PAID FOR THIS WHOLE TRIP!

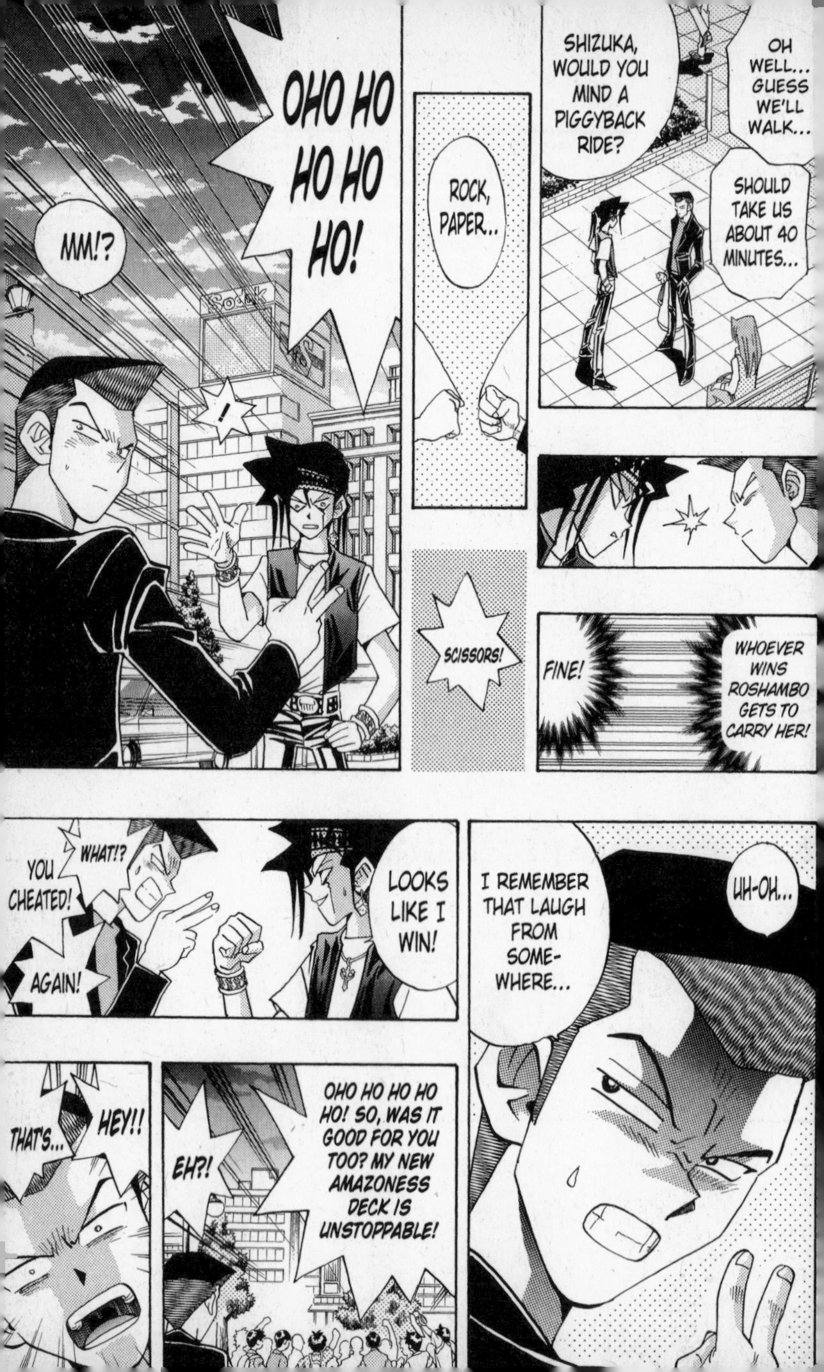
OH WELL... GUESS WE'LL WALK...
SHOULD TAKE US ABOUT 40 MINUTES...
SHIZUKA, WOULD YOU MIND A PIGGYBACK RIDE?
WHOEVER WINS ROSHAMBO GETS TO CARRY HER!
FINE!
ROCK, PAPER...
SCISSORS!
OHO HO HO HO HO!
MM!?
!
UH-OH...
I REMEMBER THAT LAUGH FROM SOME-WHERE...
LOOKS LIKE I WIN!
WHAT!?
YOU CHEATED!
AGAIN!
OHO HO HO HO HO! SO, WAS IT GOOD FOR YOU TOO? MY NEW AMAZONESS DECK IS UNSTOPPABLE!
EH?!
HEY!!
THAT'S...

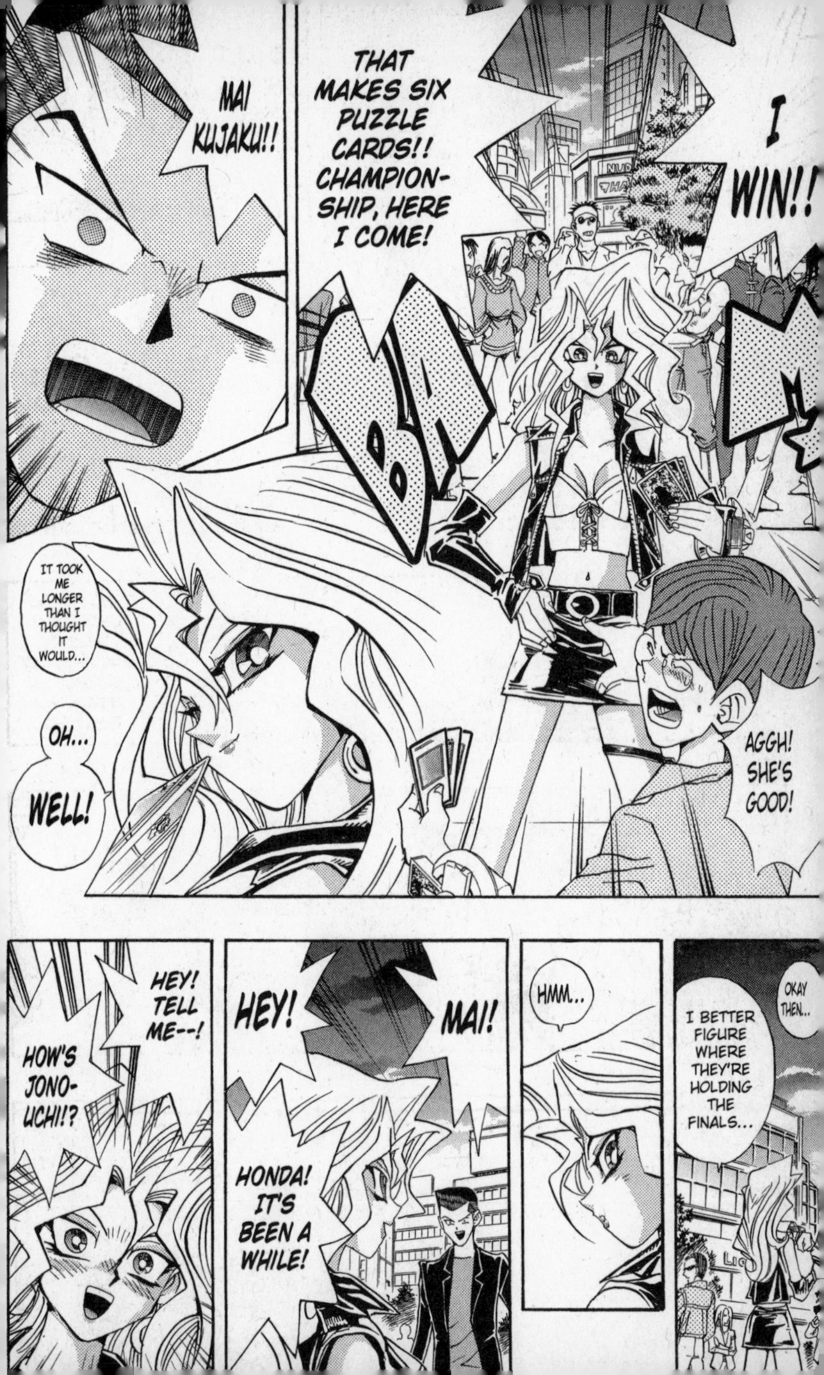

I WIN!!
M
BA
THAT MAKES SIX PUZZLE CARDS!! CHAMPION-SHIP, HERE I COME!
MAI KUJAKU!!
AGGH! SHE'S GOOD!
IT TOOK ME LONGER THAN I THOUGHT IT WOULD...
OH...
WELL!
OKAY THEN...
I BETTER FIGURE WHERE THEY'RE HOLDING THE FINALS...
HMM...
MAI!
HEY!
HONDA! IT'S BEEN A WHILE!
HEY! TELL ME--!
HOW'S JONO-UCHI!?

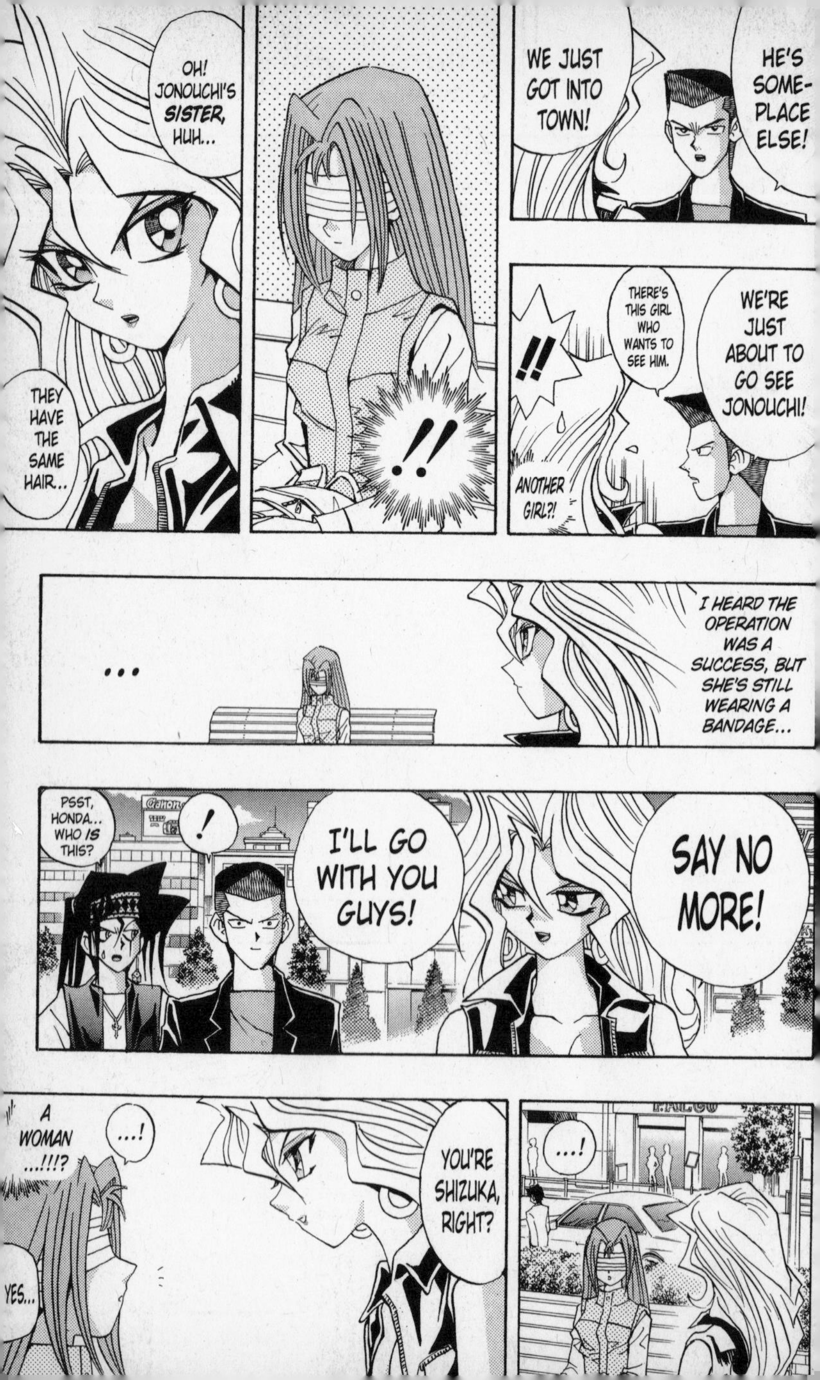
HE'S SOME-PLACE ELSE!
WE JUST GOT INTO TOWN!
WE'RE JUST ABOUT TO GO SEE JONOUCHI!
THERE'S THIS GIRL WHO WANTS TO SEE HIM.
!!
ANOTHER GIRL?!
!!
OH! JONOUCHI'S SISTER, HUH...
THEY HAVE THE SAME HAIR...
I HEARD THE OPERATION WAS A SUCCESS, BUT SHE'S STILL WEARING A BANDAGE...
...
SAY NO MORE!
I'LL GO WITH YOU GUYS!
!
PSST, HONDA... WHO IS THIS?
...!
YOU'RE SHIZUKA, RIGHT?
...!
A WOMAN ...!!!?
YES...

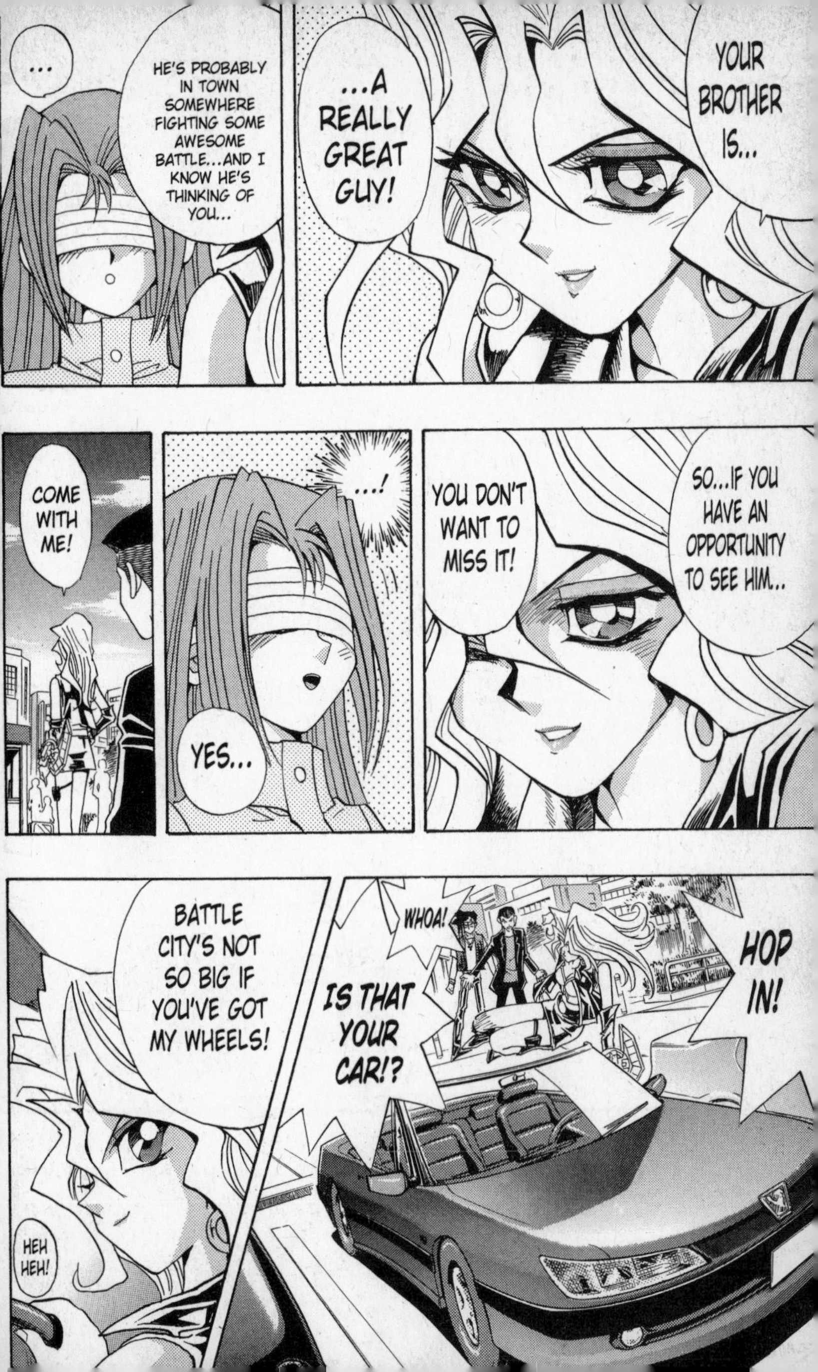
YOUR BROTHER IS...
...A REALLY GREAT GUY!
HE'S PROBABLY IN TOWN SOMEWHERE FIGHTING SOME AWESOME BATTLE...AND I KNOW HE'S THINKING OF YOU...
...
SO...IF YOU HAVE AN OPPORTUNITY TO SEE HIM...
YOU DON'T WANT TO MISS IT!
...!
YES...
COME WITH ME!
HOP IN!
WHOA!
IS THAT YOUR CAR!?
BATTLE CITY'S NOT SO BIG IF YOU'VE GOT MY WHEELS!
HEH HEH!

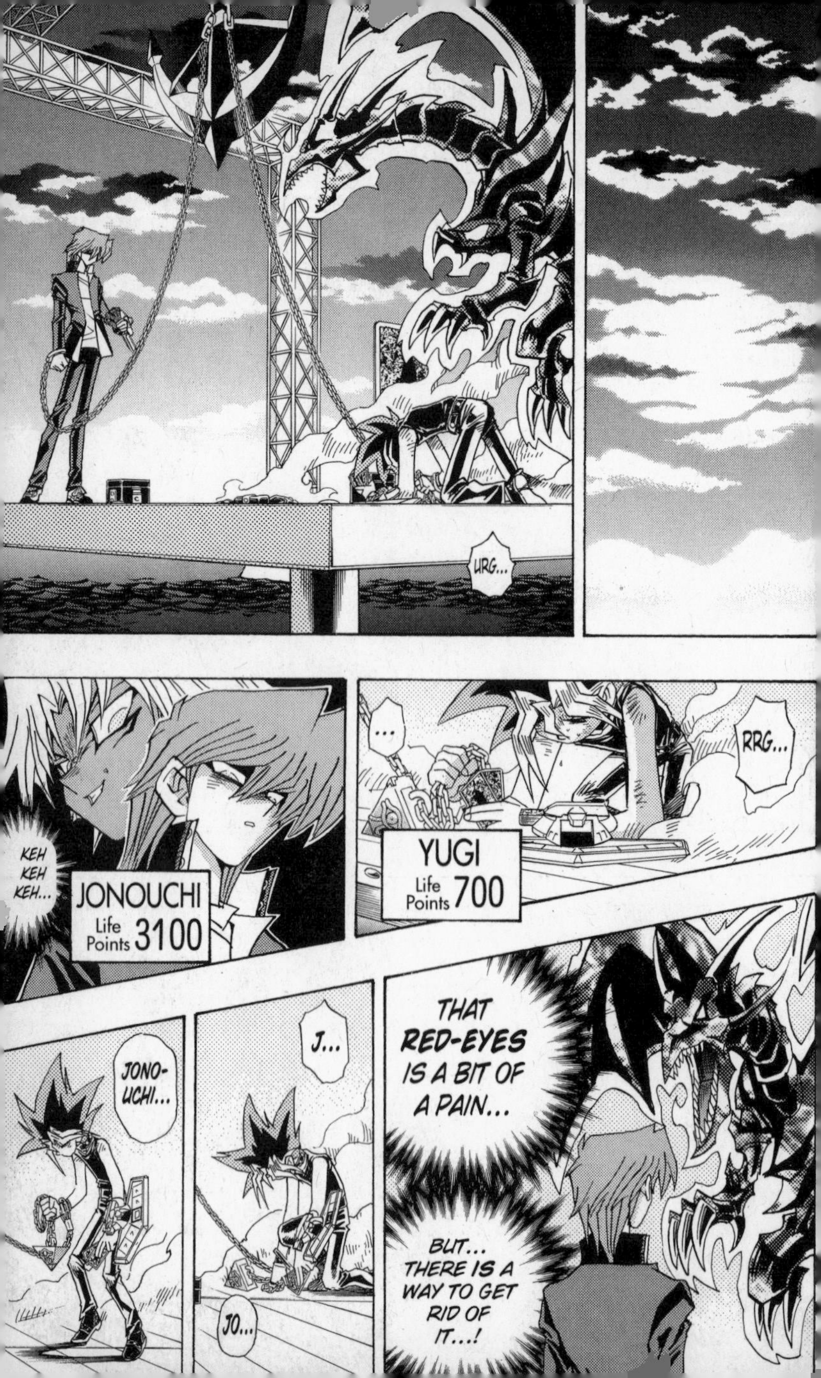
URG...
RRG...
...
YUGI Life Points 700
KEH KEH KEH...
JONOUCHI Life Points 3100
THAT RED-EYES IS A BIT OF A PAIN...
BUT... THERE IS A WAY TO GET RID OF IT...!
J...
JO...
JONO-UCHI...

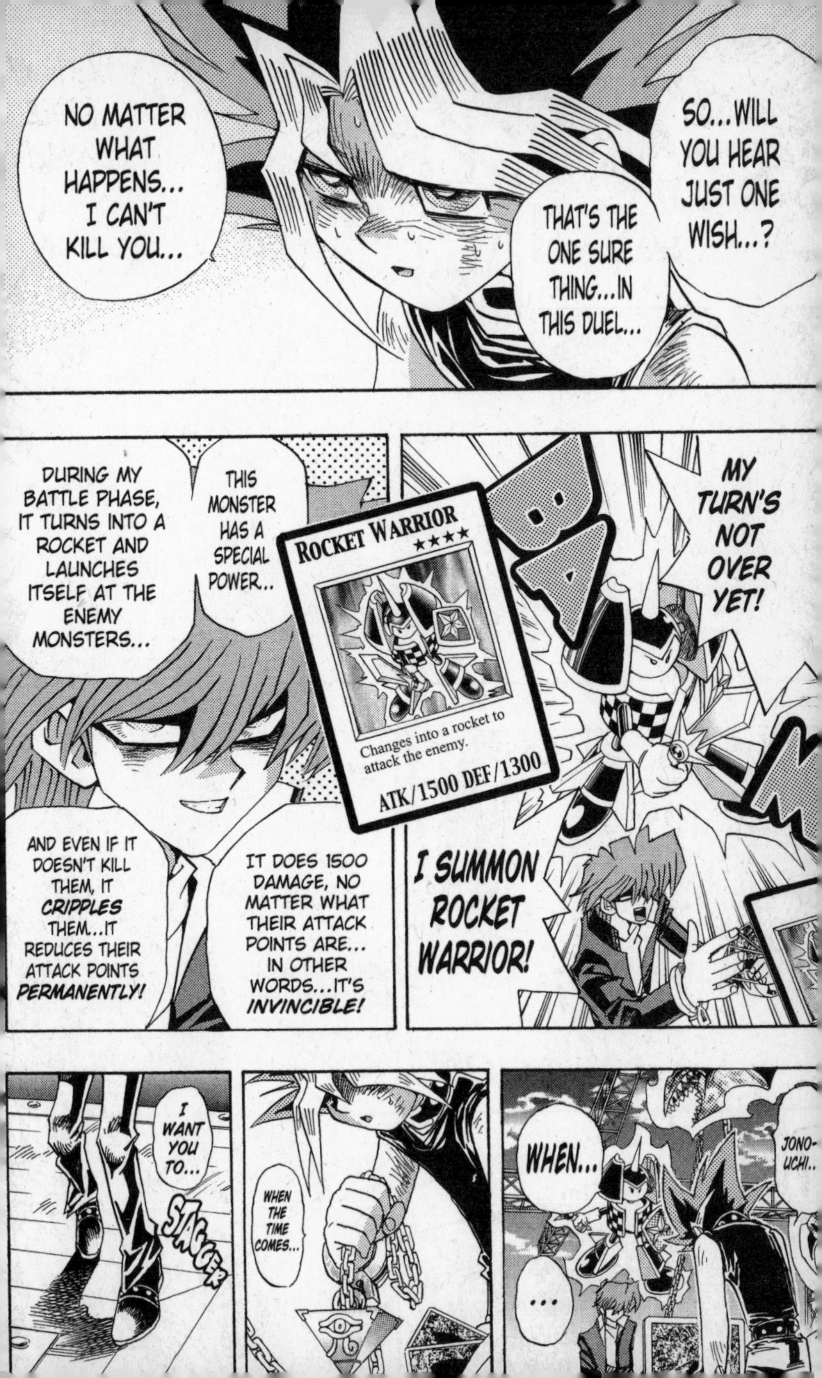
SO...WILL YOU HEAR JUST ONE WISH...?
THAT'S THE ONE SURE THING...IN THIS DUEL...
NO MATTER WHAT HAPPENS... I CAN'T KILL YOU...
MY TURN'S NOT OVER YET!
I SUMMON ROCKET WARRIOR!
ROCKET WARRIOR ★★★★
Changes into a rocket to attack the enemy.
ATK/1500 DEF/1300
THIS MONSTER HAS A SPECIAL POWER...
DURING MY BATTLE PHASE, IT TURNS INTO A ROCKET AND LAUNCHES ITSELF AT THE ENEMY MONSTERS...
IT DOES 1500 DAMAGE, NO MATTER WHAT THEIR ATTACK POINTS ARE... IN OTHER WORDS...IT'S *INVINCIBLE!*
AND EVEN IF IT DOESN'T KILL THEM, IT *CRIPPLES* THEM...IT REDUCES THEIR ATTACK POINTS *PERMANENTLY!*
JONO-UCHI..
WHEN...
...
WHEN THE TIME COMES...
I WANT YOU TO...
STAGGER

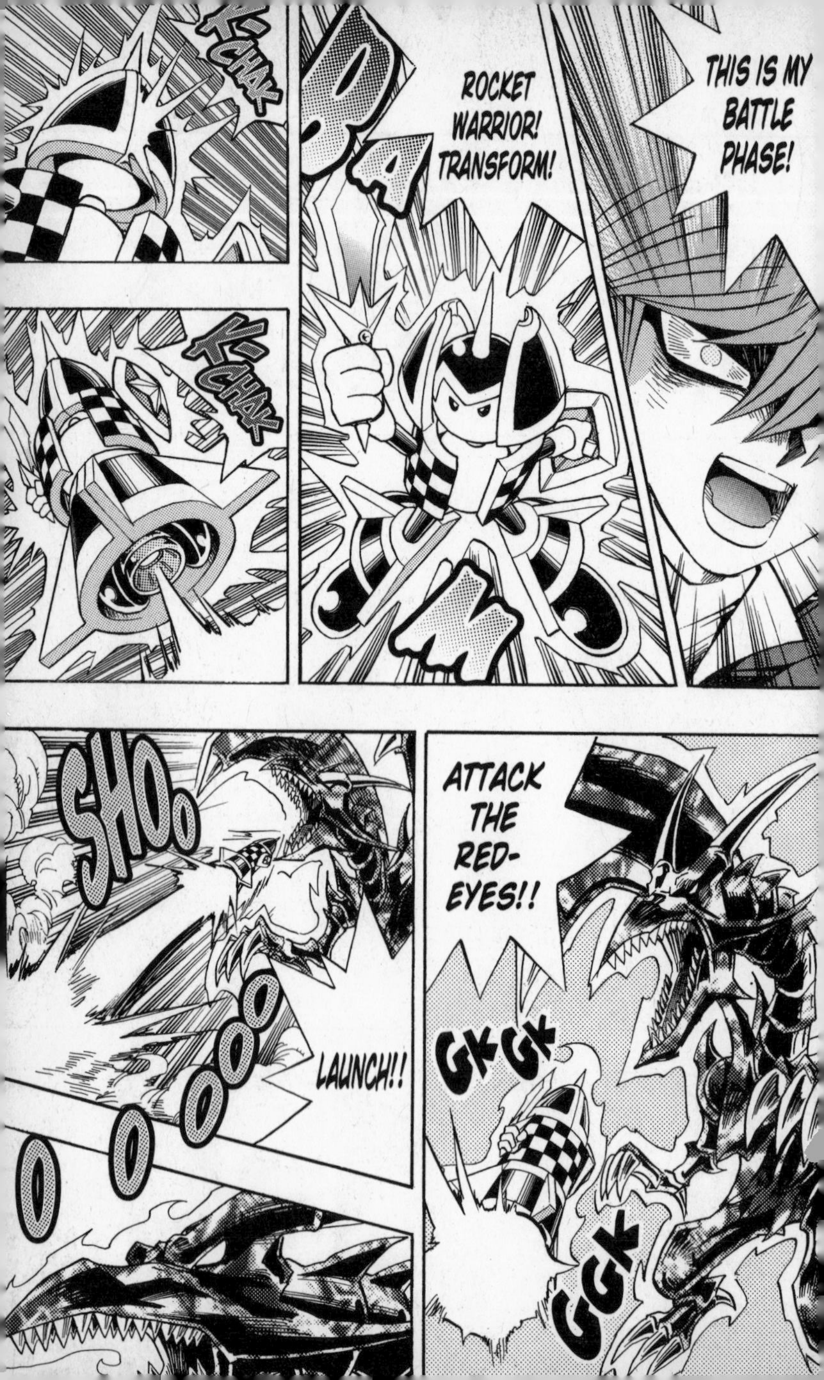
THIS IS MY BATTLE PHASE!
ROCKET WARRIOR! TRANSFORM!
BAM
K-CHAK
K-CHAK
ATTACK THE RED-EYES!!
GKGK
GGK
SHOOOOO
LAUNCH!!

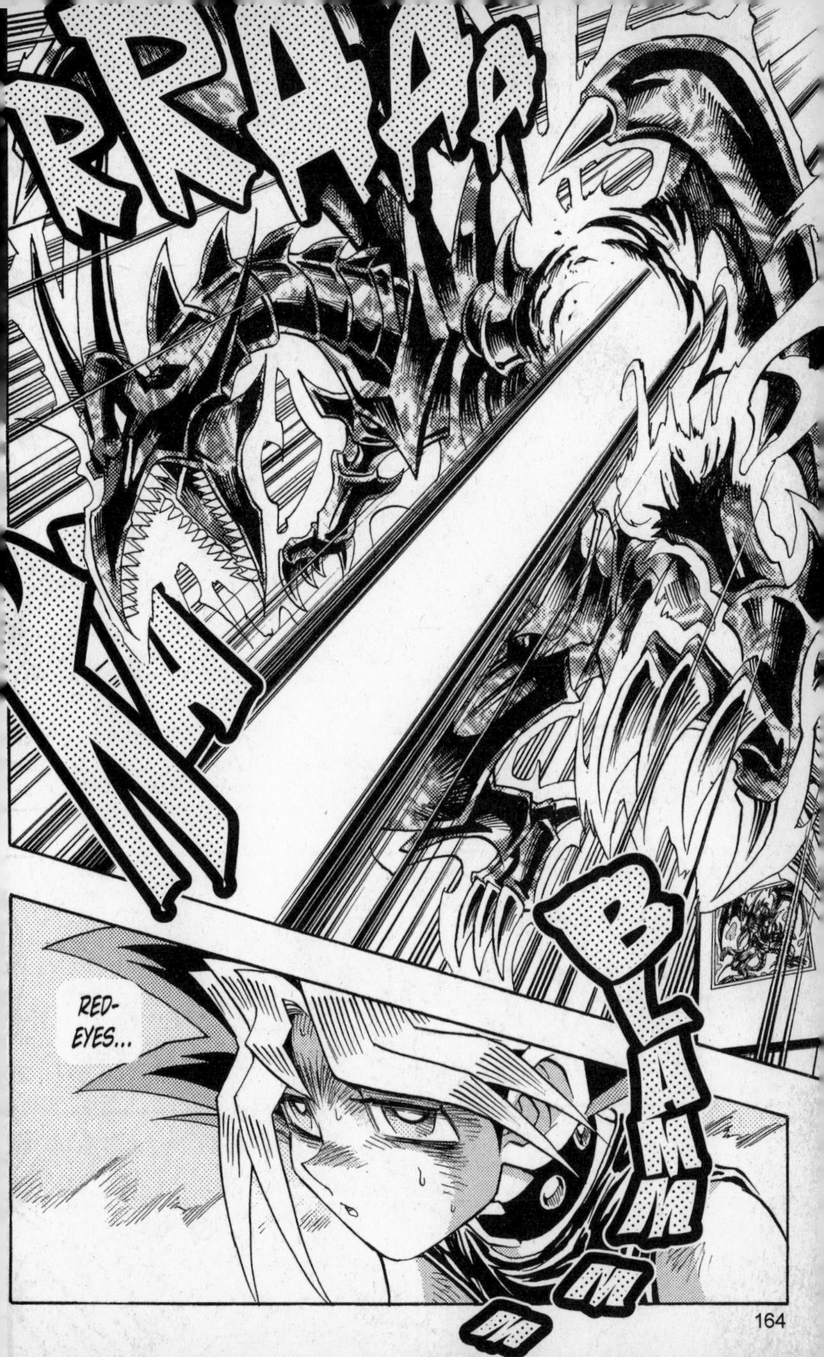
BLAMMMM
RED-EYES...

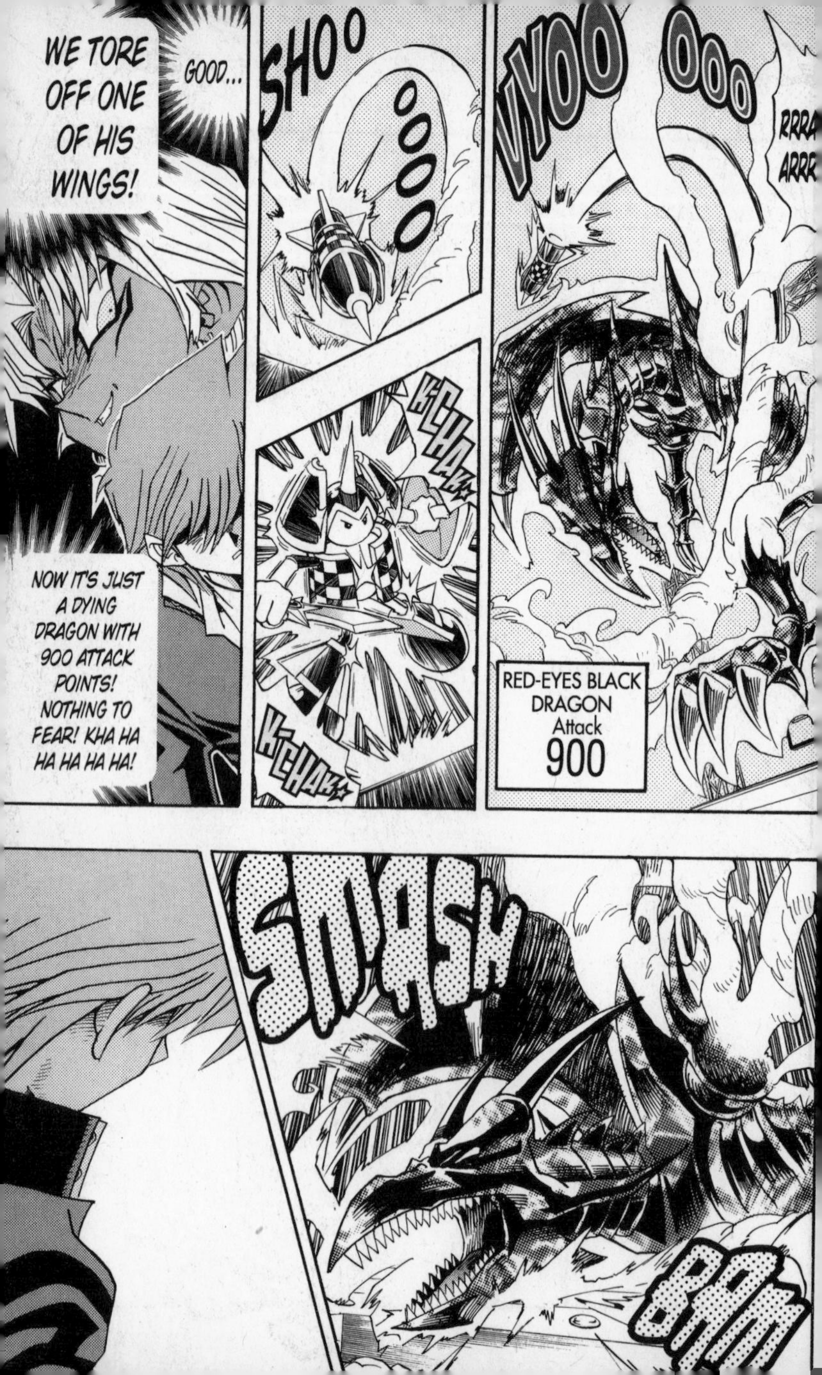
VYOO OOO
RRRA ARRR
RED-EYES BLACK DRAGON Attack 900
SHOOOOOO
K'CHAK
K'CHAK
GOOD...
WE TORE OFF ONE OF HIS WINGS!
NOW IT'S JUST A DYING DRAGON WITH 900 ATTACK POINTS! NOTHING TO FEAR! KHA HA HA HA HA HA!
SMASH
BAM

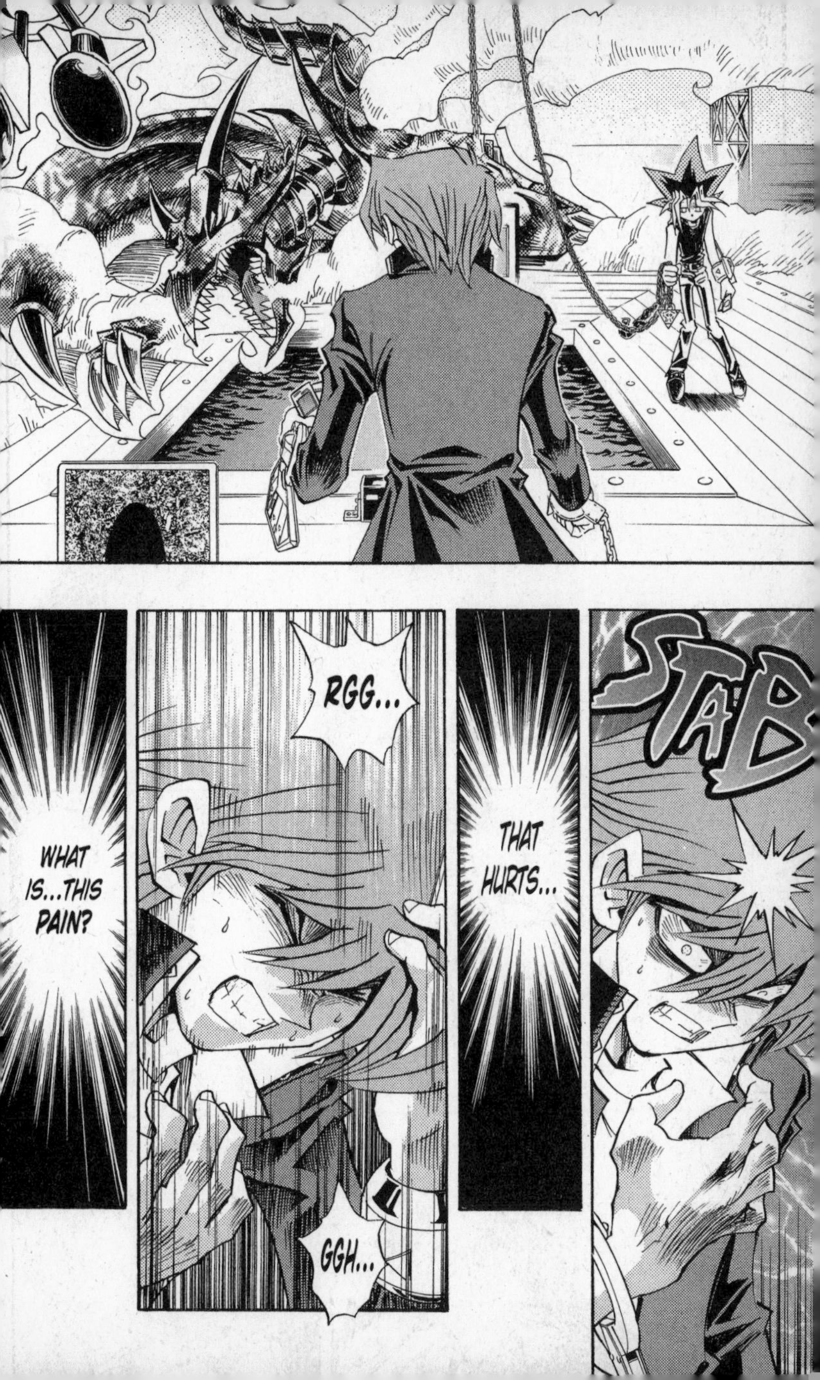
STAB
THAT HURTS...
RGG...
GGH...
WHAT IS...THIS PAIN?

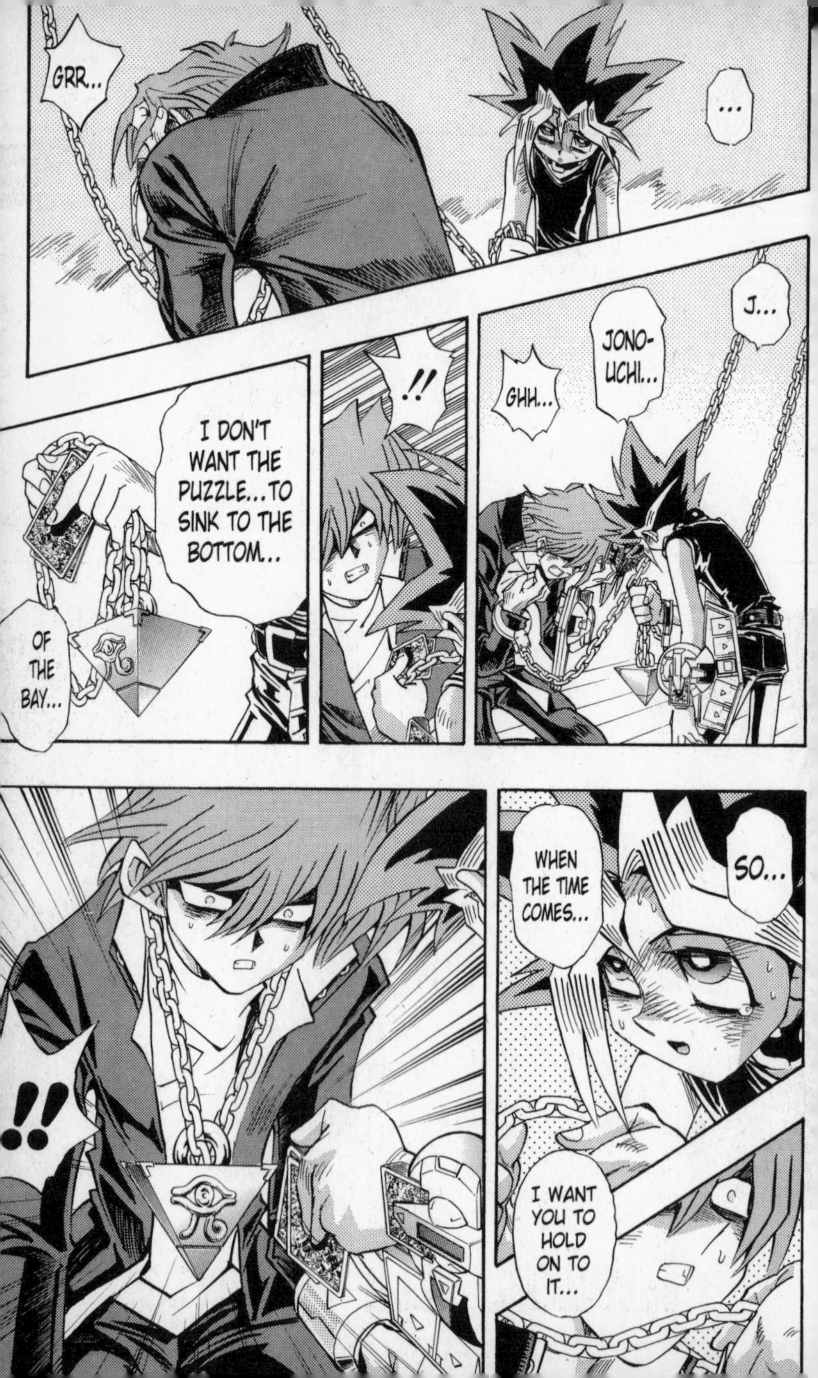
...
GRR...
J...
JONO-UCHI...
GHH...
!!
I DON'T WANT THE PUZZLE...TO SINK TO THE BOTTOM...
OF THE BAY...
SO...
WHEN THE TIME COMES...
I WANT YOU TO HOLD ON TO IT...
!!

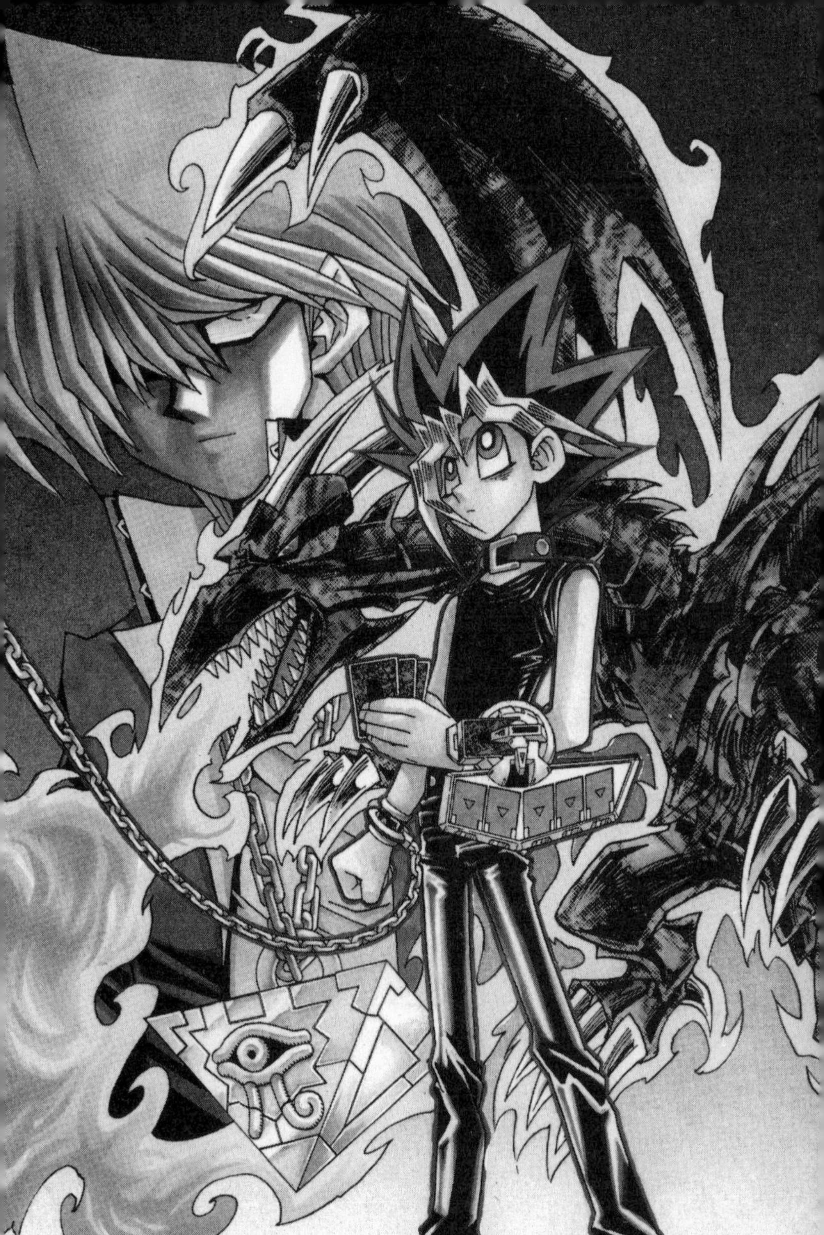

Duel 137: The Last Piece of the Puzzle

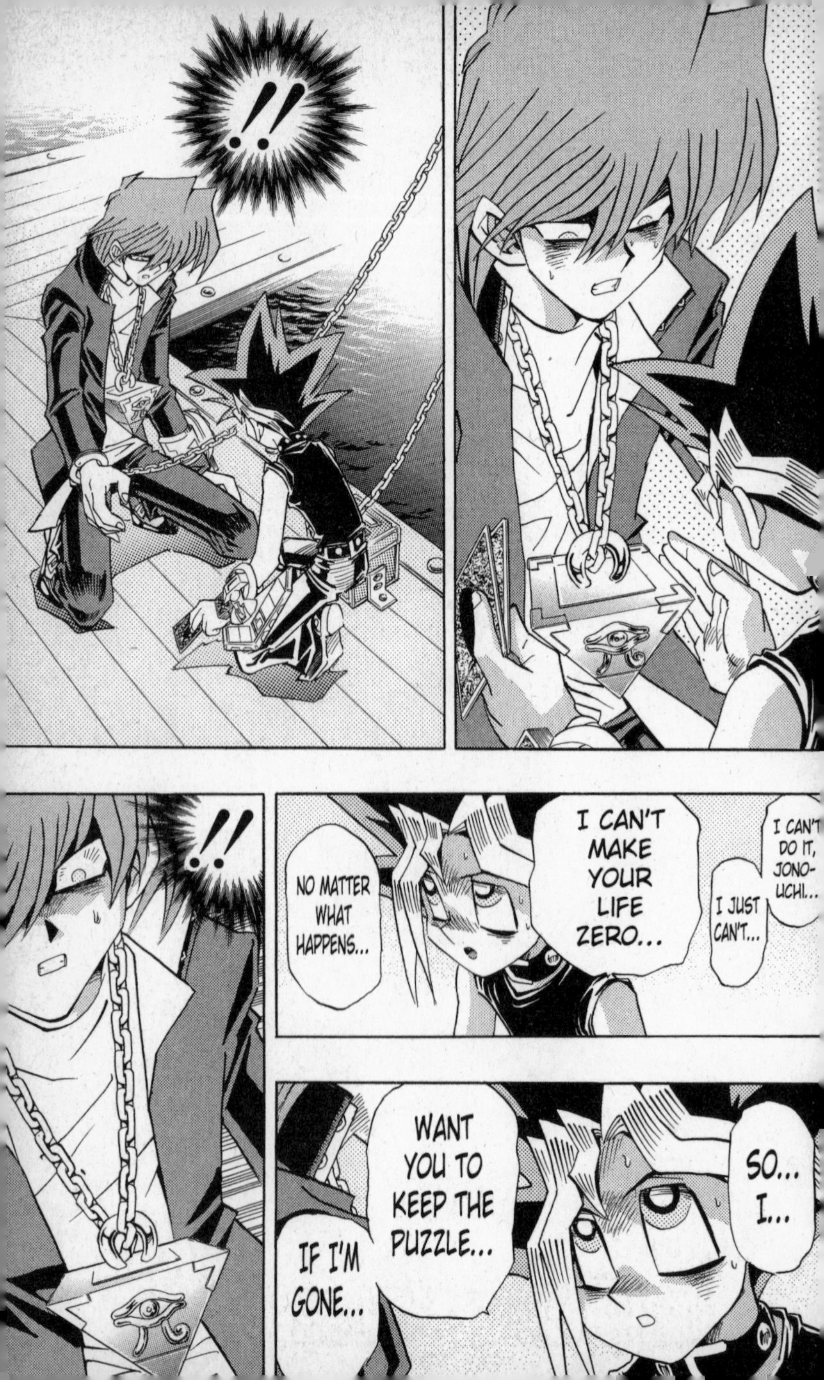
!!
I CAN'T DO IT, JONO-UCHI...
I JUST CAN'T...
I CAN'T MAKE YOUR LIFE ZERO...
NO MATTER WHAT HAPPENS...
SO... I...
WANT YOU TO KEEP THE PUZZLE...
IF I'M GONE...
!!

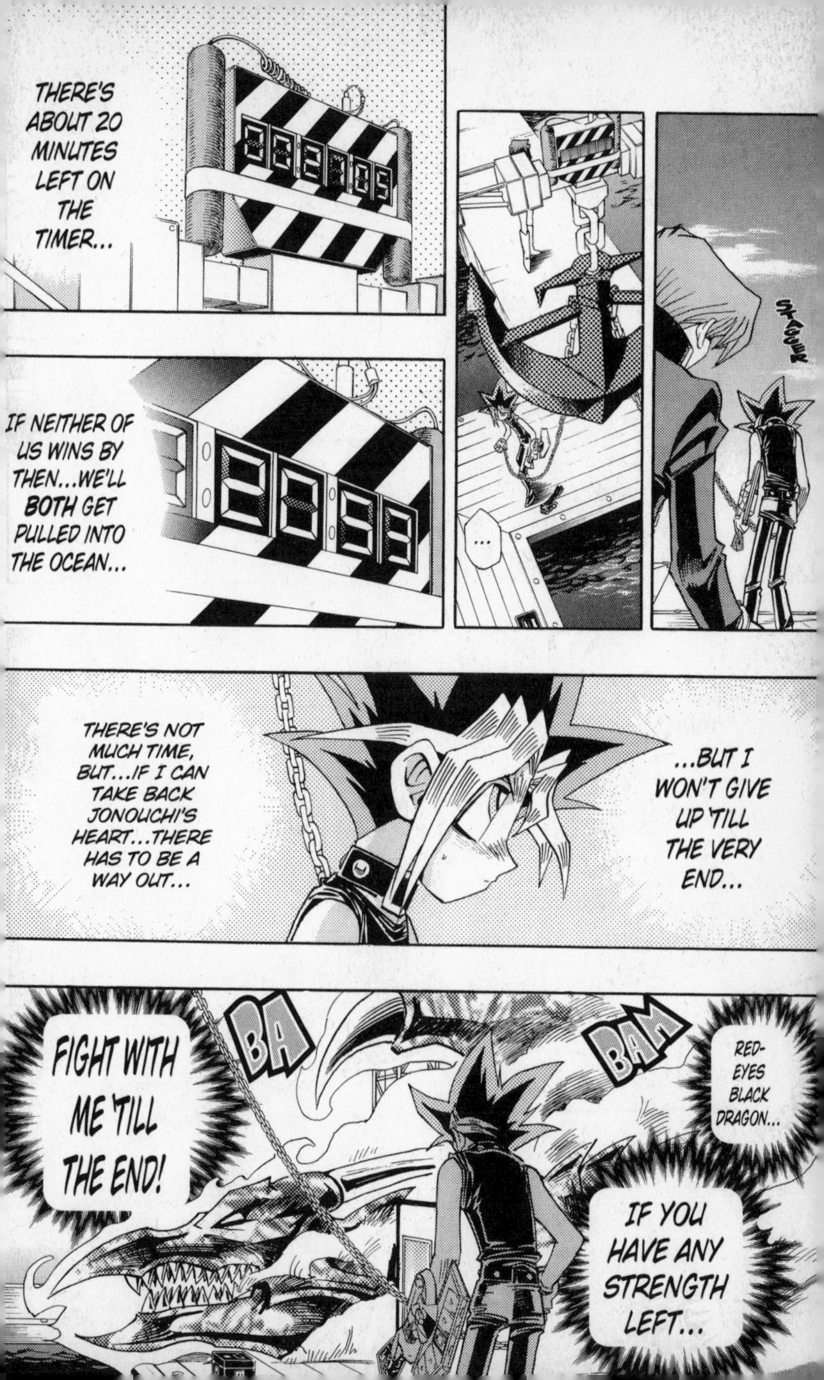
STAGGER
...
THERE'S ABOUT 20 MINUTES LEFT ON THE TIMER...
IF NEITHER OF US WINS BY THEN...WE'LL BOTH GET PULLED INTO THE OCEAN...
THERE'S NOT MUCH TIME, BUT...IF I CAN TAKE BACK JONOUCHI'S HEART...THERE HAS TO BE A WAY OUT...
...BUT I WON'T GIVE UP 'TILL THE VERY END...
BA
BAM
RED-EYES BLACK DRAGON...
IF YOU HAVE ANY STRENGTH LEFT...
FIGHT WITH ME 'TILL THE END!

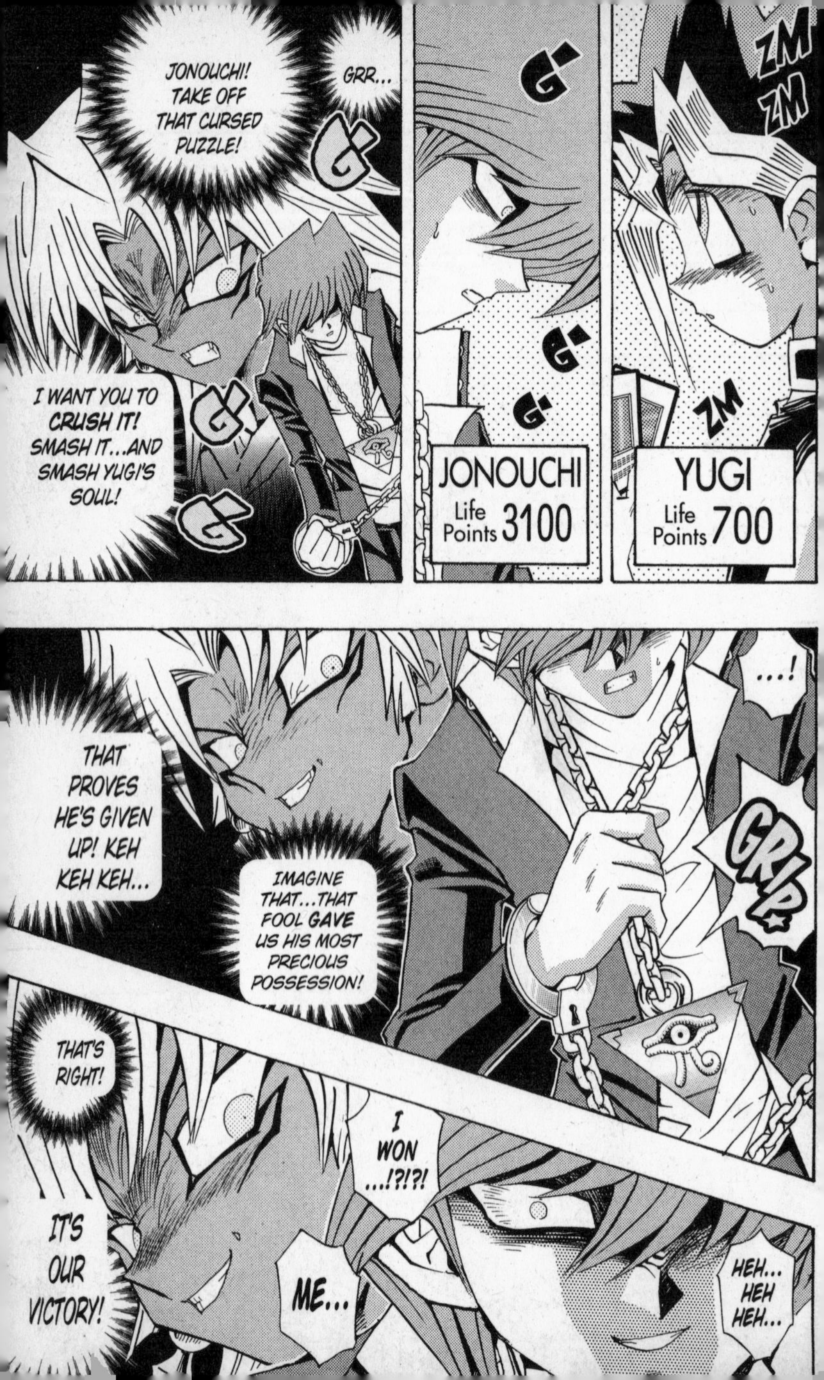
ZM
ZM
ZM
YUGI
Life Points 700
G
G
G
JONOUCHI
Life Points 3100
GRR...
JONOUCHI! TAKE OFF THAT CURSED PUZZLE!
G
I WANT YOU TO CRUSH IT! SMASH IT...AND SMASH YUGI'S SOUL!
G
G
...!
GRIP
THAT PROVES HE'S GIVEN UP! KEH KEH KEH...
IMAGINE THAT...THAT FOOL GAVE US HIS MOST PRECIOUS POSSESSION!
HEH... HEH HEH...
I WON ...!?!?!
ME...
THAT'S RIGHT!
IT'S OUR VICTORY!

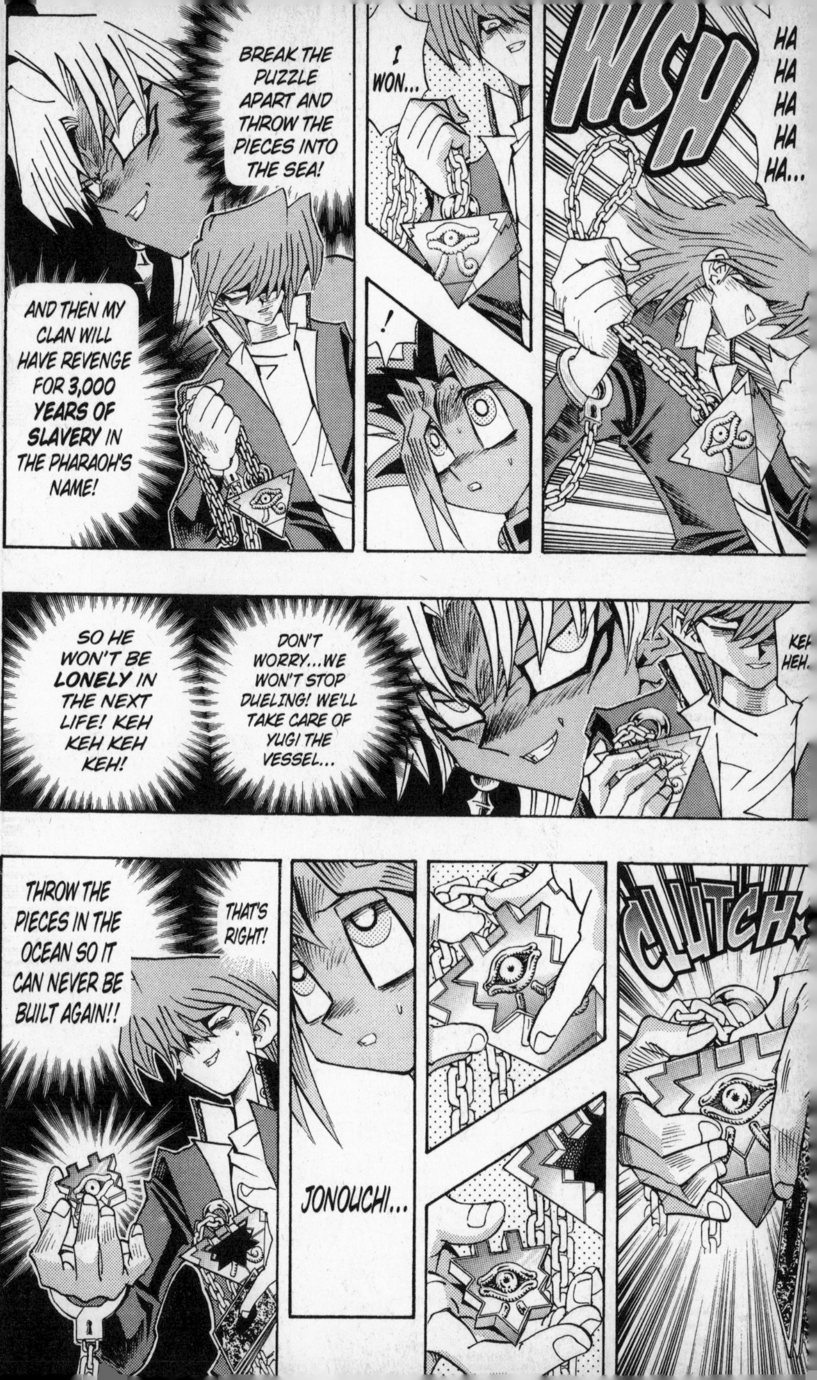
WISH
HA HA HA HA HA...
I WON...
!
BREAK THE PUZZLE APART AND THROW THE PIECES INTO THE SEA!
AND THEN MY CLAN WILL HAVE REVENGE FOR 3,000 YEARS OF SLAVERY IN THE PHARAOH'S NAME!
HEH.
DON'T WORRY...WE WON'T STOP DUELING! WE'LL TAKE CARE OF YUGI THE VESSEL...
SO HE WON'T BE LONELY IN THE NEXT LIFE! KEH KEH KEH KEH!
CLUTCH
JONOUCHI...
THAT'S RIGHT!
THROW THE PIECES IN THE OCEAN SO IT CAN NEVER BE BUILT AGAIN!!

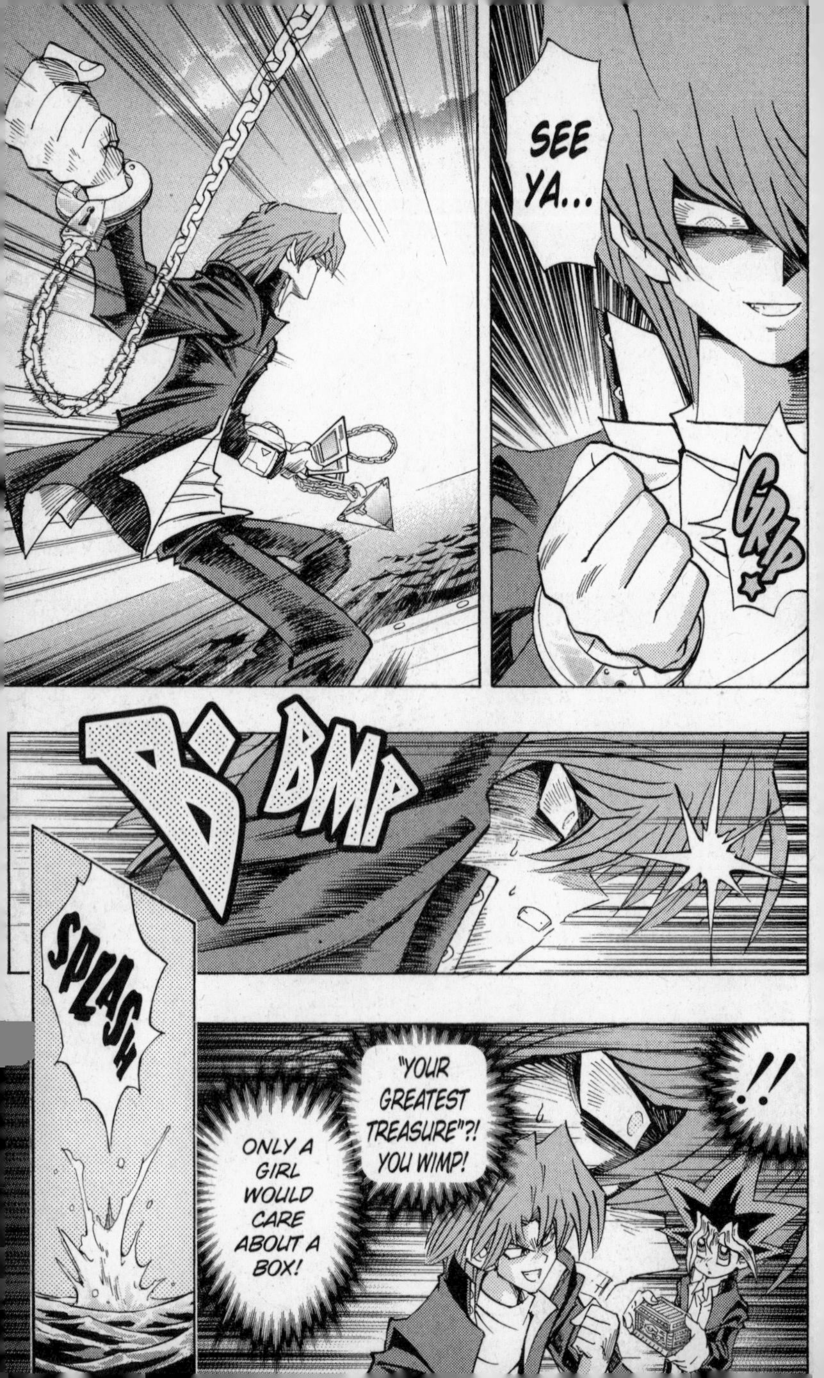
SEE YA...
GRIP
B BMP
!!
"YOUR GREATEST TREASURE"?! YOU WIMP!
ONLY A GIRL WOULD CARE ABOUT A BOX!
SPLASH

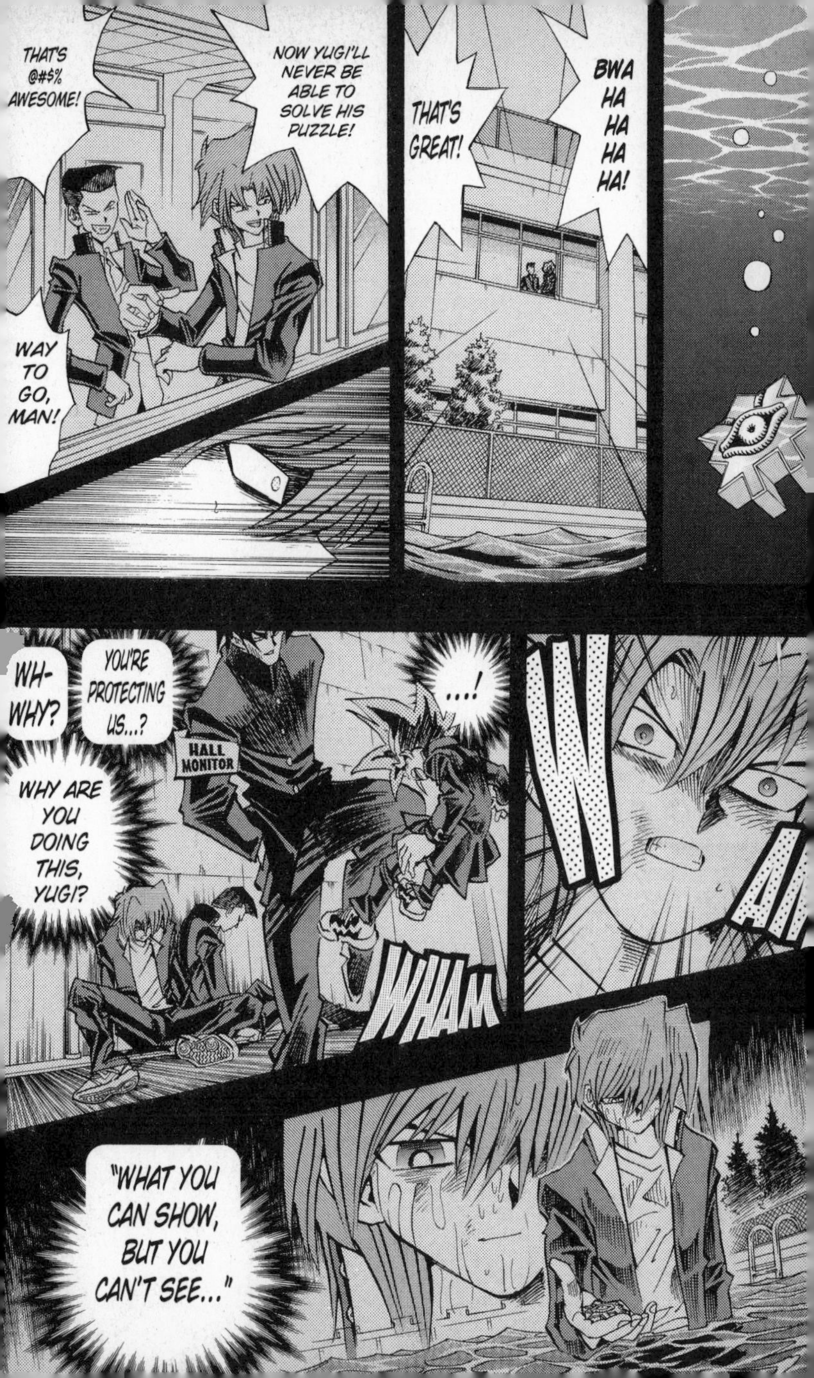
BWA HA HA HA HA!
THAT'S GREAT!
NOW YUGI'LL NEVER BE ABLE TO SOLVE HIS PUZZLE!
THAT'S @#$% AWESOME!
WAY TO GO, MAN!
...!
YOU'RE PROTECTING US...?
WH-WHY?
HALL MONITOR
WHY ARE YOU DOING THIS, YUGI?
WHAM
"WHAT YOU CAN SHOW, BUT YOU CAN'T SEE..."

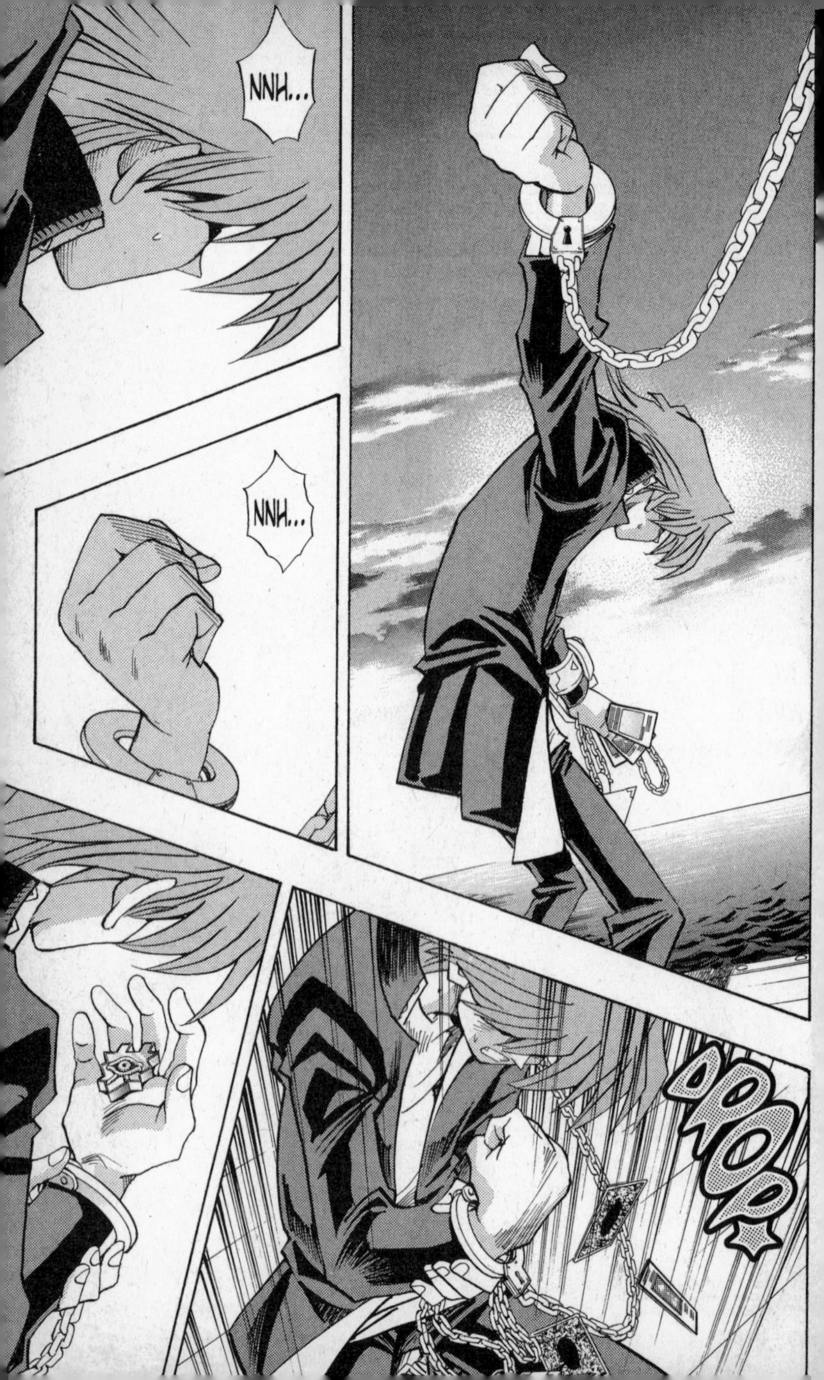
NNH...
NNH...
DROOP

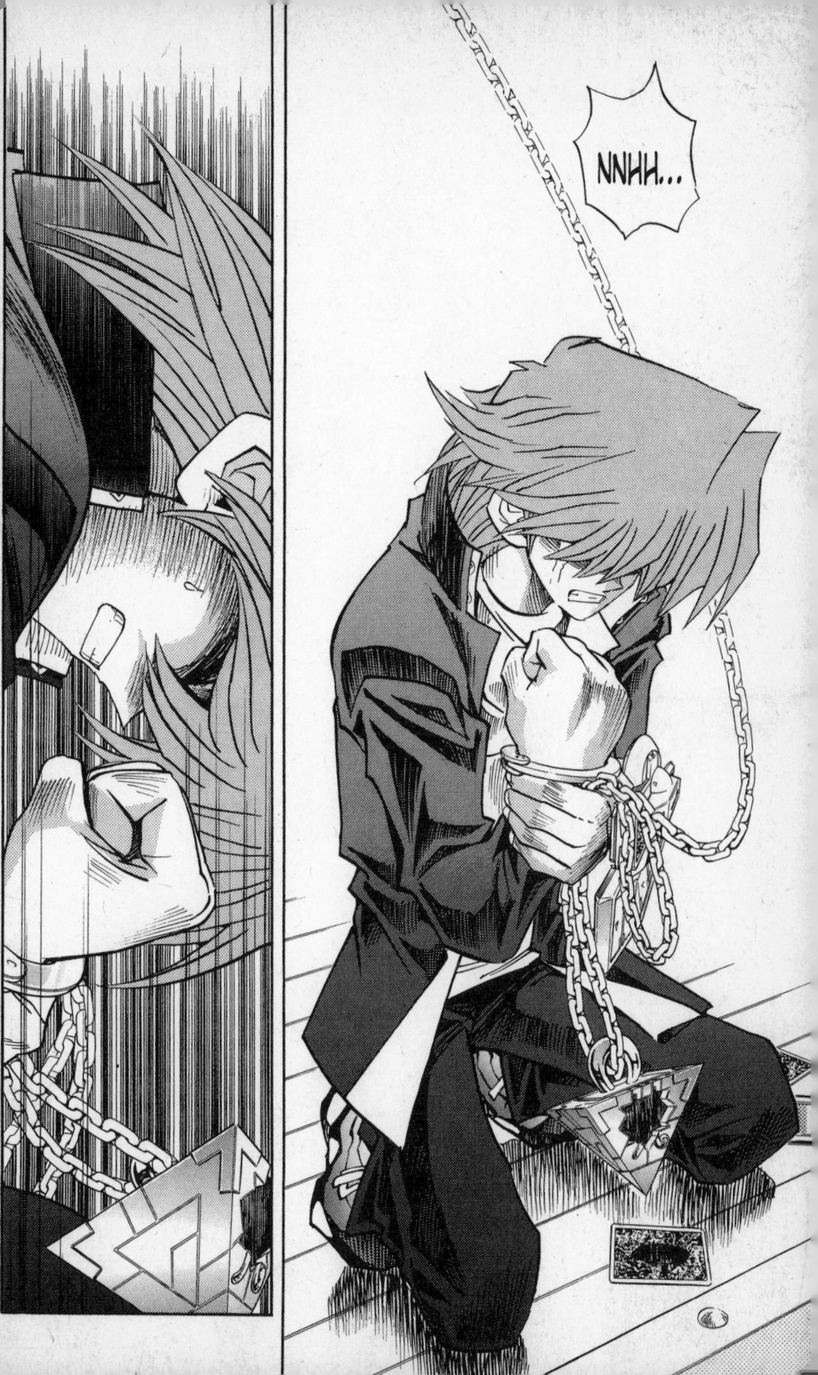
NNHH...

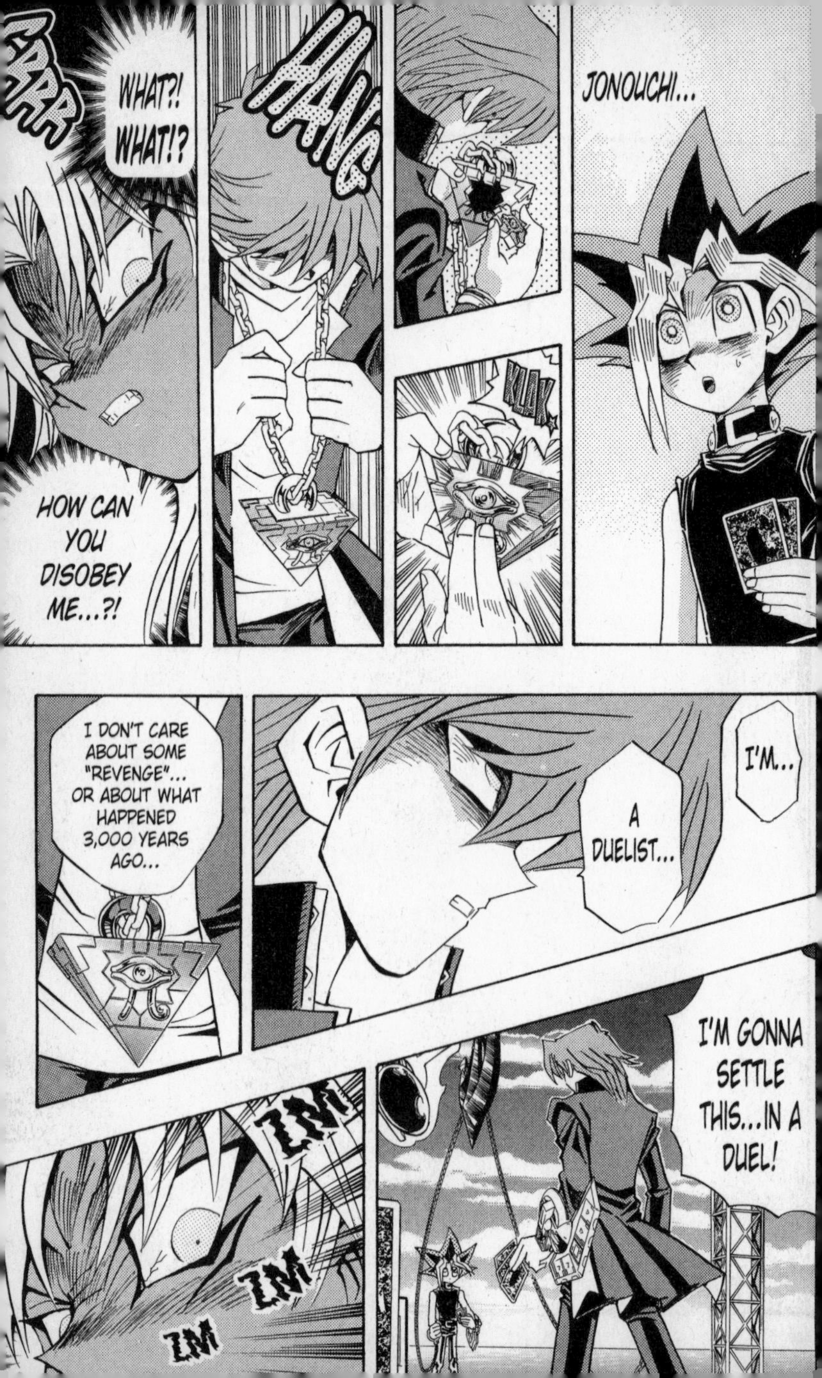

JONOUCHI...
KLIK
HANG
GRRR
WHAT?! WHAT!?
HOW CAN YOU DISOBEY ME...?!
I'M...
A DUELIST...
I DON'T CARE ABOUT SOME "REVENGE"... OR ABOUT WHAT HAPPENED 3,000 YEARS AGO...
I'M GONNA SETTLE THIS...IN A DUEL!

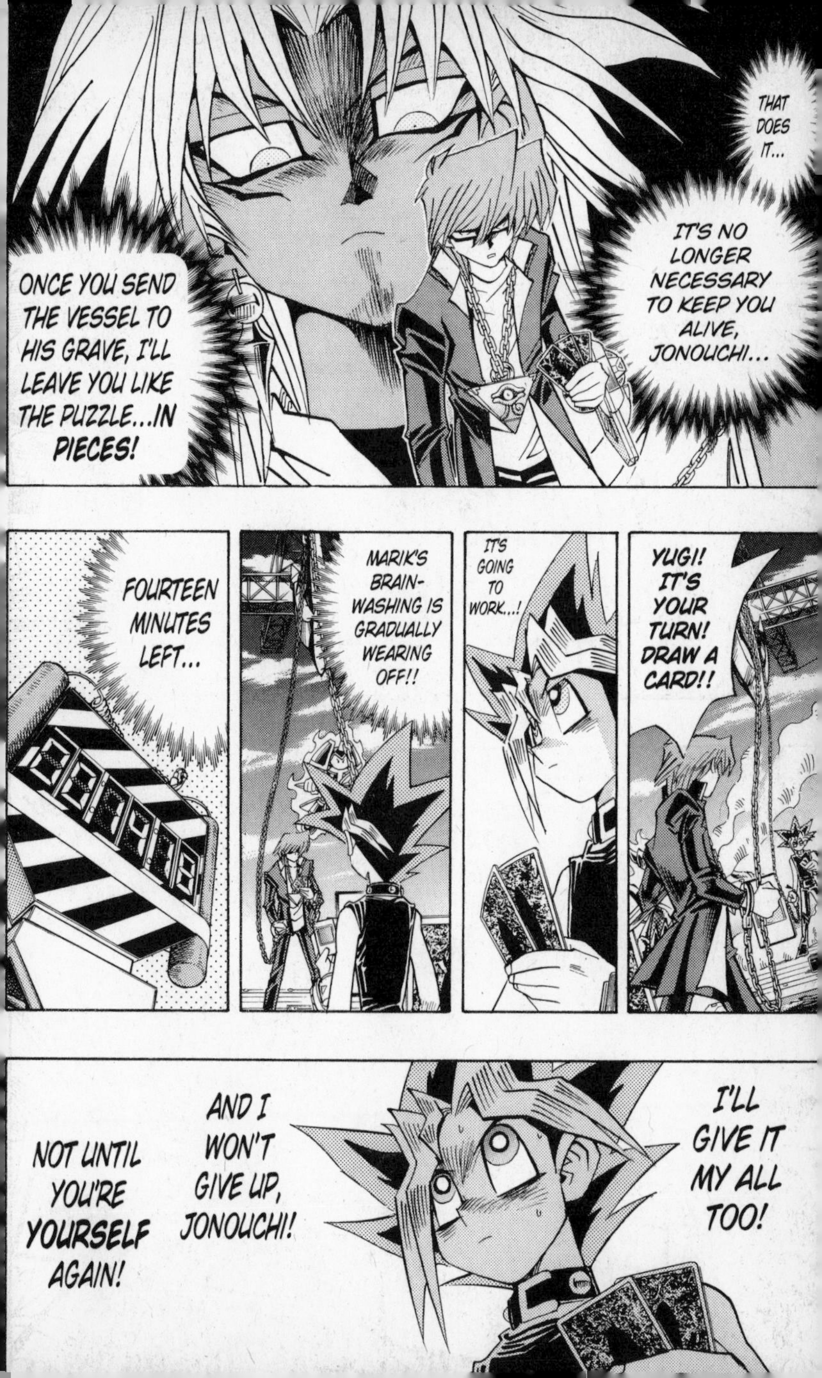
THAT DOES IT...
IT'S NO LONGER NECESSARY TO KEEP YOU ALIVE, JONOUCHI...
ONCE YOU SEND THE VESSEL TO HIS GRAVE, I'LL LEAVE YOU LIKE THE PUZZLE...IN PIECES!
YUGI! IT'S YOUR TURN! DRAW A CARD!!
IT'S GOING TO WORK...!
MARIK'S BRAIN-WASHING IS GRADUALLY WEARING OFF!!
FOURTEEN MINUTES LEFT...
I'LL GIVE IT MY ALL TOO!
AND I WON'T GIVE UP, JONOUCHI!
NOT UNTIL YOU'RE YOURSELF AGAIN!

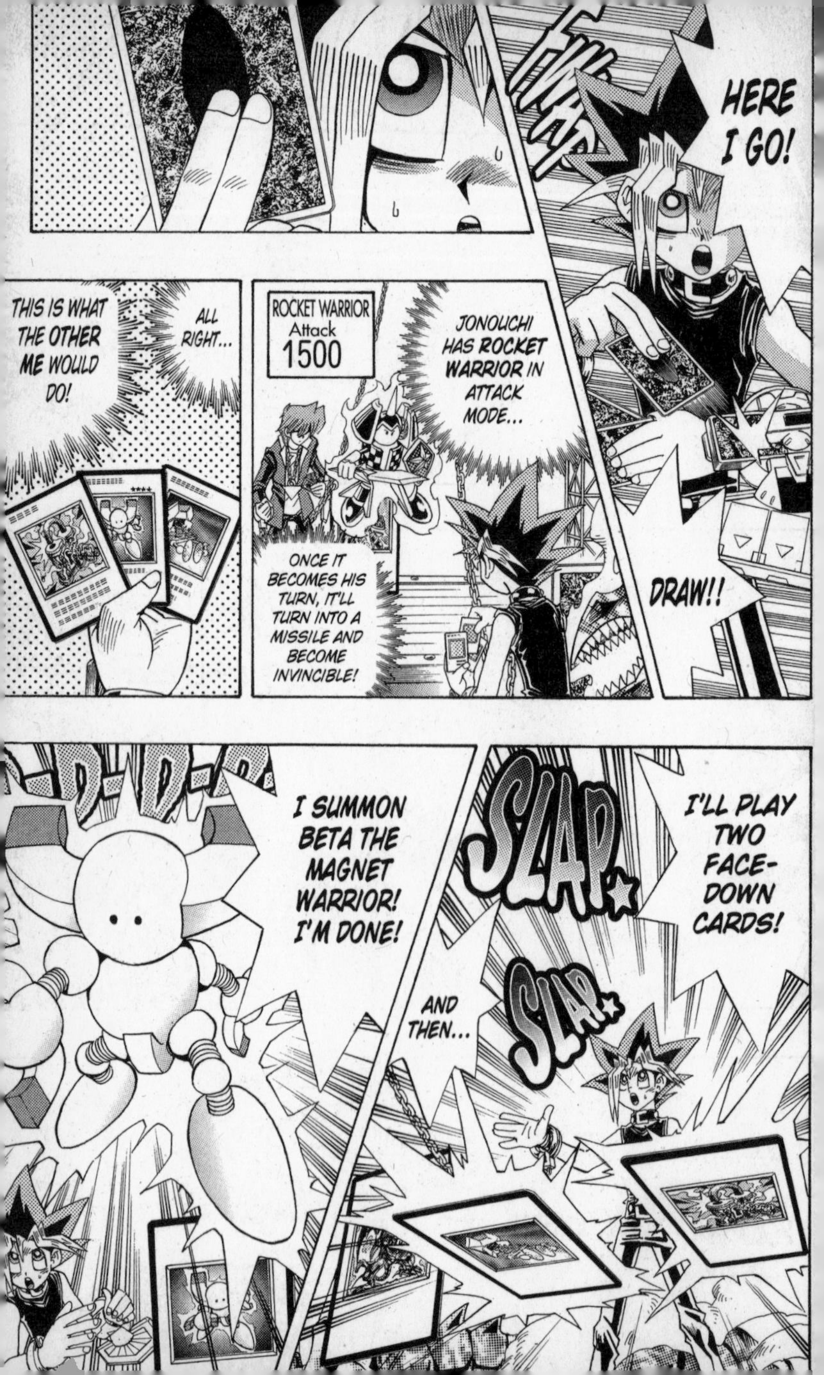
HERE I GO!
DRAW!!
ROCKET WARRIOR Attack 1500
JONOUCHI HAS ROCKET WARRIOR IN ATTACK MODE...
ONCE IT BECOMES HIS TURN, IT'LL TURN INTO A MISSILE AND BECOME INVINCIBLE!
ALL RIGHT...
THIS IS WHAT THE OTHER ME WOULD DO!
SLAP
I'LL PLAY TWO FACE-DOWN CARDS!
SLAP
AND THEN...
I SUMMON BETA THE MAGNET WARRIOR! I'M DONE!

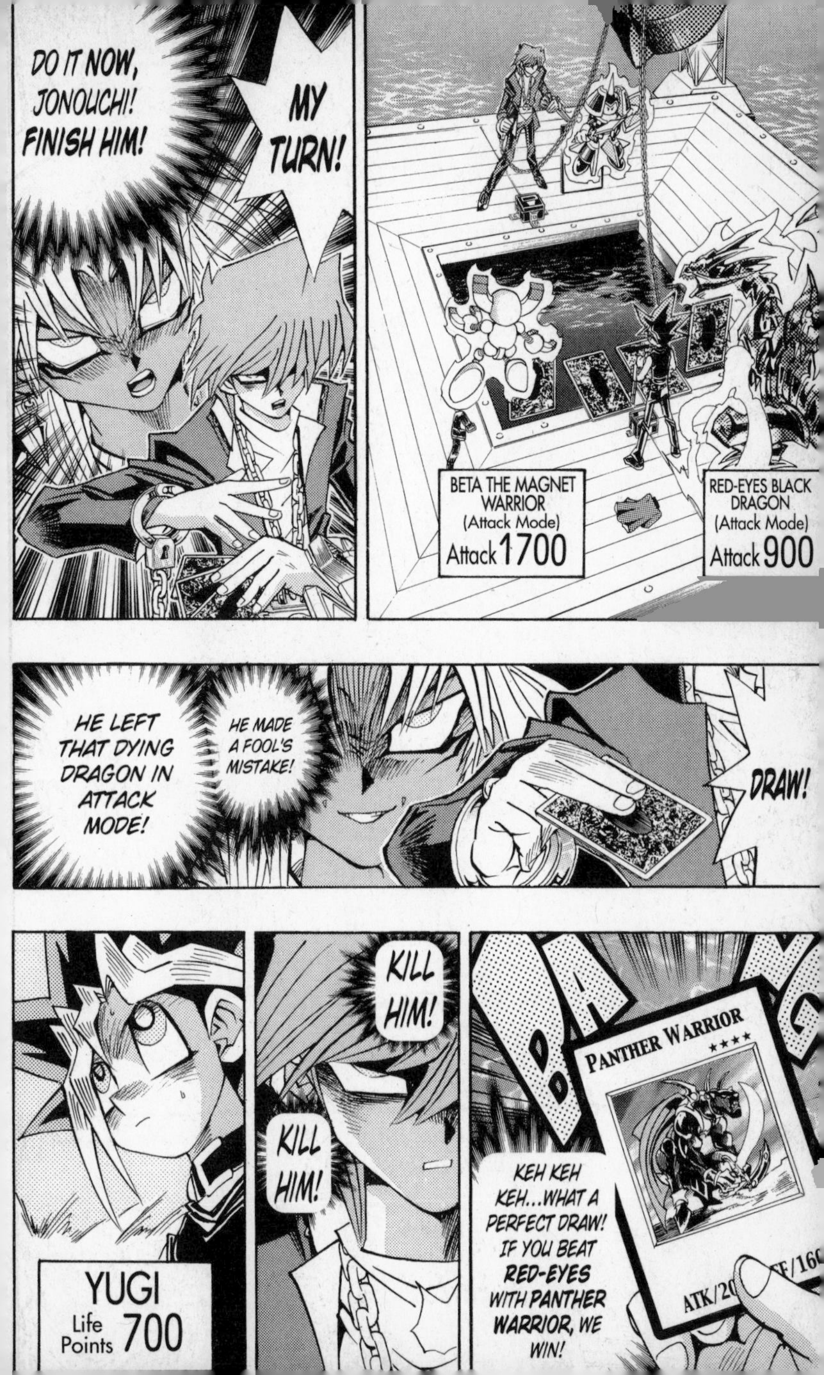

BETA THE MAGNET WARRIOR (Attack Mode) Attack 1700
RED-EYES BLACK DRAGON (Attack Mode) Attack 900
DO IT NOW, JONOUCHI! FINISH HIM!
MY TURN!
DRAW!
HE MADE A FOOL'S MISTAKE!
HE LEFT THAT DYING DRAGON IN ATTACK MODE!
PANTHER WARRIOR
KEH KEH KEH...WHAT A PERFECT DRAW! IF YOU BEAT RED-EYES WITH PANTHER WARRIOR, WE WIN!
KILL HIM!
KILL HIM!
YUGI Life Points 700

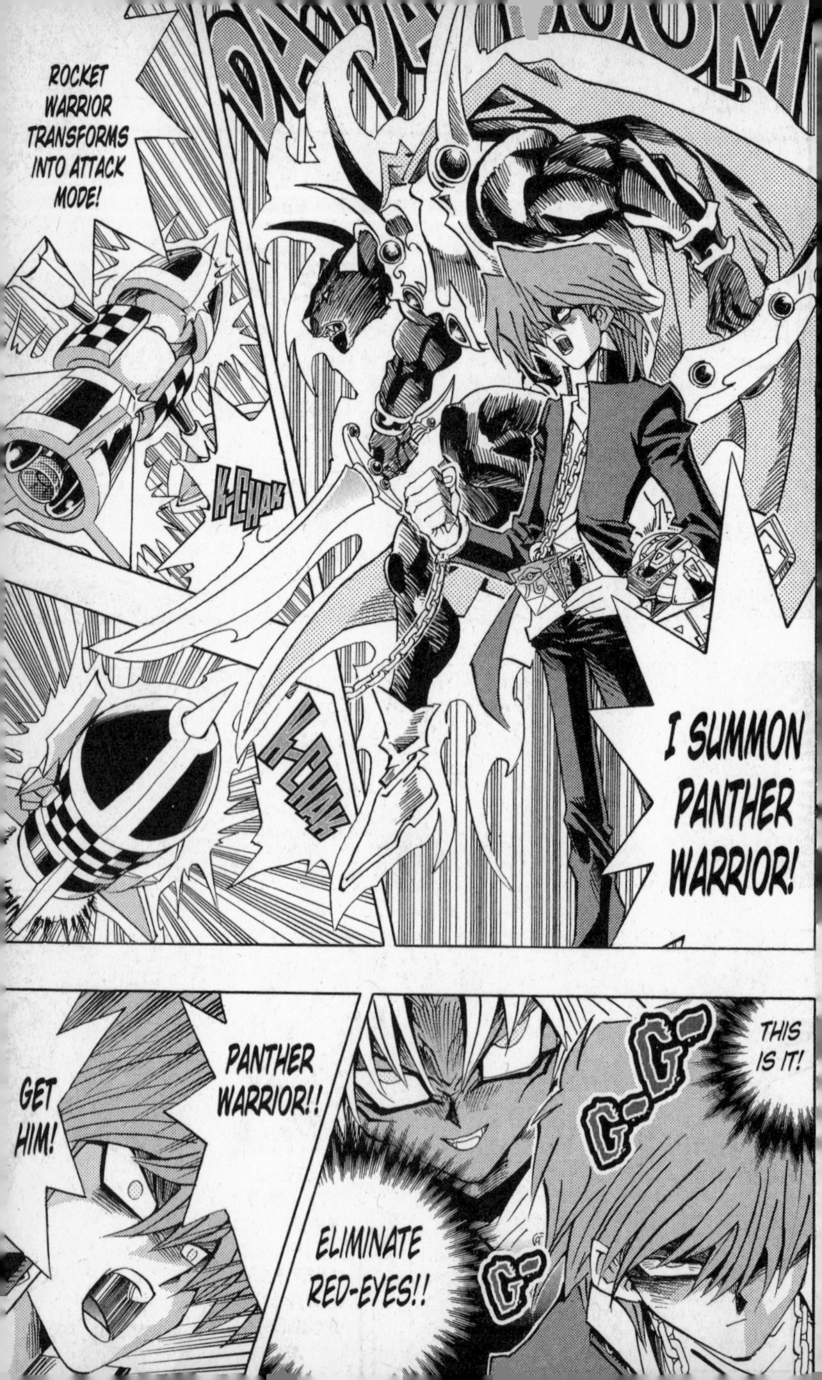

I SUMMON PANTHER WARRIOR!
ROCKET WARRIOR TRANSFORMS INTO ATTACK MODE!
K-CHAK
K-CHAK
THIS IS IT!
G-G
ELIMINATE RED-EYES!!
G
PANTHER WARRIOR!!
GET HIM!

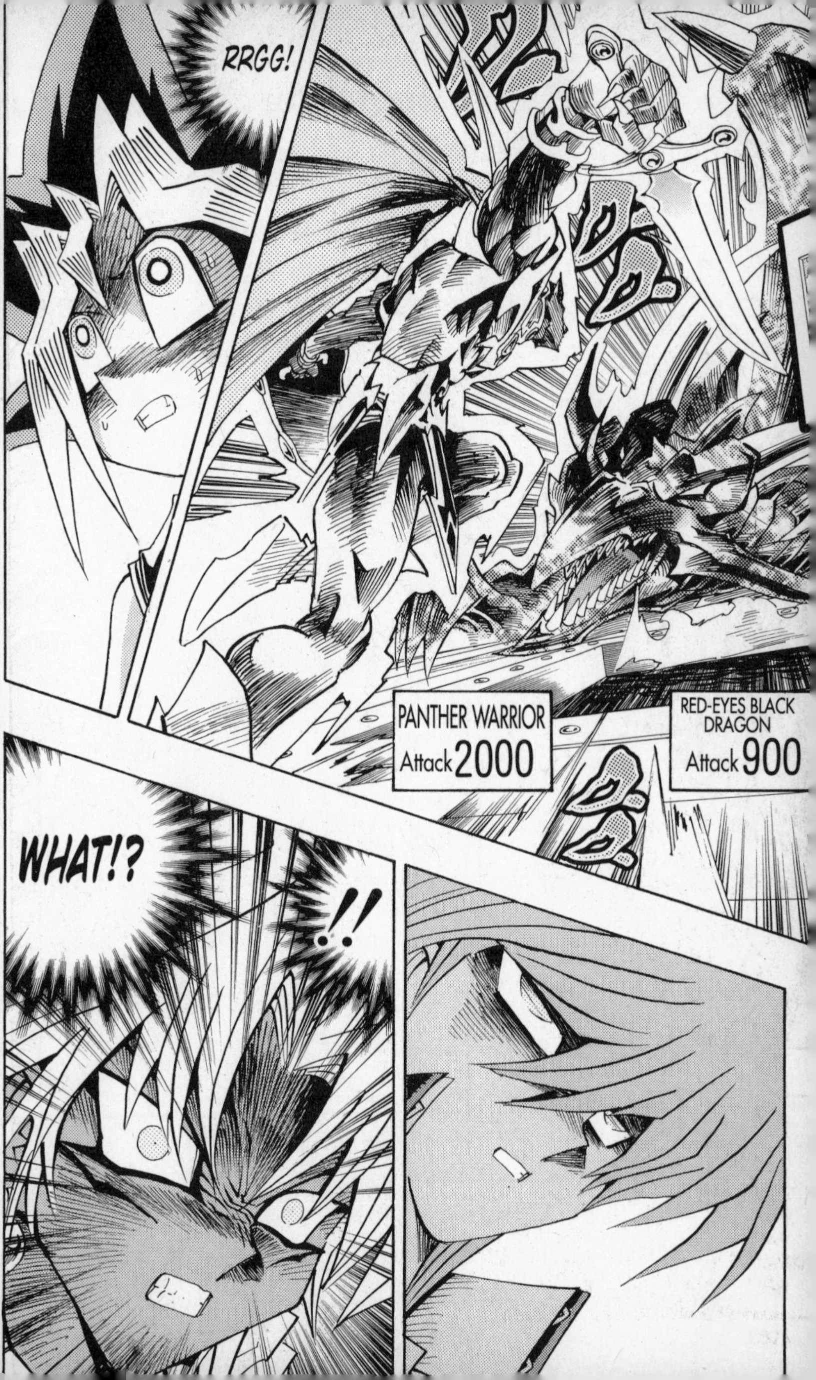
PANTHER WARRIOR
Attack 2000
RED-EYES BLACK DRAGON
Attack 900
RRGG!
!!
WHAT!?

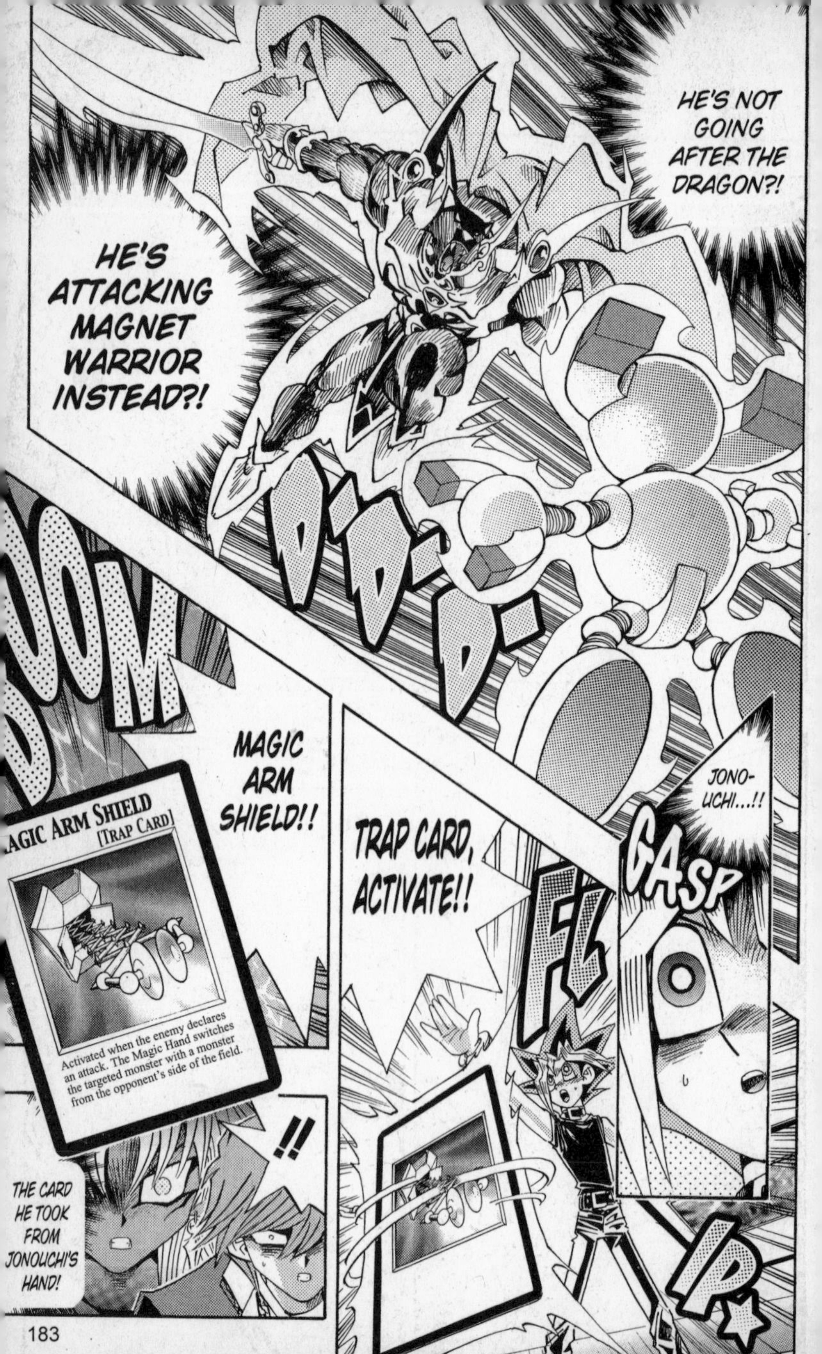
HE'S NOT GOING AFTER THE DRAGON?!
HE'S ATTACKING MAGNET WARRIOR INSTEAD?!
JONO-UCHI...!!
GASP
TRAP CARD, ACTIVATE!!
FL
IP
MAGIC ARM SHIELD!!
AGIC ARM SHIELD
[TRAP CARD]
Activated when the enemy declares an attack. The Magic Hand switches the targeted monster with a monster from the opponent's side of the field.
!!
THE CARD HE TOOK FROM JONOUCHI'S HAND!

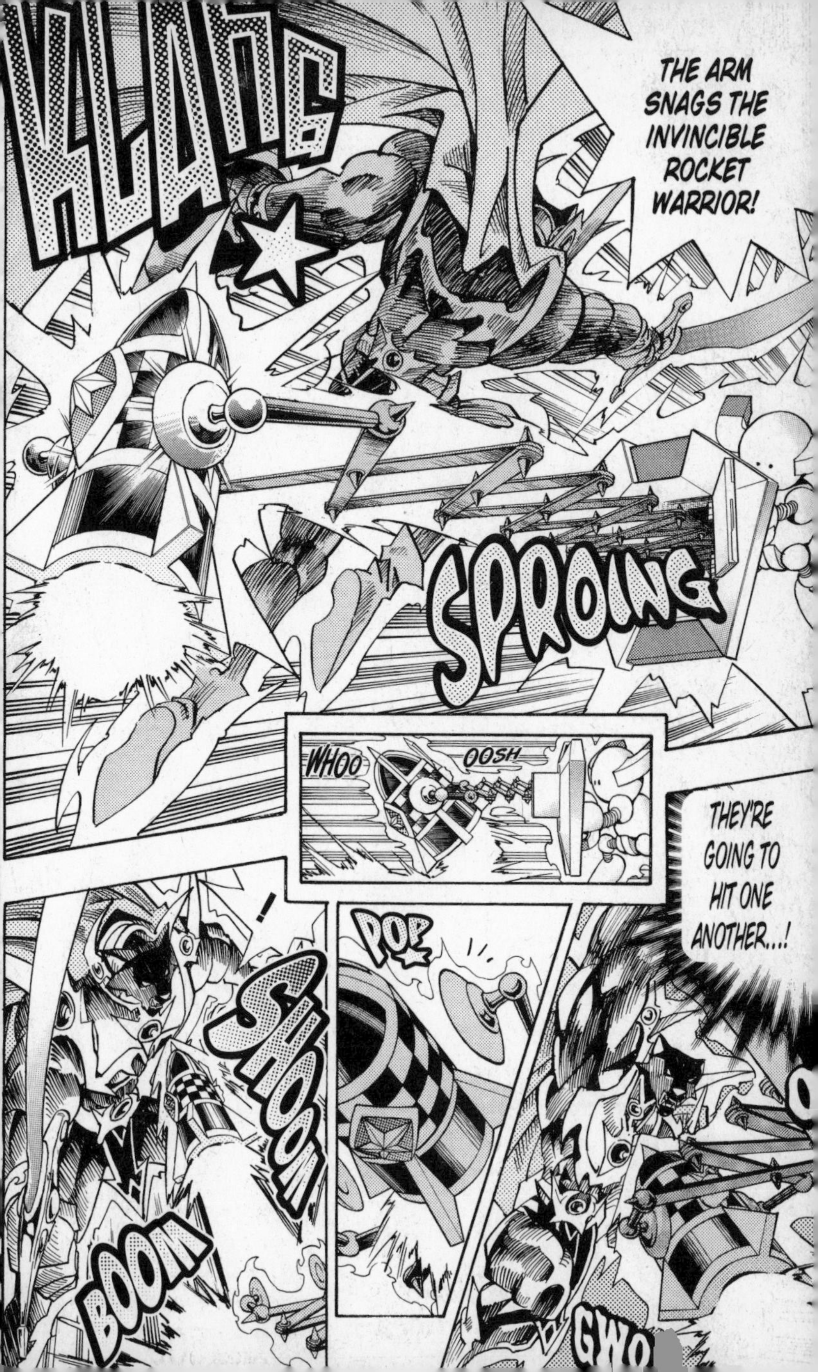

THE ARM SNAGS THE INVINCIBLE ROCKET WARRIOR!
KLANG
SPROING
THEY'RE GOING TO HIT ONE ANOTHER...!
WHOO
OOSH
GWO
POP
SHOOM
BOOM

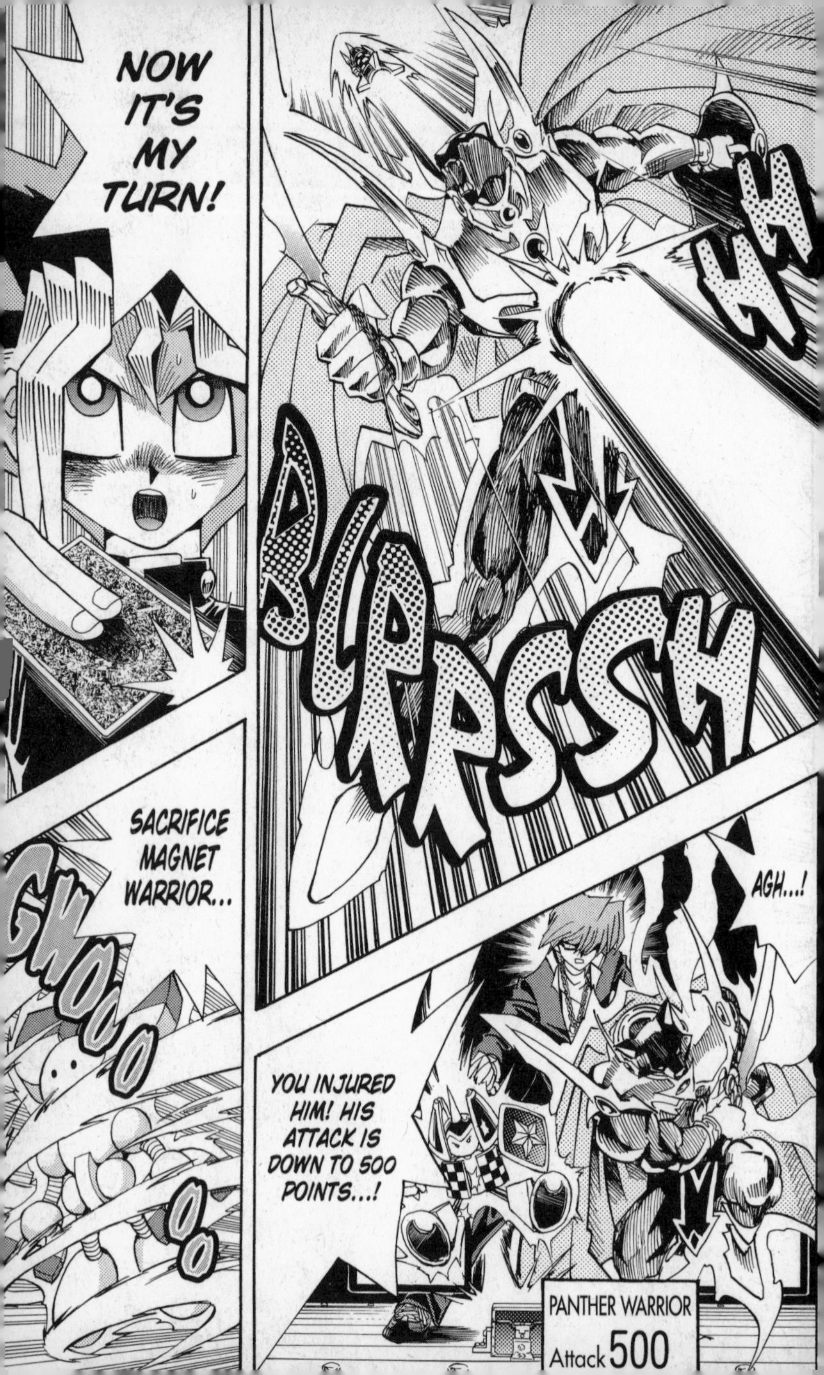

AGH...!
YOU INJURED HIM! HIS ATTACK IS DOWN TO 500 POINTS...!
PANTHER WARRIOR
Attack 500
NOW IT'S MY TURN!
SACRIFICE MAGNET WARRIOR...

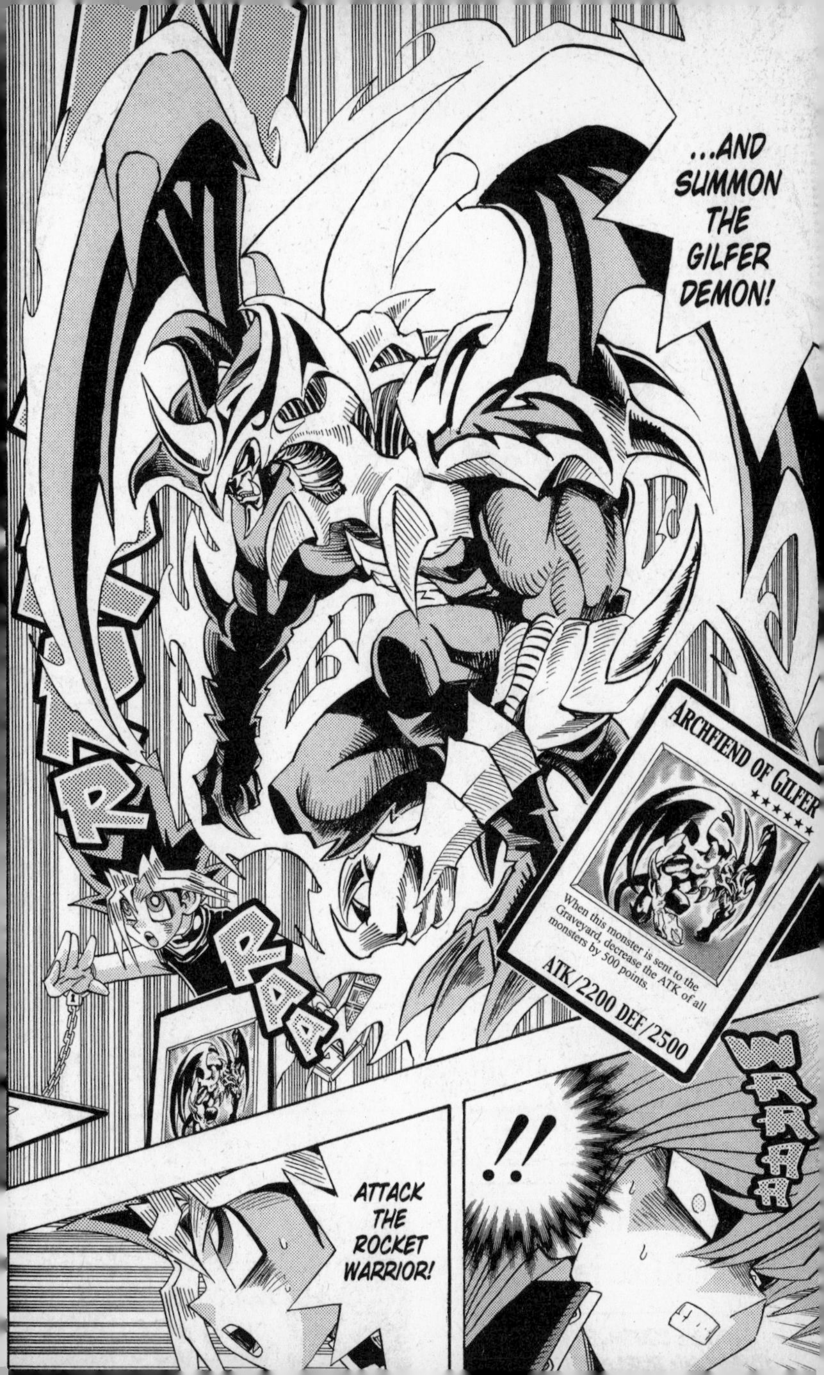
...AND SUMMON THE GILFER DEMON!
RAAA
ARCHFIEND OF GILFER
When this monster is sent to the Graveyard, decrease the ATK of all monsters by 500 points.
ATK/2200 DEF/2500
!!
ATTACK THE ROCKET WARRIOR!

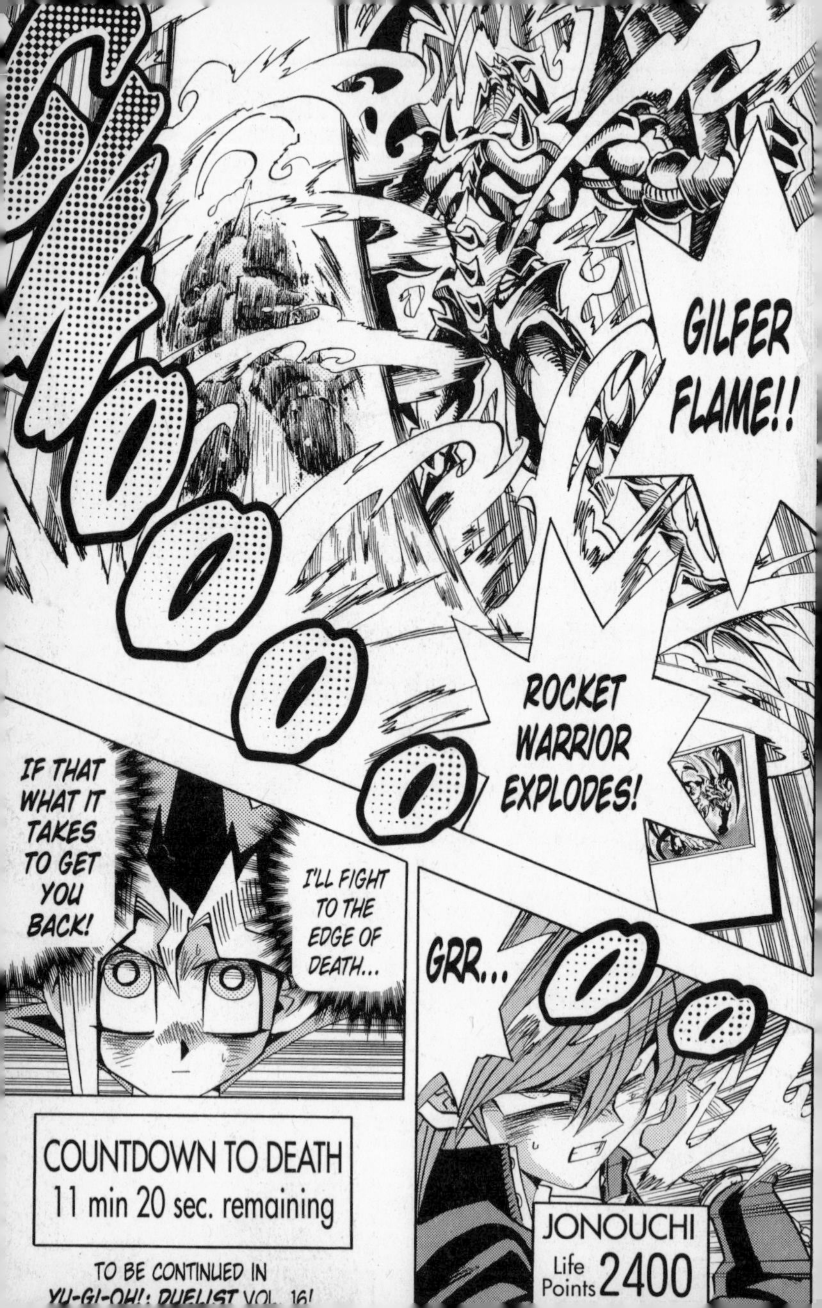
GILFER FLAME!!
ROCKET WARRIOR EXPLODES!
GRR...
JONOUCHI Life Points 2400
I'LL FIGHT TO THE EDGE OF DEATH...
IF THAT WHAT IT TAKES TO GET YOU BACK!
COUNTDOWN TO DEATH
11 min 20 sec. remaining
TO BE CONTINUED IN
YU-GI-OH!: DUELIST VOL. 16!

MASTER OF THE CARDS

©1996 KAZUKI TAKAHASHI. Manufactured by KONAMI CORPORATION. KONAMI and designs are trademarks of KONAMI CORPORATION. All rights reserved. Upper Deck Entertainment and designs are trademarks of The Upper Deck Company, LLC.

The "Duel Monsters" card game first appeared in volume two of the original **Yu-Gi-Oh!** graphic novel series, but it's in **Yu-Gi-Oh!: Duelist** (originally printed in Japan as volumes 8-31 of **Yu-Gi-Oh!**) that it gets really important. As many fans know, some of the card names are different between the English and Japanese versions. In case you play the game, or you're interested in playing, here's a rundown of some of the cards in this graphic novel. Some cards only appear in the **Yu-Gi-Oh!** video games, not in the actual collectible card game.

FIRST APPEARANCE IN THIS VOLUME	JAPANESE CARD NAME	ENGLISH CARD NAME
p.8	*Blue-Eyes White Dragon*	Blue-Eyes White Dragon
p.12	*Magnet Warrior Alpha*	Alpha the Magnet Warrior
p.13	*Teppeki no Kamen* (Mask of Iron Wall/ Invulnerability/ Impregnability)	Mask of Impregnability (NOTE: Not a real game card)
p.16	*Magnet Warrior Beta*	Beta the Magnet Warrior
p.16	*Erabareshi Mono* (Chosen/Selected One)	Chosen One
p.18	*Kamen Majû Des Guardius* (Masked Magical/Demon Beast Des Guardius)	Masked Beast of Guardius (NOTE: Not a real game card)

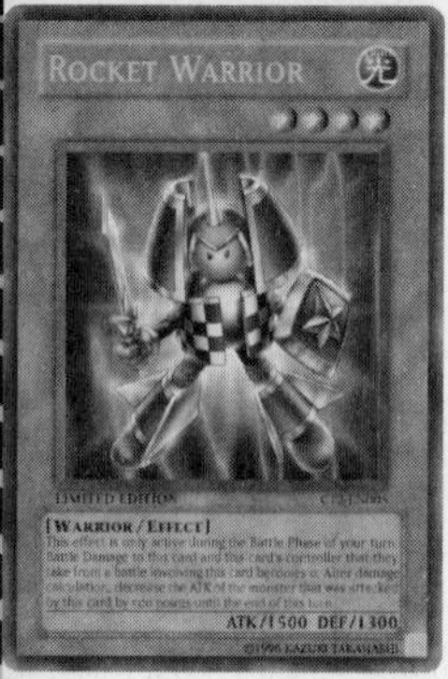
ROCKET WARRIOR
LIMITED EDITION
[WARRIOR / EFFECT]
ATK/1500 DEF/1300

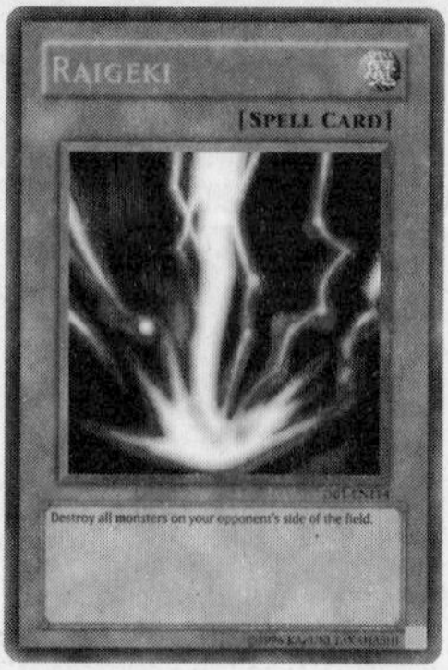
RAIGEKI
[SPELL CARD]
Destroy all monsters on your opponent's side of the field.

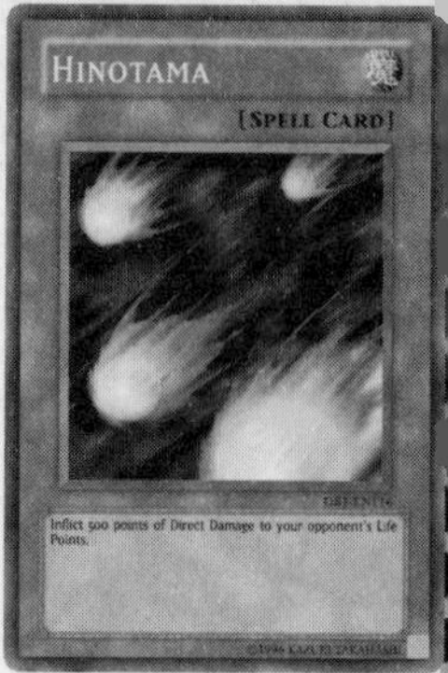
HINOTAMA
[SPELL CARD]
Inflict 500 points of Direct Damage to your opponent's Life Points.

FIRST APPEARANCE IN THIS VOLUME	JAPANESE CARD NAME	ENGLISH CARD NAME
p.20	*Jûkon no Kamen* (Mask of Cursed Grudge/Grudge Spell)	Mask of the Accursed (NOTE: Kanji on mask reads "curse/spell")
p.24	*Magnet Warrior Gamma*	Gamma the Magnet Warrior
p.25	*Jishaku no Senshi Magnet Valkyrion* (Magnet Warrior Magnet Valkyrion)	Valkyrion the Magna Warrior
p.29	*Maryoku Muryokuka no Kamen* (Mask of Magic-Power Nullification)	Mask of Dispel
p.29	*Ikeniefûji no Kamen* (Mask of Sacrificial Offering Sealing)	Mask of Restrict (NOTE: Kanji on mask reads "sacrificial offering seal")
p.32	*Obelisk no Kyoshinhei* (Obelisk the Giant God Soldier)	The God of the Obelisk (NOTE: Called "Obelisk the Tormentor" in the English anime and card game.)
p.32	*Cross Soul*	Soul Exchange
p.36	*Nuigon no Kamen* (Mask of Will/Mind)	Mask of Possession

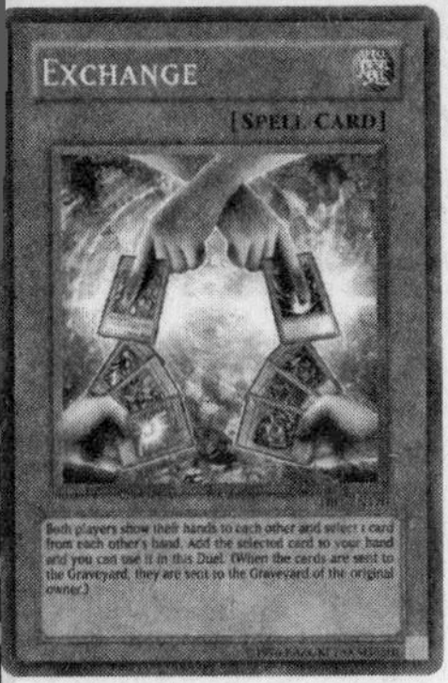
EXCHANGE
[SPELL CARD]
Both players show their hands to each other and select 1 card from each other's hand. Add the selected card to your hand and you can use it in this Duel. (When the cards are sent to the Graveyard, they are sent to the Graveyard of the original owner.)

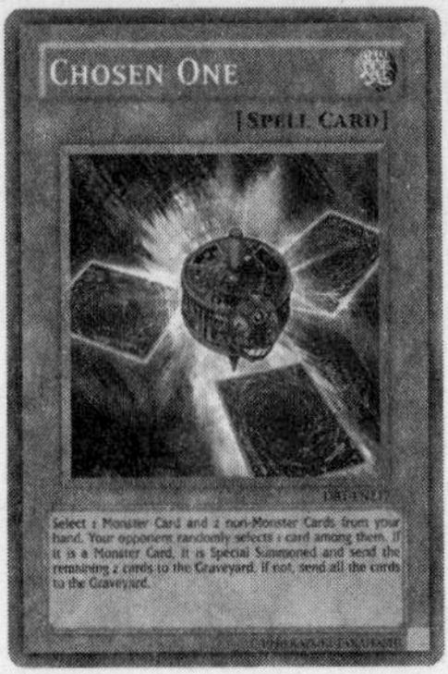
CHOSEN ONE
[SPELL CARD]
Select 1 Monster Card and 2 non-Monster Cards from your hand. Your opponent randomly selects 1 card among them. If it is a Monster Card, it is Special Summoned and send the remaining 2 cards to the Graveyard. If not, send all the cards to the Graveyard.

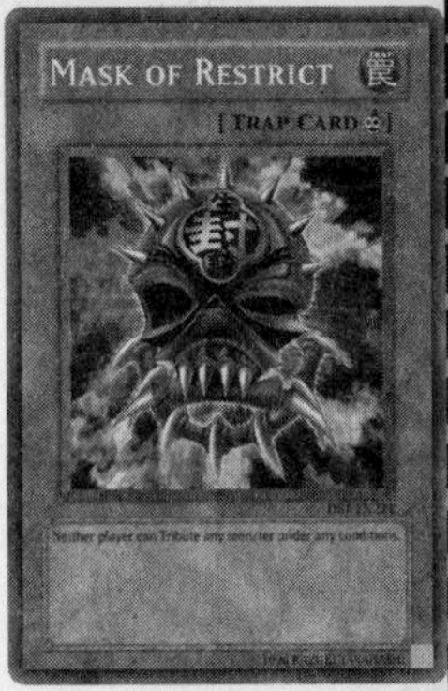
MASK OF RESTRICT
[TRAP CARD]
Neither player can Tribute any monster under any conditions.

FIRST APPEARANCE IN THIS VOLUME	JAPANESE CARD NAME	ENGLISH CARD NAME
p.39	*Yûgôkaijô* (Fusion Cancellation/Removal)	De-Fusion
p.71	*Osiris no Tenkûryû* (Osiris the Heaven Dragon)	Slifer the Sky Dragon
p.71	*Ra no Yokushinryû* (Ra the Winged God Dragon) (NOTE: The kanji for "sun god" is written beside the kanji for "Ra.")	The Sun Dragon Ra (NOTE: Called "The Winged Dragon of Ra" in the English anime and card game.)
p.71	*Death Meteor*	Meteor of Destruction
p.71	*Fire Ball*	Hinotama (NOTE: Japanese for "fireball")
p.100	*Red-Eyes Black Dragon*	Red-Eyes Black Dragon
p.103	*Baphomet*	Baphomet (NOTE: Called "Berfomet" in the English anime and card game.)
p.104	*Lightning Vortex*	Raigeki (NOTE: Japanese for "thunder attack" or "torpedo attack.")

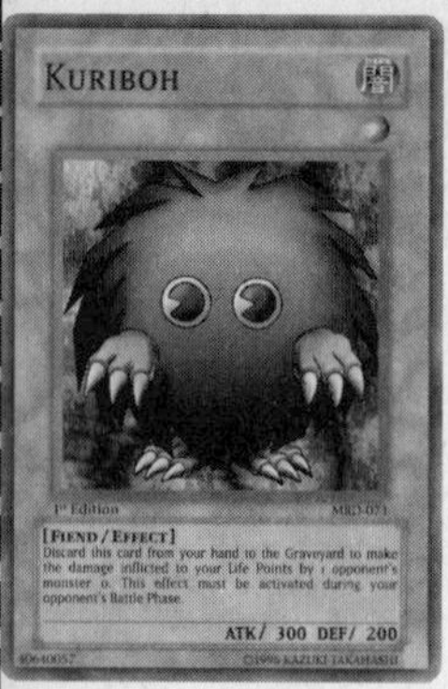
KURIBOH
[FIEND / EFFECT]
ATK/ 300 DEF/ 200

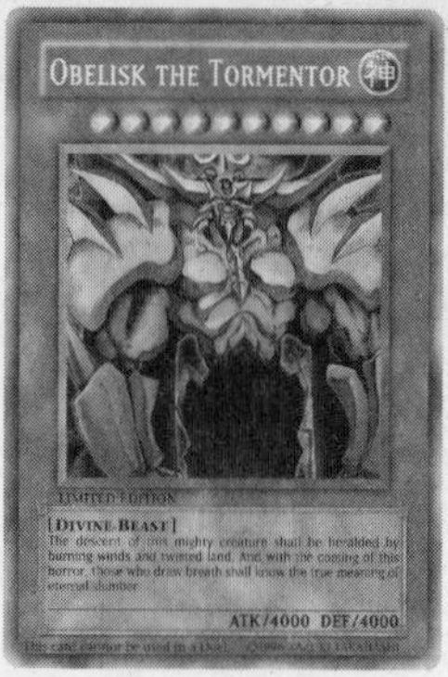
OBELISK THE TORMENTOR
[DIVINE-BEAST]
ATK/4000 DEF/4000

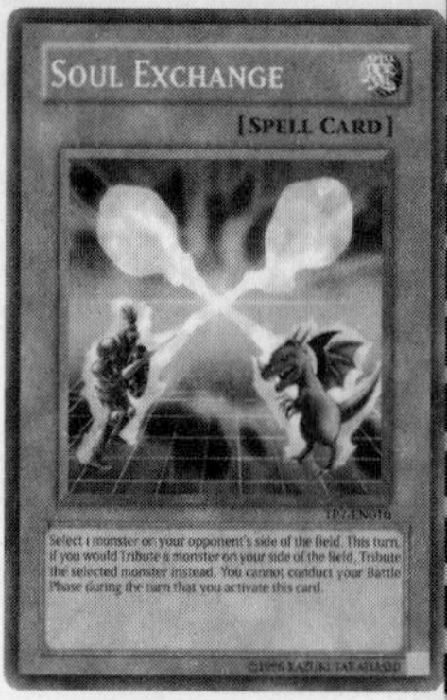
SOUL EXCHANGE
[SPELL CARD]

FIRST APPEARANCE IN THIS VOLUME	JAPANESE CARD NAME	ENGLISH CARD NAME
p.104	*Wyvern no Senshi* (Wyvern Warrior)	Alligator Sword (NOTE: Not a real game card)
p.106	*Big Shield Guardna*	Big Shield Guardna
p.112	*Rokubôsei no Jûbaku* (Binding Curse of the Hexagram)	Spellbinding Circle
p.114	*Kuribo*	Kuriboh
p.133	*Mahô Kaijo* (Magic Liquidation/Dissolution)	De-Spell
p.133	*Exchange*	Exchange
p.133	*Tefuda Massatsu* (Card Obliteration)	Card Destruction
p.162	*Rocket Senshi* (Rocket Warrior)	Rocket Warrior
p.179	*Magic Arm Shield*	Magic Arm Shield
p.180	*Shikkoku no Hyôsenshi Panther Warrior* (Jet Black Panther Warrior)	Panther Warrior
p.186	*Ankokumazoku Gilfer Demon* (Darkness/Black Magic/ Demon Clan Gilfer Demon)	Archfiend of Gilfer

IN THE NEXT VOLUME...

It's the duel Yugi and Jonouchi have been waiting for...but they never thought it would happen like *this*. Can the mighty Archfiend of Gilfer face the fury of Jonouchi's direct damage deck? Can Jonouchi overcome Marik's mind-control? And even if he does, can the two best friends escape the deadly anchor deathtrap? Who will win...and who will sleep with the fishes on the bottom of Domino Bay?

COMING AUGUST 2006!

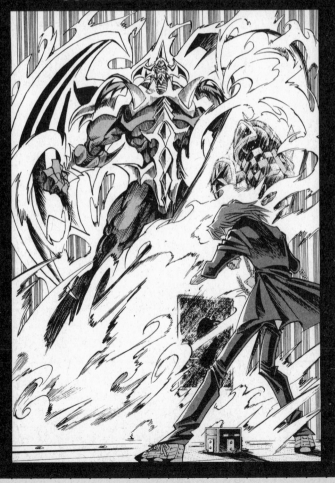

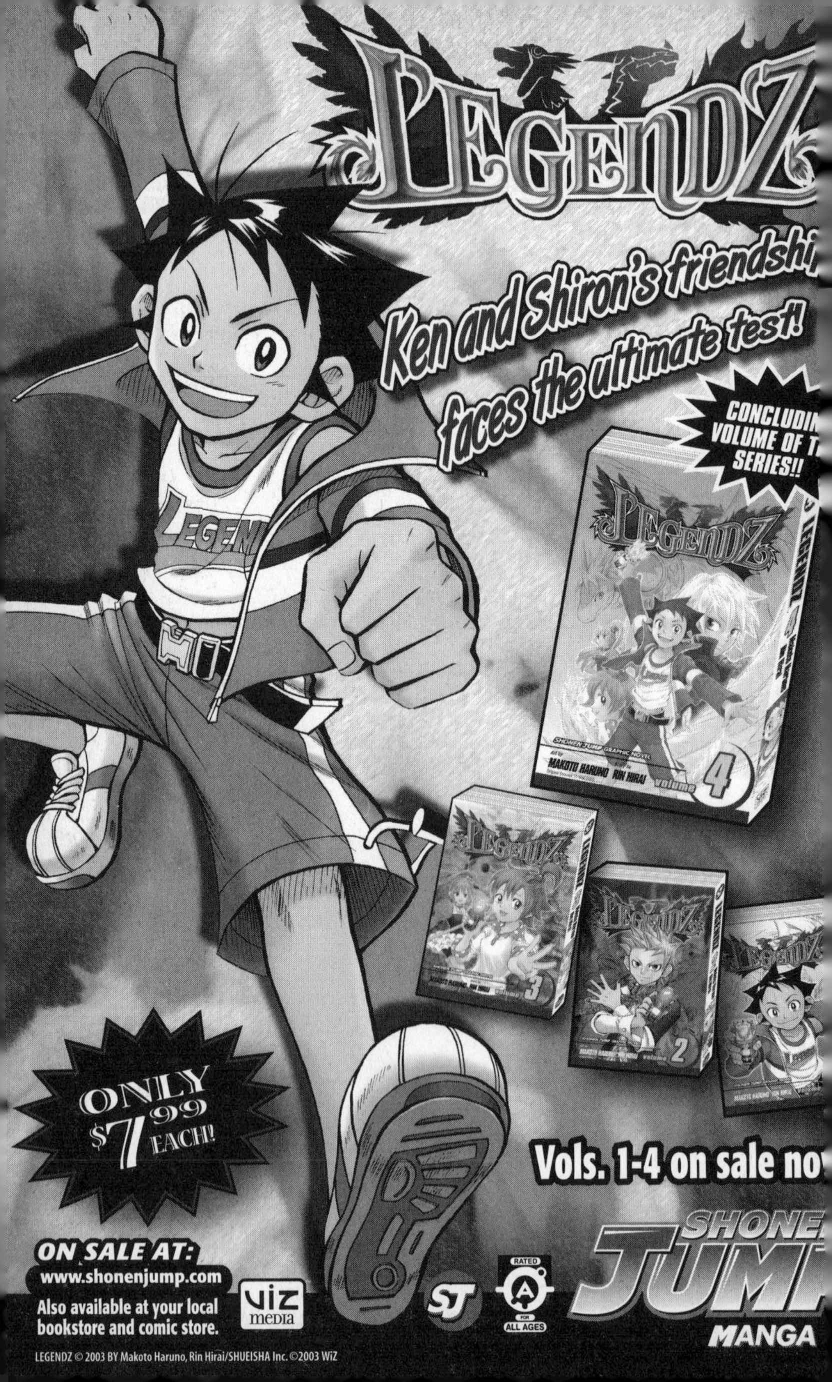

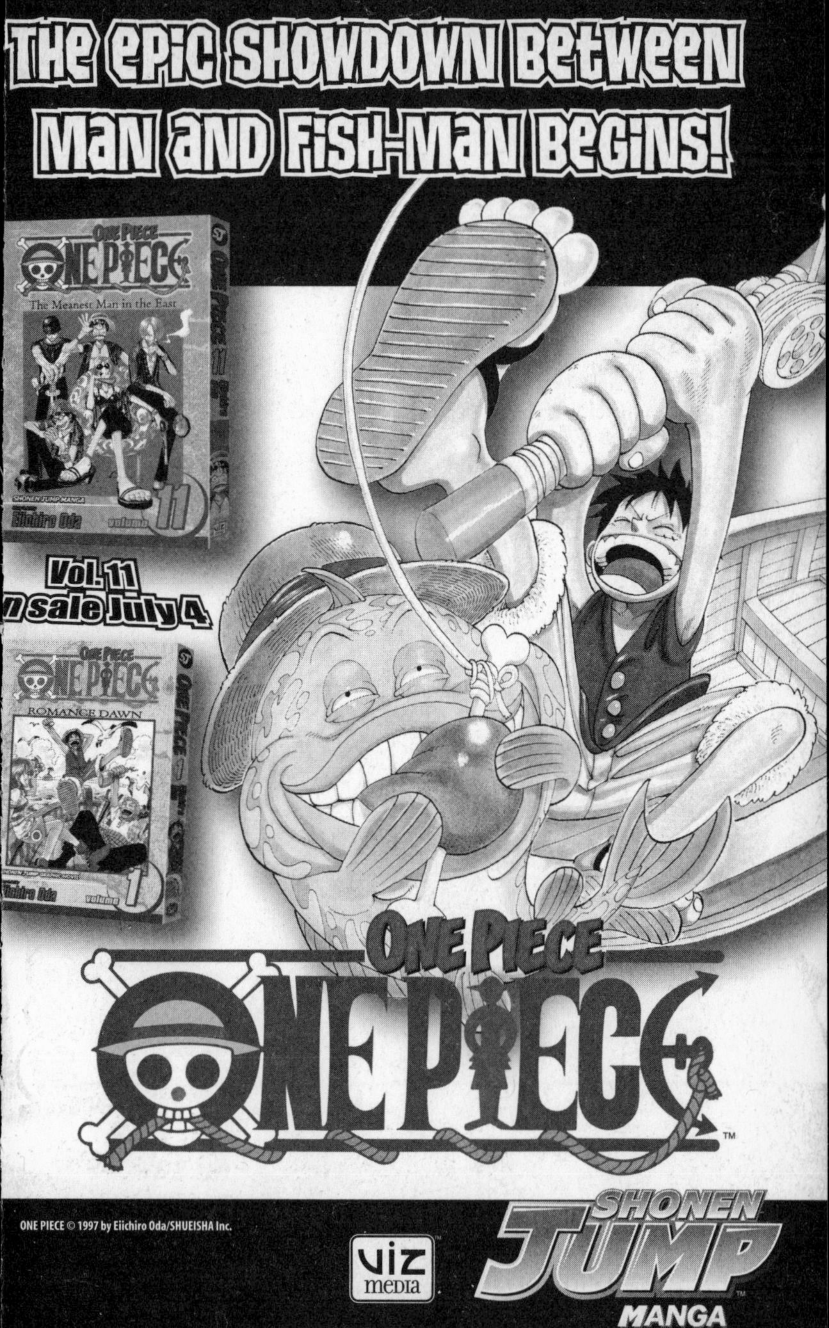
THE EPIC SHOWDOWN BETWEEN
MAN AND FISH-MAN BEGINS!
Vol. 11
n sale July 4
ONE PIECE
ONE PIECE
ONE PIECE © 1997 by Eiichiro Oda/SHUEISHA Inc.
VIZ media
SHONEN JUMP
MANGA

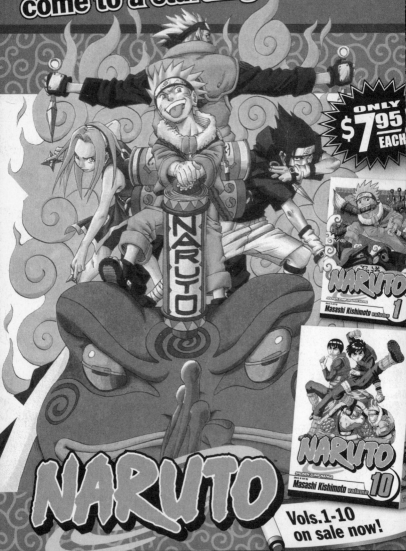

The Journeyman Ninja Selection Exams come to a startling conclusion!

ONLY $7.95 EACH

NARUTO

NARUTO 1
Story & art by Masashi Kishimoto volume 1

NARUTO 10
Story & art by Masashi Kishimoto volume 10

Vols. 1-10 on sale now!

NARUTO © 1999 by Masashi Kishimoto/SHUEISHA inc.

ON SALE AT:
www.shonenjump.com
ALSO AVAILABLE AT YOUR LOCAL
BOOKSTORE AND COMIC STORE.

RATED T TEEN

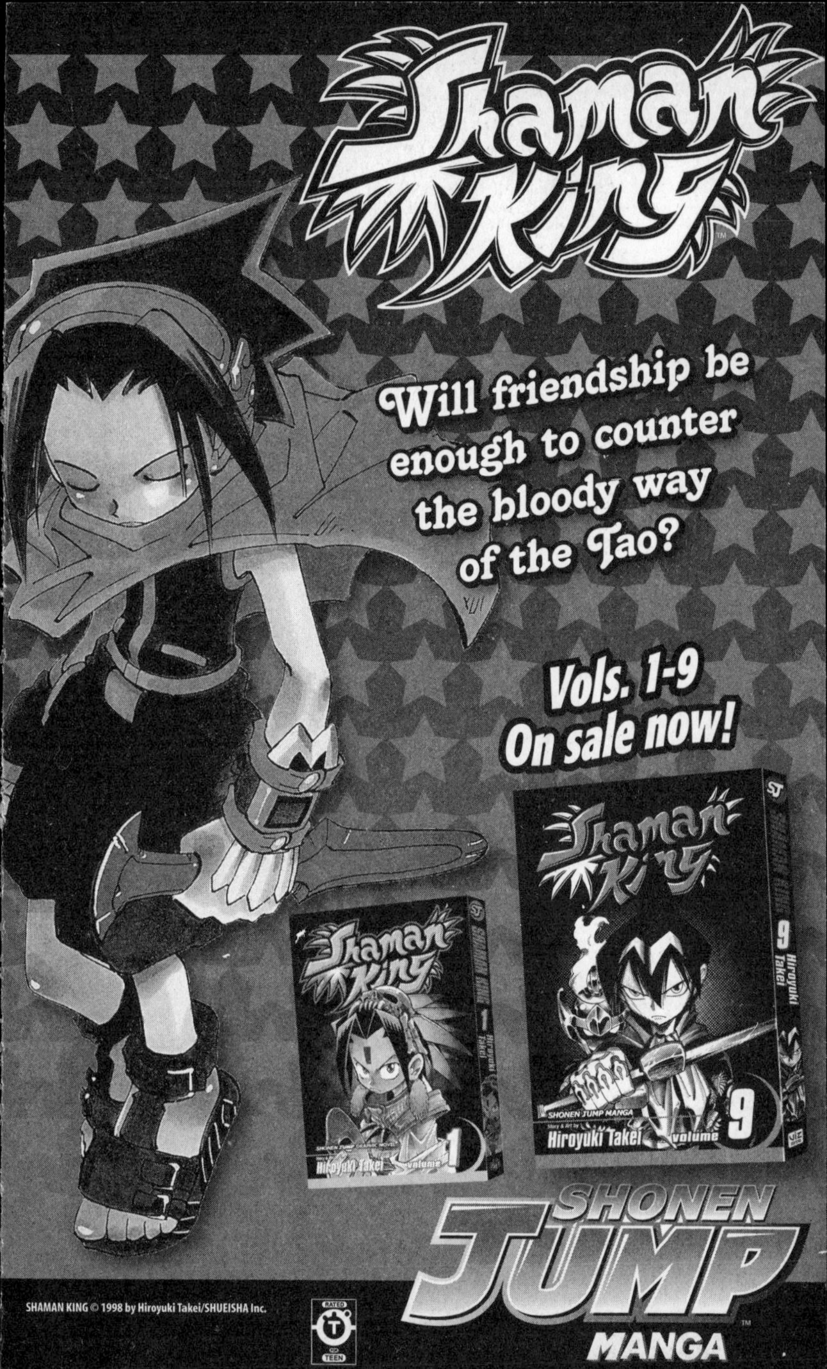
Shaman King
Will friendship be enough to counter the bloody way of the Tao?
Vols. 1-9 On sale now!
SHONEN JUMP MANGA
Story & Art by Hiroyuki Takei volume 9
Hiroyuki Takei volume 1
SHONEN JUMP MANGA
SHAMAN KING © 1998 by Hiroyuki Takei/SHUEISHA Inc.
RATED T FOR TEEN

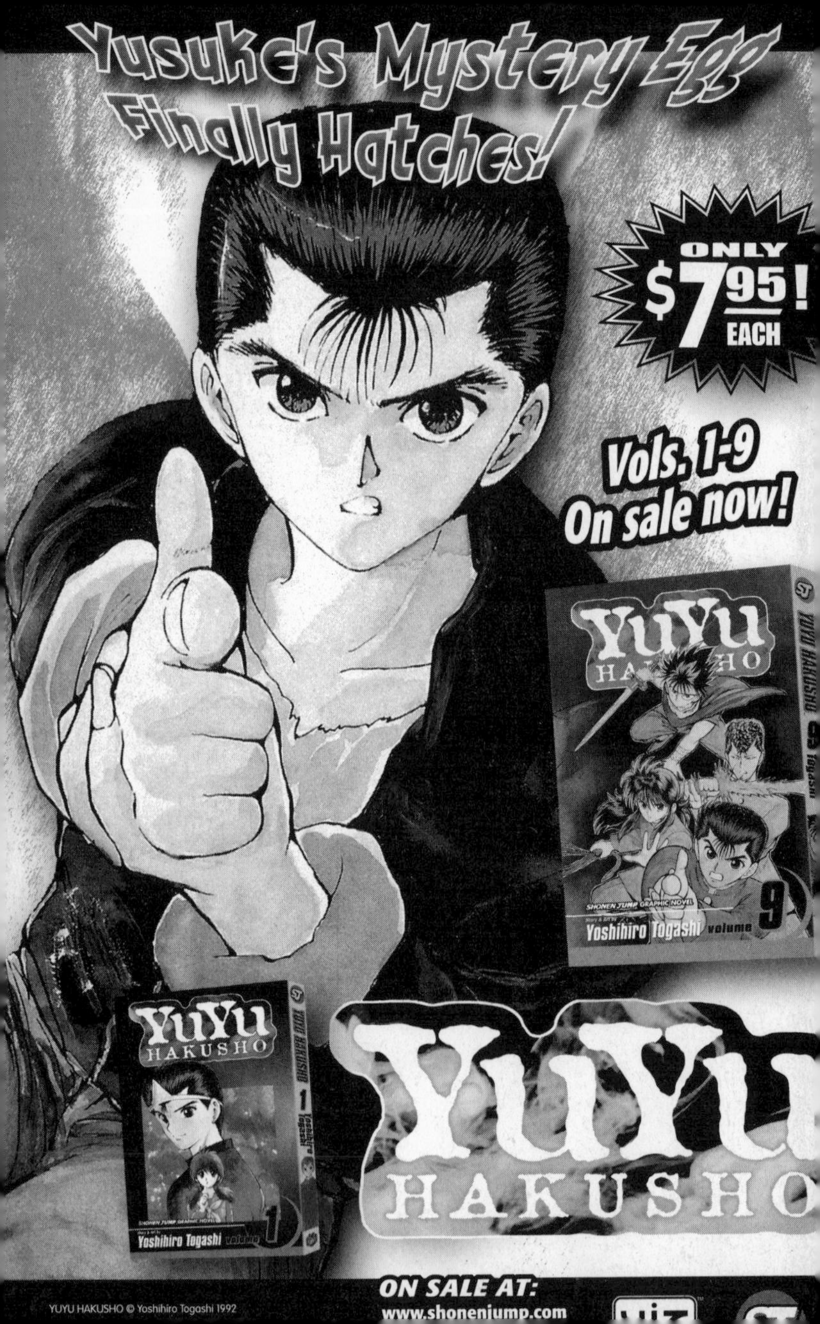
Yusuke's Mystery Egg Finally Hatches!
ONLY $7.95! EACH
Vols. 1-9 On sale now!
YuYu HAKUSHO
Yoshihiro Togashi volume 9
YuYu HAKUSHO
Yoshihiro Togashi volume 1
YuYu HAKUSHO
ON SALE AT:
www.shonenjump.com
YUYU HAKUSHO © Yoshihiro Togashi 1992

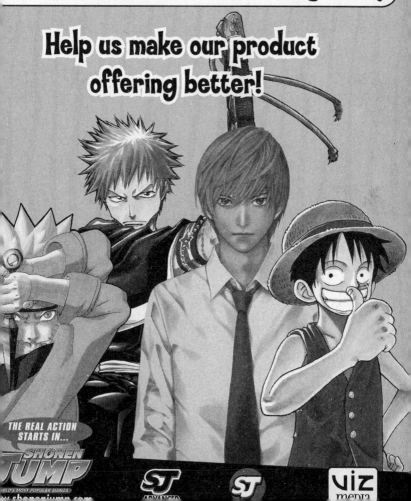

P9-EDD-798